ENTANGLED POLITICAL ECONOMY

ADVANCES IN AUSTRIAN ECONOMICS

Series Editors: Roger Koppl and Virgil Storr

Recent Volumes:

Volume 6:	Austrian Economics and Entrepreneurial Studies – Edited by Roger Koppl
Volume 7:	Evolutionary Psychology and Economic Theory – Edited by Roger Koppl
Volume 8:	The Dynamics of Intervention: Regulation and Redistribution in the Mixed Economy – Edited by P. Kurrild-Klitgaard
Volume 9:	The Cognitive Revolution in Economic Science – Edited by Elisabeth Krecké, Carine Krecké and Roger Koppl
Volume 10:	The Evolution of Consumption: Theories and Policy – Edited by Marina Bianchi
Volume 11:	Explorations in Austrian Economics – Edited by Roger Koppl
Volume 12:	Unexplored Dimensions: Karl Menger on Economics and Philosophy (1923–1938) – Edited by Giandomenica Becchio
Volume 13:	The Social Science of Hayek's 'The Sensory Order' – Edited by William N. Butos
Volume 14:	What is so Austrian about Austrian Economics? – Edited by Roger Koppl, Steven Horwitz and Pierre Desrochers
Volume 15:	Hayek in Mind: Hayek's Philosophical Psychology – Edited by Leslie Marsh
Volume 16:	The Spatial Market Process – Edited by David Emanuel Andersson
Volume 17:	Experts and Epistemic Monopolies – Edited by Roger Koppl, Steven Horwitz and Laurent Dobuzinskis

ADVANCES IN AUSTRIAN ECONOMICS VOLUME 18

ENTANGLED POLITICAL ECONOMY

EDITED BY

STEVEN HORWITZ

Department of Economics, St. Lawrence University, Canton, NY, USA

ROGER KOPPL

Department of Finance, Whitman School of Management, Syracuse University, Syracuse, NY, USA

United Kingdom – North America – Japan
India – Malaysia – China

Emerald Group Publishing Limited
Howard House, Wagon Lane, Bingley BD16 1WA, UK

First edition 2014

British Library Cataloguing in Publication Data
A catalogue record for this book is available from the British Library

ISBN: 978-1-78441-102-2
ISSN: 1529-2134 (Series)

CONTENTS

LIST OF CONTRIBUTORS

Giandomenica Becchio	Department of Economic and Social Sciences, University of Torino, Torino, Italy
James W. Bono	Economists Incorporated, San Francisco, CA, USA
George Bragues	University of Guelph-Humber, Toronto, ON, Canada
N. C. A da Costa	Advanced Studies Research Group; HCTE and Fuzzy Sets Laboratory PIT, Production Engineering Program, Universidade Federal do Rio de Janeiro, Rio de Janeiro, Brazil
Francisco A. Doria	Advanced Studies Research Group; HCTE and Fuzzy Sets Laboratory PIT, Production Engineering Program, Universidade Federal do Rio de Janeiro, Rio de Janeiro, Brazil
Steven Horwitz	Department of Economics, St. Lawrence University, Canton, NY, USA
Stuart Kauffman	Institute of Systems Biology, Seattle, WA, USA
Roger Koppl	Department of Finance, Whitman School of Management, Syracuse University, Syracuse, NY, USA
William J. Luther	Department of Economics, Kenyon College, Gambier, OH, USA

Philip Z. Maymin	Department of Finance and Risk Engineering, NYU Polytechnic School of Engineering, Brooklyn, NY, USA
Maria Pia Paganelli	Department of Economics, Trinity University, San Antonio, TX, USA
Marta Podemska-Mikluch	Department of Economics and Management, Gustavus Adolphus College, St. Peter, MN, USA
J. Barkley Rosser, Jr.	Department of Economics, James Madison University, Harrisonburg, VA, USA
Alexander W. Salter	Department of Economics, Berry College, Mt. Berry, GA, USA
Richard E. Wagner	Department of Economics, George Mason University, Fairfax, VA, USA
David H. Wolpert	Santa Fe Institute, Santa Fe, NM, USA
Moin A. Yahya	Faculty of Law, University of Alberta, Edmonton, AB, Canada

INTRODUCTION TO "ENTANGLED POLITICAL ECONOMY"

Roger Koppl

This volume celebrates and explores Richard E. Wagner's vision of entangled political economy. Wagner says political economy, "denotes an entangled network of enterprises that are constituted under different institutional arrangements that generate a continually evolving admixture of cooperation and conflict" (2010, p. 160). Just as two distant particles may be "entangled" in quantum physics such that the properties of one depends instantaneously on the properties of the other, the behavior of "private" and "public" entities are "entangled" such that the nature of each depends on the behavior of the other.

For example, Bloom (2009) finds that firms may respond to political uncertainty by "inaction in hiring and investment." It is costly to expand or contract your business, and uncertainty dampens firm responses to apparent profit opportunities. Firms "only hire and invest when business conditions are sufficiently good, and only fire and disinvest when they are sufficiently bad. When uncertainty is higher, these thresholds move out: units become more cautious in responding to business conditions" (2009, p. 638). If the firm's degree of uncertainty depends on policy, then the actions of political authorities alter the sensitivity of private enterprises to profit and loss signals. Similarly, I have argued (Koppl, 2002) that the informational efficiency of financial markets depends in part on whether

Entangled Political Economy
Advances in Austrian Economics, Volume 18, 1–13

ISSN: 1529-2134/doi:10.1108/S1529-213420140000018001

monetary policy is rule-based or discretionary. The dependency goes both ways. Smith, Wagner, and Yandle (2011) point to the radical change in central bank practices in the United States in response to the 2008 financial crisis. The prospective failure of some large "private" institutions led to "unconventional monetary policy." Regulatory capture illustrates how entanglement is a two-way street. The nature of the regulatory agency is influenced by the rent-seeking activities of the private actors. At the same time the existence of a "public" regulatory body, which may be no less zealous in the pursuit of its rents, influences the nature of the "private" enterprises in its purview.

Wagner's entanglement point is so simple, so basic, and so elementary that we may easily miss just how much it changes our understanding of political economy. A more naïve view of things is a good foil. In this naïve view, we have two types of actors: private and public. The private actors follow the logic of private interest and public actors follow the logic of public interest. From this perspective it seems only common sense to say that we need public actors ("the government") to restrain private actors ("business") whose self-seeking may be excessive and harmful. Public choice theory has replaced this naïve view with one in which there is symmetry in the motives of public and private actors. Buchanan and Tullock say, "the representative or the average individual acts on the basis of the same over-all value scale when he participates in market activity and in political activity" (1999, p. 19). Wagner pushes the point beyond the important symmetry assumption emphasized by Buchanan and Tullock.

Even if we recognize the motivational symmetry of private and public actors, we might think of each such actor as constituted independently of the other. Wagner draws our attention to a point that is hard to discover, and yet obvious once stated. The nature of a private or public actor is not given independently of the overall political-economy environment. And that means that they are shaping each other. They co-evolve. Entangled political economy contrasts with additive political economy in which "economic equilibrium is conceptualized prior to political activity, with political activity then modifying that equilibrium." Unfortunately, the model of additive political economy is used even by many otherwise very skilled and sophisticated economists.

Wagner develops the idea in *Entangled Political Economy: A Keynote Address*. He says, "the vision of entangled political economy is a feature of the effort to treat economics genuinely as a social science." This is an important and fundamental remark. It may seem only natural that we would ask social science "What shall we do?" But a science of society sets limits on what "we" can hope to do. "We" cannot somehow hand things over to supposed experts who know just what to do. Such supposed experts do not exist, somehow, above the system and beyond social-scientific inquiry. But if the policy-making process itself is subject to scientific scrutiny, then we can no longer view policy as freely chosen. And if economists are a part of the policy-making, then we must subject ourselves to the same scientific scrutiny we apply to others in society.

The insight that policy-making and economic analysis are themselves subject to scientific analysis might tempt us into a kind of scientific fatalism. Whatever happens, happens; and if you think you can do something about it, then you are just neglecting the universal principle of causation in all things. Such fatalism would be mistaken.[1] While change is hard, we have seen increasing wealth and freedom over time on all time scales. Such progress seems hard to square with fatalism. Treating economics "genuinely as a social science," Wagner explains, "doesn't mean that it is impossible to alter the pattern of social interaction and its accompanying characteristics. It means only that doing so is not a simple matter of getting a parade marshal to change the direction of march."

Finding how best to improve policy and political institutions is a great challenge. We probably don't know much about how to do it. Wagner propels us far along by replacing the vision of additive political economy with that of entangled political economy. His is a political economy of networks, complexity, and unintended consequences. It is a political economy of constitutional rules, but one in which the rules may evolve in complex ways that are hard to predict. It is a fallible political economy for a fallible world. It is a political economy that "affirms recognition that eternal vigilance is the price of liberty – and that liberty carries a significant price because the practice of liberty requires people to resist the siren call to enlist themselves as sheep in some progressivist-shepherd's flock."

Wagner's vision of entanglement has deep roots in the history of political economy, including the works of Adam Smith and Carl Menger.

"Adam Smith," Maria Paganelli notes, "analyzes the nature and causes of the wealth of nations by analyzing the interaction of the economy with politics, ethics, and the law. Similarly," she continues, "Smith presents each of these systems as a network of relations with all the other systems." Smith was in full possession of Wagner's insight that participants in the entangled economy cannot know where their agreements lead. Paganelli cites some Smithian examples of this insight, including England's precarious dependence on the colonial trade, which resulted from the special privileges extracted from an all-too-willing parliament. Because of this "unnatural" dependency, Smith explains, "The expectation of a rupture with the colonies, accordingly, has struck the people of Great Britain with more terror than they ever felt for a Spanish armada, or a French invasion."

Giandomenica Becchio notes that Wagner (2007) has cited Menger as a precursor for whom "development emerges out of specific activities in a networked manner" (p. 102). She attempts to push the Mengerian link further by exploring the somewhat neglected second edition of Menger's *Principles of Economics*. Entanglement in Menger is evident, she tells us, in "the role of biology to explain economic activity," and "the nature of 'social groups' as 'orders' and 'not organizations.'" Menger's biology-based theory of human needs, Becchio explains, "bridges the gap between biology and economics." Menger's biological perspective led him to appreciate the emergence of entities with goals or needs that exist only at the same "level" as the emergent entity. On Becchio's reading, this led Menger to recognize that "human associations" have "needs" that cannot be reduced to the needs of the associated persons. This reading of Menger may be less individualistic than that of Hayek and, perhaps, most of the modern Austrian school. Becchio suggests that this reading reflects the ideas of the Carl Menger, rather than his son Karl who edited it and published in 1923, about two years after Carl Menger's death in 1921. Becchio's interpretation seems to be consistent with a striking remark in the second edition of Menger's *Principles*: "The 'needs of human associations' [are] common needs shared by individuals who are voluntary linked in a particular association, able to provide common goods required by the members of that association. As soon as they arise, they are no longer the sum of single individuals, and they cease to be merely means to satisfy common needs: they acquire their own needs, and social goods are required to satisfy them."

Barkley Rosser helps to clarify the history of entanglement by reviewing the twin themes of self-organization and emergence. Although I have just called them "twin themes" there has been considerable debate and confusion on the relationship between self-organization and emergence, as Rosser carefully chronicles. Rosser calls them "intimately linked and frequently coinciding," while also noting that you can either one without the other. Rosser rightly notes that "emergence," like "complexity," is "a much debated term." It is useful to review the ups and downs of these terms and the variety of opinions on their interconnections, if only to reduce the chance that you will know for certain what just ain't so. The supposed impossibility of group selection is an example of something that just ain't so. (Wilson, 2004 discusses "The Rejection and Revival of Multilevel Selection Theory.") Rosser's paper includes an important take-away: The word "evolution" may indicate emergence without natural selection, natural selection without emergence, emergence through natural selection, or emergence alongside natural selection. The people who use such terms are not always clear which one they mean.

Marta Podemska-Mikluch gives us a beautiful example of applied economics in the tradition of entangled political economy. Podemska-Mikluch takes a close look at Poland's recent Medical Reimbursement Act. From the perspective of additive political economy, this case of price controls "appears to result from the costliness of following economists' recommendations. Consequently, economists explain their inability to prevent implementation of faulty policies by pointing to the constraints of the political system and shortcomings of policy-makers." This perspective may be flattering to economists. It sure is hard for those silly old politicians to understand our super-sophisticated theory. But we should more humbly recognize that public policy is not an object of choice, but an emergent phenomenon. Vital to this process of emergence was the prior existence of the National Health Fund, the Ministry of Health, and "waste caused by the overconsumption of government-subsidized medication." If policy were an object of choice, it would have been relatively easy to reduce waste by reducing the subsidies. But the National Health Fund and the Ministry of Health were actors in the political marketplace, and "the elimination of subsidies would diminish the role of [these] polity-based enterprises." The Medical Reimbursement Act added to the discretionary power of these two "Big Players" in Poland's pharmaceuticals market, thus replacing "relationships based on contract with relationships based on status."

The role of discretion is important in the 2010 Dodd–Frank Act too (Koppl, 2014, pp. 113–128). The Act creates a new regulatory regime for financial markets. Moin Yahya examines one aspect of the law, namely, its treatment of the fiduciary duties of investment advisors and broker-dealers. When the Act was being formed through Congressional hearings and the like, "sophisticated market players who have a real stake in this game" chose to offer only vague statements on what new fiduciary responsibilities to impose. This vagueness encouraged the outcome we got: The Act charged the Securities and Exchange Commission (SEC) with the task of working out a set of standards. In other words, Congress delegated the task to a regulatory body.

You might think that the sophisticated players driving this outcome would have pined for a clear set of standards that were laid down in legislation and therefore hard to change rapidly. But these players were, of course, interest groups. And these interest groups understood that it is hard to predict what rules would best serve their interest in a changing environment. "When the issue was in front of Congress, special interest groups therefore oriented their advocacy in broad terms with no specifics. The goal was to obtain a favorable legislative setup for each group that could be worked out in detail with the SEC." Yahya fleshes out this general claim with specific statements made before Congress by specific organizations. He also chronicles the next stage in this unfortunate game. In this next stage, competing interests attempted to influence that SEC study mandated by Dodd–Frank. Yahya's close analysis of the study the SEC finally produced strongly suggests that individuals had much less influence on the final product than organized interests such as the Securities Industry and Financial Markets Association (SIFMA). Indeed, in this episode SIFMA "displayed a real mastery of political lobbying."

With Dodd–Frank we see again a story in which outcomes emerge from a process in ways that are hard to capture with the model of additive political economy. The papers of both Yahya and Podemska-Mikluch discuss the importance of ambiguity and discretion in the emergent outcomes of entangled political economy. The Volcker rule provides a supporting example. Section 619 of the Dodd–Frank act adds a new section 13 to the Bank Holding Company (BHC) Act of 1956. Dodd–Frank required a group of regulatory bodies ("the agencies") to formulate a Volcker rule. The agencies released the proposed rule on November 7, 2011. It includes the following statement: "In formulating the proposed rule, the Agencies have attempted to reflect the structure of section 13 of the BHC Act ... However, the delineation of what constitutes a prohibited or permitted activity under section 13 of the BHC Act often involves subtle distinctions that are difficult both to describe comprehensively within regulation and to evaluate in practice" (Office of the Comptroller of the Currency Treasury; Board of Governors of the Federal Reserve System; Federal Deposit Insurance Corporation; and the Securities and Exchange Commission, 2011, p. 68849). The regulators seem to be saying, "Even we don't know what this rule says."

In his review of Fritz Machlup's 1940 classic, *The Stock Market, Credit, and Capital Formation*, George Bragues gives us a fine example of how "private" and "public" entities are entangled. Machlup's central question is whether financial markets somehow "absorb" capital, thus preventing it from being used in productive activities. In general, Machlup concludes, such absorption cannot and does not happen. But in boom times, there can be some absorption. Here, a rather fundamental characteristic of the stock market – whether it does or does not siphon capital out of the real economy – is a function of the larger regime of entangled political economy.

We have seen that Wagner's entangled political economy has implications for applied economics. Without such implications we might reasonably doubt the value of Wagner's entanglement insight. It clearly does have value, I think. Indeed, entangled political economy is like fractal geometry. Once you get the idea, everything changes and you see it everywhere. At root, however, it is a *theoretical* insight. And it has, therefore, theoretical implications.

Alex Salter and William Luther identify a striking theoretical implication of entanglement. We are used to thinking of chartalist and evolutionary theories of money as mutually exclusive alternatives. In common interpretations at least, chartalism says that money was invented by the state and evolutionary theories say that money emerged naturally from private trading. These views may seem irreconcilable. Salter and Luther give us a very different perspective, however. The "the locus of the debate," they explain, "is the nature of the demand for money." State theories hold that a good's "imposition and acceptance" by "powerful authorities" decides what will be money. Evolutionary theories, by contrast, try to "explain the emergence of a demand to hold money in the first place." Once framed in this way we can begin to see why Salter and Luther think a synthesis is possible.

If we accept the basic insight of entangled political economy, we are led to a "theory allowing for the interaction of government and non-government players" in the emergence of money. We should not insist on a blackboard theory that assumes away state power. Nor should we imagine that some state actor imposes order by uttering the words "Let there be money." It is the interaction of "public" and "private" entities that decides the issue. "We do not claim that government can circumvent the spontaneous order process and create a monetary order ex nihilo. Rather, we wish to emphasize that, among the set of relatively more saleable commodities, government action may be the decisive factor in creating or sustaining a monetary order."

If entanglement has deep theoretical implications, it must also matter for our modeling techniques.

Sticking relatively close to standard methods, James W. Bono and David H. Wolpert explore "game mining." Within the confines of standard game theory, the rules are the rules, and they determine what game you are playing. But in social life agents can trade, and there is no telling who will trade with whom. Bono and Wolpert consider cases in which a third party can enter an outcome-contingent contract with the players. This third party is "game mining." The game miner alters the payoffs for one of the players in a way that is known to all players as well as the miner. Among their findings is the perhaps surprising "proposition 6." This proposition shows that, in the context of two-person games, a monopolistic game miner cannot be harmed by the restriction that she contract with only one player and not both. It heightens, or at least does not reduce, competition between the two players if they know that the game miner will contract with only one of them. If the game miner has accepted a contract with one player, the other player knows that the miner will accept her contract too as long as she is not worse off with both. Thus, the miner gains nothing from being able to contract with both parties.

The paper by Bono and Wolpert opens up an interesting area of research. Among other questions, they ask, "Why aren't real game mining firms wreaking havoc on real markets?" I think this is a subtle and challenging question. They offer several plausible suggestions. It may be, as they seem to suggest, that the potential for game mining shapes the contracts people enter into such that overt game mining is relatively uncommon. The possibility of game mining may "imply that certain games should never exist because the minute they appear they will be mined into an alternate game." If that's an important phenomenon, then an invisible hand that is very different from the one that economists usually consider is profoundly shaping real-world outcomes.

It seems reasonable to wonder whether game mining might be a good way to model corruption. The game miner, perhaps, creates a conflict of interests. It may also be helpful in some cases to model the state as a monopoly game miner. Although "the state" is, as Wagner emphasizes, a congeries of officials, offices, and authorities, it may sometimes be fruitful to model the state as a monopoly game miner interfering in the games being played between "private" parties. A regulator, for example, can contract with trucking to suppress railroads or with railroads to suppress trucking. And, following "proposition 6" of Bono and Wolpert, the regulator's rents will not be diminished if it can constrain itself to contract with one side only.

Philip Maymin turns to complexity theory as a tool of entangled political economy. This is appropriate. Wagner has emphasized complexity themes in his work, as with his discussion of "degeneracy" in complex systems (Wagner, 2006). Maymin uses several tools of complexity theory to model entangled political economy, namely, cellular automata, register machines, and quantum computation. He develops an interesting voting model in which the agents can vote on redistributive schemes. In the most general case, anything can happen. Importantly, there can be collapse in social cooperation, and "the effects of redistribution are inherently intractable." Maymin shows how simple rules can generate complex results with oscillations and movement. Even in the purposefully simple contexts such as cellular automata, the system may produce the sort of complexity and turbulence Wagner describes.

da Costa and Doria go beyond the intractability Maymin discussed to arrive at formal uncomputability. They build on Rice's theorem to show how ubiquitous uncomputability is. Rice (1953) showed, in effect, that there is no algorithmic procedure that can always decide whether a given computer program has a given nontrivial property.[2] There is no general procedure for knowing ahead of time whether your program contains a bug, or is a virus, whether it outputs limericks, strategies for tic-tac-toe, or instructions for baking a cake. "Any general procedure for testing the output behavior of software is impossible, according to Rice's Theorem."

da Costa and Doria use Rice's Theorem to show that uncomputability is ubiquitous. Even finite noncooperative games may be undecidable, as they discuss near the end of their paper. Chaitin et al. (2012, p. 16) say, "undecidability and incompleteness are everywhere, from mathematics to computer science, to physics, to mathematically formulated portions of chemistry, biology, ecology, economics. The Gödel–Turing phenomenon is an all-pervasive fact that has to be understood in order to be conquered and usefully mastered." In their contribution to this volume, da Costa and Doria work out the sense in which the effects of policy in a formal model of the economy will be undecidable for at least one possible state of the economy. (They note the close similarity to Velupillai, 2007.) If the formalism is expressed "in an adequate mathematical language that includes arithmetic and is based on classical logic," then (essentially) you cannot always know what outcomes a policy will generate. If the formalism in question is a network model, "then all nontrivial economic policies which are represented by algorithmic procedures on the network are undecidable."[3]

The undecidability of network models is important for entangled political economy because network theory is an important tool of entangled political economy. "For entanglement to be possible, the entities must be conceptualized as networks of relationships where individual nodes craft particular connections with other nodes, and with those connections running through both are arenas of action" (Smith et al., 2011). But if relatively simple networks are undecidable, then it may be impossible to use policy to engineer outcomes in politico-economic systems. If there is a great and ineradicable *Ignorabimus* at the heart of mathematics, then there is an equally great and ineradicable *Ignorabimus* at the heart of economics.

Stuart Kauffman confronts this *Ignorabimus* at, perhaps, an even more fundamental level. The old-fashioned "neoclassical" economics that still has some claim to orthodoxy today is "Newtonian" in the sense that it resembles classical physics. As Kauffman puts it, "Newton taught us how to think." Fleshing this out, Kauffman invokes Laplace: "With Laplace and his Demon in the sky knowing the initial positions and momenta of all the particles, then using Newton's laws, we could deduce the entire future and past of the universe (Newton's equations are time reversible.). This is the birth of modern reductionism, the faith that there is a theory 'down there' that entails the entire unfolding of the universe." Kauffman subjects this deterministic vision to minute examination.

The Newtonian vision of neoclassical economics requires us to treat people like particles. But if we examine the Edgeworth box carefully we find "ethics at the heart of economics." The model does not tell us where on the contract curve we will end up. How then is it determined? It is determined, in part, by ethics. "We evolved as social primates," Kauffman notes, as we may therefore expect bargainers in the Edgeworth box respond to feelings of fairness just as they do in experiments such as the Ultimatum Game. In this sense, he concludes, "Ethics is central, not peripheral to the Edgeworth Box, so central to the cornerstone of the economic theory of advantages of trade that drive trade and economic activity."

Even if it were possible to treat people like particles, we would still have to give up the determinism of the Newtonian model. In any Newtonian system there is a set of initial conditions and one or more "laws of motion" for the system. They determine, or logically *entail*, the whole future history of the system. At the initial moment for the model or theory everything is there implicitly. Time roles out a tapestry that has already been woven. The "laws" that "entail" the future history of the system are "entailing laws." Kauffman rejects this Newtonian vision when he says, "[W]e can have no entailing theory for the specific goods and services and production capacities that have come to exist." As Kauffman points out, "This claim is truly radical." He approaches this point through the listing problem that has been identified earlier by Shackle (1969, pp. 3–13, pp. 47–61, pp. 278–279) and others. Kauffman asks the reader, "Can you name *all* the uses of a screwdriver?" There is, Kauffman says, no algorithm to generate all the uses of a screwdriver in part because "The evolution of novel functionalities is non-algorithmic." Generally, evolutionary systems such as the biosphere and the econosphere generate novelty. But if a system generates novelty, there can be no entailing laws for the system. Any description of the system will leave out future innovations. With respect to any description of the system, then, some events occurring within the system will be novel and therefore surprising.

Kauffman's *Ignorabimus* may be more radical than that of da Costa and Doria, who show that you may not be able to predict the future of a system even when you have a complete mathematical description of it. Kauffman shows that it is not generally possible to write out a complete mathematical description of evolving systems. In other words, da Costa and Doria allow that there might be entailing laws to write out, but you can't figure out what they imply. Kauffman shows that there are no entailing laws to write out in the first place. This perhaps more radical view is consistent with Wagner's description (in this volume) of society as "turbulent and moving" and changes as "an endogenous attribute of societal processes." It is, in other words, a very "Austrian" vision of social processes.

Kauffman uses Bergsonian language to describe evolution in the biosphere and the econosphere. "How far we are from the entailed reductionistic world view spawned by Newton. In this worldview, at least for life in its becoming, that becoming is not entailed by any law, and without any natural selection 'acting' to achieve it, evolution creates the very possibilities it shall become. More, we cannot prestate this becoming." This creativity applies no less to economic evolution: "In a rather parallel way, the evolving econosphere creates, often with no intent or foresight, its own possibilities of becoming." Kauffman draws the implication that "we cannot mathematize the detailed becoming of the econosphere." Kauffman's contrast between Newtonian models of economic growth and the unprestateable becoming of the econosphere closely parallels the contrast Wagner draws when he says, "Entangled political economy is Heraclitian in character, while orthodox or additive political economy is Ecclesiastian."

With entangled political economy, Richard E. Wagner has given us a theory that builds from a simple insight that seems hard to deny once clearly articulated: private and public entities are entangled in exchange networks such that the nature of each depends on the behavior of the other. This simple insight generates a vision of political economy that is radically different from the more orthodox "additive" or "disjunctive" political economy in which the polity is above the catallaxy and independent of it. Wagner's vision has deep roots in the history of political economy. It can be traced to Carl Menger and, before him, Adam Smith. And it matters. Once we take entanglement seriously we are led to a very different approach to policy analysis, one that rejects the model of the economist as some sort of wizardly engineer of "social outcomes." And when we recognize the error in that engineering model, we grow more interested in an applied economics that emphasizes the complex network relations that generate political economy outcomes through a jumble of voluntary exchange, extortion, cajoling, and force. We grow less interested in the sort of applied economics that emphasizes allocative efficiency or even, perhaps, constitutional design. As the contribution of Salter and Luther illustrates, we must rethink economic theory in the light of entanglement. And doing so leads to surprising results. In the case of the theory of the origin of money, it is rather as if we have been let out of a Wittgensteinian fly bottle: Much of the difference between supposedly inconsistent theories evaporates. To work up further new results in pure and applied theory, we need modeling tools suitable to entangled political economy. These would seem to include network theory and computability theory. But if social evolution is creative and, as Wagner expresses it, "Hericlitian," then mathematical modeling will be able to do only so much for us. Our "models" may have to rely on "verbal reasoning" as well as the manipulation (and ostentatious display) of mathematical symbols. We cannot predict the future knowledge that will emerge from scholarly work on entangled political economy. But we can confidently predict that the concept of entanglement will generate a growing body of research that will improve our understanding of political economy and help us to recognize how great is the challenge of generating positive social change even in fundamentally free and democratic societies. And that is an achievement for which Wagner deserves our highest admiration and our warmest thanks.

NOTES

1. In its most extreme forms, this sort of fatalism assumes that the universe is governed in all its details by a set of immutable entailing laws. An important recent challenge to this sort of view points out the impossibility of writing out such entailing laws (Longo, Montevil, & Kauffman, 2012). Kauffman's contribution to this volume applies this argument against fatalism to social science. Felin, Kauffman, Koppl, and Longo. (2015, forthcoming) and Koppl, Kauffman, Felin, and Longo (2015, forthcoming) elaborate.

2. Rice (1953) considered "classes whose elements are recursively enumerable sets of non-negative integers." He proved that "no nontrivial class is completely recursive," where complete recursiveness "may be intuitively interpreted as decidability" (p. 358). Because the partial recursive functions that define recursively enumerable sets are essentially computer programs for Turing machines, Rice says that is it not

Turing decidable which programs belong a given class if the class contains at least one program, but not all programs.

3. We are briefly characterizing Proposition 2.2 and Proposition 2.3. da Costa and Doria are careful to note that the former "is well more general" and that, therefore, the "two results aren't equivalent."

REFERENCES

Bloom, N. (2009). The impact of uncertainty shocks. *Econometrica*, *77*(3), 623–685.

Chaitin, G., da Costa, N., & Doria, F. A. (2012). *Gödel's way: Exploits into an undecidable world.* Boca Raton, FL: CRC Press.

Felin, T., Kauffman, S., Koppl, R., & Longo, G. (2014). Economic opportunity and evolution: Beyond bounded rationality and phase space. *Strategic Entrepreneurship Journal* (forthcoming).

Koppl, R. (2002). *Big players and the economic theory of expectations.* New York, NY: Palgrave Macmillan.

Koppl, R. (2014). *From crisis to confidence: Macroeconomics after the crash.* London: Institute of Economic Affairs.

Koppl, R., Kauffman, S., Felin, T., & Longo, G. (2015). Economics for a creative world. *Journal of Institutional Economics* (forthcoming).

Longo, G., Montevil, M., & Kauffman, S. (2012). No entailing laws, but enablement in the evolution of the biosphere. In *Proceedings of the genetic and evolutionary computation conference.* Philadelphia, PA.

Machlup, F. (1940). *The stock market, credit, and capital formation.* London: William Hodge and Company.

Office of the Comptroller of the Currency, Treasury; Board of Governors of the Federal Reserve System; Federal Deposit Insurance Corporation; and the Securities and Exchange Commission. (2011). Prohibitions and restrictions on proprietary trading and certain interests in, and relationships with, hedge funds and private equity funds. *Federal Register*, *76*(215), 68846–68972.

Rice, H. G. (1953). Classes of recursively enumerable sets and their decision problems. *Transactions of the American Mathematical Society*, *74*, 358–366.

Shackle, G. L. S. (1969). *Decision order and time in human affairs* (2nd ed.). Cambridge: Cambridge University Press.

Smith, A., Wagner, R. E., & Yandle, B. (2011). A theory of entangled political economy, with application to TARP and NERA. *Public Choice*, *148*, 45–66.

Velupillai, K. (2007). The impossibility of an effective theory of policy in a complex economy. In M. Salzano & D. Colander (Eds.), *Complexity hints for economic policy.* Berlin: Springer.

Wagner, R. E. (2006). Retrogressive regime drift within a theory of emergent order. *Review of Austrian Economics*, *19*, 113–123.

Wagner, R. E. (2007). Value and exchange: Two windows for economic theorizing. *Review of Austrian Economics*, *20*, 97–103.

Wilson, D. S. (2004). The new fable of the bees: Multilevel selection, adaptive societies, and the concept of self-interest. *Advances in Austrian Economics*, *7*, 201–220.

ENTANGLED POLITICAL ECONOMY: A KEYNOTE ADDRESS

Richard E. Wagner

ABSTRACT

This paper is a keynote address prepared for a conference on "Entangled Political Economy" sponsored by the Wirth Institute. In keeping with the conventions of such an address, I look both backward and forward, while placing more emphasis on looking forward. In looking backward, I compare and contrast two orientations toward political economy: additive and entangled. In looking forward, I explore some of the analytical challenges that confront efforts to pursue a vision of entangled political economy. While these challenges are substantive in character, those efforts necessarily rest on methodological presumptions. Accordingly, the paper opens by reviewing some of those methodological presumptions before turning to the substantive articulations and challenges.

Keywords: Entangled political economy; additive political economy; centralized mindset; conflicting rationalities; architecture of governance

JEL classifications: B41; D78; D85; P16

Entangled Political Economy
Advances in Austrian Economics, Volume 18, 15–36

ISSN: 1529-2134/doi:10.1108/S1529-213420140000018000

A keynote address conventionally resembles a Foreword or Preface to a collection of papers. Each author pursues his or her topic, and the task of the keynote is to supply a thematic statement that provides orientation toward the several contributions. This paper is written with that convention in mind. Entangled political economy is a theme with which I have wrestled in quite a number of publications over the past decade or so, and in doing so have used such terms as post-classical political economy, disjunctive political economy, knotted political economy, and entangled political economy. Despite this linguistic experimentation, the animating idea has remained constant and has two main strands of thought. One strand is that the marginal revolution in economics has been more negative than positive, save for the line of thought set in motion by Menger (1871 [1981], 1883 [1985]), because it led to the replacement of economics as social theory with economics as a theory of rational choice (Wagner, 2010). The other strand is that contemporary political economy reflects the infirmities introduced by the marginal revolution in creating an inapt conceptualization of its object.

As an object of inquiry, "political economy" denotes some type of relationship between the two simpler objects denoted as polity and economy. The central problem that arises immediately is that neither of these objects is directly apprehensible by a theorist. To apprehend those objects requires some preceding act of theoretical articulation, about which choices exist. Before exploring substantive matters relating to entangled political economy, I shall consider some of these methodological matters. The remainder of the paper explores aspects of entangled political economy, paying particular attention to how this orientation differs from the additive orientation that is a by-product of the marginal revolution.

POLITICAL ECONOMY: SOME METHODOLOGICAL PRELIMINARIES

Any theoretical effort entails a theorist who theorizes about some object that the theorist apprehends. When people speak of political economy, they must have an object in mind that is some compound of the simpler objects commonly denoted as polity and economy. Someone who studies economics studies an object denoted as *economy*; someone who studies politics studies an object denoted as *polity*; and someone who studies political economy studies an object that is somehow formed from those simpler objects, polity and economy. No one has observed an economy or a polity, so certainly no one has observed the object denoted as political economy. Yet people continually refer to economy, polity, and political economy. In making such references, those theorists are unavoidably creating their objects through theoretical articulation and then theorizing about some properties or qualities of those objects, after the fashion in which the prisoners were chained to the wall in Plato's allegory of the shadows on the cave.

The object of interest for all social inquiry is the entity we denote as society, or some aspect of it. There are, however, alternative analytical paths along which to conceptualize that object. One path offers conceptualizations in terms of states of being or existence at some instant of observation – as snapshots; the other path offers conceptualizations in terms of processes of becoming or development over some duration of time – as films. These alternatives are not contradictory, but they do involve a choice between foreground and background. One can recognize with Ecclesiastes that there is nothing new under the sun while relegating that observation to the conceptual background because the foreground is occupied by Heraclites's observation that a person cannot even step twice into the same river. Entangled political economy is Heraclitian in character, while orthodox or additive political economy is Ecclesiastian. Both frameworks can be reconciled, as illustrated by the aphorism: "the more things change, the more they stay the same." All the same, the relation of foreground to background asserts precedence for entangled political economy while also directing analytical attention in a different direction similar to Rescher's (2000) treatment of process philosophy.

With respect to this different direction, we should reflect for a moment on that joke about the economist who was seen looking for his lost car key beneath a lamppost. When asked if he was sure this was where he lost the key, he answered that he didn't lose it there; however, there was no light where he lost the key so his only option was to look where the light shone. Judged by the murmurings I have heard in the room when someone has told that joke, I judge that I am not alone in thinking that the joke tells an uncomfortable truth. The alternative to continuing to look under the light is to try to construct an alternative source of light where it is thought that the key might have been lost. In my estimation, orthodox political economy, as economic theory generally, looks where the light presently shines. In contrast, entangled political economy seeks to construct illumination where it is thought that the key might actually lay.

On several occasions I have invoked a comparison between a parade and a crowd of people passing through a piazza. Both are orderly social configurations, but their properties are different as are the sources of their orderliness. The parade might be a mile in length and contain 5,000 participants. The people in the piazza might likewise number 5,000, and the piazza might occupy the same amount of territory as the parade. To say that each configuration is orderly simply means that participants can operate effectively within each configuration. No one, however, would mistake a parade for a piazza. Ontologically, these are distinct objects with different sources of orderliness, and so call for different analytical frameworks. A parade can be reasonably modeled as a form of equilibrium and so can be readily reduced to an entity with point-mass status. Even though the parade is a mile long with 5,000 participants, nothing is lost by treating it as a point that moves along some announced direction at three miles per hour.

While the piazza covers the same amount of space and has the same number of participants as the parade, the piazza is a different kind of social object than a parade, and must be examined within a suitably different analytical framework. The piazza is not reducible to point-mass status because the participants are traveling in different directions, as well as spending different lengths of time in the piazza. For the parade, orderliness resides in such things as the marching and musical abilities of the members, the organizational and directional talents of the parade marshal, and on the amount of time the participants give to rehearsal. None of these attributes, however, has anything to do with the action inside a piazza. The orderliness of the piazza is rather governed by such things as the ability of people to infer other people's intentions so as to adjust walking speeds to avoid collisions, a desire to avoid treating other people as bumper cars at a carnival, and general adherence to principles of courtesy and conventions on which side of a path to walk.

A choice between theoretical frameworks is typically posed on epistemological grounds by asking which framework fits better from a given set of observations. Yet those very observations have been selected with some theoretical framework necessarily in the background if not in the foreground. If the frameworks suggest different types of relevant data, a choice between frameworks cannot be made just on the basis of goodness of fit (Ziliak & McCloskey, 2008) but must be suitable in light of the nature of the object being analyzed, as Lawson (1997, 2003) explains in his treatments of ontology and economic theory.

Consider a simple model in the spirit of Schelling (1978) and Resnick (1994). There are 100 people standing in a field that is marked by small squares. The people constitute a form of society in that its members act according to a principle of proximity: one never moves closer than two squares to a neighbor and one never allows more than four squares to arise.

To point toward substantive content, each person might occupy some point in abstract commercial space. In spatial terms, this crowd represents a stationary equilibrium. From this point of departure, suppose there is a continual sequence of two-step actions – the first step involves five people changing commercial location as acts of entrepreneurship; and the second step involves responses by the other 95 as required by the principle of proximity. Allow that process to proceed indefinitely. By epistemological standards of 5 percent significance, it is impossible to reject the claim that this social configuration is a stationary equilibrium that is subject to exogenous shocks followed by restoration of equilibrium in light of the new data.

This epistemology, however, is wrong by ontological construction. The entity is not stationary and hit by occasional shocks that induce subsequent adjustment. The entity is a moving organism, with the direction of movement set by entrepreneurs seeking new opportunities. Entrepreneurship resides inside the social system and is not a shock from outside the system. Epistemological principles of goodness of fit might suggest that static equilibrium is a suitable characterization of this society, but it isn't. For the society is in motion, and with the energy for and direction of movement set by entrepreneurial adventurers (Kirzner, 1973, 1985), and which calls to mind Schumpeter's (1934) treatment of entrepreneurship as the situs of leadership in a capitalist society. To treat the object as stationary and subject to exogenous shocks is to misrepresent the nature of the object, essentially by mistaking background for foreground. Once the object is misunderstood, mischief can easily follow, as illustrated by reducing politics to the selection of a parade marshal.

Consider again the comparison of a parade and a crowd of pedestrians, but now change that crowd to a set of spectators leaving a stadium after a game. To further clarify the scene, suppose the stadium is horseshoe-shaped and situated alongside a bend in a river, leaving the open side as the only way out. After the game, the spectators pour out of the stadium and head down the boulevard toward parking lots a mile away. Someone watching this exodus while hovering in a balloon two miles above could easily declare this object to be an *imperfect parade*. It would certainly resemble a parade in featuring people moving in an orderly fashion down the boulevard. But it wouldn't be as good as the Macy's Parade on Thanksgiving Day or the Rose Parade on New Year's Day. It would be an imperfect parade. Not everyone would be in step. Some people would walk faster than others. Some people would move diagonally rather than vertically. The reduction of an economy to a static equilibrium is to treat an economy by the image of a parade and not a piazza. Politically directed effort to make the crowd

Table 1. Five Conceptual Dichotomies Pertaining to Political Economy.

Orthodox, Additive Framework	Alternative, Entangled Framework
Society as placid and equilibrated	Society as turbulent and moving
Change as exogenous	Change as indigenous
Polity external to economy	Polity resides in economy and vice versa
Economics: science of rational choice	Economics: genuine social science
Qualities reduced to quantities via utility functions: surface heterogeneity with deep homogeneity via hedonics	Qualities kept alive via lexicographic ordering: deep heterogeneity and limited hedonics

look like a better parade is clearly capable of changing the look of the crowd when seen from above, and yet is incapable of converting that crowd into a parade. Such effort, however, is capable of generating much disruption and adverse reaction, which, to be sure, may well elicit heightened calls for increased force to try to convert the crowd into a parade.

A reasonable political economy, entangled if you will, should have as its object a pedestrian crowd and not a parade, rendering society a crowd of parades, as it were. Table 1 illustrates the distinction in terms of five dichotomies pertaining to qualities attributed to the object denoted as political economy. The orthodox framework treats society as naturally placid, while the alternative framework treats it as naturally turbulent (Wagner, 2012c). Within the orthodox framework, change comes as exogenous shocks accompanied by equilibrating responses to the new data. Within the alternative framework, change is an endogenous attribute of societal processes. In the orthodox framework, polity is external to economy; in the alternative framework, they reside inside each other. The orthodox framework arises out of a treatment of economics as a science of rational choice, where society is merely a landscape on which people act to supply inputs to the market and to take away products from the market. The alternative framework treats economics as a genuine social science which has as its object society, which in turn is not reducible to some representative or average chooser. The orthodox framework reduces quality to quantity through a universal utility function; the alternative framework keeps qualities alive through lexicographic ordering (Pirsig, 1974; Yang, 2001, pp. 24–30).

ADDITIVE POLITICAL ECONOMY

By additive political economy, I mean a scheme of thought where economic equilibrium is conceptualized prior to political activity, with political activity then modifying that equilibrium. This scheme of thought is illustrated masterfully in works of Drazen (2000), Persson and Tabellini (2000), and Besley (2006). An economy is conceptualized as an equilibrated entity, which allows it to be treated as possessing point-mass status. A polity is conceptualized as a unified locus of power that stands apart from economy and acts on economy to shift its equilibrium. The action in this scheme of thought is sequential: the first draft of the manuscript of social life is written within economy, while it is within polity where the manuscript is revised – whether perfected or worsened depends on who is asked to render judgment.

In the formulations of welfare economics that preceded public choice, the political entity was presumed in all respects to stand outside the economy, intervening into economy from some Olympian location. Public choice sought to bring the polity down to the ground level by postulating that political figures have the same talents, limitations, and interests as commercial figures. The initial thrust of the public choice formulations led to the emergence of political failure as a parallel term to market failure as summarized in Mitchell and Simmons (1994) and updated in Simmons (2011).

Starting perhaps with Becker (1983) followed by Wittman (1989, 1995), a growing chorus of scholarship in political economy has come pretty much to abolish political failure. The vehicle for this abolition is electoral competition. This competition is treated as one where candidates make proffers to voters in the form of platforms. The winning candidate is the one who attracts the most support. With uniform distributions of preferences throughout the conceptualized issue space, the winning candidate will be the one whose platform is closer to that desired by the median voter. It is further commonly presumed that candidates will fulfill their promises to create a good reputation for future elections. In these types of frameworks, a government's budget constraint can be denoted as $t \bullet Y = P + R$, where t is an average tax rate, Y is the income base on which the tax is applied, and P and R are the objects of government expenditure. Within this formulation, P denotes spending on public goods while R denotes spending on rents for politicians.

Under what would seem to be the reasonable presumption that people value public goods but not rents for politicians, the nearly inescapable conclusion is that electoral competition will tend to yield zero rents. As compared with a politician whose platform contains rents, a politician whose platform offers fewer rents will capture more votes, provided only that voters value public goods but not political rents. Should voters have preferences between politicians independently of their platforms regarding public goods, some rents can be consistent with equilibrium. Those rents, however, would be limited by the intensity of this preference differential. Electoral competition will generate outcomes in the neighborhood of Pareto efficiency even if it doesn't arrive exactly at Pareto efficiency.[1]

Fig. 1 illustrates the additive scheme of thought. It resembles a billiards table, and this image is apposite because the framework runs in terms of a political entity, P, acting upon an economic entity, E, to shift that entity to some alternative location. Following the customary left-right markers, the party of the left proposes to shift the economy in the leftward direction to E^L, while the party of the right proposes to shift it rightward to E^R. There are several notable features about this framework that are relevant to a comparison with entangled political economy as an alternative conceptual framework. One is that both economy and polity are single entities. An economy is reduced to this status through the presumption that it is in a state of equilibrium that will persist without outside shock. In the framework of additive political economy, the outside shock is supplied by polity. In this formulation, the participants in economy are members of a parade. Polity is the source of power that directs the parade, with the holder of that power designated as median voter within models of democratic regimes.

The simple model depicted in Fig. 1 reduces the world to a single two-person interaction. A median voter is stuck at E, an election determines where that voter would rather be, and the winning candidate shifts the voter to that alternative position, either E^L or E^R. It is no wonder that the new additive political economy concludes that electoral competition generates

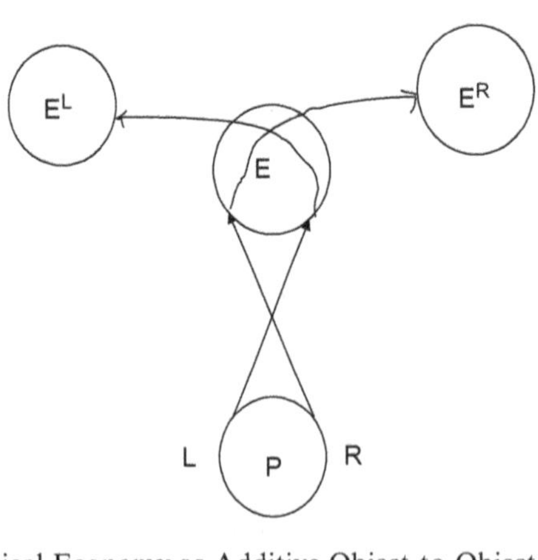

Fig. 1. Political Economy as Additive Object-to-Object Relationship.

Pareto efficient allocations, for it is really impossible to conclude anything else without presuming that the median voter wants to act charitably toward the politician by countenancing the enjoyment of rents by the politician. But then we are not talking about rents, and are back in the world of Pareto efficiency once again.

A cursory inspection might leave this formulation seeming reasonable, for it does show politics as acting on economy. Careful examination, however, shows that this formulation ignores many matters of potential significance, and must do so because there is no way this formulation can address such matters. A parade marshal acts on a parade as a unit; a parade marshal can change the direction of march in an instant. An economy is not a single entity but rather is a congeries of entities that are pursuing different plans. And polity is not some unified source of power, but rather is a collection of people who interact within some framework of rules because there is no option to such rule-governed interaction once you get beyond a mere handful of people. Polity, moreover, does not truly exist outside of economy, for it draws its support from within economy. It is no longer possible to advance meaningful statements that refer to the aggregate categories of public goods and political rents. If some political figures have alliances with some market participants, the distinction between public goods and political rents will often depend on who is making that judgment, for these depictions are constructions of judgment and not free-standing facts of nature. One person could well declare subsidized wind power to be a public good while another can declare it to be an instance of rent creation for some politically favored entity. We would, of course, expect to find suppliers of wind power to favor subsidization and declare wind power to be a public good, just as we would expect to find suppliers of other forms of energy describing those subsidies as products of rent seeking.

ENTANGLED POLITICAL ECONOMY

Additive political economy is surely an inadequate ontology through which to explore the characteristic features of the object we denote as political economy. Fig. 2 depicts in three stages how additive political economy can be transformed into entangled political economy. Panel A shows the additive point of departure, with economy denoted by a square and polity by an octagon. The lightning bolts pointing toward Panel B denote the

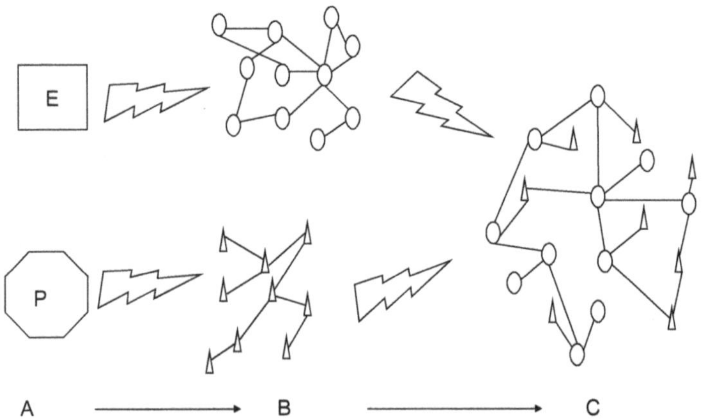

Fig. 2. Political Economy as Entangled Entity-to-Entity Relationship.

transformation of parades into piazzas: the point-mass entities shown in Panel A are transformed into incompletely connected networks of interacting participants in Panel B. As shown in Panel B, however, the two piazzas are separate venues. But they aren't separate, for they occupy the same societal territory. Panel C portrays the joining of the two piazzas, with the ovals denoting commercial entities and the triangles denoting political entities. Panel C is thus a graphical representation of entangled political economy.

This entangled system of political economy will have different properties from typical textbook versions of either market economies or democratic polities (Eusepi & Wagner, 2011; Smith, Wagner, & Yandle, 2011; Wagner, 2009). The ways in which those properties differ will depend upon the structure of connection among the entities as well as upon qualitative properties resident in the various entities. Fig. 3 illustrates three distinct patterns of entanglement. In Panel A there is no entanglement, and the image presented corresponds to standard notions of guardian or watchdog polities, where political enterprises are involved in maintaining the framework of free competition among commercial entities, and nothing else. Panel B shows modest entanglement among commercial and political enterprises. Panel C shows heightened entanglement and could well illustrate the liberal fascism explored by Goldberg (2008). The movement between the panels also illustrates a century or so of transformation in the political economies of the western democracies. As Hughes (1977) explains, a decent modicum of entanglement was present even in the colonial period of American

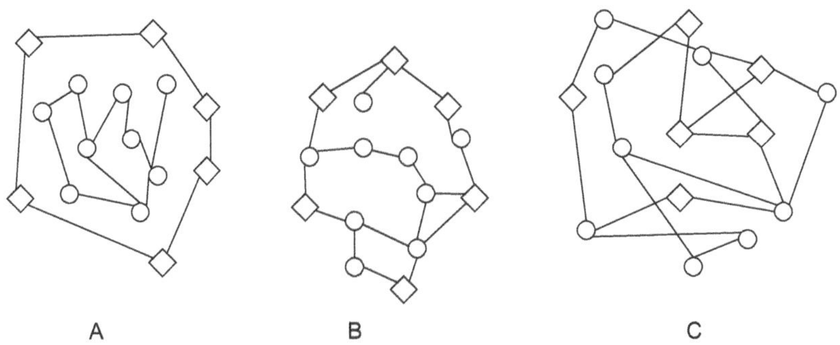

Fig. 3. Contrasting Architectures of Entanglement (○ Market Enterprises; ◊ Political Enterprises).

history, and with that entanglement gaining intensity pretty much regularly since late in the 19th century.

I have described entanglement as a pattern of connection among entities. These entities are enterprises, and enterprises are operated by people. At base, therefore, entanglement depicts a pattern of connection among people. While additive political economy, and the corresponding treatment of polities and economies, conceptualizes persons as independent actors who come together or not as they choose, entanglement recognizes that this conceptualization is more caricature or normative assertion than reality. In point of fact and similar to quantum entanglement in physics, entanglement entails some commonality in response to information among some sets of persons across entities typically denoted as political and economic. Conditions for entanglement are resident in human nature (Wagner, 2007) and are nurtured by the civilizing process that operates in all societies (Elias, 1982, 1991). The particular patterns of entanglement, however, are emergent features of human interaction and to some degree are subject to influence even if they are not open to direct control.

Entangled political economy seeks to render intelligible the changing patterns of political-economic activity within a society. Just as market theory is sometimes presented through images of an invisible hand, political activity would be presented in the same fashion. Read (1958) explains that no one can fully specify a plan that would yield pencils as a product of that plan, as against being able to assemble pencils within some pre-existing nexus of relationships. Pencils are a product of systemic interaction within some institutional arrangement that governs relationships and actions among participants. This same invisible-hand type of orientation can be brought to bear on politically organized activity, as McKean (1965) suggests and as Wagner (2007, 2012a) carries forward. Ostrom (1962) illustrates this theme in explaining that the supply of water in cities is not a product of some single plan, either private or public, but is a product of complex interaction among numerous participants, both private and public, and with some of those interactions being of mutual advantage and others not.

With respect to patterns of entanglement, Jacobs (1992, pp. 92–111) described commingling among commercial and guardian entities as being capable of generating "monstrous moral hybrids." It is easy to see how this might occur by recurring to Pantaleoni's (1911) treatment of parasitical political pricing. Market enterprises generate revenues by offering services to customers. The theory of a market economy explains how orderly patterns of activity can arise without anyone planning the entire system of interaction. Individual entities plan their activities, of course, but the entire system of interaction is spontaneously ordered and not planned. A theory of entangled political economy seeks to extend that recognition to collectively organized activity. Within this framework, patterns of collective activity emerge out of interactions among participants in political processes just as patterns of market activity emerge out of interactions among participants in market processes, which is a theme that Ikeda (1997) examines. Within an entangled system of political economy, however, both types of entity operate on the same societal landscape.

Unlike market entities, political entities cannot generate their own revenue directly through transactions with customers. To support their activities, political entities must attach themselves parasitically through taxation to market entities and activities. The nature of that attachment depends on both the form of taxation and the character of the budgetary process. In any case, political enterprises within an entangled system of political economy exist parasitically upon the activities of market enterprises within that system. The presence of parasitical relationships modifies the character of economic processes from that portrayed in the pure theory of markets, as Fig. 4 illustrates. Panel A shows a simple market relationship between two private entities denoted by the large circles. The two arrows connecting the circles denote the exchange relationship between the participants, typically services flowing in one direction and money in the other. The two tiny circles extending out from the larger circles denote the expectation of gains from trade by each participant. To provide a concrete example to carry forward, one enterprise might be a marina and the other might be an

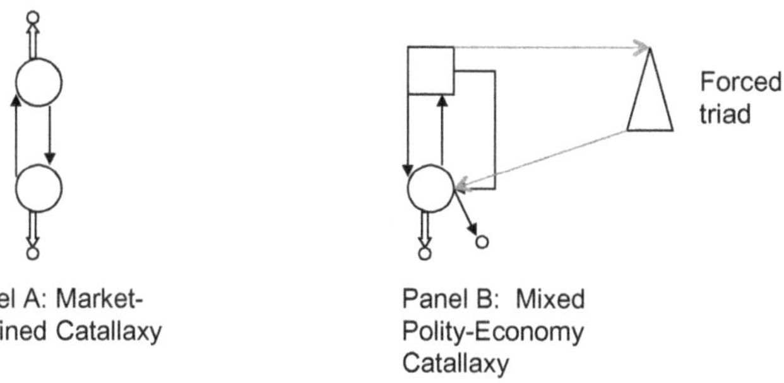

Fig. 4. Parasitical Relationships in Political Economy.

enterprise that dredges channels and replenishes eroded beaches. The marina has a beach that erodes and channels that become clogged with silt. Panel A illustrates ordinary market exchange between the two enterprises.

Panel B asks what happens when one of the entities, say the dredging enterprise denoted by the square, is a political enterprise whose cooperation the marina requires. Panel B is obviously more complex than Panel A, and in that greater complexity lays a significant part of the story of entanglement. The dredging service cannot capture profit from its services. Indeed, it will typically operate from budgetary appropriation. How, then, does the marina get the channels dredged and the beach replenished? There must be some alternative transactional structure in play; moreover, one that at relatively modest levels of entanglement might be relatively benign, while at higher levels becoming the monstrous moral hybrids that Jacobs (1992) describes. There are two forms of complexity in Panel B. One concerns the relationship between the entities. The dredging enterprise has limited capacity and confronts scarcity, as does the marina. The dredging service, moreover, is nominally nonprofit and receives no direct revenue for the service it provides. Yet, somehow there must be some kind of meeting of the minds for the "transaction" to go forward. Panel B illustrates how this might take place by showing a small circle extending southeastward from the large circle, along with the]-shaped arrow extending from the political to the market enterprise. These indicate an indirect form of transaction, similar in form to the various indirect transactions that arise in the presence of price controls, as Cheung (1975) explains for rent control. In other words, the marina would operate differently when dredging is done by a political enterprise than when it is done by a market enterprise.

Also shown in Panel B is a forced triad (Podemska-Mikluch & Wagner, 2013) to indicate the inability of a system of political pricing to operate without parasitical attachment to market transactions. In democratic settings, triadic transactions create two types of participants: those who willfully participate and those who are forced to participate. Willful participants will be those who gain from their transaction with the political enterprise, while forced participants will be those who lose. Typically, those losses will be imposed through a budgetary process through which the losers are taxed to provide the service to the willful participant. It should also be noted, however, that so-called willful participation can come under duress, as illustrated by the situation of a reluctant duelist (Ellsberg, 1956). If there were no forced triad, the transaction would not have political character and would instead be between market enterprises as illustrated by Panel A.

Entangled political economy is a framework that fits a bottom-up representation of social phenomena, as Fig. 5 illustrates (and which was first presented in Wagner, 2012b). As shown in Fig. 5, there is a micro level where all action occurs and a macro level which is not a locus of action but rather is a construction that resembles the tales told by the prisoners in

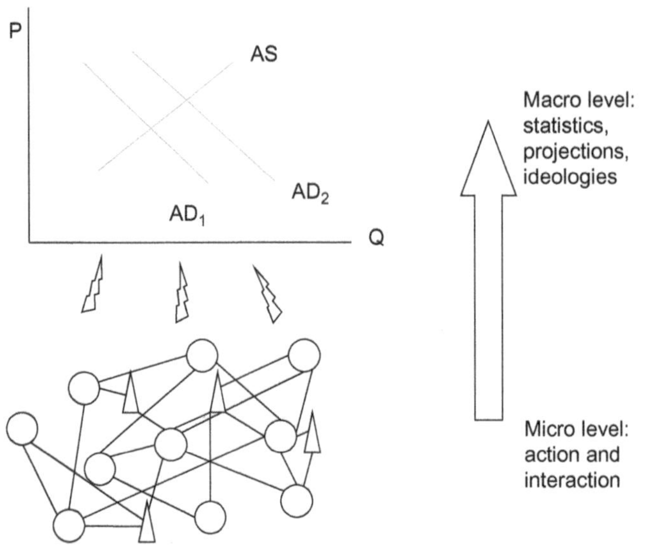

Fig. 5. Entanglement and the Micro–Macro Relationship as Part-to-Whole Ecology.

Plato's cave. As Fig. 5 is drawn, all participants are the same size and all are bound by the same kind of connective tissue. In reality, the participants are of different size and, moreover, operate with different connective tissue. How these differences play out within an evolving ecology of plans is a topic of significance for a theory of entangled political economy, as illustrated for central baking in particular by Koppl (2002).

With respect to connective tissue, transactions between commercial entities are dyadic within a framework of private property, and with multiparty transactions likewise being suitably aggregated within the dyadic rubric. When political entities enter, however, transactions become triadic and the connective tissue acquires different qualities along the lines of Schmitt's (1932 [1996]) treatment of the autonomy of the political. These differences in connective tissue can be illustrated by considering the settlement of commercial disputes between two commercial entities on the one hand and between a commercial and a political entity on the other hand. Commercial entities are residual claimants to their legal expenses, and so have incentive to settle disputes to capture those expenses. Both entities speak the same commercial language of profit and loss, so it's no surprise that most disputes between commercial entities are settled without trial.

The situation changes if one of the disputants is a political entity, for the connective tissue in such a relationship has different qualities than the tissue that connects commercial entities. Between commercial entities, the connective tissue is fabricated through mutuality of interest between equals in the sense that each desires the other's business. With relationships between commercial and political entities, the connective tissue is spun through some admixture of coercion and consent, thereby replacing relationships grounded in mutuality with relationships grounded to some extent in domination-and-subordination. A political plaintiff is not a residual claimant, so does not speak the same commercial language as a commercial defendant. A political plaintiff operates within a budgetary framework that renders budgets as inputs into some objective function. For instance, a political plaintiff who seeks higher elected office can choose to settle or pursue cases based on calculations about expected political advantage. What results in this setting is the use of budgetary appropriations as investments in seeking higher office.[2]

A word should be inserted here about the relationship between cost and choice (Buchanan, 1969) in relation to Fig. 5. The budget with which a public entity works is an item at the macro level. Action, however, occurs on the micro level. Cost is a micro and not a macro category. Cost is the obstacle to action. It is the value someone attaches to the course of action not taken because some alternative action is taken instead. Whether a trial requires $10 million or $20 million to pursue is irrelevant per se in a budgetary context because there is no residual to be claimed so there is no one for whom that magnitude is directly relevant. What is relevant and all that is relevant is the evaluation some choosing official places on the options that lie beneath that magnitude. What results is a conflict between different rationalities that pertain to different environments of action (Bourdieu, 1990; Gigerenzer, 2008; MacIntyre, 1988). Rational conduct in a dispute between two residual claimants will differ from rational conduct between a residual claimant and a political entity because action-taking entities face different sets of ground-level options even if the macro-level magnitudes are the same. In this respect, Jane Jacobs's (1992) analysis of monstrous moral hybrids arises through conflict between commercial and guardian syndromes.

FAUSTIAN BARGAINS AND CONSTITUTIONAL ARCHITECTURE

Ostrom (1984, 1996) explains that government is a form of Faustian bargain: it represents the use of an instrument of evil – the replacement of consent with force – to achieve good, recognizing that an evil instrument will be used for evil as well as for good. In this regard, statistical decision theory offers a significant lesson in starting from recognition that perfection is impossible. To the contrary, the more one type of error is avoided the more the other type of error will be committed. The more that force is used to secure outcomes that might seem to accord with notions of public good, the more that force will also be used to secure public bad. And the less that force is used to avoid public bad, the less it will be able to secure public good.

Within this framework, constitutional rules and devices are similar to experimental formats and decision rules in that they serve as filters of variable quality. A fine-grained filter might keep out most undesired sentiment, but it will also keep out some desired material. A course-grained filter might let that desired material pass through, but at the expense of also passing through much undesired material. While this setting is a difficult fact of life in experimental and statistical settings, it is doubly difficult in constitutional settings. The conductors of an experiment probably agree on the distinction between good and bad. The matter isn't so simple in constitutional settings. While it is easy enough to refer to abstract notions of public goods, rent seeking, and the like, there is nothing in reality that identifies these terms with observed objects or actions. Once again, we are back to recognition that our objects are theoretically constructed, and in a setting where it is probably rare that there would exist unanimity in particular instances of efforts to attach labels of "public goods" or "rent seeking" to particular actions. There could well exist universal agreement in the abstract that providing public goods and avoiding rent seeking are good, while at the same time there would exist considerable disagreement about how those labels apply to particular actions.

The clash between conflicting rationalities is one way of working with the Faustian character of public force through the ability of the presence or absence of force to change both the connective tissue and the architecture of social relations. As an ideal type, liberalism envisions society as constituted through horizontal relations among equals. Connective tissue is woven through material created through mutuality. As an alternative ideal type, collectivism envisions society as constituted vertically, as illustrated by shepherds tending their sheep. Connective tissue is woven with material fabricated through the hierarchical status of superior and subordinate and of domination-and-subordination. Reality, of course, is an admixture of ideal types. Indeed, the division of labor is itself a source of status and hierarchy even if at some long ago instant it might have originated in some mutual rendering of service.

The ideal type of liberalism is private property; the ideal type of collectivism is common property wherein sheep are tended by shepherds. Neither ideal type appears in pure form in reality; moreover, Carl Schmitt's concept of the autonomy of the political holds that force might be contained but will not be eradicated. Property rights are often presented by the image of a bundle of sticks, and with the owner of that bundle being able to alienate some of those sticks through market transactions. For instance, someone who owns a parcel of land might grant a right of transit to an adjacent landowner who otherwise would have to travel a longer distance. That same owner might also lease to someone else exclusive right to use a pasture on the land, and yet lease to yet another person a right to harvest berries that grow naturally on the property. All such transactions as these, however, would fall within the rubric of private property and private ordering. The uses to which that bundle of sticks is put will be a matter of dyadic interaction. But private property is not found in its ideal form because triadic participation is present and, in recent times, expanding. Public ordering can likewise act on the bundle of sticks, as illustrated by regulations of all kinds. A landowner might install a septic field, but public ordering might remove maintenance from the owner's bundle by requiring periodic public inspection and servicing. A financial regulator might require lenders to hold loan portfolios that conform to some distributive criteria regarding income, gender, and race. The reach of private property and private ordering has been generally shrinking for a century or so. That shrinkage, however, is always a consequence of actions and interactions at the micro level as depicted by Fig. 5, which means in turn that this entangled process is driven by people seeking gain at the micro level, and initiated by commercial as well as by political entities.

CONCLUDING REMARKS

This is the world of entangled political economy, which is also the world of invisible-hand political economy (Aydinonat, 2008). Fig. 5 depicts a social setting where micro level interaction is the domain largely of intention and planning, while the gamut of macro level configurations are emergent by-products of that intentional action. This doesn't mean that one must accept what one gets. It means rather that any change of direction or pattern must operate through changing the properties of interaction at the micro level. This relationship between micro and macro levels was central to the Ordo-liberalism that Eucken (1952) articulated and which was subsequently amplified and extended in such places as Kaspar and Streit (1998), Leipold and Pies (2000), Streit (1992), and Vanberg (1988). Within that framework a distinction is made between the principles that guide human interaction and the substantive features of such interaction. With respect to principles, the central issue was whether those interactions would be constituted through mutuality and reciprocity or entailed feudal-like status relationships grounded in domination-and-subordination. Given a choice for mutuality and reciprocity, attention shifted to how to control the Faustian bargain, realizing that no filter can achieve perfection. Here, the principle of market conformability comes into play. Political entities could act, but in so doing they could not contravene the market principles of private property and freedom of contract.

To be sure, the takings clause of the 5th Amendment to the American constitution fits the principle of market conformability. It says that political entities can take private property only if doing so is good for public use and only if just compensation is paid. As Epstein (1985) shows, many takings are for private use or questionable public use, and often with little compensation paid. Constitutional provisions are never self-enforcing, for the enforcement of anything is always a human quality. Strong motives often trump high principles, as Warren (1932) chronicles, which means that the Faustian bargain is always present to do its work. James Madison recognized this when he asked in Federalist 51: "What is government but the greatest of all reflections on human nature?"

Entangled political economy is old and not new. It is a concomitant of treating economics as a social science, as against treating it as a science of individual action in an equilibrated society. The downside of the marginal revolution, and a mighty big downside it has been, is the reduction of economic theory to a treatment of some rational agent in various settings. Among the marginalist troika, only Menger (1871 [1981], 1883 [1985]) kept alive the social quality of economic theory. It is often asked why there is so little money in politics in light of the attention given to rent seeking, with the presumption being that the expenses of political campaigns should be even higher. The question is posed this way because this is where the light is shining. The illumination cast by entangled political economy would show the presence of politics to be ubiquitous, so much so that we don't even think of it. Its presence can be detected in advertising on busses and billboards, in television programming, in the qualities possessed by corporate executives, and in the patterns of activity of trade associations. Entanglement affects the connective structure of societies, which in turn does the same work as technological change, as Potts (2000) explains. In other words, the vision of entangled political economy is a feature of the effort to treat economics genuinely as a social science.

This doesn't mean that it is impossible to alter the pattern of social interaction and its accompanying characteristics. It means only that doing so is not a simple matter of getting a parade marshal to change the direction of march. It is rather a matter of securing changes in conduct among a significant number of participants in the piazza to change the macro level characteristics which are not direct objects of choice. There is no necessity that the monstrous moral hybrids Jacobs (1992) sets forth will arise in full force, but the Faustian nature of the bargain that accompanies the use of governmental force affirms recognition that eternal vigilance is the price of liberty – and that liberty carries a significant price because the practice of liberty requires people to resist the siren call to enlist themselves as sheep in some progressivist-shepherd's flock (Ostrom, 1997).

NOTES

1. Actually, rents in this case wouldn't truly be rents, but would rather be a payment for a service: this is the amount the median voter would pay to be able to watch and listen to this politician relative to the alternative politician.

2. Seeking higher office is just one of numerous possibilities. Another is the pursuit of alternative employment possibilities through connections created via the selection of cases to purse or to settle. Still another is the pursuit of favored causes at public expense.

ACKNOWLEDGMENT

The author is grateful to a referee who pointed out several significant ambiguities in an earlier version of this paper.

REFERENCES

Aydinonat, N. E. (2008). *The invisible hand in economics*. London: Routledge.

Becker, G. S. (1983). A theory of competition among pressure groups for political influence. *Quarterly Journal of Economics*, *98*, 371–400.

Besley, T. (2006). *Principled agents? The political economy of good government*. Oxford: Oxford University Press.

Bourdieu, P. (1990). *The logic of practice*. Stanford, CA: Stanford University Press.

Buchanan, J. M. (1969). *Cost and choice*. Chicago, IL: Markham.

Cheung, S. N. S. (1975). Roofs or stars: The stated intents and actual effects of a rents ordinance. *Economic Inquiry*, *13*, 1–21.

Drazen, A. (2000). *Political economy in macroeconomics*. Princeton, NJ: Princeton University Press.

Elias, N. (1982). *The civilizing process*. New York, NY: Pantheon Books.

Elias, N. (1991). *The society of individuals*. Oxford: Basil Blackwell.

Ellsberg, D. (1956). Theory of the reluctant duelist. *American Economic Review*, *46*, 909–923.

Epstein, R. A. (1985). *Takings: Private property and the power of eminent domain*. Cambridge, MA: Harvard University Press.

Eucken, W. (1952). *Grundsätze der Wirtschaftpolitik*. Tübingen: J. C. B. Mohr.

Eusepi, G., & Wagner, R. E. (2011). States as ecologies of political enterprises. *Review of Political Economy*, *23*, 573–585.

Gigerenzer, G. (2008). *Rationality for mortals*. Oxford: Oxford University Press.

Goldberg, J. (2008). *Liberal fascism*. New York, NY: Random House.

Hughes, J. R. T. (1977). *The governmental habit*. New York, NY: Basic Books.

Ikeda, S. (1997). *Dynamics of the mixed economy*. London: Routledge.

Jacobs, J. (1992). *Systems of survival*. New York, NY: Random House.

Kaspar, W., & Streit, M. E. (1998). *Institutional economics: Social order and public policy*. Cheltenham: Edward Elgar.

Kirzner, I. (1973). *Competition and entrepreneurship*. Chicago, IL: University of Chicago Press.

Kirzner, I. (1985). *Discovery and the capitalist process*. Chicago, IL: University of Chicago Press.

Koppl, R. (2002). *Big players and the economic theory of expectations*. New York, NY: Palgrave Macmillan.

Lawson, T. (1997). *Economics and reality*. London: Routledge.

Lawson, T. (2003). *Reorienting economics*. London: Routledge.

Leipold, H., & Pies, I. (Eds.). (2000). *Ordnungstheorie und Ordnungspolitik: Konzeptionen und Entwicklungsperspektiven*. Stuttgart: Lucius & Lucius.

MacIntyre, A. (1988). *Whose justice? Which rationality?* Notre Dame, IN: University of Notre Dame Press.

McKean, R. N. (1965). The unseen hand in government. *American Economic Review*, *55*, 496–505.

Menger, C. (1871 [1981]). *Principles of economics*. New York, NY: University Press.

Menger, C. (1883 [1985]). *Investigations into the method of the social sciences*. New York, NY: New York University Press.

Mitchell, W. C., & Simmons, R. T. (1994). *Beyond politics: Markets, welfare, and the failure of bureaucracy*. Boulder, CO: Westview Press.

Ostrom, V. (1962). The water economy and its organization. *Natural Resources Journal*, *2*, 55–73.

Ostrom, V. (1984). Why governments fail: An inquiry into the use of instruments of evil to do good. In J. M. Buchanan & R. D. Tollison (Eds.), *Theory of public choice II* (pp. 422–435). Ann Arbor, MI: University of Michigan Press.

Ostrom, V. (1996). Faustian bargains. *Constitutional Political Economy*, *7*, 303–308.

Ostrom, V. (1997). *The meaning of democracy and the vulnerability of democracies: A response to Tocqueville's challenge*. Ann Arbor, MI: University of Michigan Press.

Pantaleoni, M. (1911). Considerazioni sulle proprieta di un sistema di prezzi politici. *Giornale degli Economisti*, *42*(9–29), 114–133.

Persson, T., & Tabellini, G. (2000). *Political economics*. Cambridge, MA: MIT Press.

Pirsig, R. M. (1974). *Zen and the art of motorcycle maintenance: An inquiry into values*. New York, NY: William Morrow.

Podemska-Mikluch, M., & Wagner, R. E. (2013). Dyads, triads, and the theory of exchange: Between liberty and coercion. *Review of Austrian Economics*, *26*, 171–182.

Potts, J. (2000). *The new evolutionary microeconomics*. Cheltenham: Edward Elgar.

Read, L. (1958). *I, pencil*. Irvington-on-Hudson, NY: Foundation for Economic Education.

Rescher, N. (2000). *Process philosophy*. Pittsburgh: University of Pittsburgh, PA Press.

Resnick, M. (1994). *Turtles, termites, and traffic jams: Explorations in massively parallel microworlds*. Cambridge, MA: MIT Press.

Schelling, T. C. (1978). *Micromotives and macrobehavior*. New York, NY: Norton.

Schmitt, C. (1932 [1996]). *The concept of the political*. Chicago, IL: University of Chicago Press.

Schumpeter, J. A. (1934). *The theory of economic development* (2nd ed.). Cambridge, MA: Harvard University Press.

Simmons, R. T. (2011). *Beyond politics: The roots of government failure*. Oakland, CA: Independent Institute.

Smith, A., Wagner, R. E., & Yandle, B. (2011). A theory of entangled political economy, with application to TARP and NERA. *Public Choice*, *148*, 45–66.

Streit, M. E. (1992). Economic order, private law, and public policy: The Freiburg school of law and economics in perspective. *Journal of Institutional and Theoretical Economics*, *148*, 675–704.

Vanberg, V. (1988). Ordnungstheorie as constitutional economics. *ORDO*, *39*, 17–31.

Wagner, R. E. (2007). *Fiscal sociology and the theory of public finance*. Cheltenham: Edward Elgar.

Wagner, R. E. (2009). Property, state, and entangled political economy. In W. Schäfer, A. Schneider, & T. Thomas (Eds.), *Markets and politics: Insights from a political economy perspective* (pp. 37–49). Marburg: Metropolis.

Wagner, R. E. (2010). *Mind, society, and human action: Time and knowledge in a theory of social economy*. London: Routledge.

Wagner, R. E. (2012a). *Deficits, debt, and democracy*. Cheltenham: Edward Elgar.

Wagner, R. E. (2012b). A macro economy as an ecology of plans. *Journal of Economic Behavior and Organization*, *82*, 433–444.

Wagner, R. E. (2012c). Viennese kaleidics: Why it's liberty more than policy that calms turbulence. *Review of Austrian Economics*, *25*, 283–297.

Warren, C. (1932). *Congress as Santa Claus: National donations and the general welfare clause of the constitution*. Charlottesville, VA: Michie.

Wittman, D. (1989). Why democracies produce efficient results. *Journal of Political Economy*, *97*, 1395–1424.

Wittman, D. (1995). *The myth of democratic failure*. Chicago, IL: University of Chicago Press.

Yang, X. (2001). *Economics: New classical versus neoclassical frameworks*. Oxford: Blackwell.

Ziliak, S. T., & McCloskey, D. N. (2008). *The cult of statistical significance*. Ann Arbor, MI: University of Michigan Press.

ADAM SMITH AND ENTANGLED POLITICAL ECONOMY

Maria Pia Paganelli

ABSTRACT

Entangled Political Economy, the idea that the economy and the polity are a nexus of interrelations often with unplanned outcomes, is close to the concept of economics that Adam Smith presents, a concept which was not shaped by strict discipline barriers. I show that Adam Smith analyzes the nature and causes of the wealth of nations by analyzing the interaction of the economy with politics, ethics, and the law. In particular, Smith presents each of these systems as a network of relations with all the other systems: the economy is entangled not just with the polity, but also with other systems of behavior such as the law and morality. Adam Smith may help expand the horizons of the entangled political economy analysis and the explanatory powers of economics.

Keywords: Adam Smith; Entangled Political Economy

JEL classifications: B12; B41; B53; D70; H1; P4

Entangled Political Economy
Advances in Austrian Economics, Volume 18, 37–54

ISSN: 1529-2134/doi:10.1108/S1529-213420140000018002

With this paper I suggest that Adam Smith would be more appropriately described as an entangled political economist rather than a traditional/orthodox political economist.

Political economy is a term with a long history and a variety of meanings (Besley, 2007). Today it seems to be limited to a relatively reductionist approach which tends either to maintain a strict division between politics and economics or to collapse politics into economics (more below). Alternative definitions and research programs are increasingly emerging to integrate, complement, or substitutes for the limits of today's political economy. For example, Boettke and Lopez (2002) call for an integration of Public Choice and Austrian research programs to generate a "unification of social sciences on the foundation of a rational choice model" (p. 112). Their approach is innovative and fruitful, but it seems limited to relax, at the same time, both the assumptions of benevolence (as Public Choice) and omniscience (as the Austrians) from traditional models. Boettke and Coyne (2003), focusing on the role of entrepreneurship, promote the role of institutions in understanding economic development. Yet they see a clean causal relation between entrepreneurs and development, that entrepreneurs are not the cause of development but their consequence. Persson and Tabellini (2004) expand the research agenda to include the effects of constitutions on economic performance and other economic policy outcomes. But here there is an analysis only of the unidirectional relationship between the constitution and the economy. And Besley (2007) goes as far as to call for a New Political Economy that resembles the original political economy of the 18th century. But his goal is to pick – picking institutions to implement and sustain good policies, as opposed to picking good policies. Picking institutions to achieve a preferred outcome implies a clear static causal relationship with no unintended consequences.

While all these works contribute to the dismantlement of discipline barriers – barriers which can be quite useful in developing specialized knowledge but also can be quite limiting by preventing communications and trade across disciplines – the idea of Entangled Political Economy takes the dismantlement of severed disciplines a step or two forward. The following section describes how Richard Wagner begins the exploration of Political Economy as an entanglement of policy and economy. Being entangled implies that a unidirectional causal relationship becomes an ineffective explanation of social phenomena. It also implies that relaxing assumptions is necessary but not sufficient, and that picking institutions becomes more challenging as institutions are constantly changing and often in unplanned directions.

As shown below, the idea of Entangled Political Economy is close to the concept of economics that Adam Smith presents, a concept which was not shaped by discipline barriers, which were still inexistent in the 18th century.

Looking at how Adam Smith works within a system of entangled political economy is relevant not because of the authority he may impose on it, but because it is an additional example of the fruitfulness of the entangled approach compared to the traditional one. Adam Smith, indeed, analyzes the nature and causes of the wealth of nations by analyzing the interaction of the economy with politics, ethics, and the law. Similarly, Smith presents each of these systems as a network of relations with all the other systems. Seeing Smith as an entangled political economist allows us to expand the domain of the analysis. As shown below, we can therefore see how Smith contributes to the literature by offering an analysis of the entanglements of politics and economics when society faces a positive shock, integrating the current literature of entanglements of politics and economics during a negative shock. Additionally, Smith presents analyses of the entanglements of the economy not just with polity, but also with other systems of behaviors such as the law and morality.

Concluding remarks end the paper suggesting that Adam Smith may therefore help expanding the horizon of the entangled political economy analysis and the explanatory powers of economics. And the more extensive the analysis, the more extensive is the call to rethink not just how we do political economy, but how we do economics in general. Thinking in terms of entangled political economy may improve our understanding of the economy, of the polity, and of human behavior in general.

The entangled political economy approach proposed by Wagner is here taken as given. I superimpose Adam Smith to Wagner's framework to expand its explanatory powers. Let us then start with a description of the Wagnerian Entangled Political Economy approach.

POLITICAL ECONOMY AS POLITICAL PLUS ECONOMY VERSUS POLITICAL ENTANGLED WITH ECONOMY

Economics tends to isolate itself. In its worst moments, it abandons interactions with other social sciences, and forms self-contained structures. The idea that interactions with other disciplines should be avoided comes from the idea that these interactions could compromise its purity.

On occasions, interdisciplinary contacts take the form of economic imperialism, where economics takes over other disciplines and dominates them rather than integrate with them. Or, when there are interdisciplinary bridges, they often are simply bridges, meaning that the two bridged disciplines remain separate and distinct. Political economy, for example, can be described not necessarily as an integrated merger of the polity and the economy, but rather as a connection, a going back and forward, between these two separate realms. Analyses in political economy are such that "market equilibrium is established theoretically prior to and independently of political action, with subsequent political intervention establishing an alternative equilibrium" (Smith, Wagner, & Yandle, 2011, p. 46).

Richard Wagner looks at the possibilities of an entangled political economy instead. Wagner recognizes that the analysis of the interactions of politics and economics in the traditional political economy is mostly like a bridge across two distinct and not permeable disciplines. As relevant and fruitful as it is, this analysis may be integrated with a different approach, increasing the explanatory power of the theory. Indeed "The conventional polarization between market and state leads theoretical thought astray by ignoring the ecological nature of human enterprise. A society contains an entangled set of enterprises, some commercial and others political. Those enterprises don't operate independently of one another in separate ponds of activity. They are entangled in a complex human ecology" (Wagner, 2012, p. 125).

For Wagner, the relation between politics and economics is not a one way street leading economics through politics. It is a complex network of reciprocal influences of economics and politics upon each other. It is an entangled and complex relation. To use his words: "Orthodox political economy pursues a sequential mode of analysis where people write the first draft of the manuscript of social life through their efforts in the precincts of market and civil society, with the state subsequently revising and polishing the manuscript. The alternative, polycentric orientation leads to a coeval or simultaneous mode of analysis, in which the manuscript of social life is generated through continual interaction among participants within the precincts of market, state, and civil society, as Eusepi and Wagner (forthcoming b) explore" (Wagner, 2012, p. 130).

Thus, within an analysis, the dominant tendency is often to go from economy to polity, or in general from the economy to another system of behavior, to analyze how the economy affects the other system. Analyses going in the opposite direction, how other systems may affect the economy, are also possible but not as frequently offered. While the traditional political economy approach reflects these tendencies, "In contrast, our framework of entangled and simultaneous political economy, as sketched in (Wagner, 2006, 2007), highlights a third possible option: the recent disturbance is a systemic feature of a constitutional system of entangled political economy" (Smith et al., 2011, p. 46), meaning that it is a continuous and complex interaction between the polity and the economy generated changes.

Another consequence of the adoption of the entangled view of political economy is the realization that the consequences of these changes are, often unpredictable, and often unintentional. The consequences of human actions may not always be intentional. This sounds, misleadingly, like a half-new point mostly because economists are generally accustomed to the idea of unintended consequences. Yet, as Wagner (2012) reminds us, this approach seems to be limited to economic rather than expand also to political economy. Indeed, in our traditional analysis of political economy, we generally think that the outcome of a political action is the result of a specific plan and intended consequences. This is a different approach from our general understanding of economic actions having a purpose for the individual actor, but not an intended social outcome. So, while we are comfortable to work within a framework of "result of human action but not human design" in economics, there is a tendency to adopt a "result of human action and human design" approach, while we analyze polities and results in traditional political economy.

But as Wagner points out, entangled political economy allows us to be consistent and to use the same approach we use in economics also in political economy. Within an entangled political economy analysis, policy outcomes may very well be the "result of human action but not the execution of any human design" (Ferguson, [1767] 1995, p. 119). So, within a traditional political economy approach, "The theoretical antinomy results because political phenomena are treated as simple products of choice while economic phenomena are treated as complex products of systemic interaction. To speak of systemic interaction is necessarily to speak of an order of organizations that is not reducible to some point–mass entity, other than by postulating that all observations pertain to equilibrium states. In contrast, the research program pursued here seeks to dissolve this antinomy by treating polity from the same scholarly orientation as economists treat economy. As an order, polity contains many organizations within its precincts, and with those organizations interacting both among themselves and with various organizations located within economy. While all organizations are oriented teleologically through plans, the resulting order emerges spontaneously through interaction among participants. Within polity there is no one organization that denotes polity, for polity is plural and not singular with respect to its organizational pattern" (Wagner, 2012, p. 122).

The analyses of entangled political economy may therefore not necessarily be elegant linear models, but rather complex representations of a network of interactions with higher explanatory power of reality. When approaching economics and politics with an entangled political economy angle, therefore, contextualization becomes central. An economic principle in a vacuum is fundamental to its own understanding. But to understand its actual functioning, we need to generate a situation where the principle is at work, which is to say, when it interacts with other systems of behavior and when it is permeable to other systems of knowledge.

This, in my understanding of Wagner, implies at least two things. First, in general, that the economic system generates a complex series of networks with all other systems, and the analysis of this complexity of networks and feedbacks allows for a deeper and more complete understanding of human actions compared to a more isolationist, linear, or unidirectional approach. Second, in particular, that within the analysis of the economy entangled with politics and other systems such as the law, morals, and science and technology, the focus should expand and include not only the interactions starting from the economy onto the other spheres, but also the interactions that have effects on the economy even if they originate elsewhere.

The appeal of entangled political economy, with both of these aspects, may be testified not just by the recent work of Wagner and his co-authors, but also by the long-lasting appeal of the work of Adam Smith, the 18th century Scottish father of our discipline. Smith is still marveled at and studied today because of the complexity and depth of his analysis. And his analysis is indeed not an imposition of a bridge between economics and politics as spheres of human conducts independent from each other, or a link between the otherwise disconnected market and state, but an analysis of the complex network of relations between economics, politics, ethics, customs, law, and institutions. Smith indeed writes before disciplinary boundaries are neatly defined, when moral philosophy covered all of the contemporary social sciences and the study of one aspect of social life in isolation would not have been an obvious approach to take. Smith's analysis does not always start from the economy to end up into polity, but it also describes the complex web of interrelation of polity and economy. Furthermore, the economy is not entangled only with polity, but also with the law and morals. And the results of these kinds of human actions are more often than not unintended. Smith's political economy is entangled political economy.

Adam Smith, indeed, analyzes the nature and causes of the wealth of nations by having a multiplicity of sources of motivation interacting with one another. The economy is always contextualized and it interacts with politics, ethics, and the law. Similarly each of these systems is presented as a network of relations with all the other systems. Studying how Adam Smith uses an entangled political economy approach helps us to see how this approach can expand to several different spheres of human behavior: not just used for the entanglements of economics and politics, but also their entanglement with the law, morals, and science. If we take Smith seriously, therefore, we can use him to extend Wagner's analysis and we can use Wagner's analysis to better understand Smith's.

ADAM SMITH

Let us now see how Adam Smith not only uses an entangled framework similar to the one that Richard Wagner describes, but that Smith also expands it and enriches it so that our understanding of human behavior may be more comprehensive. For the sake of simplicity, I limit myself to the Smith's analysis in some parts of the *Wealth of Nations* (WN) (Smith, [1776] 1981). I use the *Theory of Moral Sentiments* (TMS) (Smith, [1759] 1984) and the *Lectures on Jurisprudence* (LJ) (Smith, [1762–3, 1766] 1982) only sporadically and instrumentally and non-systematically. The inclusion of *The Theory of Moral Sentiments* (and of the *Lectures on Jurisprudence*) is an additional step that would corroborate the current analysis and increase the emphasis of how entangled human behavior is, but at this point it would excessively complicate the analysis.

Following my understanding of Wagner's analysis, I point out how Smith explores the entanglements of the economy with the polity, and how the results of the complex nexus of relations between the polity and the economy may generate unintended results. While Wagner uses a negative shock to exemplify the extent of the knotted relations between polity and economy, Smith uses a positive shock. Additionally, Adam Smith seems to use the method that Wagner describes in a more extensive way than Wagner does at the moment. For Smith, the economy is entangled not just with the polity, but also with the law and with morality. And it is the interactions of *all* these nexuses that characterize human society.

I offer a couple of examples to explain how I see Adam Smith as an entangled political economist, and how I see him as expanding entangled political economy analysis. I start by showing how in Smith the economy and the state are entangled, and how they are entangled in such a complex way to generate outcomes that none intended. I use the positive shock of the discovery of the New World. I then show how the economy and the law are entangled: the economy shapes the law just as the law shapes the economy. Similarly, I show how in Smith economy and morality are entangled, that is, how the economic affects moral just as much as the moral affects the economic.

Smith's Invisible Hand as a Wagner's Marina

The first thing I would like to notice in fleshing out the entangled relations between politics and economics is the lack of independence of market and state in Smith. As Wagner points out, traditional political economy draws a bridge between two distinct spheres of behavior, while entangled political economy sees these two spheres in continuous and porous interaction as testified by the complex nexus of their relations. When we look at Adam Smith and at his scholarship, we can see an example of the difference between political economy and entangled political economy.

Adam Smith's most famous two words are the "invisible hand." More often than not, the invisible hand today is understood and presented as a claim for free market, where by free market is generally implied as a complete absence of political intervention in the market (Grampp, 2000). This interpretation exposes Smith to a series of accusations or praises both from the left and right. It is often claimed that Smith does not believe in any regulation at all and this is why he believes in free markets. It is also often claimed that Smith believes in regulations and therefore he is in favor of interventionism. These two positions seem to be irreconcilable, and are the sources of many debates (Samuels, 2011; Stigler, 1971; Viner, 1927). Yet, if we use the entangled political economy approach, we can see why these readings of Smith may be both right and wrong. They are both right because it is true that Smith favors free markets, but it is also true that Smith favors political interventions in the market. They are both wrong because they assume Smith works with the same apparatus we do: that markets and state are separate and independent from each other.

For Smith, one cannot have a functioning market without the power of the state that guarantees and regulates property rights and contracts.

And the enforcement of contract law makes little sense in a context with no markets. Markets and state are both necessarily present in the analysis and necessarily entangled. I believe Samuels (2011) is correct in describing Smith, even if in a different context, as presenting the following view: "The market must be seen to be qualified in its operation by the impact of moral and legal rules and other institutions that are themselves a matter of choice and evolution .... The order produced by markets can only arise if the legal and moral framework is operating well" (Samuels, 2011, p. 47). And again: "Markets do not exist independently of mankind. Markets are a function of strategic actions of business people and firms, laws, and moral rules. Markets are like property, law, and morals: Each is simultaneously both a dependant and independent variable. Each, that is to say, is a function of the forces acting on and through it, and each influences those same forces" (Samuels, 2011, p. 185).

Understanding Smith's analysis of the invisible hand, regulating the relations between markets and state, in this way, as a symbiotic nexus of entangled relationships, is not far from Wagner's analysis of a marina.

A marina is an attractive place to go on vacation or just to spend a few days out of town. There are boats; there are restaurants, shops, hotels, piazzas. Wagner asks, for example, what determines the price of a hotel in that busy marina. The market? The state? Private interactions? Public interactions? In a sense, the answer is: all of the above. The price of the hotel is partially dependant on private enterprises and public enterprises, and an entangled relation of the two. The (market) price of a hotel is partly dependant on the quality of the (public) road that leads to it. In Wagner's words: "For instance, you travel between the hotel in which you stay and the marina over roads that are built and maintained by governments. Among other things, the value of the hotel and the services it offers depends on the quality of the roads. Furthermore, the river on which the marina sits requires periodic dredging by some government agency to prevent boats from running aground. The full set of activities that are undertaken within the town and its environs requires cooperation and coordination throughout an array of enterprises, private and public. That cooperation and coordination, moreover, is not that which we would recognize as a planned parade but rather resembles that of the divergent and interacting plans of the pedestrians passing through a piazza" (Wagner, 2012, p. 127). Similarly, he describes a piazza with private street vendors and public sanitation and police. Mentioning recent work of Storr (2008), Wagner explains that the entanglement is unavoidable because both collective and market activities occupy the same societal space.

Just like Smith, Wagner tells us that markets in isolations do not exist. Markets are intertwined with state activities in a way that is difficult, if not impossible to separate. In addition, Wagner notices that today considering markets in isolation may be an ineffective instrument because it tends to ignore a large part of our social and economic interactions: "The market-based theory of societal coordination, however, gives only an incomplete account of the full range of societal coordination. The domain of that incompleteness, moreover, is surely wider now when collective activity comprises a third to a half of all economic activity than when it comprised less than a tenth." (Wagner, 2012, p. 126)

Unplanned Results of Entangled Profit and Power

Another aspect of the entangled political economy we can see in Smith is the idea that the entanglement of the economy and polity is such that the desire for profits and the desire for power are knotted together, even if not always with positive consequences for society. Often the entanglement of economic profit and political power is difficult, if not impossible, to detangle. In Smith one can see that not just businesses lobby the government to expand themselves, but also that the government uses businesses to expand its power and the line that separate the two is blurred. And in all cases, the results are more often than not unplanned, or, to use the sentence of Ferguson ([1767] 1995) mentioned above, they are the results of human action but not of human design.

The idea of an entanglement of factors in determining social, political, and economic outcome in an unplanned manner is indeed one of the major contributions of the Scottish thinkers of the 18th century (Berry, 1997). In a sense following Mandeville ([1732] 1988), Adam Smith is not dissimilar to Ferguson ([1767] 1995), Robertson ([1769] 1989), or Millar ([1806] 2006) in their understanding of unplanned results of human interactions (Smith, 2009), which Wagner brings back in the analysis.

Wagner sustains that an effective arena to see the entanglements of the entangled political economy is a crisis: "Though we maintain that entanglement is a relevant organizing framework during all periods of politico-economic activity, we argue that moments of crisis are particularly useful in demonstrating this relevance because crisis accelerates interaction between the two orders as demand for political responses increases in the wake of undesirable macro-outcomes. Consequently, new relationships are formed across nodes as traditional boundaries are less respected"

(Smith et al., 2011, p. 51). He uses the reactions to the 2008 crisis as an example. Some big businesses more or less in need enable the government to expand its powers and the government crave for power enables some big businesses to gain privileges.

Adam Smith does not face nor does he describe major negative shocks to the economy. Yet, in his words, we find major shocks to the economy. The discovery of the New World is a shock to the economy, even if a positive one, in most of the cases. We can use the discovery of the New World as a parallel to see how it may be possible to expand the analysis that Wagner started. In this sense Smith's analysis completes the analysis of entangled political economy of Smith et al. (2011).

In Smith, the examples of big businesses and manufacturers obtaining privileges from the government are numerous and well described in the literature (Evensky, 2005). But what are also numerous are the simultaneous examples of the government using big businesses to expand its power. The colonial policies are an example of this complex entanglement of polity and economics. Basically, all the colonial expansions in modern time, according to Smith, seem to be due to an entanglement of search for power and search for profits, from the conquests of Columbus to the management of the East India Company. The Crown of Spain continued funding Columbus's search for Eldorado in exchange not only for half of the gold found, but also for possession of the new territories, while Columbus seeked Spanish support for his search for profits and glory (WN IV.viii. a.15, p. 51). Britain subsidized and gave privileges to the East India Company to expand its empire in the east as the East India Company searched for government's protection of its privileges (WN IV.i.e. 26–29, pp. 746–754).

Interestingly, Smith states that the consequences of the dynamics between the economy and the polity in the colonies are unplanned and unpredictable, just like Wagner suggests the consequences of entangled political economy tend to be. Wagner indeed claims: "As agreements are reached, statutes modified, and regulations written, a package of outcomes emerges that no one has chosen, not even senior members of the legislative and executive branches of government. Each participant pursues opportunities for gain within a networked system of complex interaction where the overall outcome is not a product of intentional choice" (Smith et al., 2011, p. 48). And towards the conclusion of the chapter "On the Motives for establishing new Colonies," Smith tells us something quite similar: how entangled and how unpredictable the colonial power is. Indeed "A project of commerce to the East Indies, therefore, gave occasion to the first discovery of the West. A project of conquest gave occasion to the establishment of the Spaniards in those newly discovered countries. The motive which excited them to this conquest was a project of gold and silver mines; and the course of accidents, which no human wisdom could foresee, rendered this project much more successful than the undertakers had any reasonable ground for expecting" (WN IV.vii.b.21, p. 564).

While Smith is famous, correctly or not, for the positive unintended consequences of human actions within the economy, the unintended consequences of the entanglement of the desire for power and the desire for profits, of the polity and of the economy, may not always be positive. Indeed they may be quite negative, if not fatal. The policies resulting in the long run from the development of the discovery and conquest of the new world, are an example of how damaging this entanglement can become. The following lengthy paragraph is worthy citing in full due to the power of Smith's description: The monopoly of the colony trade besides, by forcing towards it a much greater proportion of the capital of Great Britain than what would naturally have gone to it, seems to have broken altogether that natural balance which would otherwise have taken place among all the different branches of British industry. The industry of Great Britain, instead of being accommodated to a great number of small markets, has been principally suited to one great market. Her commerce, instead of running in a great number of small channels, had been taught to run principally in one great channel. But the whole system of her industry and commerce had thereby been rendered less secure; the whole state of her body politick less healthful, than it otherwise would have been. In her present condition, Great Britain resembles one of those unwholesome bodies in which some of the vital parts are overgrown, and which, upon that account, are liable to many dangerous disorders scarce incident to those in which all the parts are more properly proportioned. A small stop in that great blood-vessel, which had been artificially swelled beyond its natural dimensions, and through which an unnatural proportion of the industry and commerce of the country had been forced to circulate, is very likely to bring on the most dangerous disorders upon the whole body politick. The expectation of a rupture with the colonies, accordingly, has struck the people of Great Britain with more terror than they ever felt for a Spanish armada, or a French invasion .... The blood, of which the circulation is stopt in some of the smaller vessels, easily disgorges itself into the greater, without occasioning any dangerous disorder; but when it is stopt in any of the greater vessels, convulsions, apoplexy, or death, are the immediate and unavoidable consequences. (WN IV.vii.c.43, pp. 604–605)

Smith's analysis is parallel to Wagner's when Wagner notices that: "On a conceptual level, Jacobs (1992) describes societal processes that evolve through interaction between institutional carriers of two distinct moralities, which she describes as the commercial and the guardian moral syndromes. A central feature of her analysis is the treatment of some of the debilitating qualities of certain patterns of entanglement, and which she describes as "monstrous moral hybrids" (Smith et al., 2011, p. 48).

Entangled Law: Stage Theory as a Theory of Entanglement

Let us now look at how Smith analyzes the interaction between the economy and other systems of behaviors. Let us start from how Smith describes the interaction of the law and the economy. Here again, the relations are complex and not unidirectional. Following Montesquieu ([1748] 1989) and possibly Voltaire ([1733] 1999) and followed by Millar ([1806] 2006), Adam Smith tells us that, as societies develop more complex social and economic ties, their legal systems also increase in complexity (Berry, 1997; Smith, 2006). In different stages of development, "the laws and regulations with regard to property must be very different" (LJ: 1.33, p. 16).

A nomadic population will not need a complex legal system, and especially not a complex legal system based on property law like one would need in a society where commerce is the predominant form for the generation of wealth. There is not much private property in a nomadic economy, while there is lots of it in a commercial economy. A commercial society, with complex and multiform needs to transfer property, will have a more complex legal system based on property law and on the transfer of property (Berry, 1997).

In the earliest stages of economic development, Smith indeed tells us, "[f]ew laws or regulations will (be) requisite ..., and these will not extend to nay great length, or be very rigorous in the punishments annexed to any infringement of property" (LJ: 1.33, p. 16). But "when flocks and herds come to be reared property then becomes of a very considerable extent; there are many opportunities of injuring one another and such injuries are extremely pernicious to the sufferer. In this state many more laws and regulations much take place; theft and robbery being easily committed, will of consequences be punished with the utmost rigor. In the age of agriculture, they are not perhaps so much exposed to theft and open robbery, but then there are many ways in which property may be interrupted as the subjects of it are considerably extended. The laws therefore tho perhaps not so rigorous will be of a far greater number than amongst a nation of shepherds. In the age of commerce, as the subjects of property are greatly increased the laws must be proportionally multiplied. The more improved any society is and the greater length the several [sic] means of supporting the inhabitants are carried, the greater will be the number of their laws and regulations necessary to maintain justice, and prevent infringements of the right of property" (LJ: 1.33–4, p. 16)

The stage of economic development has, for Smith, shaped the development of the legal system. But what is interesting is that the analysis Smith gives us does not stop here. While it is true that an economic system affects its legal system, it is also true that a legal system affects its economic system. It is a complex entangled relationship that shapes the actual condition of a society.

Historically, the advent of commerce and commercial society brought about good governance and a fully developed legal system. But at the same time, the stability of the legal system allowed for commercial societies to flourish (WN III).

The most striking example of this entangled interrelation between the economy and the law is Smith's analysis of the three different kind of economic systems: the stationary, the progressive, and the declining economic systems. What characterizes each system is its level of economic growth. Smith uses the state of population growth as a proxy to evaluate economic growth. For Smith, it is the legal system that helps determining each economic state, more than the natural resources, or the technology available, or other natural variables. The law is entangled with the economy so that economy may affect the law, but at the same time the law plays a major role in determining the economic conditions.

China is "one of the richest, that is, one of the most fertile, best cultivated, most industrious, and most populous countries in the world," (WN I.viii.24, 89) but its laws are oppressive. Its population and its economy stagnate. The American colonies on the other hand are blessed with the "genius of the British constitution" (WN I.viii.26, 91) and have an expanding economy and population. So much so that a widower with several children is "frequently courted as a sort of fortune" (WN I.viii.23, 88) and is able to remarry immediately because her children are considered a valuable asset. Bengal, on the other hand, is the tragic example of the effects of bad laws on the economy. Bengal succumbed to mercantilist law which promoted monopolistic trade. Bengal, a fertile land which can support a large population sees a continuous population decline due to famine: "[Bengal is] a fertile country which had before been much depopulated, where subsistence, consequently, should not be very difficult, and where, notwithstanding, three or four hundred thousand people die of hunger in one year" (WN I.viii.25, 91).

Entangled Morality

The economy for Smith, like any other system that motivates human behavior, generates a complex nexus of relations because of its interactions with other systems such as morality. Smith shows us the economy affects morality and at the same time morality affects the economy in a complex interactive way. Smith, like (Montesquieu, [1748] 1989), but not identically, believes in the doux commerce, that is, commerce softens the spirits of people, making them more humane and compassionate. For example, the development of commerce enables the abandonment of the practice of infanticide because it grows to be considered morally repugnant (WN intro.4, 10 and WN I.viii.24, 90). The development of commerce also enables honesty to flourish and to become a habit. "Whenever commerce is introduced into any country, probity and punctuality always accompany it. These virtues in a rude and barbarous country are almost unknown. Of all the nations in Europe, the Dutch, the most commercial, are the most faithfull to their word. The English are more so than the Scotch, but much inferior to the Dutch, and in the remote parts of this country they <are> far less so than in the commercial parts of it. [...] A dealer is afraid of losing his character, and is scrupulous in observing every engagement. When a person makes perhaps 20 contracts in a day, he cannot gain so much by endeavouring to impose on his neighbours, as the very appearance of a cheat would make him lose. Where people seldom deal with one another, we find that they are somewhat disposed to cheat, because they can gain more by a smart trick than they can lose by the injury which it does their character. [...] When the greater part of people are merchants they always bring probity and punctuality into fashion, and these therefore are the principal virtues of a commercial nation"(LJ (B) 326–328, pp. 538–539). This lays out enabling conditions for economic development and growth. Yet, the prosperity now generated may in its turn generate perverse incentives, which in their turn would hinder economic development and growth.

Smith tells us indeed that large profit opportunities, such as the ones emerging from the government granting monopoly powers to some merchants in commercial societies, generate incentives for immoral behaviors which in their turn generate economic consequences which happen to be degenerative and destructive for the economy. Some big merchants and manufacturers, attracted by the rents that the government offers, disregard morality to increase their profits, thanks to the establishment and the maintenance of monopolistic privileges (Paganelli, 2009).

For Smith: "to hurt in any degree the interest of any one order of citizens, for no other purpose but to promote that of some other, is evidently contrary to that justice and equality of treatment which the sovereign owes to all the different orders of his subjects" (WN IV.viii.30, p. 654). But this is exactly what the government monopolies give incentives to do.

Merchants behave in an unjust way because "the interest of the home-consumer had been sacrificed to that of the producer ... a great empire has been established for the sole purpose of raising up a nation of customers who should be obliged to buy from the shops of our different producers, all the goods with which these could supply them. For the sake of that little enhancement of price which this monopoly might afford our produces, the home-consumers have been burdened with the whole expense of maintaining and defending that empire" (WN IV.viii.53, p. 661).

The entanglement of (im)morality and economy generates cruelty as Smith explains: "But the cruelest of our revenue laws, I will venture to affirm, are mild and gentle, in comparison of some of those which the clamour of our merchants and manufacturers had extorted from the legislature, for the support of their own absurd and oppressive monopolies. Like the laws of Draco, these laws may be said to be all written in blood" (WN IV.viii.17, 648), as well as causing disruption to an unplanned extent.

We can learn from Smith, therefore, that economy and morality are entangled in a complex nexus of relationships. The economic conditions may affect the moral code just like a moral code may affect the economic conditions of the individual and society and their relationship may not be a simple one. It may not be by accident that recent works on the morality of markets, that is of the complex of interactions and mutual influences between markets and morality, are done by scholars (such as McCloskey, 2006; Yandle, 1983; Zak & Jensen, 2008) who are deep admires of Adam Smith.

CONCLUSIONS

Entangled political economy is an approach to analyzing the relations between polity and economy which implies a complex nexus of relations between the two spheres or human behaviors. Looking at Adam Smith helps expand this approach and see its potentials for explaining human behaviors and institutions.

Smith integrates the current literature which presents an analysis of a negative shock to society and by looking at how the economy is entangled with the polity. Adam Smith also adds the possibility of seeing the unintended consequences of the complex nexus of interactions of polity and economy in a positive shock to society, such as the discovery and conquest of the New World. Smith offers the understanding that the economy is entangled not only with the polity, but also with the law, and with morals. For Smith the relation between the economy and the other systems that affect human conduct is a complex one, based on several simultaneous layers of interactions. So when we wish to understand political economy, we should consider that the economy interacts with the polity and also, simultaneously, with the law and with morality.

Using Smith to expand the understanding of an entangled political economy helps us understanding human behavior which therefore implies studying not just these different systems independently from one another, but also, and maybe in particular, their relations and interactions with each other.

REFERENCES

Berry, C. J. (1997). *Social theory of the Scottish enlightenment.* Edinburgh, IN: Edinburgh University. Press.

Besley, T. (2007). The new political economy. *The Economic Journal, 117*(524), F570–F587.

Boettke, P. J., & Coyne, C. J. (2003). Entrepreneurship and development: Cause or consequence? *Advances in Austrian Economics, 6*, 67–87.

Boettke, P. J., & Lopez, E. J. (2002). Austrian economics and public choice. *Review of Austrian Economics, 15*(2–3), 111–119.

Evensky, J. (2005). *Adam Smith's moral philosophy.* New York, NY: Cambridge University Press.

Ferguson, A. ([1767] 1995). In F. Oz-Salzberger (Ed.), *An essay on the history of civil society.* Cambridge, NY: Cambridge University Press.

Grampp, W. D. (2000). What did Smith mean by the invisible hand? *The Journal of Political Economy, 108*(3), 441.

Jacobs, J. (1992). *Systems of survival: A dialogue on the moral foundations of commerce and politics.* New York, NY: Random House.

Mandeville, B. ([1732] 1988). In F. B. Kaye (Ed.), *The fabel of the bees: Or, private vices, publick benefits.* Indianapolis, IN: Liberty Fund.

McCloskey, D. N. (2006). *The bourgeois virtues: Ethics for an age of commerce.* Chicago, IL: University of Chicago Press.

Millar, J. ([1806] 2006). *The origin of the distinction of ranks*, or, an *inquiry into the circumstances which give rise to influence and authority, in the different members of society* (Edited and with an Introduction by Aaron Garrett). Indianapolis, IN: Liberty Fund.

Montesquieu, C. de. S. ([1748] 1989). *The spirit of the laws.* Cambridge, NY: Cambridge University Press.

Paganelli, M. P. (2009). Approbation and the desire to better one's condition in Adam Smith: When the desire to better one's condition does not better one's condition and society's condition. *The History of Economics Society Bulletin, 31*(1), 79–92.

Persson, T., & Tabellini, G. (2004). Constitutions and economic policy. *The Journal of Economic Perspectives, 18*(1), 75–98.

Robertson, W. ([1769] 1989). *The history of the reign of the emperor Charles V: With a view of the progress of society in Europe, from the subversion of the Roman empire, to the beginning of the sixteenth century*. New York, NY: Harper & Brothers.

Samuels, W. J. (2011). *Erasing the invisible hand: Essays on an elusive and misused concept in economics*. New York, NY: Cambridge University Press.

Smith, A. ([1759] 1984). *The theory of moral sentiments*. Indianapolis, IN: Liberty Classics.

Smith, A. ([1762–3, 1766] 1982). Lectures on jurisprudence. In R. L. Meek, D. D. Raphael, & P. Stein (Eds.), *The Glasgow edition of the works and correspondence of Adam Smith*. Indianapolis, IN: Liberty Fund.

Smith, A. ([1776] 1981). *An inquiry into the nature and causes of the wealth of nations*. Indianapolis, IN: Liberty Classics.

Smith, A., Wagner, R. E., & Yandle, B. (2011). A theory of entangled political economy, with application to TARP and NRA. *Public Choice*, *148*(1–2), 45–66.

Smith, C. (2006). *Adam Smith's political philosophy: The invisible hand and spontaneous order*. London: Routlege.

Smith, C. (2009). The Scottish enlightenment, unintended consequences and the science of man. *Journal of Scottish Philosophy*, *7*(1), 9–28.

Stigler, G. J. (1971). Smith's travels on the ship of state. *History of Political Economy*, *3*(2), 265–277.

Storr, V. H. (2008). The market as a social space: On the meaningful extraeconomic conversations that can occur in markets. *Review of Austrian Economics*, *21*(2–3), 135–150.

Viner, J. (1927). Adam Smith and laissez faire. *The Journal of Political Economy*, *35*(2), 198–232.

Voltaire. ([1733] 1999). *Letters Concerning the English Nation* (Edited with an Introduction and Notes by Nicholas Cronk). Oxford: Oxford University Press.

Wagner, R. E. (2006). Choice, catallaxy, and just taxation: Contrasting architectonics for fiscal theorizing. *Social Philosophy Policy*, *23*(2), 235–254.

Wagner, R. E. (2007). *Fiscal sociology and the theory of public finance: An exploratory essay*. Cheltenham, PA: Edward Elgar.

Wagner, R. E. (2012). *Deficits, debt, and democracy: Wrestling with tragedy on the fiscal commons*. Cheltenham, PA: Edward Elgar Publishing.

Yandle, B. (1983). Baptists and bootleggers: The education of a regulatory economist. *Regulation*, *7*(3), 12–16.

Zak, P. J., & Jensen, M. C. (Eds.). (2008). *Moral markets: The critical role of values in the economy*. Princeton, NJ: Princeton University Press.

CARL MENGER ON STATES AS ORDERS, NOT ORGANIZATIONS: ENTANGLED ECONOMY INTO A NEO-MENGERIAN APPROACH

Giandomenica Becchio

ABSTRACT

My contribution deals with the link between Wagner's entangled political economy and Carl Menger's economic thought. It is mainly based on what Wagner himself has called "neo-Mengerianism": a new approach that considers economics as a discipline focused on the network-based interrelations among phenomena (based on human decisions) and political economy as embedded in a social framework no longer neutral from a political point of view.

Keywords: Neo-Mengerianism; emergentism; biology; social needs

JEL classifications: B13; B31; B53

Entangled Political Economy
Advances in Austrian Economics, Volume 18, 55–66

ISSN: 1529-2134/doi:10.1108/S1529-213420140000018003

> [H]uman economy and property have a joint economic origin since both have, as the ultimate reason for their existence, the fact that goods exist whose available quantities are smaller than the requirements of men. Property, therefore, like human economy, is not an arbitrary invention but rather the only practically possible solution of th[at] problem.
>
> *Menger (1871)*

> A national economy is a complex organism of economies, but it is not itself an economy (...) National economy is a multiplicity of economics joined together into a higher unity which is nevertheless not an economy itself in the strict meaning of the word.
>
> *Menger (1883)*

> Money has not been generated by law. In its origin it is a social, and not a state institution. Sanction by the authority of the state is a notion alien to it. On the other hand, however, by state recognition and state regulation, this social institution of money has been perfected and adjusted to the manifold and varying needs of an evolving commerce, just as customary rights have been perfected and adjusted by statute law.
>
> *Menger (1892)*

> The "needs of human associations"[are] common needs shared by individuals who are voluntary linked in a particular association able to provide common goods required by the members of that association. As soon as they arise, they are no longer the sum of single individuals, and they cease to be merely means to satisfy common needs: they acquire their own needs, and social goods are required to satisfy them.
>
> *Menger (1923)*

INTRODUCTION

Wagner's work is based on the too often forgotten fact that economics, or better said political economy, had been emerged as a part of humanities within the history of social sciences: Adam Smith as well as other Founder Fathers, was a professor of moral philosophy. The initial aim of political economy was to understand why some societies flourish while others stagnate. As it is well known during the last century, a massive introduction of formalism and the import of physics into the methodological framework of political economy led the discipline to struggle for its own scientific status. The transformation of political economy into economic science (economics) led the discipline to forget any fruitful interaction and interconnection with the other social sciences.

During the last few years, Wagner has been proposing to replace economics as regarded by mainstream economists with a new form of political economy, which he named "entangled economy." In Wagner's entangled economy, political institutions as well as economic ones are no longer performing uniquely on efficiency: their mutual interaction is much more complex than a linear function has the ability to be maximized. For instance, according to Wagner, both State and market "describe a process of interaction among participants and not some coherent set of optimizing choices" (Wagner, 2010, p. 160). This new way of considering institutions is able to re-build the forgotten tie between economics and the other social sciences.

Wagner considers Carl Menger as a forerunner of his approach. Wagner suggests a new way of reading Menger's work to the history of economics and he suggests a "neo-Mengerian" approach, where entangled political economy would be rooted. Menger's vision of society as a complex organism, not reducible to some average or representative individual is the starting point for what Wagner has in mind: (1) a new approach that considers economics as a discipline focused on the network-based interrelations among phenomena, specifically based on human decisions, and (2) economics as necessarily embedded in a social framework and no longer neutral from a political point of view (Wagner, 2007).

A possible interpretation of Menger's thought through the notion of entangled economy is fascinating. The aim of this paper is to go one step further on Wagner's interpretive reading of Menger by introducing the second edition of Menger's *Principles* (1923) in order to strengthen this interpretation. Although the still unavailable translation into English of the second edition of Menger's *Principles* makes things more complicated, the possibility to show a sort of entangled political economy in Menger's works is both challenging and definitely possible. Wagner developed his concepts by considering Menger's first edition of his *Principles* (1871) as well as Menger's book on methodology (1883).

In the second edition of his *Principles*, Menger described economic activity as a complex biological development of the human species and he reconsidered the role of institutions (basically the State, but also money) as orders and not as organizations (Becchio, 2011; Cangiani, 2006; Ikeda, 2008; Polanyi, 1971; Yagi, 1993). There are two parts where the reader can recognize an entangled political economy approach: (1) the role of biology to explain economic activity, (2) the nature of "social groups" as "orders" and "not organizations." In this passage Menger introduced a shift from his original individualism to a new approach that considers the active and ineludible role of social institutions (including the State) in economic activity.

From Biology to Economy in Menger 1923

Menger had never considered economy as a model where equilibrium can be reached: he regarded economy as an open system based on multiple dynamics amongst individuals and between them and their environment (the so-called Mengerian organicism). In his latest work (1923), he explicitly introduced biology to explain the origin of the economy: namely, he discussed the relation between the subject (individuals) and the object (individual choices to achieve an economic good) of economy, by stating the importance of understanding how cerebral forms of learning are working, and how they are influenced by the environment where subjects are living.[1] If an individual is located in a particular eco-system, the only way to understand the mechanism of their knowledge (that will lead to an economic choice) is to consider actions, interactions, and feedback as emerging forms emanating from the external environment.

Adopting the concept of emergentism[2] developed the rejection of a sharp dualism in the social sciences. John Stuart Mill was the first philosopher who used the term in order to explain some properties of dynamics of some physical and social realities (Mill, 1843).[3] Menger often quoted Mill; Menger had already explained the distinction between some social planned phenomena (legislation) and some other social unintended phenomena (money and language), to be intended as the results of a spontaneous emergence as outlined in his methodological book (1883). In fact he wrote, "the problem which science has to solve consists in the explanation of a social phenomenon of a homogeneous way of acting on the part of the members of a community" (…) "the general nature of the process to which those social phenomena owe the origin which are not the result of socially teleological factors, but are the unintended result of social movement" (Menger, 1883, pp. 152–158).

As it is well recognized, this way of describing social facts (including economy) was carried out by Menger in a strong opposition to Gustav Schmoller, who supported a historical point of view, according to which social phenomena are historically determined and cannot follow any regularity, much like natural phenomena. Menger, who supported a possible analogy between some social phenomena and natural organisms, delved further on this aspect in his latest work: before dealing with how to get resources in a context of scarcity, economy is a research on how some human needs arise. Moreover, he stated that a theory of human needs (i.e., how a need arises in human minds) bridges the gap between biology and economic theory (i.e., how an individual is able to get an economic good to satisfy their original need): "the needs inherent in human nature are the starting point of any economic inquiry.... The theory of human needs (the knowledge and understanding of their nature) is of fundamental importance for economic science" (Menger, 1923, p. 1).

At that time Menger had neither instruments nor applicable data that would enable him to explain how neurological mechanisms worked in the human brain. Nonetheless, he clearly intuited that biological changes in human minds due to an increase of a need represent the starting point of an inquiry into the nature of economy.

Menger went on: he introduced the idea that biological impulses are determined by the interaction between individuals and their natural environment. He underlined how many similar mechanisms of biological feedback between humans and their environment are shared among many animals. Interestingly, human beings and some other animal species have similar social dynamics that enable a rational organization of social life: economy is the highest rational form to organize social life, henceforth economic activity is grounded on biological structures.

The central role of environment in the changes of species, as well as the tendency of organisms to become more and more complex, was Lamarck's theoretically ideas. Although Lamark's concepts on animal evolution have been discredited later, they were adopted by Menger through Schäffle (Streissler, 1990).[4] On one hand, they are compatible with the classical cause-effect explanation previously adopted by Menger, and, on the other hand, they would have allowed Menger to find a general description of how brains work when humans and animals are affected by an external stimulus. Another fundamental idea in Lamarck, that is, the spontaneous generation of more complex living forms from the simplest ones, is compatible with the Mengerian idea of spontaneous order in describing the origins of institutions.[5] Incidentally, on this issue, the connection between Menger and Herbert Spencer's idea of super-organic evolution seems to be plausible.[6]

The spontaneous organicism was central in Menger's methodological work as well as in his article on the origin of money (1892), and became the core of the revised version of his *Principles*. It is worthy to keep in mind that Hayek maintained that Menger's aim was "to trace the complex phenomena of the social economy to their simplest elements which are still accessible to certain observation" (Hayek, 1978, p. 276). Nevertheless, according to Hayek, by starting from these known elements it's possible to combine only certain stable structures: "Carl Menger was quite aware of this limitation of the predictive power of the theory he developed and he felt that more could not be achieved in this field" (278).[7]

On Social Needs and Goods

The use of biology to describe the complexity of an economy allowed Menger to take into account not only individuals as economic agents, but also groups as economic agents: like individuals, social groups have their own needs (social needs). Social groups have a double nature: they can be regarded either as the sum of the individuals that form a group, or as something for more complex than merely a collection of individuals. According to Menger "societies, associations, corporations, communities, and the States" are complex social groups:[8]: he defined them as "human associations" (p. 7). Similar to other economic agents, human associations have their own needs (Bedürfnisse menschlicher Verbände) to be satisfied by proper economic goods (social goods). Social goods are the means to satisfy social needs.

According to Menger, there are three kinds of social goods: (a) common goods, (b) collective goods, and (c) goods of human associations.

Common goods (a) satisfy common needs: a common need of many individuals may be satisfied by each of them separately (the need for drinking water by separate house wells) or jointly by a single well (e.g., owned by a monopolist).

Collective goods (b) satisfy collective needs: they arise when people who share the same common need (private schools, as well as private waterworks provided by private firms in order to get a profit" (p. 8)[9]) require goods able to satisfy any individual need and a delegate agency is able to provide those goods demanded by the community as a whole, not just by single individuals (this is the difference between (a) and (b)). They correspond to the modern meaning of "collective" or "public goods." This social group is composed by the sum of all individuals who share the same common need.

The third kind of social needs (c), the "need of human associations," is a set of needs shared by individuals who are voluntary linked in a particular association ("institution") and able to provide goods required by the members of that association in order to satisfy not an individual need commonly shared, but to satisfy a need of the human association as a whole. The difference between (b) and (c) is that as soon as these human associations arise, they cease to be merely means to satisfy collective needs (b): they acquire their own needs (c). They are no longer the sum of single individuals (b) but a whole that is more than the sum of its parts (c). Institutions become new economic agents with their own needs, which have the ability to influence individual choices. When the need of education (as well as of getting drinking water) is intended as a collective need (b), it can be satisfied by private firms, when it is intended as a need of human associations (c), it can be provided by the State ("der Staat") or the community ("die Gemeinde") (p. 9). This means that in the latest Menger, the historical and cultural development (also effected by the biological interaction between humans and environment) has been bringing about the emergence of new economic agent. As already stated, this new economic agent is different from individuals as well as from the sum of individuals.[10]

This addition of a more complex economic agents (human associations) to individual agents, led Menger to shift from a pure individualistic approach to a more complex perspective: it's not the simple idea according to which social pressure and social rules can influence individuals' choices, rather it's the introduction of human association as a new economic agent. And this approach is quite similar to the German Historical school point of view. It should be noted at this point the fact that Menger's personal *querelle* against Schmoller did not cancel the deep influence that the old German Historical School (mainly Roscher) had on Menger (Ikeda, 1995; Ikeda, 2008; Yagi, 1993).[11] It was Hayek who had always tried to shade Menger's affinities with German tradition, and who had insisted on Menger's similarities with Scottish tradition (Hayek, 1934, p. 406).[12]

The introduction of human associations should not be regarded as an eventual distance from individualism in the latest Menger text, rather as a development of his initially strict individualism toward a more complex approach. He was not interested in any ontological definition: he never claimed that the human associations can be considered as a sort of "Uber-economic-agent." Menger was interested in the causal connection amongst events: human needs are the cause of economic goods; and goods become economic when they are the effects of human needs in a context of scarcity. Human needs are individual as well as social, because along with individuals there are some particular social groups (human associations) whose nature is too complex to be considered just as a sum (of individuals). Human associations exist on complex levels of order magnitude higher than individuals that spontaneously emerge during human history.

CONCLUSIONS: THE MEANING OF ENTANGLED POLITICAL ECONOMY IN NEO-MENGERIANISM

A few relevant elements in Menger's *Principles* lead the reader to consider him as a possible forerunner of Wagner's entangled economy. The link between human needs and economic goods as a form of ecological approach to economics represents the most relevant aspect of the affinity between his late work and Wagner's entangled economy. Wagner himself, when presenting "neo-Mengerian" approach, starts from an inquiry into the relation between mind and society, and between society and environment.

The urgency of reconnecting economy and polity, that is fundamental in an entangled economy, was present in Menger. Wagner mainly refers to Menger 1883: when he recalls the distinction between the two "exact" address and "empirical-realistic," but instead of considering the former as the most important one (as it has always been done in order to emphasize the distance between Menger and German historicists), Wagner stressed the importance of the latter, that is related with any possible application between economy and its historical context (Wagner, 2010, p. XX). Entangled economy is as well implicitly present in the last Menger publication: because of the nature of human associations, any tentative consideration of economic activity as a set of rules separate from polity is incoherent, and, in a certain way, it is a naïve representation of economy that does not take an account of the complexity of social orders.

"Entangled, not separated," as Wagner writes about the nature of politics, markets, and political economy, when he invites economists to avoid the old fashioned contraposition between markets and states, economy and polity. States like markets are "polycentric networks of human relationships," they are not "organizations that exist apart." The four quotations from Menger at the beginning of this paper represent how he developed the idea that the State, market, and money are not organizations: rather they are orders, or better said, networks, where agents spontaneously coordinate their choices and where there is no room for a sharp distinction between economy and polity.

In the first edition of his *Principles* (1871), Menger adopted a strict individualism: only individuals exist as economic agents. A decade later, in his methodological book (1883), Menger started to consider a national economy as an organism where economic laws (that exist) are applied in a context that has been developing in a more and more complex way. A decade later in his article on the origin of money (1892), the role of the State starts to be seen as necessary to fix and to adjust a social institution like money. In his last work (1923), that was composed after 20 years of studies and researches in anthropology and sociology Menger clearly considered "human associations," including states as an economic agents: they have their own needs that require special economic goods (social goods).

Human associations are not merely organized by individuals: they are spontaneous orders where economy and polity are connected in a natural and complex way. This final passage makes Menger a legitimate forerunner of Wagner's entangled political economy and it paves the way to the neo-Mengerianism, that is, a new reading of Menger's thoughts as a whole.

NOTES

1. Modern biology has passed from the romantic concept of "organicism" to the modern concept of "organizationalism": if organism and organizations are considered complementary and isomorphic, their functions can be described as a whole in terms of the theory of self-organizations. In 1945, Schrödinger showed that living organizations don't obey the second thermodynamic principle and later von Neumann pointed out the differences between living machines (self-organized systems) and artificial machines (simply organized systems) (von Neumann, 1966).

2. From a methodological point of view, many economists evoked the concept of emergence as compatible with individualism: they "invert[s] the causal arrow of the structural determinists: instead of top-down causation, [and] focus on bottom-up causation, which they often refer to as emergence" (Sawyer, 2005, pp. 1, 95). Against this kind of position, Israel proposed a different approach to the epistemological status of the science of complexity (Israel, 2005). He claimed that the hope of superseding reductionism by means such as "emergence" is fallacious, because science of complexity proposes forms of reductionism even more restrictive than the classical ones. Israel is strongly adverse to the notion of complexity because of the absence of any rigorous definition.

3. A modern concept of emergentism is due to the *General System Theory* by Ludwig von Bertanlaffy (Bertanlaffy, 1950). From a historical point of view, its forerunners were the nineteenth century Darwinian organicists like Schäffle and Spencer. In 1938, Ablowitz defined "emergence" as a non-addictive, non-predictable or deductible, hierarchical element: "the essential newness of the theory itself lies in its emphasis on unpredictability, for in no previous philosophy has this concept been so central: it is thus a kind of philosophical analogue to the Heisenberg principle of uncertainty in the behavior of electrons" (Ablowitz, 1938, p. 12). And, being aware of the possible "mystical" development of the application of emergence, he added: "however, like alcohol, it is stimulant only in proper doses: many who have used it have gotten drunk in the attempt to apply it to everything" (*ibid*., p. 16).

4. At that time, Schäffle was very popular in Germany, and Menger read and quoted him in his works. The possible connection with biology and the constructive use of biological metaphor in Menger's thought (which he shared with German thinkers) seems sharply in contrast with the recent interpretation by Hodgson (2005), who argues that even if biological metaphor was not directly attacked by Menger, he indirectly criticized it to such an extent that its usage diminished in Germany.

5. This theme was central in his *Untersuchungen* and it was presented in the chapter on the origin of money in the first edition of his *Principles*.

6. Menger was an eager reader of Spencer's *Principles of Sociology* (Spencer, 1876–1897). In Menger's library (held at the Hitotsubashi University, Tokyo) there are many books by Spencer, including Spencer's *Encyclopedia of Social Facts* (in eight volumes, Spencer, 1867–1897), where Menger wrote copious notes and marginalia. Spencer's *Encyclopedia* is an enormous collection of data about language, markets, political organizations, etc., that he collected worldwide. Spencer used those data in order to write his *Principles of Sociology*. Menger's notes reveal he was mainly interested in understanding the origin of money and the nature of labor as well as trade.

7. Hayek wrote: "if we were to derive from our knowledge of individual behavior specific predictions about changes of the complex structures into which the individual actions combine, we should need full information about the conduct of every single individual who takes part" (p. 277).

8. The German equivalents are "Gesellschaften, Genossenschaften, Korporationen, Gemeinden, Staat, Volks- und Weltwirtschaft" (Menger's words).

9. In Menger's words: "… Es kann dies durch auf Gewinn hinzielende individualwirtschaftliche Unternehmungen (z. B. durch eine Privatschule, private Wasserleitung, usf.).

10. Summing up, the distinction among needs-goods of type (a), (b), and (c) is: (a) I'm thirsty, I use my well; (b) I am thirsty, and I also need to go to school, therefore I use a well, and I go to school: they both are provided by a private firm; (c) the State (or the community), as a new more complex economic agent needs drinkable water and a system of education, therefore the State will choose whether to provide a public waterworks and a public system of education or to allow some private firms to supply them. The State (or the community) has its own aims ("Zwecke"), and it has the right ("Recht") to choose how to get goods to satisfy them (p. 9).

11. There are many similarities in fact between Menger and (at least) the old German Historical School. The struggle between Menger and Schmoller was mainly a personal issue that faded away after a few years. Also, the influence of Roscher was central in Menger's thinking, and this is not well recognized to any significant degree: historians seemed to consider Menger as a watershed in German-speaking countries by highlighting the break between him and the German economists of the Historical School during the *Methodenstreit*. Unfortunately, the idea of a sharp division between Menger and the German School is still the dominant point of view among historians of economic thought. Reading the second edition of Menger's *Principles*, the "German influence" on Menger is even stronger above all if we think about the rise of institutions in the new first chapter (on human needs) where a kind of "holistic approach" to social goods seems to be present.

12. Some authors had already underlined the presence of two methodological approaches in Menger's writings (Shearmur, 1990); "in Menger's vision an 'organistic' approach to social phenomena in no way conflicts with an atomistic analysis in terms of exact economic theory" (Krabbe, 1988, p. 58); as well as the differences between Menger's and Hayek's point of view on institutions: Menger's organic approach (compatible with what he called "the exact orientation of theoretical

research") versus Hayek's subjectivism based on the central notion of cultural evolution and on the coordination of individual actions in a framework of dispersed knowledge (Garrouste, 1994).

REFERENCES

Ablowitz, R. (1938). The theory of emergence. *Philosophy of Science*, *6*(1), 1–16.

Becchio, G. (2011). Existe-t-il une "doctrine-Menger" qui soit "heterodoxe"? In G. Campagnolo (Ed.), *Sur la lecture et l'interpretation des grundsätze der volkwirtschaftlehre (seconde version-1923) par Karl Polanyi* (pp. 167–186). Publications de l'Universite de provence coll. Aix en Provence: Episteme.

Cangiani, M. (2006). From Menger to Polanyi: Toward the substantive economy. *The History of Economic Thought*, *48*(1), 1–15.

Garrouste, P. (1994). Menger and Hayek on institutions: Continuity and discontinuity. *Journal of the History of Economic Thought*, *16*(2), 270–291.

Hayek, F. A. (1934). Carl Menger. In F. A. Hayek (Ed.), *The collected works of Carl Menger* (Vol. 1). Reprinted as volume 17 of Series of Reprints of Scarce Tracts in Economics and Political Science. London: London School of Economics and Political Science.

Hayek, F. A. (1967). The theory of complex phenomena. In F. A. Hayek (Ed.), *Studies in philosophy, politics, and economics* (pp. 22–42). London: Routledge & Kegan Paul.

Hayek, F. A. (1978). *New studies in philosophy, politics and economics*. Chicago, IL: University of Chicago Press.

Hodgson, G. (2005). Decomposition and growth: Biological metaphors in economics from the 1880s to the 1980s. In K. Dopfer (Ed.), *The evolutionary foundations of economics* (pp. 105–148). Cambridge: Cambridge University Press.

Ikeda, Y. (1995). Carl Menger in the 1860s: Menger on Roscher's grundlagen. In G. Meijer (Ed.), *New perspectives on Austrian economics*. London: Routledge.

Ikeda, Y. (2008). Carl Menger's monetary theory: A revisionist view. *European Journal of the History of Economic Thought*, *15*(3), 455–473.

Israel, G. (2005). The science of complexity: Epistemological problems and perspectives. *Science in Context*, *18*(3), 479–509.

Krabbe, J. J. (1988). Menger's valuation of nature: An atomistic and "organistic" approach. *Journal of Economic Studies*, *15*, 55–63.

Menger, C. (1883). In L. Schneider (Ed.), *Investigations into the method of the social sciences with special reference to economics*. New York, NY: New York University Press.

Menger, C. (1892). On the origin of money. *Economic Journal*, *2*, 239–255.

Menger, C. (1923). *Grundsätze der volkswirtschaftslehre. Zweite auflage*. Wien, Leipzig, Hölder-Pichler-Tempsky A.G.

Menger, C. (1981 [1871]). *Principles of economics*. New York, NY: New York University Press.

Mill, J. S. (1843). *A system of logic*. London: John Parker.

Neumann, V. J. (1966). *Theory of self-reproducing automata*. Urbana, IL: University of Illinois Press.

Polanyi, K. (1971). Carl Menger's two meanings of "economics". In G. Dalton (Ed.), *Studies in economic anthropology*. Washington, DC: American Anthropological Association.

Sawyer, R. K. (2005). *Social emergence. Societies as complex systems*. Cambridge: Cambridge University Press.
Shearmur, J. (1990). From Hayek to Menger. In B. Caldwell (Ed.), *Carl Menger and his legacy in economics* (pp. 189–212). Durham: Duke University Press.
Spencer, H. (1867–1874). *Descriptive sociology: Encyclopaedia of social facts representing the constitution of every type and grade of human society, past and present, stationary and progressive, classified and tabulated for easy comparison and convenient studies of the relations of social phenomena*. London: Williams and Norgate.
Spencer, H. (1876–1897). *Principles of Sociology* (Vol. 3). New York, NY: D. Appleton and Co.
Streissler, E. (1990). The influence of German economics on the work of Menger and Marshall. In B. Caldwell (Ed.), *Carl Menger and his legacy in economics* (pp. 31–68). Durham: Duke University Press.
Wagner, R. (2007). *Fiscal sociology and the theory of public finance*. Northampton: Edward Elgar.
Wagner, R. (2010). *Mind, society and human action*. New York, NY: Routledge.
Yagi, K. (1993). Carl Menger's grundsätze in the making. *History of Political Economy*, *25*(4), 697–724.

NATURAL SELECTION VERSUS EMERGENT SELF-ORGANIZATION IN EVOLUTIONARY POLITICAL ECONOMY

J. Barkley Rosser, Jr.

ABSTRACT

Political economies evolve institutionally and technologically over time. This means that to understand evolutionary political economy one must understand the nature of the evolutionary process in its full complexity. From the time of Darwin and Spencer natural selection has been seen as the foundation of evolution. This view has remained even as views of how evolution operates more broadly have changed. An issue that some have viewed as an aspect of evolution that natural selection may not fully explain is that of emergence of higher order structures, with this aspect having been associated with the idea of emergence. In recent decades it has been argued that self-organization dynamics may explain such emergence, with this being argued to be constrained, if not overshadowed, by natural selection. Just as the balance between these aspects is debated within organic evolutionary theory, it also arises in the evolution of political economy, as between such examples of self-organizing

Entangled Political Economy
Advances in Austrian Economics, Volume 18, 67–91

ISSN: 1529-2134/doi:10.1108/S1529-213420140000018004

emergence as the Mengerian analysis of the appearance of commodity money in primitive societies and the natural selection that operates in the competition between firms in markets.

Keywords: Evolution; emergence; natural selection

JEL classifications: B52; B53

> This is the doctrine of Malthus, applied to the whole animal and vegetable kingdoms. As many more individuals of each species are born than can possibly survive; and as, consequently, there is a frequently recurring struggle for existence, it follows that any being, if it vary however slightly in any manner profitable to itself, under the complex and sometimes varying conditions of life, will have a better chance of surviving and thus be *naturally selected.* From the strong principle of inheritance any selected variety will tend to propagate its new and modified form. Darwin (1859, p. 4)

> Every resultant is either a sum or a difference of the co-operant forces: their sum, when their directions are the same – their difference, when their directions are contrary. Further, every resultant is clearly traceable in its components, because these are homogeneous and commensurable. It is otherwise with emergents, when, instead of adding measurable motion to measurable motion, or things of one kind to other individuals of their kind, there is a co-operation of things of unlike kinds. The emergent is unlike its components insofar as these are incommensurable, and it cannot be reduced to their sum or their difference. Lewes (1875, p. 412)

INTRODUCTION

Evolutionary theory has seen a debate go back and forth between a view that natural selection operates at the lowest possible level of an ecosystem, parts of an organism for Charles Darwin, who did not know about genes, and later the level of the gene, and a view that the most important part of evolution is the appearance of higher order structures such as multi-cellular organisms or consciousness in human beings, the process of emergence. While most see these two as ultimately inseparable, emergence emerges from the lower level processes and only succeeds through natural selection, strict natural selection evolutionists tend to downplay any selective process really operating at the higher level, while at the other extreme certain emergentists argue that emergence can transcend or move beyond natural selection, leapfrogging it as it were. Stricter natural selection advocates argue that this is a form of "order for free" that cannot really occur. We note that Darwin himself has been cited by both camps, although most tend to think of him as being more firmly in the first camp of those stressing lower level natural selection operating gradually over long periods of time in a continuous manner.

A parallel debate has occurred in political economy among those who think about the evolution of political economic systems. Competition among firms and among societies and systems involves a process of natural selection. However, is what is most important the competition at the lowest individual level or level of firms, the strictly micro, or does the process of the emergence of higher order structures such as larger scale markets or nations move the locus of evolution to this higher level? How do these levels interrelate? Is the emergence of higher order political economic structures an independent process that does not arise from lower level natural selection processes, or does this simply move the natural selection process to this higher level?

The evolution of human beings has increasingly operated through the political economic systems that they live within. Those living in more productive systems have survived and reproduced better than those who do not. This process resembles evolutionary natural selection as it operates more broadly within nature. Thus, the evolution of such systems has become central to the evolution of the species as a whole. This view first found expression with such figures as Spencer (1851) and Darwin (1871), although the principal mechanism by which this cultural evolution operated was through the Lamarckian (1809) mechanism of the inheritance of acquired characteristics.[1] Among those coming to agree with this view late in his life was Hayek (1979, 1988),[2] although many others did so as well (Alchian, 1950; Boulding, 1978; Hodgson, 1993; Marshall, 1890; Nelson & Winter, 1982; Rosser, 1992; Schumpeter, 1911; Veblen, 1898).

It was Spencer (1852) who first coined the term "natural selection," although it was Malthus (1798) who inspired not only him but also both Darwin and Alfred Russel Wallace in their independent breakthroughs in discovering the "Darwinian" theory of organic evolution (Darwin & Wallace, 1858). The lack of knowledge of how inheritance operated through genetics later led to a long period in the late 19th and early 20th centuries, in which the Lamarckian theory of inheritance of acquired characteristics came to dominate under the influence of Spencer and others until the neo-Darwinian synthesis combined knowledge of Mendelian genetics[3] with probability theory to put the standard Darwinian theory onto a more solid scientific foundation (Fisher, 1930; Haldane, 1932; Wright, 1931). Natural selection was central to this synthesis and continued to be even among those who would later disagree with details of the synthesis such as its emphasis on a continuous gradualism (Eldredge & Gould, 1972)[4] or its disallowance of multi-level selection (Crow, 1955; Hamilton, 1972; Price, 1970, 1972). This remained true also for some who allowed for elements of pure randomness unconnected to natural selection to operate as well, most prominently one of the main developers of the neo-Darwinian synthesis, Wright (1951).

A particular problem with the continuous gradualism view was the matter of how it came to be that higher order structures came to appear, such as the appearance of multi-cellular organisms evolved out of single cell ones. This is the problem of *emergence*, which Hayek also stressed, a term originally due to Lewes (1875), although he drew it from Mill's (1843) invocation of "heteropathic laws."[5] However, this problem had been understood as an issue even earlier for evolutionary theory, notably by Lamarck (1809) himself, although his solution involved elements of vitalist theory that would come under criticism by Lyell (1830–1832) and others (including Darwin). Following the influence of Lewes, there developed in Britain the school of "emergentists" who would come to prominence in the 1920s (Alexander, 1920; Morgan, 1923), although their views fell into disfavor with the rise of the neo-Darwinian synthesis in the 1930s.[6] Nevertheless, this emergentist view would gain a revival with the appearance of the complexity revolution in the 1990s, most prominently in connection with ideas of dynamic self-organization (Kauffman, 1993, 1995; Kauffman & Johnsen, 1991). While advocates of this view always insisted that these self-organizing processes developed within the framework of natural selection, critics argued that they underplayed the important role of natural selection (Gould, 2002).

A similar debate exists within the realm of evolutionary political economy. Among those listed above, those more in tune with the de-emphasizing any sort of emergence or self-organization include Marshall, Alchian, and Nelson and Winter, with the rest more open to such ideas, even if the dynamically complex form of self-organization promulgated by Kauffman was not necessarily a part of the views of most of the earlier adherents. Nevertheless, particularly within the Austrian tradition, the idea of self-organization developed drawing upon ideas from the Scottish Enlightenment developed, with Menger's (1892) theory of the spontaneous emergence of commodity money in primitive societies seminal in this regard. Hayek (1937, 1948, 1952) would also develop ideas of emergence and self-organization even before he came to apply these more specifically to discussions of evolutionary political economy later in his career (Koppl, 2009; Lavoie, 1989; Lewis, 2012; Rosser, 1999, 2010, 2011, 2012; Wagner, 2010, 2012).

NATURAL SELECTION AND EVOLUTIONARY POLITICAL ECONOMY

As noted above, it was the vision of Malthus of humans competing over scarce resources as their populations increased that independently inspired both Darwin and Wallace to see natural selection as the central key to their theories of organic evolution, even as Malthus never concerned himself with such applications to non-human situations.[7] Indeed, whereas natural selection in organic evolution underlies the dynamic processes that would lead a group of finches migrating to the Galapagos Islands to gradually differentiate into a set of differentiated species, each adapted to a particular ecological niche on the islands, particularly in terms of the kind of food they would eat, Malthus never posited such dynamic processes in human societies. He was notorious for being one of the great pessimists of the "dismal science" of economics. There was no hope of betterment for humanity because its sinful lust would constantly lead it to expand its population whenever conditions improved until those improvements would be undone as population pressed against the means of subsistence, leading to the infamous checks of war, famine, and pestilence. His pessimism was deeply rooted in the disasters of the French Revolution that he observed in his youth, leading him to turn against the sunny optimism of his father, a friend of the anarchist William Godwin and admirer of Condorcet. While he would become the first professor of Political Economy in Britain, he also became a cleric of the Church of England, seeing only the balm and strictures of religion as the ultimate resolution for the doomed and sinful poor. While his friend and rival Ricardo disagreed with him on many matters, he adopted substantial portions of Malthus's gloomy vision in his formulation of the Iron Law of Wages as underlying the tendency to secular stagnation of the economy.

While he did not provide the link between the economist Malthus and the biologists Darwin and Wallace, the crucial figure in communicating between the social and biological from 1850 until into the early 20th century in Britain was Herbert Spencer, with few today realizing the immense influence he exercised in his own day. While today Darwin is viewed as on a pedestal far above the somewhat obscure and odd Spencer, in their own day Darwin looked up to Spencer as probably the greater and vaster intellect, if not for the profundity of his knowledge of evolution and biology, then for his ability to brilliantly provide a vast integrative synthesis that crossed the social and biological sciences. Darwin disagreed with Spencer on various matters, particularly on Spencer's attachment to Lamarckian inheritance of acquired characteristics, but he never publicly aired this disagreement and declared to a fellow biologist in 1870 that "I suspect that hereafter he [Spencer] will be looked at as by far the greatest living philosopher in England; perhaps equal to any that have lived" (Darwin, 1959, pp. 2, 301).

In any case, it was Spencer who first coined both the terms "natural selection" (Spencer, 1852) and also "survival of the fittest" (Spencer, 1864). In fact he also used the term "evolution" prior to Darwin, who did not use it all in the first edition of his *Origin of Species*. It was only with subsequent editions that "survival of the fittest" and "evolution" would enter into that ultimately seminal volume, although both Darwin and Wallace came to "natural selection" on their own under the influence of Malthus. Thus, in many ways, Spencer was more the father of modern evolutionary theory as we know it than either Darwin or Wallace, despite his Lamarckian sympathies.[8]

Spencer would also play a crucial role in influencing the economists who would specifically draw upon and cite Darwin and evolution as important in economics, although these figures would move beyond him, partly explaining the decline of his influence and fame. Arguably the first[9] of these was Alfred Marshall who touted biology as the "Mecca" of economics in the Preface to his *Principles of Economics* (1890), even as in his more detailed analysis Marshall drew more heavily on physics concepts rather than biological or evolutionary ones. Nevertheless he followed the pro-laissez faire ideas of Spencer, if not as vigorously, given that he also drew strongly on John Stuart Mill whose liberalism gradually moved away from the purer classical form that Spencer advocated and that apparently Darwin also agreed with (Weikart, 2009). More than any of these, Spencer cross-referenced his ideas in biology and sociology to support each other, influencing Clements (1916) in supporting a "hands off" conservationist approach to nature that should be allowed to proceed through its given dynamic succession,[10] just as in human societies he argued that laissez faire would allow the full working out of evolutionary processes that would move humanity to a higher level of society and morality, even if along the way to this higher state the social laissez faire evolution implies society "excreting its unhealthy, imbecile, slow, vacillating, faithless members" (Spencer, 1851, p. 324).

While he would later moderate these views and support charity for the poor as well as hold to a firm pacificism, it was such sentiments that led him to be derided by later observers as the father of a supposedly inhuman "social Darwinism" (Hofstadter, 1944; Leonard, 2009). This designation and the ill-repute that this concept fell into in the wake of World War II may be responsible as much as anything for the current obscurity of

Spencer, although it must also be admitted that he was superseded by others in the many fields in which he wrote, thus also obscuring his important role in developing ideas in these numerous areas.

In any case, in economics Marshall certainly superseded Spencer, who was better known for his work in sociology, biology, philosophy, and psychology than in economics or political economy (Marshall being the figure more than any other who turned "political economy" into just "economics" in the English language tradition). While much of his formal static analysis drew on physics foundations, in considering the dynamics of firms and industries Marshall would invoke natural selection and evolutionary ideas. Firms were not static entities in some unchanging equilibrium, but went through a life cycle, from youth to age and death as they competed with each other. The competition between firms and even industries operated through natural selection as they rose and fell in succession. Following Spencer, although also the older political economists going from Adam Smith through J.S. Mill, he would see a free market as bringing about the proper functioning of this process of natural selection.

Veblen (1898) would criticize Marshall quite vigorously, coining the term "neoclassical" that he used pejoratively in doing so. He would stress the dynamics of the economy in criticizing static marginal analysis, while not noticing that Marshall left the door open for that as well. Veblen certainly applied the idea of natural selection to the competition between firms and industries, particularly stressing the development of the latter over time. However, in this latter analysis he also moved somewhat in the "saltationalist"[11] direction that Schumpeter (1911) would more fully embody, recognizing the possibility of dramatic technological breakthroughs that could discontinuously alter the face of the economy as it transformed in a manner that suggested the emergent self-organizing alternative.[12]

As Hodgson (1993) and Gould (2002) note, Darwin's star fell in the early 20th century due to the general ignorance regarding genetics, only overcome with the development of the neo-Darwinian synthesis in the 1930s and 1940s. The revival of Darwin's standing with this emergence laid the groundwork for the influential paper of Alchian (1950). Arguably more than any other he represented the introduction of this gradualist Darwinian view of evolution based fully on natural selection into microeconomics. Again, the emphasis as with Marshall was on the competition of firms and industries, particularly the former. Alchian's argument became the battering ram against the arguments of proto-behavioralists who kept pointing to such inconvenient facts such as that firm managers generally do not know what their marginal costs are, thus making them incapable of consciously following the recommendations for profit-maximization put forward by Marshallian neoclassical economics. Alchian's argument laid an instrumentalist "as if" foundation that Friedman (1953) would more clearly articulate. It does not matter whether or not economic agents consciously know how to maximize or optimize. Those who come closest to actually doing so will make the most profits and thus survive and grow faster than their rivals and will thus displace them and dominate them in an industrial process of natural selection, following very much on the model of Spencer and Marshall and seeing such processes as improving the efficiency and progress of the economy over time.

For our purposes perhaps the latest stage of this focus on natural selection without some accompanying focus on emergence or self-organization comes with the influential work of Nelson and Winter (1982), even as some of their neo-Schumpeterian followers have been more open to such emergentist ideas (Dopfer, Foster, & Potts, 2004; Foster & Metcalfe, 2012; Potts, 2000). They would draw on ideas of "universal Darwinism" most fully articulated by Dawkins (1976, 1983; see also Hamilton, 1964), particularly the concept of the "meme," which they identified with "routines" in industrial processes. Memes are the fundamental objects of natural selection and thus of evolution. Whereas for Darwin this was the organism, for the neo-Darwinians and their more fervent followers such as Dawkins, this would be the gene. For biological evolution, the gene was the meme. But for Nelson and Winter, it was industrial routines, although this has been a matter of ongoing controversy ever since (Witt, 2004). In any case, if Marshall and Alchian focused on the firm as the locus of evolutionary natural selection, just as Darwin (and Wallace) focused on organisms as the locus in biology, so Nelson and Winter sought to move to the micro underpinnings beneath individual firms and even industries to the fundamental units and interstices that underlie the technological and institutional progress of an economy and society. For them, this fundamental unit was routine, which could spread from firm to firm and industry to industry, maintaining an identity and existence of their own that would follow the trilogy identified by Hodgson (1993) as fundamental to evolution: variability, inheritance, and natural selection.[13]

EMERGENCE AND SELF-ORGANIZATION

While there might be emergence without self-organization and self-organization without emergence, the two seem intimately linked and frequently coinciding, as well as being deeply linked with various forms of complexity.[14] Self-organization is the spontaneous appearance of order in a system without any external driving force. The term was first used explicitly by Ashby (1947) to mean a system moving on its own toward some sort of attractor or equilibrium, with cyberneticists and then general systems theorists picking it up from him, with Hayek then picking it up from them. Hayek looking back sees it in Menger and even earlier in the works of the Scottish Enlightenment and such ideas as Adam Smith's "invisible hand," although none of these used the precise term. Some have also claimed that Descartes (1637) posited it in thinking how the universe might have developed without God, and also in Kant (1790) when in discussing teleology he posited organs that are both ends and means and thus self-organize on their own. Where self-organization may differ from emergence is that this order that it has may not involve any sort of higher level structure.

The first thing we must recognize about the term emergence is that like "complexity," it is a much debated term, particularly within philosophy from where it originally, well, emerged. The first to use the term, or more precisely "emergent," was George Lewes in one of the opening quotations of this paper. He refers to the "co-operation of things of unlike kinds" that result in an outcome that is not the simple sum or difference of these kinds, that is different from them in some qualitative way, and that cannot be "reduced" to them in some sense. He was initially inspired by examples of various chemical reactions where two chemicals come together to form another unlike the original two, with such examples being the original key to J.S. Mill's "heteropathic laws" (Mill, 1843).

By the 1920s, such ideas had developed further into the British *emergentist* school led by Alexander (1920), Morgan (1923), and Broad (1925), with these emphasizing more specifically the idea of emergence involving the appearance of new hierarchical levels, particularly in evolution, with these exhibiting "novelty" or "surprise." Such ideas had been around from the beginning of evolutionary theory with Gautieri (1805) and Lamarck (1809) both linking such emergence of higher levels with vitalist forces, an argument also pursued later particularly by Broad. Corsi (2005, p. 77) notes that "Gautieri rapidly sketched a series of steps linking the inorganic to the organic, minerals to crystals, zoophytes to plants and animals, and finally to man." For some of the 1920s emergentists this moved further on into contemplating the emergence of ever higher states of consciousness and knowledge.

This movement would fall into disrepute in evolutionary and some other discussions with the rise of the gene-focused neo-Darwinian synthesis as well as the triumph of even more reductionist quantum mechanics in physics during the 1930s and 1940s. Holistic evolutionists advocating direct "group selection" such as Goldschmidt (1940) and Wynne-Edwards (1962) were ridiculed and pushed aside (Dawkins, 1976; Williams, 1966), with their arguments never really being revived. The future of emergentist evolutionary theory would depend on more specifically "ground up" arguments based on specified microfoundations out of which the emergence would be shown to arise.

To return to an effort to more precisely define "emergence," an influential definition due to philosopher van Cleve (1990) is the following:

> If P is a property of w, then P is emergent if and only if P supervenes with nomological necessity, but not with logical necessity, on the properties of w.

Pretty obviously as with many definitions this just shifts the issue to the meaning of the terms "supervenes" and "nomological," with much debate over these ensuing. McLaughlin (1997, appendix) argues that *supervenience* involves the appearance of the novel or unexpected along the lines of the 1920s British emergentists. "Nomological" refers to arising from physical laws, in contrast to logical necessity. The emergence of consciousness in the mind in Hayek's (1952) *The Sensory Order* is seen as a good example (Lewis, 2012). A related, although unresolved issue is whether or not this new higher level can downwardly cause events at the lower levels (Hayek, 1952; Kim, 1993). Such emergence involving the appearance of higher levels exhibiting these characteristics was labeled *anagenesis* by Boulding (1978), who drew on it for his own theory of emergent economic evolution.[15]

MECHANISMS OF EMERGENT SELF-ORGANIZATION

After the development of the neo-Darwinian synthesis and the general collapse of the emergentist movement, it took some time for evolutionists to gradually learn mechanisms that could operate within the general understanding given by that synthesis while nevertheless allowing for emergent self-organizing phenomena to operate nevertheless. Arguably the first such mechanism studied was that of what is now called *multi-level selection*. When this occurs something resembling group selection operates, but it does as a result of interactions at the level below that of the group that bring about this emergence at the higher level. Curiously, the foundations for this understanding were based on work by two of the founders of the neo-Darwinian synthesis, namely J. B. S. Haldane and more importantly, Wright (1932), whose use of *fitness landscapes* underpinned his earlier study of how random migrations that separate sub-populations with distinctive genetic patterns from larger ones with different patterns can be the basis of a form of random evolution not necessarily based on natural selection, per se. This initially controversial phenomenon is known as the *Sewall Wright Effect*.

It was Wright's close friend and associate, Crow (1955), who encouraged Wight to move to the University of Wisconsin–Madison in the mid-1950s, who first developed the key mathematical condition under which this multilevel selection could occur, although this has not been properly recognized. This condition involves when an "altruistic" gene might survive and reproduce even as it is making it more likely that other genes will survive and reproduce through actions or processes that are damaging to the individual, per se. This is the essence of cooperation and has its parallel in the problem of game theory first studied at about the same time known as the *prisoner's dilemma*, in which agents may collectively do better if they cooperate, but in which the Nash equilibrium is for them not to do so. The condition developed by Crow allows for the emergence of cooperation in both a conscious human situation over time as well as its equivalent in non-human species, even when the basic incentive and reward structure favors not cooperating on the parts of individual agents or genes. This involves distinguishing changes in fitness within a group versus changes in fitness across groups, with the emphasis on fitness clearly keeping this consistent with natural selection.

Let B_w be the within-group genic regression on the fitness value of the trait as defined in Wright (1951) and B_b be the between-group genic regression to the fitness value. Let V_w be the variance among individuals within a group and V_b be the variance among means across groups. For an altruistic trait, one expects B_w to be negative while B_b to be positive. Thus, as sufficient condition for the altruistic trait to increase in frequency is given by

$$B_b/(-B_w) > V_w/V_b \tag{1}$$

Eq. (1) would be rediscovered in variations later by Hamilton (1972) and by Price (1970, 1972), who published their findings in more widely read outlets than did Crow, leading to this condition being known as the "Hamilton-Price equation." As it is, the expectation is that V_w is likely to be substantially larger than V_b, which led to skepticism that this would be a rare outcome. In order to increase the between-group fitness effect there must be ability of individuals within a group to recognize who will be a cooperator, with this easier for smaller and more isolated groups. Henrich (2004) has labeled this the "greenbeard" problem and it has been at the core of human groups learning how to cooperate to achieve common goals (Ostrom, 1990).[16] Within organic evolution this seems most common for the social insects, who while only a small number of the species in existence, have been highly successful at surviving and reproducing and have come to represent a much larger amount of the biomass on earth than their proportion among the number of species would lead one to expect (Wilson, 2012).

A deep argument has arisen over whether such altruism must be of a reciprocal nature (Trivers, 1971), development of punishment mechanisms to enforce cooperation that appear to be hardwired into human morality (Gintis, 2000). As it is, the subject of how to distinguish pure form from reciprocal altruism has been a matter of intense study and controversy (Binmore & Shaked, 2010; Fehr & Schmidt, 1999, 2010).

A variation on multi-level selection has been that of *hypercyclic morphogenesis* (Rosser, 1991, chapter 12), based on combining Turing's (1952) idea of self-organizing morphogenesis with the hypercycle idea due to Eigen and Schuster (1979), the latter developed initially to explain the successful emergence of multi-cellular organisms out of unicellular ones, one of the deepest problems of evolution and one as clearly exhibiting emergence as much as any other. Central to this is efficient transmission of information. Darwinian natural selection operates on these self-reproducing "quasi-species" based on their ability to transmit information. Key is their ability to stabilize themselves against the accumulation of errors in reproduction, with Eigen and Schuster proposing the existence of a "threshold of information content" for a system that if exceeded will generate an "error catastrophe" and the "disintegration of information due to a steady accumulation of errors" (Eigen & Schuster, 1979, p. 25). If V_m is the number of symbols, σ_m is the degree of superiority of "master copy" in selective advantage and exceeds one, and q_m is the quality of symbol copying, then the threshold is given by

$$V_m < \ln \sigma_m/(1 - q_m) \tag{2}$$

Eq. (2) brings us finally to the models of emergent self-organization that came out of the Santa Fe Institute and its relatives starting about two decades ago, with key work by Langton (1990), Kauffman and Johnsen (1991), Holland (1942), Kauffman (1993, 1995), and Crutchfield (1994, 2003). Most of this involved studying various computer simulation models to see patterns of higher order patterns emerging out of less well ordered systems, often posed as doing so "at the edge of chaos," although this was not a strict mathematical form of chaos. The original inspiration for this came from Thompson (1917), who saw order arising to fit optimal patterns. As Kauffman (1993, p. xiii) has put it, "this single force view [of Darwin's, e.g. natural selection]... fails to stress, fails to incorporate the possibility that simple and complex systems exhibit order spontaneously." Drawing on fitness landscapes and work of Crow and Kimura (1970), Kauffman in particular has argued that as the number of parts in a system (genes in a genotype) that are indirectly involved in the adaptation process increases from zero to one less than the number of parts directly connected, the fitness landscape will change from having a single optimum to becoming random, the *complexity catastrophe.* The so-called "edge of chaos" where spontaneous emergent self-organization can occur is most likely between these two extremes.

This argument and its extensions by others has come under a variety of criticisms. Some come from harder line physics and computational perspectives as represented by McCauley (2004, p. 77) who argues that proper explanation involves the discovery of ergodicity and invariances, and that "we may know how a cell mutates to a new form, but we do not know how a fish evolves into a bird." McCauley cites the work of Moore (1990) to argue that true emergence only occurs with full unpredictability and surprise in complex Turing machines or their systemic equivalents.

From the standpoint of more traditional evolutionary thinking among evolutionary biologists, objections come from those who argue that this approach amounts to getting "order for free" (Gould, 2002, pp. 1200–1214). While expressing admiration for work done by Kauffman and his associates, Gould argues that emergent self-organization fails to fully explain detailed evolutionary developments, which must rely more on natural selection at all stages in a more fully Darwinian mode, even as Gould accepts some non-Darwinian elements in evolution such as the random Sewall Wright Effect. Thus Gould argues that emergent self-organizing models are too general and unable to explain the evolution of "such a phyletically localized, complex, and historically particular structure as the tetrapod limb" (Gould, 2002, p. 1213). In effect, Gould throws the complexity of actual evolutionary processes back at those who put it forward as a complement to natural selection with variability and inheritance.

In their own defense, those arguing for the independent importance of emergent self-organization insist that all these processes necessarily operate within the broader rubric and constraint of natural selection, even if particular processes may not immediately reflect the direct working of natural selection. If what emerges from such self-organization is not able to sustain itself, is not able to survive and reproduce, then it will not persist. For emergent self-organization to play an important role in evolutionary processes, what emerges must be able to be naturally selected at the levels at which it is organized, even if it might appear to be that there is at a more detailed level of analysis.

EVOLUTIONARY EMERGENCE IN POLITICAL ECONOMY

As Lewis (2012) argues, following on Caldwell (2004), it was in his 1937 paper that Hayek began to develop his ideas of spontaneous order and emergence in economics, although he had apparently worked on such ideas earlier in his earlier writings on psychology not published up to that point, but that would later appear in *The Sensory Order* (Hayek, 1952). It has been widely argued that this turn arose partly from some of his frustrations with ongoing arguments about capital theory. Indeed, while most identify emergence with spontaneous order, Harper and Endres (2012) argue that they should be distinguished, with true spontaneous order more complex than emergence, which can have a consciously planned aspect to it. True spontaneous order looks like what McCauley says that Moore argues for, full unpredictability in principle associated with the complete lack of any higher level planning (Buchanan & Vanberg, 1991), although presumably individual agents in a system may be engaging in planning.

As it is, while Menger's arguments about the spontaneous emergence of money constitute the archetypal example, he did not fully lay out what was involved in such emergence or how it related to broader concepts. It was Hayek within the Austrian tradition who did this most thoroughly, and whose ideas themselves on this only gradually emerged over time. Indeed, it appears that although the work was published later, it was his psychological work that underpins his ideas on the subject. In this he was studying ultimately the emergence of consciousness from the nervous system, and he drew on the work of earlier Gestalt psychologists in this (McDougall, 1923), although he would later also be influenced strongly by general systems theory (von Bertalanffy, 1968). Thus, he saw the nervous system operating to develop "organized fields" of "complex sensory phenomena" in accumulating layers, or looking from the top down:

> The fact that the whole system of sensory qualities must in this sense be regarded as one organized field need not prevent us, however, from occasionally speaking of

> different fields as sub-systems within which the elements are differentiated by a more dense and complex system of relations. (Hayek, 1952, p. 77)

In the final chapter of that book he famously pushed this argument to an extreme point while noting arguments of Gödel (Koppl & Rosser, 2002) regarding the limits to self-awareness:

> ... even though we may understand its *modus operandi* in general terms, or, in other words, possess an explanation of the principle on which it operates, we shall never, by means of the same brain, be able to arrive at a detailed explanation of its working in particular circumstances, or be able to predict what the results of its operations will be. To achieve this would require a brain of a higher order of complexity, though it might be built on the same general principles. Such a brain might be able to explain what happens in our brain, but it would in turn still be unable fully to explain its own operations, and so on. (Hayek, 1952, pp. 188–189)[17]

It is not immediately obvious that these arguments apply to his discussion of spontaneous order in socio-economic systems. That discussion referred to older arguments from the Scottish Englightenment, and took the following form:

> What the economists understood for the first time was that the market as it had grown up was an effective way of making man take part in a process more complex and extended than he could comprehend and that it was through the market that he was made to contribute "to ends which were no part of his purpose." (Hayek, 1948, pp. 14–15)

Eventually he would combine these strands of argument into a broader perspective on emergence and complexity. He would directly link this formulation to the older arguments made by the members of the British emergentist school, tracing back the origins of their arguments through Lewes to Mill as described above in this paper and also argued by Lewis (2012). Thus:

> The "emergence" of "new" patterns as a result of the increase in the number of elements between which simple relations exist, means that this larger structure will possess certain general or abstract features which will recur independently of the particular values of he individual data, so long as the general structure (as described, e.g., by an equation) is preserved. Such 'wholes', defined in terms of certain general properties of their structure, will constitute distinctive objects of explanation for a theory, even though such a theory may be merely a particular way of fitting together statements about the relations between individual elements ... What we single out as wholes will be determined by the consideration whether we can isolate recurrent patterns of coherent structures of a distinct kind which we do in fact encounter in the world in which we live. (Hayek, 1967, p. 26)

While it is not explicitly clear in this quote, from this time on Hayek increasingly linked such emergence to evolutionary processes that operate at the level of Lamarckian multi-level selection within human societies. Particular spontaneous socio-economic orders are naturally selected and persist if they are successful in competition with other such orders. He argued for the superiority of such spontaneously emerged orders, with British natural law being a favorite example of his along with competitive markets.

In his final writings (Hayek, 1988) he sharply contrasted such evolutionarily emerged spontaneous orders with centrally directed or planned orders imposed according to supposedly rational plans from above. He saw the source of the *fatal conceit* of such efforts as being in France, with its long tradition from Descartes[18] in philosophy (if not earlier) through Colbertiste *dirigisme* in ancient régime economic policy, to the more fully idealized utopias of Saint–Simon and others. This had earlier manifested itself in how France came to be a nation, the nation where the term "nationalism" was invented. Essentially the province around Paris, the Ile de France, simply conquered the rest and imposed its language and rules on the rest over a long period of time. After the French Revolution, Napoleon Bonaparte imposed his own order upon this nation from the center, reordering its provinces into departments, establishing his own centrally imposed law code upon the nation, as well as a new currency and bureaucracy and so on. He even attempted to spread this to the rest of Europe by force of arms in imitation of his royal predecessors within France, only to fail in this effort, as would Hitler so fail in the 20th century. Nevertheless, for all of Hayek's denunciation of French political and economic traditions, it remains a nation and one that is reasonably free in terms of personal liberties and not entirely unsuccessful economically, although that reflects that it has always held back from full-blown central planning and control and moved to being democratically ruled a long time ago.

While the French model looks more like what we have seen in history, in more recent times we have seen nations and groupings of nations into higher structures emerge from lower levels in a more self-organized and cooperative manner, if consciously so in contrast with pure spontaneous order. So, the United State came into being as a result of a freely organized entity out of the former colonies, even if it was maintained during the Civil War by force. Switzerland also emerged out of its cantons agreeing to form a higher unity, although this unity was also challenged at times largely on grounds of religious differences and conflicts, only becoming set in its modern form in 1848.[19] Recently still we have seen the effort to reinvent the Roman Empire or the Napoleonic or Hitlerian visions in a democratic and freely cooperating way in the form of the European Union and its sub-part, the Eurozone. That these entities are facing serious challenges and may not survive shows that not all such entities persist and survive, although this may yet be the case for the EU and the Eurozone, a topic beyond this paper.

Although he does not see himself in much agreement with Hayek, Mirowski (2007) has put forth a view that this observer thinks shares much of this evolutionary spontaneous self-organization perspective. He controversially argues that markets are algorithms, not just like algorithms, and that market systems spontaneously emerge out of each other and compete with each other in an evolutionary process of natural selection. This is clearly linking together these two processes, much as Hayek does: spontaneous and emergent self-organization with natural selection. Even as these orders may emerge, they may also fail to survive or reproduce. Thus, futures markets emerged from spot markets, options markets from futures markets, derivatives markets from options markets, and then recently various forms of higher order derivatives markets such as credit default swaps and collateralized debt obligations. The latter in particular have almost completely disappeared in the wake of the financial crisis of 2008, although one cannot say for certain that they will not yet re-emerge at some later time in some form or other. Mirowski's argument has come under criticisms both in terms of the real nature of markets (Kirman, 2007) as well as on logical and computational grounds (Zambelli, 2007). However, it would seem that the core of his argument still may hold even if one modifies his arguments to account for those criticisms, with what is left still resembling in many ways the view that Hayek eventually developed after a long period of intellectual evolutionary emergence.

Nevertheless, the matter of emergence also shows up in the old debate about the microfoundations of macroeconomics. In mid-20th century this issue was ignored as it was viewed that it was too hard to model such emergence due to the problem of the "fallacy of composition," a real issue. However, modeling was simply done at an aggregate level without any effort to specify anything about microfoundations. The reaction against this after the late 1960s led to assuming that the aggregate economy resembles a representative micro agent with rational expectations operating with in a dynamic stochastic general equilibrium (DSGE) framework, which would come to dominate both research and policy discussions. However, problems with this approach were pointed out by Kirman (1992) and others, and recently efforts have been made to explicitly model microfoundations as interacting heterogeneous agents complexly generating macroeconomic phenomena as emergence (Delli Gatti, Gaffeo, Gallegati,

Giulioni, & Palestrini, 2008). Such efforts have been seen as increasingly useful since the crisis of 2008 that the DSGE approach was unable to model, with such models that show how financial crashes can occur providing substantial alternatives (Gallegati, Palestrini, & Rosser, 2011).

CONCLUSIONS

This paper makes no claim on ultimately resolving the debate between the natural selection and self-organization views of evolution in the broader sense. Nor does it do so even within the context of the cultural evolution of humans within the political economic context. Nevertheless, it seems that both processes are at work at many junctures, if not always and everywhere. Political economic systems do evolve through competing with each other in a process resembling biological natural selection, although with much more marked Lamarckian elements than in the biological realm. And in both realms it would appear that we observe moments of phase transition or discontinuity where a higher order structure emerges out of lower order ones without there necessarily being some higher order planner or director who brings about this emergence. The most dramatic examples in economics have involved those old ones of the spontaneous emergence of commodity monies as described by Menger as well as the spontaneous order of markets and natural law described by Hayek. New efforts have appeared that attempt to model macroeconomic events as emerging from interacting agent-based models. While these examples exist, they do not necessarily rule out other processes or disprove the arguments of more conventional economists who eschew such evolutionary arguments in favor of more static equilibrium models.

NOTES

1. This process has often been labeled "social Darwinism," a term used pejoratively to describe Spencer's views in particular (Hofstadter, 1944), although this involved considerable misrepresentation on various grounds (Leonard, 2009; Weikart, 2009).

2. See Caldwell (2004), Marciano (2009), Marmefelt (2009) for further discussion.

3. While Mendel (1866) appeared not long after *Origin of the Species*, it remained unknown to Darwin and those interested in evolution until William Bateson translated it into English in 1901 and invented the term "genetics" in 1906,

with Johannsen (1909) coining "gene," "genotype," and "phenotype," thus laying the groundwork for the later neo-Darwinian synthesis (Rheinberger, 2012).

4. The early Mendelians such as Bateson and Johannsen called themselves "saltationalists" and criticized the continuity arguments of Darwin and early probability followers such as Galton, emphasizing the discrete nature of genotypes and phenotypes, although the neo-Darwinian synthesis would integrate these views showing that even though genotypes (and phenotypes) might be discrete, distributions of characteristics could still be described by continuous normal distributions over populations that were expected to change only gradually over time.

5. See Rosser (2012) for further discussion.

6. A coincident factor in this was the simultaneous triumph of quantum mechanics over the deterministic position of Einstein. Einstein also became more focused on larger scale phenomena, particularly gravitation and its role in a possible unified field theory, whereas quantum mechanics focused on subatomic particles as well as stochasticity, rather like the gene-level focus of the neo-Darwinians. While this may seem irrelevant, the emergentists had attempted to address many disciplines in their vision of evolution proceeding from subatomic particles to groups of humans, if not further, this process itself crossing the disciplines as one moved from physics through chemistry to biology and ultimately to social science and philosophy with humans.

7. While Malthus was the primary influence from economics onto Darwin and Wallace, for Darwin more particularly he was also influenced by the earlier work of the Scottish enlightenment on matters involving neither biology nor economics. Thus, he admired both Adam Smith's discussion of the evolution of languages in the third edition of his Smith (1767) as well as the discussion of the evolution of laws and customs by Hume (1779).

8. On the other hand, it must be noted that even to this day in France, Lamarck is given the superior position above all of these as the true father of evolution, and there is no question that Darwin drew copiously on his work.

9. Perhaps the first economist to notice Darwin's work was Karl Marx in 1860 who wrote to Engels that "although it is developed in the crude English style, this is the book which contains the basis in natural history for our view" (Marx, 1942, p. 126). However, they tended to prefer his analysis of biological evolution while viewing humans as operating differently due to their ability to control production, with their unhappiness with Darwin on this front at least partly due to his admiration for Malthus, whom they despised. Nevertheless, one can argue that their historical materialism was an example of emergent evolution with its stages of modes of production appearing as phase transitions out of Hegelian dialectics, with the neo-Darwinian Haldane influenced by them.

10. Clements's ideas of a unique successional path for each environment has become as extinct as the idea of the ubuiquity of single equilibria in economics (Holling, 1992).

11. This term implying discontinuity comes from the Latin for "jump," as used in the phrase *natura non facit saltum*, "nature does not make jumps," first coined by Leibniz and quoted in the Prefaces to both Darwin's *Origin of Species* and Marshall's *Principles of Economics*, indicating their fundamental belief in gradualism (Rosser, 1992, 2011, chapter 6).

12. For Schumpeter (1911, p. 64), such saltationalist evolutionary emergence in technology is given by "… that kind of change arising from within the system which so displaces the equilibrium point that the new one cannot be reached from the old one by infinitesimal steps. Add successively many mail coaches as you please, you will never get to a railway thereby."

13. See also Hodgson and Knudsen (2006) for further discussion of the usefulness but limits of universal Darwinism.

14. A prominent form of complexity that has little to do with either of these is computational complexity, of which there are a variety of definitions. For a debate over the greater relevance for economics of dynamic versus computational complexity, see Rosser (2009), Velupillai (2009).

15. Rosser et al. (1994) would posit the moment of such an emergence as being the *anagenetic moment*, drawing on a model of entrainment of lower level oscillators generating a higher order structure due to Nicolis (1986). As with Hayek, Nicolis was studying emergence in brains and mental phenomena.

16. An early advocate of this argument for human evolution was the anarchist Kropotkin (1902).

17. Despite the apparent absoluteness of this, a few pages later Hayek partly allows for the individual to understand his or her own "mental events" by means of introspection, using the term *verstehende* for this process, an idea much emphasized by Koppl (2006, 2009).

18. We note the irony here that Descartes (1637) may well have also been one of the earliest formulators of the idea of self-organization.

19. However, as in France, the name of the nation is derived from the name of one of its cantons, Swyz.

REFERENCES

Alchian, A. A. (1950). Uncertainty, evolution, and economic theory. *Journal of Political Economy*, *58*, 211–222.

Alexander, S. (1920). *Space, time and deity*. London: Macmillan.

Ashby, W. R. (1947). Principles of the self-organizing dynamic system. *Journal of General Psychology*, *37*, 125–128.

Binmore, K., & Shaked, A. (2010). Experimental economics: Where next? *Journal of Economic Behavior and Organization*, *73*, 87–100.

Boulding, K. E. (1978). *Ecodynamics: A new theory of societal evolution*. Beverly Hills, CA: Sage.

Broad, C. D. (1925). *The mind and its place in nature*. London: Routledge & Kegan Paul.

Buchanan, J. P., & Vanberg, V. J. (1991). The market as a creative process. *Economics and Philosophy*, *7*, 167–186.

Caldwell, B. J. (2004). *Hayek's challenge: An intellectual biography of F. A. Hayek*. Chicago, IL: University of Chicago Press.

Clements, F. E. (1916). *Plant succession: Analysis of the development of vegetation*. Washington, DC: Carnegie Institute.

Corsi, P. (2005). Before Darwin: Transformist concepts in European natural history. *Journal of the History of Biology*, *38*, 67–83.

Crow, J. F. (1955). General theory of population genetics: Synthesis. *Cold Spring Harbor Symposia on Quantitative Biology*, *20*, 54–59.

Crow, J. F., & Kimura, M. (1970). *An introduction to population genetics*. New York, NY: Harper & Row.

Crutchfield, J. P. (1994). The calculi of emergence: Computation, dynamics, and induction. *Physica D*, *75*, 11–54.

Crutchfield, J. P. (2003). When evolution is revolution – Origins of innovation. In J. P. Crutchfield & P. Schuster (Eds.), *Evolutionary dynamics: Exploring the interplay of selection, accident, neutrality, and function* (pp. 101–133). Oxford: Oxford University Press.

Darwin, C. (1859). *On the origin of species by means of natural selection or the preservation of favored races in the struggle for life*. London: John Murray.

Darwin, C. (1871). *The descent of man and selection in relation to sex*. London: John Murray.

Darwin, C., & Wallace, A. R. (1858). On the tendency of species to form varieties; and on the perpetuation of varieties and species by means of natural selection. *Journal of the Linnean Society (Zoology)*, *3*, 45–62.

Darwin, F. (1959). *The life and letters of Charles Darwin* (Vol. 2). New York, NY: Basic Books.

Dawkins, R. (1976). *The selfish gene*. Oxford: Oxford University Press.

Dawkins, R. (1983). Universal Darwinism. In D. S. Bendall (Ed.), *Evolution from molecules to men* (pp. 403–425). Cambridge: Cambridge University Press.

Delli Gatti, D., Gaffeo, E., Gallegati, M., Giulioni, G., & Palestrini, A. (2008). *Emergent macroeconomics: An agent-based approach to business fluctuations*. Milan: Springer.

Descartes, R. (1637). *Disours de la Méthode pour bien Conduire sa Raison, et Chercher la Vérité dans les Sciences (Discourse on the Method)*. Leiden: Jean Le Maire.

Dopfer, K., Foster, J., & Potts, J. (2004). Micro meso macro. *Journal of Evolutionary Economics*, *14*, 263–279.

Eigen, M. & Schuster, P. (1979). *The Hypercycle: A Principle of Natural Self-Organization*, Berlin: Springer.

Eldredge, N. J., & Gould, S. J. (1972). Punctuated equilibria. In D. J. M. Schopf (Ed.), *Models in paleobiology* (pp. 82–115). San Francisco, CA: Freeman Cooper.

Fehr, E., & Schmidt, K. (1999). A theory of fairness, competition, and cooperation. *Quarterly Journal of Economics*, *114*, 817–868.

Fehr, E., & Schmidt, K. (2010). On inequity aversion: A reply to Binmore and Shaked. *Journal of Economic Behavior and Organization*, *73*, 101–108.

Fisher, R. A. (1930). *The genetical theory of natural selection*. Oxford: Oxford University Press.

Foster, J., & Metcalfe, J. S. (2012). Economic emergence: And evolutionary economic perspective. *Journal of Economic Behavior and Organization*, *82*, 420–432.

Friedman, M. (1953). *The methodology of positive economics*. Chicago, IL: University of Chicago Press.

Gallegati, M., Palestrini, A., & Rosser, J. B., Jr. (2011). The period of financial distress in speculative markets: Interacting heterogeneous agents and financial constraints. *Macroeconomic Dynamics*, *15*, 60–79.

Gautieri, G. (1805). *Slanco sulla Genealogica della Terra e sulla Construzione Dinamica dell Organizzazione, Seguito da una Ricerca sull'Origine del Vermi Abitanti le Interiora degli Annali*. Jena: Sassonia.

Gintis, H. (2000). Strong reciprocity and human sociality. *Journal of Theoretical Biology, 206*, 169–170.
Goldschmidt, R. (1940). *The material basis of evolution*. New Haven, CT: Yale University Press.
Gould, S. J. (2002). *The structure of evolutionary theory*. Cambridge: Belknap Press of Harvard University Press.
Haldane, J. B. S. (1932). *The causes of evolution*. London: Longmans and Green.
Hamilton, W. D. (1964). The genetical evolution of social behavior. *Journal of Theoretical Biology, 7*, 1–52.
Hamilton, W. D. (1972). Altruism and related phenomena. Mainly in the social insects. *Annual Review of Ecology and Systematics, 3*, 192–232.
Harper, D., & Endres, A. M. (2012). The anatomy of emergence, with a focus upon capital formation. *Journal of Economic Behavior and Organization, 82*, 352–367.
Hayek, F. A. (1937). Economics and knowledge. *Economica, 4*, 33–45.
Hayek, F. A. (1948). *Individualism and economic order*. Chicago, IL: University of Chicago Press.
Hayek, F. A. (1952). *The sensory order: An inquiry into the foundations of theoretical psychology*. London: Routledge & Kegan Paul.
Hayek, F. A. (1967). The theory of complex phenomena. In F. A. Hayek (Ed.), *Studies in philosophy, politics, and economics* (pp. 22–42). Chicago, IL: University of Chicago Press.
Hayek, F. A. (1979). *Law, legislation and liberty: A new statement of the liberal principles of justice and political economy* (Vol. 3). The political order of a free people. London: Routledge.
Hayek, F. A. (1988). *The fatal conceit: The errors of socialism*. London: Routledge.
Henrich, J. (2004). Cultural group selection, coevolutionary processes, and large-scale cooperation. *Journal of Economic Behavior and Organization, 53*, 3–35.
Hodgson, G. M. (1993). *Economics and evolution: Bringing life back into economics*. Ann Arbor, MI: University of Michigan Press.
Hodgson, G. M., & Knudsen, T. (2006). Why we need a generalized Darwinism and why generalized Darwinism is not enough. *Journal of Economic Behavior and Organization, 61*, 1–19.
Hofstadter, R. (1944). *Social Darwinism in American thought 1860–1915*. Philadelphia, PA: University of Pennsylvania Press.
Holland, J. H. (1942). *Adaptation in Natural and Artificial Systems*. 2nd edition. Cambridge, MA: MIT Press.
Holling, C. S. (1992). Cross-scale morphology, geometry, and dynamics of ecosystems. *Ecological Monographs, 62*, 447–502.
Hume, D. (1779). *Dialogues concerning natural religion*. Edinburgh, IN: Pinter.
Johannsen, W. (1909). *Elemente der exacten Eflichkeitslehre*. Jena: Gustav Fischer.
Kant, I. (1790). *Kritik der Urteilskraft (Critique of judgment)*. Augsburg: Adweichungen.
Kauffman, S. A. (1993). *The origins of order: Self-oganization and selection in evolution*. Oxford: Oxford University Press.
Kauffman, S. A. (1995). *At home in the universe*. Oxford: Oxford University Press.
Kauffman, S. A., & Johnsen, S. (1991). Coevolution to the edge of chaos: Coupled fitness landscapes, poised states, and coevolutionary avalanches. *Journal of Theoretical Biology, 49*, 505.
Kim, J. (1993). *Supervenience and mind*. Cambridge: Cambridge University Press.

Kirman, A. (2007). The basic unit of economic analysis: Individuals or markets? A comment on "markets come to bits" by Phil Mirowski. *Journal of Economic Behavior and Organization*, *63*, 284–294.
Kirman, A. P. (1992). Who or what does the representative agent represent? *Journal of Economic Perspectives*, *6*(2), 117–136.
Koppl, R. (2006). Austrian economics at the cutting edge. *Review of Austrian Economics*, *19*, 231–241.
Koppl, R. (2009). Complexity and Austrian economics. In J. B. Rosser, Jr. (Ed.), *Handbook of complexity research* (pp. 393–408). Cheltenham, PA: Edward Elgar.
Koppl, R., & Rosser, J. B., Jr. (2002). All I have to say has already crossed your mind. *Metroeconomica*, *53*, 339–360.
Kropotkin, P. A. (1902). *Mutual aid: A factor of evolution*. New York, NY: McClure Phillips.
Langton, C. G. (1990). Computation at the edge of chaos: Phase transitions and emergent computation. *Physica D*, *42*, 12–37.
Lamarck, J. B. de. (1809). *Philosophie Zoologique, ou Exposition des Considérations Relatives à l'Histoire Naturelle des Animaux* (Vol. 2). Paris: Dentu.
Lavoie, D. (1989). Economic chaos or spontaneous order? Implications for political economy of the new view of science. *Cato Journal*, *8*, 613–635.
Leonard, T. C. (2009). Origins of the myth of social Darwinism: The ambiguous legacy of Richard Hofstadter's social Darwinism in American thought. *Journal of Economic Behavior and Organization*, *71*, 37–51.
Lewes, G. H. (1875). *Problems of life and mind (first series) 2*. London: Tribner.
Lewis, P. (2012). Emergent properties in the work of Friedrich Hayek. *Journal of Economic Behavior and Organization*, *82*, 368–378.
Lyell, C. (1830–1832). *The principles of geology: Or, the modern changes of the earth and its inhabitants as illustrative of geology* (Vol. 3). London: John Murray.
Malthus, T. R. (1798). *An essay on the principle of population as it affects the future improvement of society with remarks on the speculations of Mr. Godwin, M. Condorcet and other writers*. London: J. Johnson.
Marciano, A. (2009). Why Hayek is a Darwinian (after all)? Hayek and Darwin on social evolution. *Journal of Economic Behavior and Organization*, *71*, 52–61.
Marmefelt, T. (2009). Human knowledge, rules, and the spontaneous evolution of society in the social thought of Darwin, Hayek, and Boulding. *Journal of Economic Behavior and Organization*, *71*, 62–74.
Marshall, A. (1890). *Principles of economics*. London: Macmillan.
Marx, K. (1860/1942). *Selected correspondence of Karl Marx and Friedrich Engels*. New York, NY: International Publishers.
McCauley, J. L. (2004). *Dynamics of markets: Econophysics and finance*. Cambridge: Cambridge University Press.
McDougall, W. (1923). *Outline of psychology*. London: Methuen.
McLaughlin, B. P. (1997). Emergence and supervenience. *Intellectica*, *2*, 25–43.
Mendel, G. (1866). Versuche über pflanzen hybriden. *Verhandlung Naturforsch Vereines Brunn*, *4*, 3–47. [William B. (1901). Experiments in plant hybridization. *Journal of Royal Horticultural Society*, 26, 1–32].
Menger, C. (1892). On the origins of money. *Economic Journal*, *2*, 239–255.
Mill, J. S. (1843). *A system of logic: Ratiocinative and inductive*. London: Longmans Green.

Mirowski, P. (2007). Markets come to bits: Evolution, computation, and markomata in economic science. *Journal of Economic Behavior and Organization*, *63*, 209–242.

Moore, C. (1990). Undecidability and unpredictability in dynamical systems. *Physical Review Letters*, *64*, 2354–2357.

Morgan, C. L. (1923). *Emergent evolution*. London: Williams and Norgate.

Nelson, R. R., & Winter, S. G. (1982). *An evolutionary theory of economic change*. Cambridge: Belknap Press of Harvard University Press.

Nicolis, J. S. (1986). *Dynamics of hierarchical systems: An evolutionary approach*. Berlin: Springer.

Ostrom, E. (1990). *Governing the commons the evolution of institutions of collective action*. Cambridge: Cambridge University Press.

Potts, J. (2000). *The new evolutionary microeconomics: Complexity, competence and adaptive behaviour*. Cheltenham, PA: Edward Elgar.

Price, G. (1970). Selection and covariance. *Nature*, *227*, 520–521.

Price, G. (1972). Extensions of covariance selection mathematics. *Annals of Human Genetics*, *35*, 485–490.

Rheinberger, H.-J. (2012). Biology – A systemic redefinition? *Max Planck Research*, *2*, 12–16.

Rosser, J. B., Jr. (1991). *From catastrophe to chaos: A general theory of economic discontinuities*. Boston: Kluwer.

Rosser, J. B., Jr. (1992). The dialogue between the economic and ecologic theories of evolution. *Journal of Economic Behavior and Organization*, *17*, 195–215.

Rosser, J. B., Jr. (1999). On the complexities of complex economic dynamics. *Journal of Economic Perspectives*, *13*(4), 169–192.

Rosser, J. B., Jr. (2009). Computational and dynamic complexity in economics. In J. B. Rosser, Jr. (Ed.), *Handbook of research on complexity* (pp. 22–35). Cheltenham, PA: Edward Elgar.

Rosser, J. B., Jr. (2010). How complex are the Austrians? In R. Koppl, S. Horwitz, & P. Desrochers (Eds.), *What is so Austrian about Austrian economics?* (pp. 165–179). Bingley: Emerald Group.

Rosser, J. B., Jr. (2011). *Complex evolutionary dynamics in urban-regional and ecologic-economic systems: From catastrophe to chaos and beyond*. New York, NY: Springer.

Rosser, J. B., Jr. (2012). Emergence and complexity in Austrian economics. *Journal of Economic Behavior and Organization*, *81*, 122–128.

Rosser, J. B., Jr., Folke, C., Günther, F., Isomäki, H., Perrings, C., & Puu, T. (1994). Discontinuous change in multi-level hierarchical systems. *Systems Research*, *11*(3), 77–94.

Schumpeter, J. A. (1911). *Theorie der Wirtschaftlichen Entwiklung*. Leipzig: Duncker & Humboldt. [Redvers O. (1934). *The theory of economic development*. Cambridge: Harvard University Press).

Smith, A. (1767). Considerations concerning the first formation of languages. Appendix. In *The theory of moral sentiments* (3rd ed.). London: Miller, Kincaid, and Bell.

Spencer, H. (1851). *Social statics: Or, the conditions essential to happiness specified and the first of them developed*. London: John Chapman.

Spencer, H. (1852). A theory of population, deduced from the general law of animal fertility. *Westminster Review*, *57*, 468–501.

Spencer, H. (1864). *Principles of biology*. London: Williams and Norgate.

Thompson, D'Arcy W. (1917). *On growth and form*. Cambridge: Cambridge University Press.

Trivers, R. L. (1971). The evolution of reciprocal altruism. *The Quarterly Review of Biology, 46*, 34–57.
Turing, A. M. (1952). The chemical basis of morphogenesis. *Philosophical Transactions of the Royal Society B, 237*, 37–72.
van Cleve, J. (1990). Magic or mind dust: Panpsychism vs. emergence. *Philosophical Perspectives, 4*, 215–226.
Veblen, T. B. (1898). Why is economics not an evolutionary science? *Quarterly Journal of Economics, 12*, 373–397.
Velupillai, K. V. (2009). A computational economist's perspective on computational complexity. In J. B. Rosser, Jr. (Ed.), *Handbook of complexity research* (pp. 36–83). Cheltenham, PA: Edward Elgar.
von Bertalanffy, L. (1968). *General systems theory*. New York, NY: George Braziller.
Wagner, R. E. (2010). *Mind, society, and human action: Time and knowledge in a theory of social economy*. London: Routledge.
Wagner, R. E. (2012). A macro economy in an ecology of plans. *Journal of Economic Behavior and Organization, 82*, 433–444.
Weikart, R. (2009). Was Darwin or Spencer the father of laissez-faire social Darwinism? *Journal of Economic Behavior and Organization, 71*, 20–28.
Williams, G. C. (1966). *Adaptation and natural selection*. Princeton, NJ: Princeton University Press.
Wilson, E. O. (2012). *The social conquest of earth*. New York, NY: Liveright Publishing.
Witt, U. (2004). On the proper interpretation of 'evolution' in economics and its implications for production theory. *Journal of Economic Methodology, 16*, 361–375.
Wright, S. (1931). Evolution in Mendelian populations. *Genetics, 16*, 97–159.
Wright, S. (1932). The roles of mutation, inbreeding, crossbreeding, and selection in evolution. *Proceedings of 6th International Congress of Genetics, 1*, 356–366.
Wright, S. (1951). The genetical theory of populations. *Annals of Eugenics, 15*, 323–354.
Wynne-Edwards, V. C. (1962). *Animal dispersion in relation to social behavior*. Edinburgh, IN: Oliver & Boyd.
Zambelli, S. (2007). Comments on Philip Mirowski's article: Markets come to bits: Evolution, computation, and markomata in economic science. *Journal of Economic Behavior and Organization, 63*, 345–358.

PUBLIC POLICY: OBJECT OF CHOICE OR EMERGENT PHENOMENA? LEARNING FROM THE IMPLEMENTATION OF THE MEDICAL REIMBURSEMENT ACT IN POLAND

Marta Podemska-Mikluch

ABSTRACT

The recurring implementation and continuous maintenance of price controls implies a deep incongruence between public policy and economic common sense. Yet, economists do not tire of concluding their papers with policy recommendations as if oblivious to the ineffectiveness of their efforts. By assuming that policy is an object of choice, economists have no alternative but to naively hope for a decision-maker sensitive to economic logic. An alternative approach is to think of policy, not as an object of choice but as an outcome of a competitive process. From this perspective, the often-lamented disregard for economic principles is not a characteristic of a deficient policymaker, but a systemic quality of institutional

Entangled Political Economy
Advances in Austrian Economics, Volume 18, 93–110

ISSN: 1529-2134/doi:10.1108/S1529-213420140000018005

arrangements. I illustrate my argument with the analysis of the implementation of rigid prices for reimbursed pharmaceuticals in Poland.

Keywords: Entangled political economy; healthcare; price controls: centralized mindset

JEL classifications: B41; D78; D85; P16

The recurring implementation and continuous maintenance of price controls suggest that policymakers remain immune to economists' advice. Why do practitioners of the dismal science share Cassandra's sad fate? Some explain this puzzle by pointing out the constraints of the political system; others focus on the inadequacies of those in charge. Such explanations challenge economists to design and recommend policies that are politically plausible and economically sound. This, however, so far appears to be an empty set.

The search for the Holy Grail of public policy presumes the existence of a decision-maker in charge of choosing a policy. All standard political economy models of neo-Walrasian economics involve some type of a decision-maker. In some cases, it is a benevolent dictator, in others a special interest group, but most commonly a median voter, is thought to be responsible for choosing a policy from options proposed by various individuals and groups within the society. No matter which kind of a decision-maker is considered, the implication is the same: policy is an object of choice. Conceptualized in this manner, the process of policy formation is not much different from shopping at a supermarket where one picks and chooses the ingredients for the optimal policy (Wagner, 2010). As a result, much of the story is missed, that is, unintended consequences that are generated in interactions between individuals pursuing their plans and goals.

In contrast, from the neo-Mengerian perspective, policy formation is approached as an emergent process, not an object of choice (for an in-depth analysis and comparison of the neo-Walrasian and the neo-Mengerian research programs, see Wagner, 2010). The neo-Mengerian approach conceptualizes society as a polycentric order where there is no entity capable of acting teleologically upon the others (Polanyi, 1951). Thus, policies cannot be chosen, but rather, emerge from interactions among individuals in the pursuit of their various plans and goals. The neo-Mengerian approach illuminates multiple aspects of policy formation that are unintelligible from the neo-Walrasian perspective. I illustrate three of them in the ensuing analysis. First, the emergent approach allows for the consideration of how policies change the way in which individuals interact with one another and what happens when relationships based on contract are replaced by relationships based on status (Maine, 1906; Wagner, 2007a). Second, the potential for acquisition of discretionary authority becomes one of the main driving forces in the process of policy formation, and is a key generator of Big Players (Butos & Koppl, 1993; Koppl, 2002; Koppl & Yeager, 1996). Third, the inability to anticipate specific interpretations infuses uncertainty among investors, reinforcing Wagner's assertion that policy is an inferior method of calming turbulence (Wagner, 2012a).

I illustrate my argument with the analysis of the recent implementation of the Medical Reimbursement Act in Poland. The Act, which was signed in May 2011 and went into effect in January 2012, introduced fixed prices and fixed profit margins for reimbursed medications; from now on reimbursed drugs are to be sold at the same price in every pharmacy. The prices are no longer determined in the market but instead are established by the government in negotiations with the pharmaceutical companies, and then published in a bi-monthly bulletin. The severity of this policy highlights the deep divide between public policy and the basic principles of economics. Poland's experience with a centrally commanded economy and its relatively enthusiastic adoption of market-oriented reforms (Hayo, 2004) render the sudden implementation of these Soviet-like policies particularly puzzling.

The paper opens with the overview of the Medical Reimbursement Act in the context of major characteristics of the healthcare industry in Poland. The section "Public Policy as an Object of Choice" summarizes the literature on the neo-Walrasian treatment of policy formation. The section "Public Policy as an Emergent Phenomenon" discusses the entrepreneurial component of policy formation and contrasts the neo-Walrasian and neo-Mengerian conceptualizations of the process. The section "Two Perspectives on the Implementation of Medical Reimbursement Act" offers an analysis of the implementation of the Medical Reimbursement Act in Poland from the two contrasting perspectives. The section "Conclusions" concludes the paper.

REIMBURSEMENT ACT AND THE POLISH HEALTHCARE SYSTEM

Some argue that the healthcare industry is unique, and therefore, the efficiency of healthcare provisioning cannot be evaluated in the same way as other, not-so-unique, industries (Arrow, 1963). Building on this argument, others assert that the uniqueness of healthcare and its importance render it too sensitive to leave it unprotected from the market forces (Krugman, 2006). While I see no reason to treat healthcare as exceptional, I believe that its importance makes it necessary to leave it open to the workings of the market system. But I have no hope of settling this discussion here. Rather, I focus solely on the role of price controls in the provision of pharmaceuticals. In this regard, Kyle's findings allow me to discuss price fixing in the pharmaceutical market within the general context of price restrictions (Kyle, 2007). Kyle analyzes entry strategies employed by pharmaceutical manufacturers in the presence of price controls and finds that price controls, understood either as a cap on the ex-manufacturer's price or the amount a national health service pays for a pharmaceutical product (the reimbursement price), cause a reduction in the number of innovative products available in a given country. This result is exactly what one should expect if the pharmaceutical markets were to operate in the same way as markets for other goods and services.

Healthcare coverage in Poland is compulsory and expensive. Employees have about 8.5 percent of their salaries deducted for medical and social insurance payments (*Social Insurance in Poland*, 2012). The self-employed are to make contributions on a monthly basis: currently, all business owners pay 623 PLN a month, which is equivalent to about $200 (Zakład Ubezpieczeń Społecznych, 2013). To understand the weight of this burden on the Polish entrepreneur, the reader should remember that Polish GDP per capita is still less than a half of that in the United States. In 2012 per capita GDP (PPP) was $22,162 in Poland and $49,965 in the United States (World Bank, 2013). The steep medical insurance contributions are one of the reasons why the Doing Business survey ranks Poland on the 124th in the ease of starting a business category (The World Bank Group, 2012).

The steep contributions do not translate into wide availability of high-quality healthcare, as documented by the OECD (Boulhol, Sowa, Golinowska, & Sicari, 2012). The researchers report that while the insured and their dependents are entitled to free primary care, specialist outpatient care, hospital treatment, dental treatment, and ambulance transportation, the quality of the services remains lacking. As a result, most Poles choose to pay for private care on top of the mandatory contributions. For example, even though dental treatments are covered by the national healthcare insurance, most people choose to pay for private services. Moreover, while it is acceptable to approach specialists directly without a referral from a general practitioner, most Poles prefer to only visit specialists privately, avoiding the queues and dramatically boosting the quality of received services. Interestingly enough, both private and public visits take place in the same facility and even in the same office.

Another insight into the Polish healthcare system comes from the popular health expenditure statistics, collected by the World Health Organization (2012). According to the estimates, in 2010, 7 percent of GDP was spent on healthcare in Poland. That same year public sector expenditure on healthcare was 11 percent of general government expenditures. For comparison, the respective numbers for the United States are 17.6 percent and 22.4 percent. This same year, private expenditure on health as a percentage of total expenditure on health was 27.8 in Poland and 51.8 in the United States.

The purchase of medications is also highly subsidized in Poland. The insured pay only a part of the price, the government refunds the pharmacies for the rest. Until the implementation of the Medical Reimbursement Act in 2012, only the refundable amount was established in the negotiations between the pharmacies and the government, the selling price was decided by individual pharmacies. The competition between pharmacies was so fierce that many priced medication below the refundable amount and intentionally incurred a loss. The consumers were great winners of this contest as many medications could be purchased for as little as one *grosz*, an equivalent of about one-third of a U.S. cent (Watoła, 2010).

But since all good things come to an end, this consumer paradise did not last. From the beginning of 2012 Polish pharmacies are no longer able to compete through prices. This change was brought on by the Medical Reimbursement Act, which was signed in May 2011 and went into effect in January 2012. The Act introduced fixed prices and fixed profit margins for reimbursed medicines. From now on, reimbursed drugs are to cost the same price in every pharmacy. The prices are established by the government agency in negotiations with the pharmaceutical companies and then published in a bulletin and updated every 2 months. Medical Reimbursement Act goes well beyond establishing a maximum or a minimum price, it dictates exact prices. Its resemblance to Soviet-like policies is hard to ignore.

The Act was supposed to grant broad access to the most advanced drugs and lower the public costs of healthcare. Now, after the reform, the responsible politicians argue that the new, government mandated, prices are still lower than the prices charged by the pharmacies before the reform. This is hard to believe given that the pharmacies are no longer able to offer deep discounts. Moreover, analysts argue that the government, not the consumers, accumulates most of the savings. WHO established that the amount paid by the consumers increased 7 percent and the amount refunded by the government decreased 9 percent in the aftermath of the reform. The missing 2 percent can probably be explained by lower consumption as the patients are still working through the medications purchased before the law went into effect (Baker & McKenzie, 2012).

PUBLIC POLICY AS AN OBJECT OF CHOICE

When viewed from the neo-Walrasian perspective, the disjunction between public policy and economic common sense appears to result from the costliness of following economists' recommendations. Consequently, economists explain their inability to prevent implementation of faulty policies by pointing to the constraints of the political system and shortcomings of policymakers. In such accounts, policymakers are portrayed as self-interested, and therefore, insensitive to how others are affected by the given policy (Tullock, 2008). Depending on a model, among the typical suspects are misinformed or biased voters, greedy interest groups, and power-hungry politicians. Which player is deemed responsible for a mistaken policy depends on the model. But while models differ, in all cases it is the shortcomings of those in charge that cause the disjunction between economic principles and political practice.

Neoclassical economics did not venture into the institutional questions. Its analysis took place in a world where institutional problems were already solved and conflict was always resolved through voluntary exchange as characterized by an Edgeworth box (Podemska-Mikluch & Wagner, 2013). Only with the rise of Public Choice did economists start to ask about the political process and inquire about how public policies came to be adopted. But just like the economic literature in general is dominated by the analytical framework of the neo-Walrasian economics, Public Choice also became populated with equilibrium models despite its spontaneous order origins (Wagner, 2008, 2012b).

As a result, most of its models characterize public policy as equilibria among self-interested participants of the political process. There still remain disagreements regarding the nature of the equilibria, the line of incongruity centered on the relative importance of voting, interest groups, and bureaucracy. But in general, policies are believed to reflect the interests and constraints of persons assigned the decision-making authority. In democracies such authority, by definition, belongs to the people. In order to fit a democracy into a monocentric framework, economists use the median voter model which reduces the process of policy formation to a single person's optimization problem (see Mueller, 2003 for a summary of the vast literature). One example of this approach is the popular pure transfer model portraying the redistributionist tendencies of the majority (Meltzer & Richard, 1981). The model is built on the reasonable assertion that voters are no different from economic agents and therefore are motivated by self-interest. Due to their self-interest, voters elect redistributive policies: the government grows as the median income increases relative to the income of the decisive voter.

The median voter model does an even better job of explaining the incongruity between public policy and economics when it is expanded to account for informational problems. The cost of obtaining information may lead voters to be less than perfectly informed about the costs and benefits of public programs. This gives room for the activity of the interest groups as well as allows for the consideration of principal-agent problems among elected representatives and the bureaucracy. The information problems allow the candidates, interest groups, and the bureaucracy to manipulate ignorant voters. For example, in separate works Austen-Smith and Congleton developed models in which campaign messages and financial support are shown to affect electoral outcomes (Austen-Smith, 1987; Congleton, 1989, 1991). Caplan takes the argument a step further and argues that the voters are not only ignorant, but also biased about the costs and benefits of political programs (Caplan, 2001, 2008). Caplan models irrationality as a normal good for which, as we know, demand increases as price decreases. The author believes that private repercussions of biased beliefs about politics and economics are virtually nonexistent, which allows voters to remain irrationally ignorant.

Much has been written on the differences between these approaches, and there continues a debate on whether it is self-interest, ignorance, or irrationality that determines the nature of the equilibria in the median voter models. But while the different strings of the median voter literature may appear to be idiosyncratic, their similarities run deep. They all are based on the conceptualization of society as a monocentric organization, in which market-based enterprises are believed to operate within an institutional framework established, protected, and regulated by a polity.

PUBLIC POLICY AS AN EMERGENT PHENOMENON

In contrast, the neo-Mengerian perspective treats society as an emergent polycentric order, not an organization (Hayek, 1973). These different treatments relate to different conceptualization of the source of orderliness in a society. In the neo-Walrasian framework, with its presumption of a central decision-maker, societal orderliness is implicit. On the other hand, in the neo-Mengerian framework, the source of orderliness and the mechanism of conflict resolution are at the very core of investigation; the analysis is centered on how individuals coordinate their conflicting plans. To illuminate the difference between organizations and orders, Wagner uses an example of parades and crowds (Wagner, 2010). While both are orderly, the sources of orderliness differ between them. Organizations and parades are hierarchical; their orderliness is thought to come from some central decision-maker. In contrast, orders and crowds are polycentric; their orderliness emerges through interactions among the individuals "each of whom pursues an individually chosen path or objective while also engaging in continual readjustment in response to the similar efforts of other spectators." A similar account of orderliness being generated from the bottom-up can be found in Shelling (1978) and Resnick (1997).

As was mentioned in the introduction, in many ways, proposals for policy reforms are analogues to market innovations. Since entrepreneurship is an omnipresent aspect of human action, it occurs in all environments (Boettke & Coyne, 2003; Mises, 1949). Independent of institutional environment, entrepreneurs respond with innovative ideas to previously unnoticed profit or rent opportunities (Holcombe, 2002; Kirzner, 1978; Tullock, 1967). Given this commonality, it is worth considering that the subsequent step is also common to the two environments; that in politics, like in markets, the success and failure of entrepreneurs are determined in interactions among many individuals, not by a choice of a single decision-maker. Both neo-Walrasian and neo-Mengerian perspectives allow for a significant role of an entrepreneur in their frameworks. However, the frameworks differ in how the success and failure of entrepreneurs are determined. They also differ in conceptualization of the relationship between the activities of entrepreneurs and the institutional environment in which these activities take place.

In the neo-Walrasian framework, the manner in which the success of an entrepreneur is determined depends on the environment in which the entrepreneur is thought to operate. The success of market entrepreneurs depends on market forces and the success of political entrepreneurs depends on the preferences of the decision-maker, typically the median voter. Thus, political entrepreneurs are portrayed as competing over the support of the decision-maker, usually through electoral competition. Whoever's reform proposal attracts the support of the median voter, succeeds. As a result, in the neo-Walrasian framework electoral competition occupies central stage of analysis. On the other hand, in the neo-Mengerian framework, elections are almost of no consequence. The success and failure of political entrepreneurs are determined in the interactions among individuals, no matter the institutional environment in which these entrepreneurs operate.

The two frameworks also differ in how they conceptualize the relationship between the activities of entrepreneurs and the institutional environment in which these activities take place. In the neo-Walrasian framework, this relationship is one-directional, while in the neo-Mengerian framework, it is bidirectional. For example, Baumol argues that the distribution of entrepreneurs between productive, unproductive, and destructive activities depends on the relative pay-offs offered by different realms of activity (Baumol, 1990). In Baumol's account, the decision over the rules under which the entrepreneurial activity takes place is independent of the activities of the entrepreneurs. His analysis is oriented on the one-directional relationship of how institutions, including various policies, affect entrepreneurs (Podemska-Mikluch & Wagner, 2010).

In the neo-Mengerian framework, the relationship between entrepreneurs and institutional environment is bidirectional. Environment affects the nature of entrepreneurial activity and is not immune to it. Those entrepreneurs who operate within the environment of alienable property are residual claimants to the profit and losses generated by the investment (Wagner, 1997). In contrast, entrepreneurs operating in the world of inalienable property work with taxes extracted through a budgetary process and are not responsible for the losses or have a claim over the gains. Thus, while market-based entities can extract profits directly, polity-based enterprises operate within the framework of inalienable property and need to extract profits indirectly. For this reason, polity-based enterprises must act parasitically upon market-based enterprises. In order to extract profits, polity-based enterprises alter the rules of exchange between market-based enterprises. These changes obliterate some of the market-based entities while strengthening others. The process continues as long as polity-based enterprises are capable of attaching themselves to market transactions; as long as they are able to alter the rules of exchange.

These two approaches to political entrepreneurship lead to two different conceptualization of interactions between market and polity-based enterprises.

The neo-Mengerian approach portrays polity- and market-based enterprises as interacting on the same field, with the relationship between them entangled, not hierarchical (Smith, Wagner, & Yandle, 2011; Wagner, 2009). Due to the presumption of hierarchical social structure, the neo-Walrasian framework presumes the government as capable of improving upon the outcomes generated in interactions among market-based enterprises. The polity is thought to act teleologically upon the market. But when the society is approached as a polycentric order, polity-based enterprises are incapable of acting teleologically upon the market. Instead, polity-based enterprises can only affect relative prices by rendering some activities more costly than the others. In effect, regulation leads to a constitutive change: a change in rules of interaction. As noticed by Wagner, legislation can only affect constitutive rules but cannot be used to determine the allocative outcomes (Wagner, 2002).

TWO PERSPECTIVES ON THE IMPLEMENTATION OF MEDICAL REIMBURSEMENT ACT

The neo-Walrasian tradition associates price controls with a horizontal line running either below or above equilibrium on the supply and demand graph. The specific level of prices is selected by policymakers, who are acting on the behalf of the median voter or some interest group. At first glance, the implementation of the Medical Reimbursement Act, and especially its ban on advertising, easily fits the interest group explanation. However, upon closer inspection, most aspects of the process turned out to be unintelligible from the centralized perspective.

Choice versus Interaction

In the years before the implementation of the Medical Reimbursement Act, entry into the pharmaceutical sales market was easy, and new pharmacies were being opened around the clock (Zawisza, 2012). This relative ease of starting a pharmacy allowed international pharmaceutical chains to grow their market share. Newly opening franchises were using loss leaders, freebie marketing, and loyalty programs in order to attract customers. As a result, patients enjoyed variety of benefits, for example many of the chained pharmacies offered diabetics needles and glucose free-of-charge with the purchase of insulin. These aggressive marketing strategies put significant pressure on the individual, well-established, long existing pharmacies, usually owned and operated by licensed pharmacists.

In order to maintain their license, Polish pharmacists must maintain membership in the Polish Pharmaceutical Chamber, a professional association that represents their collective interests. Since the profitability of individually owned pharmacies was threatened by the growth of international chains, the chamber began lobbying for a policy requiring the presence of an experienced, licensed pharmacist on the premises during the pharmacy's hours of operation. This policy never went into effect. But the chamber found a different way of going after the pharmaceutical chains: based on the chamber's efforts, the Medical Reimbursement Act introduced the complete prohibition of pharmacy advertising as well as outlawed any encouragement to purchase reimbursed drugs (Baker & McKenzie, 2012).

The wording of the Article 49 Paragraph 3 of the Reimbursement Act illustrates the thoroughness of this aspect of the act:

> It shall be forbidden to use any kind of encouragement in relation to medicines, foodstuffs for special nutritional purposes or medical products subjected to refund from public resources, especially directed to beneficiaries, entrepreneurs and their employees or entitled people including sale conditioned by various factors, discounts, packets, customer loyalty schemes, donations, awards, presents, gifts, trips, lotteries, draws, all forms of commodities, tie-in transactions, facilitations, sponsored shopping or services, any kinds of coupons, tokens and any not specifically mentioned benefits.

Of course, there is no guarantee that the ban on advertising will restore the position of individually owned pharmacies. No legislation has the capacity to put an end to the competitive process; it can only alter the form that competition takes. The franchises can now be expected to search for alternative ways of attracting and retaining customers. Moreover, Tollison and Wagner were right on point when they remarked that politics always gives us policies that are in need of reform (Tollison & Wagner, 1991). Thus, there is no guarantee that the modification in relative prices and consequent change in rules of interaction brought on by the Medical Reimbursement Act will remain unaltered. Nothing stops pharmaceutical chains from lobbying for a rule that would tip the scale again in their favor. One hypothetical possibility would be to attach a requirement of disabled-persons access to some building reform in the future. Since the independent pharmacies are usually located in older, often historical buildings, and the franchises usually occupy modern, newly constructed locations, this law would increase operating costs for the older pharmacies while leaving franchises unaffected. This move would likely gather significant support in the Bootleggers and Baptists form (Yandle, 1983).

The malleable character of public policy is well illustrated by the fact that the first amendment to the Medical Reimbursement Act was passed just two weeks after the original bill went into effect (Money.pl, 2012). The original version of the Medical Reimbursement Act established penalties for doctors who prescribed an inappropriate drug on medical basis, prescribed a drug in a manner that was not consistent with the list of reimbursable medicines, or prescribed a drug to a patient who was not covered by public health insurance. It also required that doctors specify the level of reimbursement to which the patient was entitled. In response, many doctors went on strike and refused to prescribe reimbursable medicines. They also refused to be financially responsible in case they accidentally provide medical services to the uninsured as checking patients' status is constrained by the low level of computerization. The chaos created by the strike, and especially patients' helplessness in trying to obtain a prescription for a reimbursable medication, were extensively covered in the media. Policymakers responded by passing an amendment that encompassed all of the physicians' demands – an illustration of the open-ended character of policy formation.

It is also worth noting that in defending the ban on advertising, the Ministry of Health argued that the public money used to pay for drug reimbursement should not be mixed up with commercial concerns. The Pharmaceutical Chamber added that pharmacies are supposed to provide patients with unbiased information, and not overwhelm them with confusing advertising. These commentaries highlight the role of narrative and preponderance of credence goods in electoral competition (Wagner & Yazigi, 2014). As explained by Martin, ideas play a much greater role in the environment of inalienable property due to its looser feedback mechanism (Martin, 2010).

Contract and Status

Proponents of the Medical Reimbursement Act justified the reform with the desire to eliminate waste caused by the overconsumption of government-subsidized medication. They argued that when the pharmacies were free to lower the prices of reimbursed drugs, patients were prone to buy more than they otherwise would. For example, in the interview for one of the national newspapers the vice-minister of health pointed out that in

2010 consumers returned about 75 tons of expired medications in the waste management program (Watoła, 2010). But why introduce price controls when a simple measure of decreasing or eliminating subsidies would contribute directly to eradication of waste? The difference seems to lie in the fact that while the elimination of subsidies would diminish the role of polity-based enterprises, in this case the National Health Fund and the Ministry of Health, price fixing had the contrary effect.

Due to the Medical Reimbursement Act, prices of medications are no longer determined in the market but instead are established by the government in negotiations with the pharmaceutical companies and then published in a monthly bulletin. Being invited to negotiations is of crucial importance as, due to the Medical Reimbursement Act, the success of pharmaceutical manufacturers depends much more on the discretion of the National Health Fund and much less on how well they serve the patients. Thus, industry leaders can be expected to invest heavily in securing an invitation. Effectively, the reform creates positions of dominance and subordination and replaces relationships based on contract with relationships based on status (Maine, 1906; Wagner, 2007a). As noted by Wagner, alteration in how people relate to one another is a commonly ignored aspect of policy formation:

> Relationships based on contract are relationships among equals whereas relationships based on status inject positions of domination and subordination into society. The continuing debates over such elements of the welfare state as social security and medical care have been largely treated as debates over financial projections and implicit rates of return. This debate, however, also involves matters of how people relate to one another, and of the competencies they are to develop. (Wagner, 2007b, p. 196)

Discretion

The transformation of relationships based on contract into relationships based on status leads to the raise of big Players, whose "discretionary actions have a disproportionate affect on the market" as defined by Butos and Koppl (1993) and further developed by Koppl and Yeager (1996). Due to its vagueness, the Medical Reimbursement Act contributed to the emergence and consolidation of Big Players in the pharmaceutical market, namely National Health Fund and Ministry of Health. The newly implemented reimbursement standards are imprecise, flexible, and easily altered which provides Big Players with the capacity for advancing some manufacturers while hindering others.

In most countries, reimbursement policies cluster medicines into limit groups. All medicines within each limit group constitute therapeutic equivalents and are considered interchangeable. However, the actual equivalence itself depends on the criteria by which the grouping is performed, allowing an easy entry for political discretion. Natalia Lojko, an attorney specializing in pharmaceutical law, explains that flexibility in defining limit groups creates a great amount of ambiguity and allows the National Health Fund to make arbitrary changes in drug clusters:

> Drug equivalence within a group depends on criteria of their incorporation into the group. The worst-case scenario for patients and at the same time the best one for the public payer is when the limit group is broadly fixed, broader than actual therapeutic equivalency. Since essentially it means that reimbursement limit – that is the basic amount of money for co-payments obliging the National Health Fund and simultaneously its upper limit, is established on the level of the cheapest or one of the cheapest drugs within the group; it is established on the level of a fairly inexpensive drug. Having a big group it is easy to assume that there are more inexpensive drugs. At the same time, such broad grouping means that less expensive equivalent may not be available for a given patient at all, only because it is a reimbursement equivalent and not the therapeutic one.[1]

Uncertainty

The efficient-market hypothesis presumes that once a new policy is announced, the information it contains becomes publicly available and therefore it will be instantly reflected in asset prices (Malkiel & Fama, 1970). Yet, legislative changes seem to introduce a great deal of uncertainty. For example, the uncertainty regarding the interpretation of the advertising ban led to a dramatic decline in the number of on-line pharmacies. Out of 160 on-line pharmacies existing in 2011, 30 decided to close after the bill was signed into law. Their owners cited the inability to anticipate the interpretation and implication of the advertising ban as the reason for exiting the market (Czubkowska, 2012). Given that any element of an Internet portal can be considered a form of advertising, they worried that the advertising ban could be interpreted as equivalent to a ban on on-line pharmacies.

Since in the neo-Walrasian framework the government is presumed to act teleologically upon the market, there is no room for matters of interpretation. In contrast, the neo-Mengerian approach portrays polity- and market-based enterprises as interacting on the same field. As a result, political reforms do not decide allocative outcomes but rather change relative prices to which agents respond in a heterogeneous manner (Wagner, 2002). Thus, from the neo-Mengerian perspective, the exit of on-line pharmacies is explained as resulting from uncertainty regarding how the policy is interpreted and how others respond to it. In its explanation of uncertainty, the neo-Mengerian framework expands upon Higg's treatment of regime uncertainty (Higgs, 1997). According to Higgs, regime uncertainty describes the pervasive lack of confidence among investors as they fail to foresee how future government action will affect their private-property rights. But since polity-based enterprises are incapable of acting teleologically on the market, the uncertainty comes not only from a failure to predict future legislative changes, but also from the inability to reasonably anticipate all impacts of policies that are already in place.

CONCLUSIONS

In recent decades, economists have devoted tremendous intellectual effort to the design of policy recommendations. With their opinions selectively ignored, some ventured into the search for policies that are not only consistent with basic principles of economics but are also politically plausible. Whether such policies exist remains an open question but much evidence warrants doubt (Boettke, 2010). However, even if the Holy Grail of public policy exists, there is nothing that would render it immune to erosion through the political process (Wagner, 2006).

The neo-Walrasian focus on the costs and benefits of public policy; on the financial projections regarding its impact, leaves little room for the consideration of how the policy impacts heterogeneous agents. In most cases, the standard approach reduces voluminous legislation to a change in a single variable, with the analysis oriented on the comparison of equilibrium states before and after the change. For instance, implementation of price controls is usually portrayed as a movement of a single line on the supply and demand graph. However, Ockham's Razor must be used with care so that simple does not turn into simplistic. Even the most verbose lawyer could not write legislation longer than a couple of pages if he or she were only restating the neo-Walrasian conceptualization of price controls. And yet, the Medical Reimbursement Act is 77 pages long. Anyone who attempts to read the act will quickly realize that its length is not due to the inefficiency of legal jargon, but rather results from an abundance of provisions and exclusions that protect some groups while hurting others.

And while it would be naïve to expect that the adoption of the emergent approach could resolve the incongruence between public policy and economic common sense, we can hope for a less ambitious, yet nevertheless significant outcome: an adoption of the emergent approach turns the attention of the economist from policy design to the investigation of social life. By approaching public policy as emergent phenomena and object of an ongoing competition, economists free themselves from the efforts of convincing and educating the mythical decision-maker and can instead focus on the investigation of the complexities that penetrate social life. Keeping Pareto's (1935) distinction between residues and derivations in mind, economists are bound to make a greater impact by helping people filter through the derivations, instead of attempting to fix the residue.

NOTE

1. http://liberte.pl/rewolucja-refundacyjna/

REFERENCES

Arrow, K. J. (1963). Uncertainty and the welfare economics of medical care. *The American Economic Review*, *53*(5), 941–973.

Austen-Smith, D. (1987). Interest groups, campaign contributions, and probabilistic voting. *Public Choice*, *54*(2), 123–139.

Baker, & McKenzie. (2012). *Do Trzech Razy Sztuka. Ustawa Refundacyjna Po Publikacji Trzech Pierwszych Wykazów*. Pricewaterhouse Coopers. Retrieved from http://www.pwc.pl/pl/publikacje/ustawa-refundacyjna-po-publikacji-trzech-pierwszych-wykazow.jhtml

Baumol, W. J. (1990). Entrepreneurship: Productive, unproductive, and destructive. *Journal of Political Economy*, *98*(5), 893–921.

Boettke, P. J. (2010). Is the only form of "reasonable regulation" self regulation?: Lessons from Lin Ostrom on regulating the commons and cultivating citizens. *Public Choice*, *143*(3), 283–291.

Boettke, P. J., & Coyne, C. J. (2003). Entrepreneurship and development: Cause or consequence? *Advances in Austrian Economics*, *6*, 67–87.

Boulhol, H., Sowa, A., Golinowska, S., & Sicari, P. (2012). *Improving the health-care system in Poland*. OECD Economics Department Working Paper No. 957. OECD Publishing.

Butos, W., & Koppl, R. (1993). Hayekian expectations: Theory and empirical applications. *Constitutional Political Economy*, *4*(3), 303–329.

Caplan, B. (2001). Rational ignorance versus rational irrationality. *Kyklos*, *54*(1), 3–26.

Caplan, B. (2008). *The myth of the rational voter: Why democracies choose bad policies*. Princeton, NJ: Princeton University Press.

Congleton, R. D. (1989). Campaign finances and political platforms: The economics of political controversy. *Public Choice*, *62*(2), 101–118. doi:10.1007/BF00124328

Congleton, R. D. (1991). Information, special interests, and single-issue voting. *Public Choice, 69*(1), 39–49.

Czubkowska, S. (2012). Ustawa Wypędza Farmaceutów z Sieci. Rynek E-aptek Wart 200 Mln Zł Przestanie Istnieć. *Dziennik Gazeta Prawna*, January 4.

Hayek, F. A. (1973). *Law, legislation and liberty: A new statement of the liberal principles of justice and political economy*. Chicago, IL: University of Chicago Press.

Hayo, B. (2004). Public support for creating a market economy in Eastern Europe. *Journal of Comparative Economics, 32*(4), 720–744.

Higgs, R. (1997). Regime uncertainty: Why the great depression lasted so long and why prosperity resumed after the war. *Independent Review, 1*(4), 561–590.

Holcombe, R. G. (2002). Political entrepreneurship and the democratic allocation of economic resources. *The Review of Austrian Economics, 15*(2–3), 143–159.

Kirzner, I. M. (1978). *Competition and entrepreneurship*. Chicago, IL: University of Chicago Press.

Koppl, R. (2002). *Big players and the economic theory of expectations*. New York, NY: Palgrave Macmillan.

Koppl, R., & Yeager, L. B. (1996). Big players and herding in asset markets: The case of the Russian ruble. *Explorations in Economic History, 33*(3), 367–383. doi:10.1006/exeh.1996.0020

Krugman, P. (2006). Health care confidential. *New York Times*, January 27.

Kyle, M. K. (2007). Pharmaceutical price controls and entry strategies. *Review of Economics and Statistics, 89*(1), 88–99.

Maine, H. S. (1906). *Ancient law, its connection with the early history of society and its relation to modern ideas*. 4th American from the 10th London edition. New York, NY: Henry Holt and Co. Retrieved from http://oll.libertyfund.org/title/2001

Malkiel, B. G., & Fama, E. F. (1970). Efficient capital markets: A review of theory and empirical work. *The Journal of Finance, 25*(2), 383–417.

Martin, A. (2010). Emergent politics and the power of ideas. *Studies in Emergent Order, 3*, 212–245.

Meltzer, A. H., & Richard, S. F. (1981). A rational theory of the size of government. *Journal of Political Economy, 89*(5), 914–927.

Mises, L. V. (1949). *Human action: A treatise on economics*. New Haven, CT: Yale University Press.

Money.pl. (2012, February 8). *Ważna Nowelizacja Ustawy Refundacyjnej Znosi Kary Dla Lekarzy*. Retrieved from http://www.money.pl/fb/artykul,1021714.html

Mueller, D. C. (2003). *Public choice III* (3rd ed.). Cambridge: Cambridge University Press.

Pareto, V. (1935). *The mind and society*. Harcourt, IA, Brace.

Podemska-Mikluch, M., & Wagner, R. (2013). Dyads, triads, and the theory of exchange: Between liberty and coercion. *The Review of Austrian Economics, 26*(2), 171–182.

Podemska-Mikluch, M., & Wagner, R. E. (2010). Entangled political economy and the two faces of entrepreneurship. *Journal of Public Finance and Public Choice, 27*(2–3), 3–18.

Polanyi, M. (1951). *The logic of liberty; reflections and rejoinders*. Chicago, IL: University of Chicago Press.

Resnick, M. (1997). *Turtles, termites, and traffic jams: Explorations in massively parallel microworlds*. Cambridge, MA: MIT Press.

Schelling, T. C. (1978). *Micromotives and macrobehavior*. New York, NY: Norton.

Smith, A., Wagner, R. E., & Yandle, B. (2011). A theory of entangled political economy, with application to TARP and NRA. *Public Choice, 148*(1), 45–66.

Social Insurance in Poland. (2012). *Warsaw: The Social Insurance Institution*. Retrieved from http://www.zus.pl/pliki/ulotki/Ubezpieczenia%20spoleczne%20informacje%20fakty%20wer%20angielska.pdf

The World Bank Group. (2012). *Doing business 2013: Smarter regulations for small and medium-size enterprises*. Washington, DC: World Bank Publications.

Tollison, R. D., & Wagner, R. E. (1991). Romance, realism, and economic reform. *Kyklos*, *44*(1), 57–70.

Tullock, G. (1967). The welfare costs of tariffs, monopolies, and theft. *Economic Inquiry*, *5*(3), 224–232.

Tullock, G. (2008). Public choice. In S. N. Durlauf & L. E. Blume (Eds.), *The new Palgrave dictionary of economics* (2nd ed., pp. 722–727). Basingstoke: Nature Publishing Group.

Wagner, R. E. (1997). Parasitical political pricing, economic calculation, and the size of government: Variations on a theme by Maffeo Pantaleoni. *Journal of Public Finance and Public Choice*, *15*, 135–146.

Wagner, R. E. (2002). Complexity, governance and constitutional craftsmanship. *American Journal of Economics and Sociology*, *61*(1), 105–122.

Wagner, R. E. (2006). Retrogressive regime drift within a theory of emergent order. *The Review of Austrian Economics*, *19*(2–3), 113–123.

Wagner, R. E. (2007a). Value and exchange: Two windows for economic theorizing. *The Review of Austrian Economics*, *20*(2), 97–103.

Wagner, R. E. (2007b). *Fiscal sociology and the theory of public finance: An exploratory essay*. Northampton, MA: Edward Elgar Publishing.

Wagner, R. E. (2008). Finding social dilemma: West of babel, not east of Eden. *Public Choice*, *135*(1), 55–66.

Wagner, R. E. (2009). Property, state, and entangled political economy. In W. Schafer, A. Schneider, & T. Thomas (Eds.), *Markets and politics: Insights from a political economy perspective* (pp. 37–49). Marburg: Metropolis.

Wagner, R. E. (2010). *Mind, society, and human action: Time and knowledge in a theory of social economy*. New York, NY: Routledge.

Wagner, R. E. (2012a). Viennese kaleidics: Why It's liberty more than policy that calms turbulence. *The Review of Austrian Economics*, *25*(4), 283–297.

Wagner, R. E. (2012b). Choice vs. interaction in public choice theory: Discerning the legacy of the calculus of consent. In D. R. Lee (Ed.), *Public choice, past and present: The legacy of James M. Buchanan and Gordon Tullock* (pp. 65–79). New York, NY: Springer.

Wagner, R. E., & Yazigi, D. (2014). Form vs. substance in selection through competition: Elections, markets, and political economy. *Public Choice*, *159*(3), 503–514. doi:10.1007/s11127-013-0065-y

Watoła, J. (2010). Koniec Leków Za Grosz. *Wyborcza.pl*, September 14. Retrieved from http://wyborcza.pl/1,76842,8372172,Koniec_lekow_za_grosz.html

World Bank. (2013). *World development indicators 2013*. Washington, DC: World Bank. Retrieved from http://elibrary.worldbank.org/content/book/9780821398241

World Health Organization. (2012). Global Health Data Repository: Poland. Retrieved from http://www.who.int/countries/pol/en/index.html

Yandle, B. (1983). Bootleggers and baptists-the education of a regulatory economists. *Regulation*, *7*, 12.

Zakład Ubezpieczeń Społecznych. (2013). *Ubezpieczenia Społeczne. Serwis ZUS*. Retrieved from http://www.zus.pl/default.asp?p=1&id=35

Zawisza, A. (2012). Bańka Apteczna Może Pęknąć. *Przegląd*. January 21.

DODD-FRANK, FIDUCIARY DUTIES, AND THE ENTANGLED POLITICAL ECONOMY OF FEDERALISM AND AGENCY RULE-MAKING

Moin A. Yahya

ABSTRACT

Making law in America is not a simple task. It can be legislated by Congress, enforced by the executive, interpreted by the courts, and augmented by a massive body of rules created by administrative agencies such as the Securities and Exchange Commission (SEC). The Dodd-Frank Wall Street Reform and Consumer Protection Act (2010) (Dodd-Frank was passed) with an eye to preventing future financial crises. Four years later, many details of Dodd-Frank have yet to be finalized as the SEC is still in the process of developing the regulations that the legislation required them to create. Even once the regulations are finalized by the SEC, the regulations will be challenged by various parties in the courts. The regulations will be either upheld or rejected. Those that are upheld will then face numerous challenges when applied in specific cases,

Entangled Political Economy
Advances in Austrian Economics, Volume 18, 111–138

ISSN: 1529-2134/doi:10.1108/S1529-213420140000018006

while those rejected will have to be redone all over again. The process of developing these regulations is cumbersome and attracts many of the special interests that were present in the legislative phase of Dodd-Frank and who will also be present in the litigation phases of testing Dodd-Frank in the courts. This paper focuses on the requirement that investment advisors and broker-dealers be deemed as owing fiduciary duties to their clients as a case study for the entangled political economy theory. The paper shows how the development of a simple rule such as whether these fiduciary duties should be owed or not requires years of back and forth between the legislative, executive, administrative, and judicial branches.

Keywords: Dodd-Frank; entangled political economy; law and jurisprudence; fiduciary duties of investment advisors and broker-dealers; rule-making

JEL classifications: G11; G18; K22; P48

INTRODUCTION

When the term "political economy" is used by social scientists, it invokes models of an economy initially operating in a politically unconstrained manner only to be then affected by political interference, which renders the outcome somewhat sub-optimal.[1] Those models typically posit an economy that can be characterized by some market failure, which then invites regulation by a regulator. The regulator then seeks to correct the perceived market failure, but is also constrained by political realities, which render the regulation ineffective or not as effective as could be absent the political constraints. The direction of the interaction tends to be one-way, with the economy existing first, and the political regulation coming second.

Other models have recognized that private actors may seek to create a market failure, such as a monopoly, whereby they expend as much as the expected monopoly profits to receive the right to be the monopolist.[2] These models reverse the flow from the market actors to the political sphere, but the flow is nonetheless one-way.

The eminent political economist Richard Wagner has formalized a more nuanced way to model the political process.[3] Rather than the process of regulation coming from political actors to affect a passive economy or the process of political capture coming from the market actors, political economy can be modeled as a two-way interactive process. In this process, the market players seek their private interests both in the market as well as political theater, while political actors also interact onto the marketplace with various political motivations. The various private interests can shape the political preferences of the political actors, which in turn allow the private interests to sometimes capture rents in the marketplace or minimize the impact of any regulation by political actors. The process is ongoing, and figure 2 of Smith et al. (2011, p. 47) illustrates the model of what they call entangled political economy. It is this figure, which will be used in this paper to illustrate the process with respect to the treatment of fiduciary duties of broker-dealers and investment advisers by the most recent act of Congress regulating the financial markets.

The *Dodd-Frank Wall Street Reform and Consumer Protection Act* (2010) (Dodd-Frank) was signed into law by President Obama on July 21, 2010.[4] The President stated that this bill was in response to the deep recession that hit the United States in 2008, especially since "the primary cause [of the recession] was a breakdown in our financial system."[5] The President listed many goals of Dodd-Frank, which should be no surprise, since Dodd-Frank is a voluminous bill containing hundreds of provisions. The President then went on to state that Dodd-Frank would now ensure that "ordinary investors – like seniors and folks saving for retirement – will be able to receive more information about the costs and risks of mutual funds and other investment products, so that they can make better financial decisions as to what will work for them."[6] In this statement, the President was alluding to a possible new treatment of the fiduciary duties of investment advisors and broker-dealers.

This paper will use Dodd-Frank's treatment of such fiduciary duties to illustrate Wagner's paradigm of entangled political economy. While the focus of this paper may seem narrow, one can only see the details of an entangled political economy by looking at each component of Dodd-Frank. Indeed, focusing on one such component, fiduciary duties, will allow the observer to see how financial regulation is truly formed. This paper could then serve as a template for future research on financial regulation through the lens of entangled political economy.

The concept of fiduciary duties is a legal doctrine developed by the states with their various legal mechanisms. Until recently, even though the federal government regulated securities under the aegis of the Securities and Exchange Commission (SEC), when it came to state-developed legal doctrines, such as fiduciary duties, the federal government deferred to what was developed by the states. Dodd-Frank tasked the SEC with examining the question of whether a uniform fiduciary standard should be imposed on broker-dealers and investment advisers, which, if happens, would upset a delicate balance that had been in place between the federal and state legal systems.

The goal of this paper, while not aiming to comment on the merits of imposing these fiduciary duties, is to examine the entangled political economy that drove the question being proposed in Dodd-Frank and the subsequent way the SEC has gone about answering the question. The paper will show, the entangled political economy process has resulted in the question, not being answered in the legislation itself, but in subsequent agency rule-making by the SEC. Ultimately, this example will demonstrate that the entangled political economy paradigm is the proper methodology for understanding financial regulation today.

In order to understand this issue more clearly, a bit of machinery needs to be introduced. Therefore, the paper will be organized as follows. The section "Entangled Political Economy and the Making of Law" will provide a basic overview of the interaction between federal law and state law, including how such laws are made. The section "Fiduciary Duties for Broker-Dealers and Investment Advisors: before and after Dodd-Frank" will then address the question of fiduciary duties for broker-dealers and investment advisors, and how Dodd-Frank will affect this question. The section "Dodd-Frank and Fiduciary Duties: Entangled Political Economy in Action" will finally then provide some insight into the entangled political economy aspect of this question. The section "Concluding Thoughts" will conclude.

ENTANGLED POLITICAL ECONOMY AND THE MAKING OF LAW

This section is somewhat lengthy but necessary for the reader to appreciate the pre-existing state of entangled political economy that drives the creation and application of laws in the United States. It will also allow the reader to appreciate at the end of the paper the future of any regulatory endeavors by the federal government, especially when it comes to financial regulation.

In the United States, there are two basic levels of government: the federal government and the states. Within each level of government, however, there are at least four methods that laws are made and enforced. The first is at the legislative level. The second is at the executive level. The third is at the regulatory agencies level, and the fourth is at the judicial level.

At the legislative level, members of the various legislatures enact all sorts of laws. These laws usually require or prohibit certain conduct. The various members of the legislatures are undoubtedly subject to the political pressures that much of the public choice literature has spoken about.[7] In designing the laws they pass, however, the legislators have many options for how to proceed. They can either specify with great detail the type of commands they wish to be executed. They can also simply outline their broad wishes and leave the executive or one of the regulatory agencies to promulgate regulations that give effect to the laws they pass. This method is very common at the federal level, and Dodd-Frank is no different. Dodd-Frank contains both highly detailed prescriptions as well as rule-making delegations to the SEC.[8]

After the legislation is passed, the executive level is charged with implementing the various laws passed by the legislative branch, as well as developing rules pursuant to "fill in the blanks" provisions of the enacted laws. This means that the executive not only gets to create the rules that give effect to the law passed, but it also gets discretion in how to implement the laws. This creates another layer of entanglement in the political economy sphere. Parties that could not achieve their goals in the legislature, or chose not to pursue their goals there, can now pursue their objectives at the executive level. They can either spend resources to affect the creation of new rules or to lobby for favorable enforcement of the laws and rules.

At the administrative agency level, the enacted legislation may specify that new rules must be promulgated at the agency level. These rules can also be enforced by the various agencies, thereby creating another level of entanglement. At the state level, some of the agencies are run by elected members. This creates another level of complexity to the model.

Finally, all of these laws, regulations, and rules must be enforced by one level or another of the judiciary. The question of where the laws are enforced is also the subject of political economy. There are state courts and federal courts. State courts can also create common laws, something, in theory, the federal courts cannot. But federal courts can adjudicate state law issues, if the litigants are "diverse" or from two different states. At the federal level, judges are appointed by the President with the approval of the Senate for life, but at the state level there are numerous ways they can be chosen. In some states the judges are appointed, while in others they are elected. The election of judges creates a whole level of political economy that just adds another level of complexity and entanglement. Many legal scholars have written on the question of how the interaction between the various judicial branches has affected the laws of the United States.[9]

Indeed, when it comes to analyzing the development of legal doctrines by state courts, public choice theory has been very useful for the analysis. For example, Professor Krauss used public choice to explain the outcome of a dispute between a Canadian company that purchased a funeral home in Mississippi and a local businessman.[10] The dispute out as a $3.5 million dispute, but the trial resulted in a $500 million jury award in favor of the local businessman. Krauss explains that this result happened, because the trial judge allowed the local businessman's plaintiff's lawyer to make many wild accusations against the Canadian company. In addition, even though it emerged that the jury had actually miscalculated the damages, the judge did nothing to correct this.

Krauss explained this result by explaining that many state judges are elected. They are elected by their local voters. Hence, state judges have an incentive to redistribute wealth away from out-of-state defendants to in-state plaintiffs.[11] But not only are the plaintiffs in these disputes local, their lawyers are also local lawyers who contribute to the judges' election campaigns. The out-of-state defendants, however and even sometimes their lawyers, are from out of the state. They, therefore, have no opportunity to contribute to the judges' campaigns. This results in the trial judges favoring the plaintiffs and their lawyers during the trial. This can result in harsh results from the jury against the out-of-state defendants.

The situation doesn't get any better on appeal. Many of the state appellate and state supreme court judges are also elected. In the now infamous case of *Texaco v. Pennzoil, Co.*,[12] the lawyers for the losing defendant argued on appeal that the trial judge had been biased because he accepted donations from the plaintiff's lawyer. The appellate court (also elected) rejected this claim by stating (quoting from another case):

> It is not surprising that attorneys are the principal source of contributions in a judicial election. … If a judge cannot sit on a case in which a contributing lawyer is involved as counsel, judges who have been elected would have to recuse themselves in perhaps a majority of the cases filed in their courts. Perhaps the next step would be to require a judge to recuse himself in any case in which one of the lawyers had refused to contribute or, worse still, had contributed to that judge's opponent.

But lest the reader think that this problem is only confined to elected judges, it should be noted that even the non-elected federal courts can become susceptible to public choice pressures. When it comes to enforcing federal laws, for many types of cases and circumstances, the parties, especially the one initiating a lawsuit, can choose from among many federal judicial forums to bring their case. If, for example, someone wishes to challenge a federal law as being unconstitutional, he or she may bring the suit in any one of the 50 states where a federal court is located (provided a proper plaintiff is found). This leads to what is known as forum shopping. In other words, parties will search for sympathetic courts that may rule in their favor. Such forum shopping has been documented in the areas of bankruptcy[13] and patents.[14]

Just a few years ago, for example, a private special interest group managed to temporarily thwart the re-opening of the United States border to Canadian beef, even after the United States Department of Agriculture (USDA) had determined that such beef was safe.[15] The organization representing American ranchers, in addition to its lobbying efforts at the federal legislative and executive levels, also poured resources into the judicial arena. They found a federal court in Montana with a sympathetic judge whom they convinced to shut the United States border to Canadian beef. The order was overturned on appeal, but the episode demonstrates the ability of special interest groups to use the federal courts to achieve their ends even when they have failed at the legislative and executive level.

State and federal courts have their own dynamic entanglement. As stated earlier, while federal courts can hear "diverse" cases, that is, cases where both litigants are from different states, there are ways to defeat diversity. For example, if A is from California, B is from Virginia, and C is from California, and if A sues B and C in California, then only a California state court can hear the case. Creative lawyers will therefore sue a local defendant in addition to the out-of-state target in order to avoid the case being heard by the federal court. Later after the case has started and after it is too late to transfer the case back to the federal court, the plaintiff dismisses the lawsuit against the local defendant or settles. Creative parties who wish to extract rents using the judicial process can do so even in the face of institutional settings designed to prevent that.

Whether it is best to have the federal or state courts develop legal doctrine and apply them can be analyzed under the rubric of competitive federalism. The concept of competitive federalism has much support among lawyers and political economists alike.[16] Federalism works best when states compete on matters that do not spill over, that is, the competition does not lead to a race to the bottom. Hence, when it comes to state courts creating new legal doctrines, federalism encourages states to experiment with various doctrines. As Justice Brandeis famously pronounced:

> It is one of the happy incidents of the federal system that a single courageous state may, if its citizens choose, serve as a laboratory; and try novel social and economic experiments without risk to the rest of the country.[17]

As long as, however, the results of the experiments stay within the states so that there are no externalities visited upon the other states, federalism works best. When, however, states impact others, especially negatively, then this is when there is a proper role for federal intervention. Hence, if state courts are taxing out-of-state defendants unfairly, then federal laws should ensure that federal courts and laws pre-empt state law.

A state court will develop various legal doctrines that are applied in that state. Those doctrines may also be applied by a federal court if it is adjudicating a claim regarding a citizen of that particular state. Additionally, other state courts may look to these doctrines for guidance. In fact, many legal doctrines have been created in the courts, starting with the common law courts in England and then the state courts in the United States. One such doctrine is that of fiduciary duties.

FIDUCIARY DUTIES FOR BROKER-DEALERS AND INVESTMENT ADVISORS: BEFORE AND AFTER DODD-FRANK

The concept of fiduciary duties arose from old English law many centuries ago. To understand what it entails consider the following stylized story. The year is 1300, and the place is a manor somewhere in England. A dying father has a very young son and an adult brother as his only next of kin. He has a considerable amount of money, or more likely land, that he wishes his son to have. The ailing father is concerned that if he leaves to his son the money in his will, the son, who is too young to know better, may squander the money either through imprudent financial decisions or simply wasting the money frivolously. So instead, the father turns to his brother, the young son's uncle, and tells him that he will leave the money to him on the condition that he looks after the son.

The uncle agrees. The father asks him further to cultivate the money or land so that when the son reaches the age of majority, the son can then take over and be comfortable in his life. The uncle agrees. The father executes a will leaving his assets to his brother, and even states that these assets are being left to his brother in the hopes that the brother look after the son. Perhaps the language is stronger, so that the assets are being left on condition that the uncle looks after the nephew and manage the assets for the benefit of the son during his years as a minor. Regardless of what conditions, stipulations, or other wishful language, once the father died, the son's uncle now owned the assets outright, and he was free to do whatever he pleased with the assets.

The uncle could escort the little boy to an orphanage and leave him there sharing none of the assets his brother left him with the son. If the son hired a lawyer and sued, the courts of law would side with the uncle. The uncle owned the assets in law and had *legal* title to the assets. All the conditions in the will were mere desires and had no legal impact on the assets. This harsh result in this stylized fact pattern illustrates the harsh origins of the English common law treatment of assets that were meant for the benefit of one group, but that were being held by another group.

By the 1600s, however, English law had developed several legal mechanisms that would allow young children to be protected from their greedy uncles. Specifically, three concepts were created by the English courts. The first was the concept of equity. Originally separate courts that were run by clergy, courts of equity or chancery courts were established to ameliorate the harshness of the common law. The son who lost his case against his uncle in the regular, or common law, courts could now go to a court of equity and seek some redress. The courts of equity did not disturb the verdict of the common law courts. Hence, the legal title of the assets remained with the uncle. Instead, the courts of equity acted upon a person. In other words, the courts of equity commanded the uncle to look after the son, not to waste the money or the land he inherited, and to prudently manage the assets for the benefit of the son while he is a minor.

In other words, the courts of equity imposed a trust upon the assets and declared the uncle a trustee holding the assets in trust for the benefit of the minor. The concept of trusts, therefore, was the second legal concept that helps the orphan. The third was the concept of fiduciary duties. The trustee, or the uncle, was held by the courts to be a fiduciary toward his nephew, and this meant that he was required to act within certain fiduciary duties.

Over time, the law classified many relationships as being fiduciary relationships. The law creates these relationships through judicial pronouncements, that is, the common law, or through legislative pronouncements, that is, statutory law. In such a relationship, typically, there is a principal and an agent, whereby the agent owes the principal certain fiduciary duties. The principal, in our example, would be the son, while the agent would be the uncle. In some fiduciary relationships, the principal and agent are clear, such the doctor-patient, attorney-client, and partner-partnership relationship. In others, the agent is clear but the principal is not.[18]

These duties are sometimes characterized as positive and negative. Sometimes, they are known as duties of loyalty and care. The negative duties are essentially duties of loyalty. While the duty of loyalty can be expressed in positive terms, that is, the fiduciary must act in the best interests of the trust, it is easier to state them in terms of what the fiduciary or trustee is not allowed to do. Typically, the negative duties are the duty to refrain from making self-dealing and stealing opportunities belonging to the trust. In other words, the trustee cannot use any of the trust's assets for his own personal usage or even use any proprietary information only learnt because of his involvement with the trust for personal gain. The trustee cannot use the assets of the trust as his personal piggybank. Suppose the assets were agricultural land, for example, and the land required fertilizer. The trustee, generally speaking, could not sell the land fertilizer from his personal fertilizer company.

The positive duties are not as clear to define. The trustee is expected to take a level of care that ensures that the trust's assets provide for the young son during his minor years while leaving sufficient assets in the trust for the son to assume once he reaches the age of majority. How exactly the trustee is supposed to do this is the question that this paper will shed some light on. These legally imposed fiduciary duties presuppose an inability on the agent's part to establish these duties, or rules of the relationship, through the normal contracting mechanisms. The law assumes such an inability either due to some systemic asymmetric information or some inability of the agent to rationally bargain. A patient who knows little about medicine could be an example of the former, while a young child who is unable to look after his daily affairs let alone outline complex financial arrangements is an example of the latter.[19]

With respect to portfolio management, the question of fiduciary duties is quite nuanced. In our son and uncle example, let us first move the time of these two to the modern day where the son has inherited an amount of cash in the bank that the uncle must now look after. There are many scenarios that could result during their lifetime. The first is the basic trustee beneficiary relationship, where the son is a helpless minor at the mercy of his uncle. The uncle could be very financially sophisticated or have no financial skills whatsoever.

Suppose after growing up, the son decides that his uncle, who is actually a financial genius, should continue to manage his account. The son, being in his early twenties, is no longer worried about there being food on the table and is actually more concerned with the growth of his assets. It turns out that the son is himself quite financially sophisticated and wishes to play the market himself. It also turns out the uncle is a stockbroker who can carry out trades for the son. In another scenario, the son simply hands over his cash to the uncle who also manages a mutual fund.

Finally, the son who has dreams of striking it rich and who has been reading about the fantastic returns hedge fund managers can generate (alas he has been reading older copies of *Business Week*) decides to hand his cash over to his uncle, who happens to run a hedge fund. He instructs the uncle to "go crazy" and to "work his magic" on the funds in the trust. As one can see, there are many situations where imposing a fiduciary duty may or may not be the appropriate policy decision. This is because what exactly the fiduciary duties are depends on what the standard of care is.

There are two types of brokers: pure brokers and investment advisors. Brokers simply execute their clients' orders, known as broker-dealers.[20] They are usually paid by commissions. Some broker-dealers may also provide advice to their clients. Investment advisers are supposed to only give advice, but in reality many are active managers who manage the client's assets. These advisers charge fees that are related to the size of the assets, and these advisers are best known as managing mutual funds or hedge funds.

To see the issues surrounding fiduciary duties of brokers and advisors, briefly consider the situation of trust managers. Trust managers who manage trust funds set up for young children or charities or who manage pension plans are also fiduciaries. Once upon a time, trust managers were only allowed to invest in low-risk assets such as treasury bills. Modern portfolio theory, however, tells us that the optimal investment is a combination of the risk-free asset and the efficient portfolio frontier. Individual investors are supposed to choose a combination of these two assets, the exact ratio of the two assets being determined by the individual's risk tolerance.[21] Today, trust managers are allowed to make investments in diversified portfolios, but it is still unclear how much leeway the law allows such managers when making investment decisions.[22]

If broker-dealers and investment advisors, however, are to be deemed fiduciaries, it should become obvious how this can be very onerous. After all, how is the broker or advisor to determine what the investor's indifference curve (between risk and return) looks like, let alone what combination of assets to invest in. What does a broker do with the wildly optimistic client who wants all his money to be invested in a high-yield hedge fund? Or for that matter, what does the broker do with a very self-confident investor who insists that he or she knows best but keeps losing money?

The problem is that the relationship between individuals who trade in stocks, bonds, or other assets for their own personal portfolios and their brokers is not obviously a fiduciary relationship. A day-trading investor who trades to make money quickly, or who actually has a realistic plan for long-term investing, have very different view of their brokers than future retirees who are at the mercy of their pension plan managers. Some of these day-traders consider themselves, and may actually be, more sophisticated than their brokers.

If brokers are deemed to be fiduciaries, there can be serious implications. For example, brokers might not be allowed to sell their clients stock that they personally own, because this would be a form of self-dealing creating a conflict of interest. For that matter, getting paid on commission could also be deemed a conflict of interest.

Brokers would have to advise clients all the time. They would have to advise against making certain trades if they believed those trades were adverse to their clients' interest even if the client thought otherwise. They may even have to watch out for such behavior and prevent them from making these trades, just as bartenders are required to stop serving extremely drunk patrons.

Although the Securities Exchange Act (SEA) provides some basic requirements for brokers, brokers are governed by a self-regulating organization, the Financial Industry Regulatory Authority (FINRA). At present, the laws concerning their fiduciary duties vary, and because of this, broker-dealers face many uncertainties regarding their duties.[23] They are not explicitly deemed to be fiduciaries, but that may change depending on the circumstances. They are required to deal with their clients in a fair and honest manner, and they cannot engage in fraud.[24]

But they are not fiduciaries, unless they have an active role in managing their client's account. Broker-dealers are also required to register with their state regulatory agency and are therefore subject to various state regulations. Some states, such as California, deem brokers to be fiduciaries, while others do not.

Broker-dealers may also find themselves facing quasi-fiduciary responsibilities. For example, if a broker recommends a particular investment or investment strategy to their clients, this then triggers "suitability requirements." Brokers must understand their client's specific financial situation and needs. Conceptually, these requirements relate to modern portfolio theory which discusses investing in the optimal portfolio frontier in ratios that depend on investors' tolerance for risk.

In order to determine the investor's indifference curve, brokers administer a questionnaire that determines whether the client in more "income" oriented or more "growth" oriented. Hence, the elderly widow who is investing to keep up her retirement income should not receive the same recommendation as a young high-income professional in his or her twenties.[25] That being said, suitability requirements, currently, do not translate into strict fiduciary duties for brokers. No disclosure is required of the broker's conflicts of interest or that the broker does not believe that the investment is contrary to the client's best interest.

Investment advisers also face legal ambiguities. They are regulated by the Investment Advisers Act, which lays out the obligations of those managing other people's money. The Investment Company Act also lays out the duties of investment companies that mange other people's money. With respect to investment advisers, section 36(b) of the Investment Company Act states that "the investment adviser of a registered investment company shall be deemed to have a fiduciary duty with respect to the receipt of compensation for services, or of payments of a material nature, paid by such registered investment company, or by the security holders thereof, to such investment adviser or any affiliated person of such investment adviser."

This means that there are duties of disclosure that come with any transaction that the investment adviser conducts on behalf of the client. They must disclose their actual and potential conflicts of interest. They also have a duty of best execution. This means that the advisor must execute trades in the cheapest and most efficient manner. If, however, they receive any payments from other brokers, then they must disclose these payments. What exactly constitutes best execution, however, is another question. Johnsen (2009) explain why, for example, "soft-dollar" payments might actually be efficiency enhancing, and should therefore not be required in the disclosure requirements.

Because they are fiduciaries, they are also expected to only receive a reasonable fee for their services. This generates much litigation as Ribstein (2010) explains. For example, with respect to mutual funds, a mutual fund adviser-manager cannot charge what is "so disproportionately large that it bears no reasonable relationship to the services rendered and could not have been the product of arm's-length bargaining" (Ribstein, 2010, p. 302). Although this is impossible to determine practically, it doesn't stop plaintiffs from suing their mutual fund managers. The American legal system is expensive and most funds will settle the lawsuit regardless of the merit. The average annual settlement works out to an average of $125,000 for each of the approximately 8,000 mutual funds in the United States (Ribstein, p. 310).

At this stage, nonetheless, there is a fine balance between the brokers and advisors on one hand and their customers on the other hand. It has been developed over the years through various legal channels, including state and federal courts. Dodd-Frank changes this balance.

Dodd-Frank requires the SEC to examine the state of legal obligations for brokers and investment advisors. Indeed, the SEC issued a study in January 2011, which contains a detailed examination of these duties in 208 pages.[26] The study recommended that a uniform fiduciary standard for both broker-dealers and investment advisers be imposed upon them. If the SEC chooses to enact a uniform fiduciary standard, it will issue new regulations, which will no doubt be promptly challenged in the courts.

While the results of enacting a uniform standard are unclear at this stage, the purpose of this paper is to discuss the entangled political economy that has led to the current status and discuss where it may lead in the future.

DODD-FRANK AND FIDUCIARY DUTIES: ENTANGLED POLITICAL ECONOMY IN ACTION

Dodd-Frank like any massive post-disaster legislation comes as a result of perceived public pressure on legislators to be seen taking action. The process of passage, as alluded to by the President involved an almost one sided partisan effort to pass this legislation:

> Passing this bill was no easy task. To get there, we had to overcome the furious lobbying of an array of powerful interest groups and a partisan minority determined to block change. ... And I also want to thank the three Republican senators who put partisanship aside ... and voted for reform.[27]

The "intense lobbying" right away should alert the reader behind the scenes entanglement that affected the passage of Dodd-Frank. Indeed the President's statement contains the type of political economy messaging such as "[n]ow, for all those Americans who are wondering what Wall Street reform means for you, here's what you can expect ...."[28]

The President went on to list transparency of fees in credit cards, the elimination of "abusive practices" in the mortgage industry, and transparency for "ordinary investors – like seniors and folks saving for retirement" regarding mutual funds and other investment opportunities. The final appeal was to the idea that Americans would never again have to "foot the bill for Wall Street's mistakes." All of these statements were received by applause from those in attendance, again indicating how measured the signing statements were considering that the bulk of the legislation is actually very technical and beyond the grasp of most in the room let alone "ordinary" Americans.

To see the degree of entanglement just on the discrete question of whether fiduciary duties should be extended to broker-dealers, the process is broken down into two stages. The first is before the enactment of Dodd-Frank when the legislation was pending before Congress, and the second is after Dodd-Frank when the rule-making is in the hands of the SEC.

Before Dodd-Frank in Congress

The political appeal to abusive practices by Wall Street and its impact on ordinary Americans was the reason for the political push to regulate broker-dealers and investment advisers. One way to regulate them was to impose fiduciary duties on them. Hence, when Congress posed the question of whether such duties should be imposed in the legislation itself, what is striking is that so few of the affected players answered the question in detail when the issue was still before Congress in the legislative phase. In contrast, as will be seen below, far more answered it and opined on the question in much more detail once the issue was in front of the SEC.

This suggests that those sophisticated market players who have a real stake in this game prefer to create the rules at the SEC level of rule-making instead of the Congressional legislative phase. For that matter, even the consumer groups who could have seized the political moment of outrage at Wall Street also chose not to contribute much on this question at the legislative phase. This also indicates that all the market actors were more interested in the question being posed by Congress and answered by the SEC. To understand why, consider what Macey (1992, p. 108) has argued, namely that "agency structure and design reduce the agency costs associated with broad delegations of authority to administrative agencies." This, he argued, allows special interest groups who may "not know what issues will affect them in the future or even what their preferences will be with respect to future controversies" to "generate outcomes that continually reflect the interests of the original interest group." He concludes that "[t]his state of affairs has obvious benefits for interest groups."

When the issue was in front of Congress, special interest groups therefore oriented their advocacy in broad terms with no specifics. The goal was to obtain a favorable legislative setup for each group that could be worked out in detail with the SEC. This can be seen in the various testimonies in front of the various House and Senate Committees that examined the legislation.

For example, in testimony unrelated to the fiduciary duties question but on other matters in the legislation, the Securities Industry and Financial Markets Association (SIFMA) displayed a real mastery of political lobbying. SIFMA posed a series of questions to the House Financial Services Committee which included:

> Should the government play a role in encouraging affordable rental housing funded by multifamily lending? Arguably, all of these things stem from, or have been historically bolstered by, Federal engagement in the mortgage finance system.

SIFMA then answered "yes," going on to state that "[n]ational mortgage markets should be maintained, and liquid secondary markets are necessary for them to exist." This, of course, serves the association's members well. But to justify this, SIFMA immediately stated that:

> The broader economy is well served when mortgage rates are generally affordable to a large number of appropriately qualified consumers, given the important contribution of housing and all of its ancillary industries to GDP and employment. Therefore, our perspective is that some form of government support for mortgage markets should be provided ....[29]

In other words, the association members are happy to continue the provision of the politically motivated goals of Congress but with the price of government support for mortgage markets.

Not wanting to miss some of the action during the legislative session, an association of real estate appraisers also testified on a variety of bills, Dodd-Frank being the least important of the bills they addressed.[30] Nonetheless, in a passing reference to Dodd-Frank, they sought the enactment of a provision in Dodd-Frank that "enhances appraiser oversight and enforcement and clarifies certain provisions to enhance commercial real estate collateral analysis." While this provision was ostensibly proposed to make sure that loans were properly securitized, it nonetheless managed to get the attention and political lobbying of those who would directly benefit from such provisions.

The National Association of Hispanic Real Estate Professionals also made a presentation supporting the creation of "an Office of Minority and Women Inclusion at each of the major federal financial regulatory agencies."[31] The National Association of Real Estate Brokers also voiced their support for the creation of this office.[32] Arguing that "minority real estate professionals have virtually been shut out of business opportunities made available through Federal government agencies." This shutout came about, for example, by "the bundling of contract solicitations that limit a successful response to large, highly capitalized, general market firms with a performance history of doing business with Federal agencies dealing with the financial crisis." These solicitation requirements, therefore, "immediately bar minority and woman-owned businesses from participating in the bidding process." To remind the committee of who is behind the association, the testimony closed by stating that the "over 60,000 African Americans in the real estate industry are counting on your support and your continued vigilance." Indeed many such testimonies were given supporting the creation of the office. Other testimony included consumer public interest groups supported provisions that would prohibit binding arbitration provisions in financial services disputes.[33]

None of the testimony by the special interest groups that I could find supported (or even opposed) the creation of a uniform standard, which may explain why the legislation delegated to the SEC the task of studying whether such a uniform standard should be imposed.

At this juncture, the reader should see that the sophistication of all parties driving an abstention on answering the question is almost collusive. By not answering the question, Congress, in a sense, was forced to leave the question to the SEC. The entangled political economy paradigm would indeed suggest such a result. As Wagner (2014) states "there is a micro level where all action occurs and a macro level which is not a locus of action but rather is a construction that resembles the tales told by the prisoners in Plato's cave."

After Dodd-Frank at the SEC (and Congress)

Once Dodd-Frank became law, the dynamics changed. The shifting of the task from Congress to the SEC meant that a new round of lobbying began. Under principles of administrative law, when an agency engages in a study or proposes new rules, interested parties must have an opportunity to make submissions to the agency. The agency is then required to examine the submissions and respond to them. In this case, the SEC established a cross-divisional staff task force.

This time, unlike the lackluster commentary in Congress, the task force "solicited comments and data as part of the Study and received over 3,500 comment letters."[34] The task force "also met with interested parties representing investors, broker-dealers, investment advisers, other representatives of the financial services industry, academics, state securities regulators, the North American Securities Administrator Association ... and the Financial Industry Regulatory Authority ('FINRA') ...." In other words, all those special interests that were able to completely bypass the first round of the legislative process now got their chance to affect the shape of the proposed rules. An examination of the submissions and meetings shows that 111 entities have been meeting with the SEC for over two years now, while just about 2,850 unique letters were submitted, also over a two year period. Given that over 3,500 letters were submitted, and only 2,850 were unique, it should be obvious that there were many mass mailed letters submitted to the SEC.

The format, that is, unique versus mass mailed, of the submissions discloses the types of efforts made when commenting on the question of fiduciary duties to the SEC. The SEC on its comments page indicated that 264 submissions were received using a template letter, which it called Letter Type A. Similarly, the SEC received 22 Letters of Type B, 3 of Type C, 145 of Type D, 43 of Type E, 6 of Type F, and 8 of Type G. In other words, 491 comments were really only making the point of seven submissions.

The Type A letters were from life insurance producers who sell various insurance products.[35] The representative letter's author voiced concerns that these producers are already subject to state regulators' supervision as well as FINRA and the SEC. To add another layer of duties on top of what is already required of them, the author advocates that this "most certainly will result in increased compliance costs ... with no measurable benefit to investors. Over time, ... it will reduce product choice and access for investors." The author argues that rather than increasing liability and uncertainty for these insurance producers, what the SEC should do is focus on specific conduct it feels is harmful instead of a blanket declaration that brokers-dealers are now fiduciaries.

However, a group of financial planners and investment advises filed Letter Type D, where this group advocated for the imposition of the fiduciary standard. The submissions, were in the nature of quality control for all industry participants. The author of the letter stated that his

> clients recognize and understand that the advice I give them is in their best interests, because: my loyalty is to them first; I will advise them with utmost good faith; I will manage any conflicts of interests that may harm them and disclose those conflicts to them; I get paid for the advice I give them and the investments I select for them; I am

required to choose from the best investments available keeping their interests first; and I can charge a fee or commissions based on their needs and preferences.

Frequently regulated firms will want the state to regulate and regulate more often in order to raise rivals' costs, which confers a competitive advantage on the incumbent firms. This letter has the ring of that type of submission.

Many of the letters submitted were written by individual customers of broker-dealers, university professors, and other public interest types. The letters by the customers either expressed outrage at their treatment by their brokers or advisers, while some stated that they did not even know there were two separate legal duties for the brokers and advisers. For example, one customer submitted that they were "tired of the lies and thievery by people working in investments, insurance, banking, credit." The customer stated that "[w]e little investors are not making money AND we are not getting good advice from our PAID 'investment' guys working the in computer gambling dens in the Big Firm's basement either." For this bad behavior, the customer urged the "SEC to eliminate this kind of crap and other fraudster-moves like it," and implored the SEC to "set some standards – tough ones – for what is to be available online too, as well as tightening up the standards overall." The customer assuaged the SEC over concerns that tightening up standards would be onerous for industry by closing with: "Don't worry about the investment industry players – they'll always make out."[36]

Indeed, it was interesting that SIFMA supported the creation of a uniform federal standard despite this being adverse to its members' interests at first glance.[37] Reasons for this support can easily be discerned when looking through the lens of entangled political economy. It is easier to develop one uniform standard at the federal level than trying to influence 50 states' jurisprudence. Indeed, SIFMA and others must feel more confident with their ability to influence the development of the law in the federal regulatory arena than the consumer groups who also made various submissions on the subject.

In order to deal with all of these concerns, the industry players displayed deft legal strategy. For example, SIFMA's submission to the SEC on the issue of a uniform standard displays good legal maneuvering on many fronts. The submissions conceded the imposition a uniform standard, but then go one to explain why such a uniform standard would be undesirable. Hence, instead of rejecting the imposition of a standard outright, which would put SIFMA outside the political economy arena, it entered the fray but in a manner that allows it to influence the outcome. In response the Consumer Federation of America, took issue with the points raised by SIFMA. Indeed, their letter states that:

> Last year, SIFMA submitted a letter outlining its views on an appropriate framework for rulemaking in this area. The SIFMA letter does a good job of highlighting the key issues the Commission will need to consider in developing a rule proposal. We agree with many of their points but disagree, sometimes strongly, with others. In order to make it as easy as possible for the Commission to determine both our points of agreement and where our views diverge, we have chosen to use their letter as a starting point for our own discussion of the same issues.[38]

This shows that SIFMA was quite successful in framing the discussion to the point that even those on the opposite end had to frame their discussion in light of SIFMA's submissions.

But SIFMA's submissions went beyond just sending three letters and nine meeting with the SEC. In 2011 and 2012, SIFMA has made numerous appearances in front of various Congressional committees regarding various financial issues that affect its members. The committees or subcommittees ranged from the ones dealing with capital markets to health, employment and labor issues. In each one of these submissions the representative of SIFMA went of their way to remind the Congressional subcommittee of their support for a uniform fiduciary standard, and thereby leverage that support in exchange (presumably) for favorable treatment of its members by Congress. For example, after thanking the committee members, SIFMA reminded them that:

> SIFMA and its members remain committed to being constructive participants in the process of establishing a uniform fiduciary standard for broker-dealers and investment advisers, and ensuring uniform examination, oversight, and enforcement of that standard. [SIFMA] stand[s] ready to provide any further assistance requested by this Subcommittee on these critically important topics.[39]

In another hearing, SIFMA stated that:

> SIFMA strongly supported that provision of Dodd-Frank [that authorizes the SEC to establish a uniform fiduciary standard of care for brokers and advisors when providing personalized investment advice] and [SIFMA] recently submitted a letter to the SEC encouraging the Commission to move forward with such a rule. I have submitted our letter with my testimony for the record.[40]

Not to be outdone, the Consumer Federation of America submitted five letters and met twice with the SEC, almost each time to rebut what SIFMA had submitted. Similarly, customer and labor groups also testified in front of Congress on a variety of matters relating to these fiduciary duties even though it was the SEC and not Congress after 2010 that would be creating the new rules.[41] The fact that SIFMA and its opponents continue to show up in front of Congress simultaneously with their submissions to the SEC shows how entangled the political economy of rule-making can be.

At the end of the day, the comments all impacted the creation of the SEC's study. The SEC study, which ultimately recommended a uniform standard, was just over 160 pages long. There were over 700 footnotes, most of which were citations to the various submissions made by all the interested parties. This translates into an average of four citations per page of the study. Almost all of the citations, however, were to interested organizations and very few to individuals. This means that despite over 3,000 submissions (many from ordinary citizens), it was the properly documented and study-supported submissions that ruled the day at the SEC.

This SEC study simply recommends the creation of a uniform standard with very little details on what the standard would entail. That is the task for another round of rule-making at the SEC with all the entangled political economy in play. Perhaps, because of the fatigue from the last round of compiling the study and the political uncertainty prior to the 2012 presidential election, no final rules have emerged from the SEC.

At the end of the day, the SEC report recommended the imposition of a uniform fiduciary standard. The SEC report also attempted to define with some precisions the nature of the duties of care that would now be required of brokers and advisors. Many commentators, however, have called these duties vague, cosmetic, and falling short of any real reform.[42] The reason should be clear from the earlier discussion: they are hard to define. Fiduciary duties are more in the nature of spontaneous order developed rules developed over the centuries in the English and state courts, rather than centrally planned rules developed overnight. For this, even if the SEC imposes its uniform standard, there may be no real reform.

When the final rules arrive, if at all, the various parties will undoubtedly challenge them in the courts. Additionally, the rule will be applied through various legal actions by the SEC that will refine, define, and re-define what the yet-to-be-issued rules will say. Judicial challenges will also play a role in the process of defining the rules. This will lead to another round of judicial entanglement as explained above.

While the fiduciary duties rule has not been developed to be challenged, to illustrate this point, consider that there has already been at least two legal challenges to other specific provisions of Dodd-Frank. In one challenge, among others, a bank, the Competitive Enterprise Institute, and several states sued to challenge the constitutionality of the Consumer Financial Protection Bureau, created by Dodd-Frank as well as the constitutionality of the appointment of its director.[43] In another challenge, various business groups challenged the validity and constitutionality of rules promulgated by the SEC requiring the disclosure on companies that use "conflict minerals" originating from several African countries.[44]

In both cases, the trial judges dismissed the legal challenges. In one of the cases, the trial judge was appointed by President Clinton to the bench, while the other was appointed by President Obama.[45] The parties in both cases have appealed to the court of appeal, which may have a different political composition, and which may yield a different result. Even if these two cases end on appeal the same way they ended at the trial level, other challenges will flow from other provisions of Dodd-Frank. The entanglement will continue as described in the section "Entangled Political Economy and the Making of Law" and illustrated in Fig. 1. Even when the legal challenges die down, more rule-making will take place at the SEC, which will then revive the process of legal challenges, and the entanglement will continue.

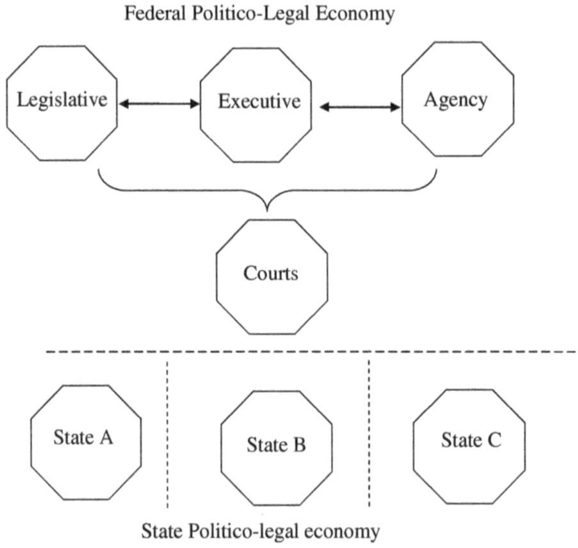

Fig. 1. Interaction Between State and Federal Law-making.

CONCLUDING THOUGHTS

The paper proposed to use the question of fiduciary duties for broker-dealers and investment advisers as an illustration of the paradigm of entangled political economy. The question has yet to be answered in detail precisely because the process of making these rules are subject to an entangled political economy and not the classical one-way political economy. From the question being posed by Congress but not being answered to rule-making at the SEC (which has yet to answer the question in detail) to the ultimate legal challenges that will ensue, the whole process can be properly characterized by the entangled political economy paradigm.

Wagner (2012) observes that the macro-economy is not a simple aggregation of micro-economies, but rather a complex interaction of the various micro-economies that constitute the macro-economy. This paper argues that Dodd-Frank's treatment of fiduciary duties can be seen as the sum of various interactions between different actors throughout various stages of the development of rules. At this stage, all that is certain is that there is now a shift of power from the state courts and legislatures, where these doctrines and duties had developed over the years, to the federal SEC and federal courts.[46] Dodd-Frank and the efforts of the SEC to try to impose a uniform fiduciary standard on broker-dealers and investment advisors represent the latest step in a political economy saga. The saga started during the New Deal with the imposition of federal regulations on broker-dealers and then investment advisors. Over the years, the federal government has been grabbing more and more of the authority to enforce the laws. The federal government has also been grabbing the authority to create legal doctrine, something that has traditionally resided in the states. Dodd-Frank, in addition to creating more federal enforcement, has now also waded into the creation of legal doctrine.

This means that despite any hope for finality in the legislation will not be achieved, as the political entanglement will not end there. The entangled political economy will now shift to the federal arena, while the state arena may still be a ground of activity in the future. Those interests that may feel left out of the federal process may then try to devise novel ways of re-entangling the process at the state level, for example. The result will undoubtedly be another round of legislation down the road. What does emerge from this process, however, is a new entangled political economy that can be seen in Fig. 1. There the dotted line between the federal and state politico-legal systems may become a bold line or stay dotted depending on how the parties involved are able to affect the various politico-legal systems.

The reader should remember that the question of fiduciary duties was but one of hundreds of questions that Dodd-Frank either addressed directly or delegated to the SEC to answer. The story told here of this one aspect can be repeated for each of these questions. Indeed, the entanglement in one question can spill over to the entanglement in another. At the end of the day, Dodd-Frank, like Wagner's (2012) macro-economy, cannot be thought of as a simple aggregate of its various sections, but rather as a complex entangled system resulting from the entanglement that is behind the hundreds of questions being addressed by Dodd-Frank. The story developed in this paper can serve as a template to further understand financial regulation in the United States. Understanding the political economy of the development of legal doctrine at both the federal and state levels as well as the interaction between the two levels is important to get a complete picture of what is happening in today's financial markets.

NOTES

1. Stigler (1971) and Peltzman (1976).
2. Posner (1975).
3. Wagner (2013) and Smith, Wagner, and Yandle (2011).
4. Obama (2010).
5. Obama (2010).
6. Obama (2010).
7. Tullock (1994) provides a good overview of various political systems, while Potters and Sloof (1996) provide a survey of the empirical models concerning political influencing by interest groups.
8. The question of why legislators may delegate the creation of rules to another agency has been the subject of much work by political scientists and public choice scholars (Macey, 1992).
9. See for example Olson (1992, 2003); Clements and Yahya (2007); Krauss (2001); and Helland and Tabarrok (2000).
10. Krauss (2001).
11. Krauss (2001).
12. 729 S.W.2d 768 (Tex. App. 1987).
13. Zywicki (2006).
14. Moore (2001).
15. Clements and Yahya (2007).
16. Johnsen and Yahya (2004, p. 404).
17. New State Ice Co. V. Liebmann, 285 U.S. 262, 311 (1932, Brandeis J. dissenting).

18. See Valsan and Yahya (2011, 2013) for more details. Valsan and Yahya (2013) provide an overview of the current fiduciary duties of portfolio managers.
19. Cooter and Freeman (1991) provide a good overview.
20. Laby (2010) provides a good overview of this area.
21. See the classic article on this (Merton, 1972).
22. Valsan and Yahya (2013).
23. The SEC has a good outline of broker-dealers duties in http://www.sec.gov/divisions/marketreg/bdguide.htm
24. Valsan and Yahya (2013).
25. Root (1991) explains why this does not make sense in light of modern financial theory.
26. SEC (2011).
27. Obama (2010).
28. Obama (2010).
29. Statement of Kenneth E. Bentsen, Jr., Executive Vice President, Public Policy and Advocacy, Securities Industry and Financial Markets Association to Committee on House Financial Services, Roll Call, Inc., September 29, 2010. (2010 WL 3972567).
30. Statement of Leslie Sellers, MAI, SRA President Appraisal Institute to Committee on House Financial Services Subcommittee on Oversight and Investigations, Roll Call, Inc., May 17, 2010 (2010 WL 1987601).
31. Statement of Alexander Chaparro President National Association of Hispanic Real Estate Professionals to Committee on House Financial Services Subcommittee on Oversight and Investigations, Roll Call, Inc., May 12, 2010 (2010 WL 1900475).
32. Statement of Vincent Wimbish President and Chief Executive Officer National Association of Real Estate Brokers to Committee on House Financial Services Subcommittee on Oversight and Investigations, Roll Call, Inc., May 12, 2010 (2010 WL 1900473).
33. Statement of Edmund Mierzwinski Consumer Program Director U.S. Public Interest Research Group to House of Representatives Committee on House Judiciary, Roll Call, Inc., April 28, 2010 (2010 WL 1695757).
34. SEC (2011, p. ii). All the comments can be found on the SEC's website at http://www.sec.gov/comments/4-606/4-606.shtml
35. http://www.sec.gov/comments/4-606/4606-1059.htm
36. http://www.sec.gov/comments/4-606/4606-2772.htm
37. http://www.sec.gov/comments/4-606/4606-2952.pdf
38. http://www.sec.gov/comments/4-606/4606-2973.pdf
39. Statement of John Taft, Chairman Securities Industry And Financial Markets Association to Committee on House Financial Services Subcommittee on Capital Markets and Government Sponsored Enterprises, Roll Call, Inc., September 13, 2011 (2011 WL 4048538).
40. Statement of Kenneth E. Bentsen, Jr. Executive Vice President Securities Industry and Financial Markets Association to Committee on House Education and the Workforce Subcommittee on Health, Employment, Labor and Pensions, Roll Call, Inc., July 26, 2011 (2011 WL 3156143). See also Statement of Chet Helck CEO, Global Private Client Group Raymond James Financial, Inc. (Chairman elect

of SIFMA) to Committee on House Financial Services, Roll Call, Inc., June 6, 2012 (2012 WL 202586).

41. See, for example, Statement of Barbara Roper, Director, Investor Protection Consumer Federation of America to Committee on Senate Banking, Housing and Urban Affairs, Roll Call, Inc., July 12, 2011 (2011 WL 2690203).

42. SEC (2011, p. 121, p. 162) and Jordan (2012).

43. State Nat. Bank of Big Spring v. Lew, 2013 WL 3945027 (D.D.C., 2013).

44. National Ass'n of Mfrs. v. S.E.C., 2013 WL 3803918 (D.D.C., 2013).

45. Sunstein, Schkade, Ellman, and Sawicki (2006) have conducted an extensive study of whether the political affiliation of federal judges matters for the outcome of cases. While it does not matter for most cases, when the question is political or unclear, then the political backgrounds matter.

46. Bainbridge (2012) has documented how corporate governance, generally, has slowly drifted from being developed by the states to being developed by the federal government.

ACKNOWLEDGMENTS

The author would like to thank Professor Roger Koppl for inviting them to the 2012 Wirth Institute's biennial conference on the Austrian School of Economics (Entangled Political Economy) Lake Louise, Alberta September 14–15, 2012. Professor Koppl also provided very helpful comments as did the conference participants and an anonymous referee, for which the author is very grateful. Any remaining errors are the author's.

REFERENCES

Bainbridge, S. (2012). *Corporate governance after the financial crisis*. New York, NY: Oxford University Press.

Clements, R., & Yahya, M. A. (2007). Private interests, public borders, and NAFTA's chapter 11: Lessons from the mad cow saga. *Alberta Law Review*, *45*(2), 381–400.

Cooter, R., & Freeman, B. J. (1991). The fiduciary relationship: Its economic character and legal consequences. *New York University Law Review*, *66*(4), 1045–1076.

Dodd-Frank Wall Street Reform and Consumer Protection Act. (2010). Pub. L. 111–203 [HR 4173], 124 Stat. 1376, 12 U.S.C.A. § 5301-5641.

Helland, E., & Tabarrok, A. (2000). Runaway judges? Selection effects and the jury. *Journal of Law, Economics, & Organization*, *16*(2), 306–333.

Johnsen, B., & Yahya, M. A. (2004). The evolution of Sherman act jurisdiction: A roadmap for competitive federalism. *University of Pennsylvania Journal of Constitutional Law*, *17*(2), 403–472.

Johnsen, D. B. (2009). The SEC's 2006 soft dollar guidance: Law and economics. *Cardozo Law Review*, *30*(4), 1545–1613.

Jordan, R. (2012). Thinking before rulemaking: Why the SEC should think twice before imposing a uniform fiduciary standard on broker-dealers and investment advisers. *University of Louisville Law Review*, *50*(3), 491–526.

Krauss, M. I. (2001). NAFTA meets the American torts crisis: The Loewen case. *George Mason Law Review*, *9*(1), 69–98.

Laby, A. B. (2010). Fiduciary obligations of broker-dealers and investment advisers. *Villanova Law Review*, *55*(3), 701–742.

Macey, J. R. (1992). Organizational design and political control of administrative agencies. *Journal of Law, Economics, & Organization*, *8*(1), 93–110.

Merton, R. C. (1972). An analytic derivation of the efficient portfolio frontier. *Journal of Financial and Quantitative Analysis*, *7*(4), 1851–1872.

Moore, K. A. (2001). Forum shopping in patent cases: Does geographic choice affect innovation. *North Carolina Law Review*, *79*(4), 889–938.

Obama, B. (2010). Statement by President Barack Obama upon signing H.R. 4173, *White House Press Release*, July 21, 2010, 2010 U.S.C.C.A.N. S26, 2010 WL 4068938 (Leg. Hist.).

Olson, W. K. (1992). *The litigation explosion: What happened when America unleashed the lawsuit*. New York, NY: Truman Talley Books.

Olson, W. K. (2003). *The rule of lawyers: How the new litigation elite threatens America's rule of law*. New York, NY: Truman Talley Books.

Peltzman, S. (1976). Toward a more general theory of regulation. *Journal of Law and Economics*, *19*(2), 211–240.

Posner, R. A. (1975). The social costs of monopoly and regulation. *The Journal of Political Economy*, *83*(4), 807–828.

Potters, J., & Sloof, R. (1996). Interest groups: A survey of empirical models that try to assess their influence. *European Journal of Political Economy*, *12*(3), 403–442.

Ribstein, L. E. (2010). Federal misgovernance of mutual funds. *Cato Supreme Court Review 2009–2010*, 301–331.

Root, S. D. (1991). Suitability – the sophisticated investor – and modern portfolio management. *Columbia Business Law Review*, *1991*(3), 288–357.

SEC (Securities and Exchange Commission). (2011). *Study on investment advisers and broker-dealers*. Retrieved from http://sec.gov/news/studies/2011/913studyfi nal.pdf

Smith, A., Wagner, R. E., & Yandle, B., (2011). A theory of entangled political economy, with application to TARP and NRA. *Public Choice*, *148*(1), 45–66.

Stigler, G. J. (1971). The theory of economic regulation. *The Bell Journal of Economics and Management Science*, *2*(1), 3–21.

Sunstein, C. R., Schkade, D., Ellman, L. M., & Sawicki, A. (2006). *Are judges political?: An empirical analysis of the federal judiciary*. Washington, DC: The Brookings Institution.

Tullock, G. (1994). Thoughts about representative government. *European Journal of Political Economy*, *10*(1), 27–39.

Valsan, R. D., & Yahya, M. A. (2011). Fiduciary responsibility and financial distress. In H. K. Baker & G. S. Martin (Eds.), *Capital structure and corporate financing decisions: Theory, evidence, and practice*. Hoboken, NJ: Wiley.

Valsan, R. D., & Yahya, M. A. (2013). Fiduciary duties and responsibilities of portfolio managers. In H. K. Baker & G. Filbeck (Eds.), *Portfolio theory and management*. New York, NY: Oxford University Press.

Wagner, R. E. (2012). A macro economy as an ecology of plans. *Journal of Economic Behavior and Organization*, *82*(2), 433–444.

Wagner, R. E. (2014). Entangled political economy: A keynote address. In S. Horwitz & R. Koppl (Eds.), *Entangled political economy* (Vol. 18). Advances in Austrian Economics. Bingley, UK: Emerald Group Publishing Limited.

Zywicki, T. J. (2006). Is forum shopping corrupting America's bankruptcy courts? *Georgetown Law Journal*, *94*(4), 1141–1196.

HAS FRITZ MACHLUP STOOD THE TEST OF TIME? REVISITING HIS MONETARY ANALYSIS OF THE STOCK MARKET☆

George Bragues

ABSTRACT

It has often been alleged that the financial markets, with all their speculative excesses, wastefully absorb resources that could be better employed in the real economy. Fritz Machlup, originally a student of Ludwig von Mises, dealt with that charge in the aftermath of the 1929 crash. His defense of the stock market remains germane to our time. In it, he argues that the stock exchange offers an important alternative mechanism of allocating savings to investment, while generally being a way station through which money travels on its way to the real economy either to finance capital projects or to be spent on consumer goods. To the extent the stock market ever absorbs capital, it is only during stock

☆A version of this paper was presented at the third biennial Wirth Institute Workshop on Austrian Economics held in Lake Louise, Alberta, Canada, September 14–15, 2012.

Entangled Political Economy
Advances in Austrian Economics, Volume 18, 139–160

ISSN: 1529-2134/doi:10.1108/S1529-213420140000018007

market booms. Yet these are generated by the uncertain course of central bank monetary expansion. Bull and bear markets cycles are, at bottom, politically driven events.

Keywords: Stock market; monetary policy; credit; central banks; capital; business cycles

JEL classifications: B22; B31; E32; E42; E44; E50; E58; G10; G12; N20

INTRODUCTION

Ludwig von Mises called it a "masterpiece." No other book written by a disciple of his would ever be commended by the great Austrian economist in the same terms (Hulsmann, 2007, pp. 478–479). The book to which Mises referred was entitled *The Stock Market, Credit, and Capital Formation* and its author was Fritz Machlup. A member of Mises' private seminar that met regularly on Fridays at the Austrian Chamber of Commerce during the 1920s and 1930s, Machlup initially earned his livelihood in the cardboard manufacturing business before moving to the United States. There, he taught at the University of Buffalo, Johns Hopkins, Princeton, and then at New York University, where he ended his illustrious academic career (Haberler, 1983). Strangely enough, the book that Mises so lavishly praised did not figure prominently in establishing Machlup's reputation. The former doctoral student of Mises is best known today for his pioneering work on the economics of information. If the citation count at Google Scholar is any guide, Machlup's other spheres of influence included the theory of the firm, the methodology of the social sciences, the economics of competition and monopoly, as well as international monetary economics. Indeed, his book on the stock market has thus far only garnered 1/50 of the citations that his most famous work has on the production and distribution of knowledge. In his memoriam to Machlup, Gottfried Haberler never once mentions his analysis of equity trading.

That analysis, however much it has been neglected, is well worth revisiting. Making this effort relevant today is that the financial markets, of which the stock market looms largest in the popular mind, have come under widespread attack for having assumed an outsized, and hence detrimental, role in the economy and society. In the 1920s and 1930s, when Machlup originally wrote and subsequently revised his book on the stock exchange, analogous charges were leveled against the world of high finance. While the particulars in the indictments have changed, the general line of argument remains the same now as it was then – to wit, that the markets draw resources, particularly when they are booming, from other areas of the economy into less optimal, if not wasteful, activities (Mitchell, 2007). Machlup rejected the idea that the equity market is a kind of vampire sucking vitality from the rest of the community. The bourse, he thought, is no different from the banks in constituting a mechanism by which capital is allocated to firms. Furthermore, he maintained that share price bubbles are not caused by factors internal to the stock market, but are rather owing to the inflation of the money supply by government authorities. Only when this happens, Machlup observes, can the stock market be said, if only temporarily, to engross resources. Examining this thesis more than 80 years since the initial publication of *The Stock Market, Credit, and Capital Formation*, the book's main arguments stand the test of time.

WHERE THE MONEY GOES

Machlup's book was originally part of a now largely forgotten debate about the equity market's impact on the quantity of credit.[1] On one side were those who argued that trading in corporate shares absorbed credit, thereby making it unavailable to the real economy and raising its price in the form of higher interest rates. Chief among those taking this position were Reisch (1929, 1930), Reed (1930), and Palyi (1932). On the other side were those who denied that any sustained absorption takes place, viewing the stock exchange instead as a way station through which money travels on its way to the real economy either to finance capital projects or to be spent on consumer goods. Machlup endeavored to defend this latter position and was joined by Cassel (1929), Hahn (1927), and Barger (1935). Arrayed against Machlup was not just a group of economic writers, but also central bank officials at the US Federal Reserve (Fed). For in the late stages of the 1920s bull market in equities, the Federal Reserve Board (1930, p. 1) had concluded that speculative excesses on the stock exchange were draining capital away from agricultural and industrial enterprises. It consequently sought to restrict bank loans collateralized by equities. In doing so originally, the Fed only had moral suasion at its disposal, but its quiver was subsequently augmented after Congress gave it authority to mandate capital reserve levels for loans backed by shares as part of the 1933 Banking Act, more popularly known as Glass-Steagall (Barger, 1935, pp. 764–765). In its inquiry into stock exchange practices that Congress launched after the 1929 crash, more commonly known as the Pecora Commission (1934), it expressed greater concern about the way margin credit exacerbates market volatility, as easy access to share collateralized loans drives prices up and then a subsequent fall in prices is accelerated as investors are forced to sell because of margin calls (pp. 9–11). Even so, the Pecora Commission made the point that credit provided to the stock market takes money away from the rest of the economy and so, besides empowering the Fed to regulate margin lending, it prohibited non-bank companies from putting short-term funds to work in the broker call loan market: "Loans by nonbanking lenders tend to decrease bank deposits and reduce the lending power of banks to commerce and industry" (p. 13). Evidently, America's political classes went with Machlup's opponents.

This is hardly proof, of course, that he was on the wrong side. In light of the vehement passions directed at the financial sector in the 1930s, one is entirely justified in suspecting that politicians, reflecting popular anger, too readily accepted dubious conceptions of how the stock market works. All one might do to buttress this suspicion is to apply a bit of economic logic. Even if we were to concede that the trading of shares absorbs capital, so removing it from other uses, one can still argue that this result is economically efficient. Like any scarce good available on the marketplace, capital should go to whoever can use it best, that is, the parties most likely to generate the best returns upon investing that capital. Such parties will naturally be willing to place higher bids for available capital – that is, offer its suppliers a better expected rate of remuneration – than those with less promising investment opportunities. From this it follows that if the stock market has outbid other economic agents for capital, it must be because it contains the greatest prospective yields. Ergo, the public is a gainer by the stock market's appropriation of capital.

While not dismissing this reasoning outright, Machlup (2007) does not think it wise to rely on it entirely without examining the matter further (pp. 3–5). For one thing, not everyone accepts the underlying premise that the most profitable use of a resource is always the most socially optimal outcome. Or as many economists would nowadays put it, market failures cannot automatically be discounted. More tellingly, Machlup points out that the credit allocation process does not actually occur within a purely free market. Government is involved: "The modern organization of money and credit," Machlup (2007) writes, "is such that it enables the banks to 'create' credit (i.e., to grant credit in excess of the proceeds of intended savings) and thus makes the credit supply dependent on considerations of a politico-economic nature" (pp. 4–5). Once the state enters the scene to manipulate the availability of credit, the question inevitably arises as to its distribution. Whether to have more or less money implies determining who should gain or lose it – a point that Machlup makes echoing Lasswell's (1950) famous definition of politics as consisting in, "who gets what, when, and how."

Having laid out why it is not enough to invoke an invisible hand type argument linking private and public interests, Machlup (2007) commences his inquiry by describing the place of the stock market in the capital formation and allocation process. By capital, Machlup strictly means humanly produced resources capable of generating future consumption goods – thus following Bohm-Bawerk's (1930, pp. 36–41) definition of capital. However, when people talk about this in the context of financial market discussions, the term "capital" is often used differently to denote money available for the acquisition and construction of the means of producing future goods. In the first sense, capital is made up of things like factories, machines, equipment, and computers; in the second, it consists of dollars in a bank account somewhere earmarked to buy those things. Looking to maintain Bohm-Bawerk's formulation while simultaneously making it amenable to the financial markets universe, Machlup opted to retain the equation of capital to future goods, calling these real capital, and then further qualifying that term with the word "money" to specify funds ready at hand for the purchase of the capabilities of producing future goods. Accordingly, the stock market encompasses the trading of titles to real capital, the transactions thereof being settled in money capital (Machlup, 2007, p. 11). Where such titles are offered by companies in return for money capital, in what is called the primary market, the stock exchange manifests its most distinguishing function as an allocator of capital. It enables firms to obtain money capital which they can use over the long-term, indeed theoretically throughout their entire lives as going concerns. At the same time, those who have supplied that capital in the hopes of generating a return are not necessarily bound to any particular firm over the long-term, but can transfer their titles to another part. "The chief advantage," Machlup writes, "of the security method of lending and borrowing is that credit obtained through the issue of securities is a long-term one for the borrower ... while from the point of view of the capitalist it is not a long-term loan at all, and has in fact no definite term" (p. 23). This exit option renders the purchase of shares more attractive than it would otherwise be if people were permanently stuck with their investment position, affording companies a valuable source of financing beyond the banking system.

Exercises of the exit option take place on what is called the secondary market. Except for a few highly anticipated initial public offerings (IPO), such as that for Facebook in the spring of 2012, what most people experience as the stock market most of the time is the secondary market. Measured by dollar volume, this segment was 79 times larger than its primary counterpart in 2012, leaving the stock market vulnerable to the criticism that its contribution to society is negligible at best in offering the well-to-do a venue to gamble their wealth by continuing shifting ownership stakes amongst themselves (World Federation of Exchanges, 2012).[2] Those who happen to engage in this activity full time as professional speculators tend to draw particular ire. How can an institution, it is asked, be redeemed which provides hospitable grounds for an occupation in which money can be gained without producing an authentic good or service and, moreover, always at the expense of others not lucky enough to correctly guess the direction of prices? Machlup's (2007) answer is that the professional stock trader provides liquidity to the market (pp. 23–25, 35–36). There is no guarantee, after all, that a long-term investor looking to remove their savings from the market, or shift those elsewhere, will find a counter-party with a similar time horizon at the very instance they wish to execute their transaction. Professional traders bridge this gap by assuming the risk of holding shares as these get transferred amongst savers. "The speculator," Machlup says, "jumps into the breach and takes over the title to capital goods for a temporary period with his own money capital" (pp. 35–36). Standing by always ready to buy and sell, speculators allow investors to liquidate their positions at the prevailing rate, instead of having to lower their offering price to find takers. As a result, speculators reduce stock price volatility rather than raise it, contrary to what is often said against them. By thus adding to the attractiveness of the stock market as an arena in which to place one's nest egg, speculators further that institution's role in directing money capital from savers, unwilling or incapable of transforming it into real capital, to firms willing and capable of doing so. Nor can speculators, as Machlup rightly indicates, be faulted for hoarding money capital, since they have a strong interest in actively using their funds to make bets (p. 36).

Nowadays, anyone skeptical of Machlup's defense of speculation is apt to invoke the emergence of high frequency trading. Using an array of intricate and complex algorithms, high-frequency traders use computers to scan the market for short-term market inefficiencies and supply-demand imbalances, entering and exiting positions very quickly, often holding them for mere seconds. While they typically only earn an infinitesimal amount on each trade, their ability to continually repeat this feat means profits can accumulate enough to make the overall strategy worthwhile. Singled out by many as the cause of various market disturbances, including the flash crash that struck US equity markets on May 6, 2010, high-frequency trading made up slight over half of the number of shares traded as of 2012 (Clark, 2012). Only a few academic studies have been published thus far on this activity, and though no consensus has been reached thus far, the literature tends to favor the view that high-frequency traders add liquidity to the secondary market and reduce volatility (Brogard, 2010; Hasbrouck & Saar, 2013; Hendershott, Jones, & Menkveld, 2011). One might counter, of course, that the pervasiveness of high-frequency traders means that the market become highly vulnerable to negative shocks should they suddenly decide to cease transacting, as they did for a short period on the afternoon of the flash crash (Securities and Exchange Commission, 2010). By that logic, any major provider of the liquidity, including market makers and stock exchange specialists, is to be seen as a danger, inasmuch as these too can also wreck havoc by abruptly exiting from trading.

Strengthening the case that speculators do not dam up the flow of money capital, Machlup (2007) painstakingly maps all the possible outcomes of their trading (pp. 25–40). The broadest division is between what can happen after the purchase of shares on the primary versus the secondary market. Consider first the buying of newly issued equity on the primary market. As Machlup reckons it, one of five events can occur. First, the company offering the shares uses the proceeds to pay off an existing a bank loan – a reminder, by the way, that IPOs, as well as seasoned equity offerings tendered by already existing publicly traded companies, do not necessarily lead to new real capital formation. The funds, as they would be in this instance, can be used to adjust the relative proportions of debt and equity in the firm's capital structure. This does not foreclose the prospect of new capital goods eventually being produced. Insofar as the money from the sale of the shares ends up in the hands of the company's original lenders to use as they see fit, they could decide to invest the proceeds in constructing real capital or relend it to someone who will. The second scenario that Machlup envisions is where the company immediately uses part of the monies obtained in augmenting its real capital, by adding new equipment, for example, and then putting the rest into money market securities with a view to delaying further capital investments until a later date. Here, a portion of the speculator's funds have gone into real capital, while the rest has gone to borrowers in the money market to use at their discretion.

Thirdly, the company can purchase already constructed capital goods from whoever produced them. In thus receiving the speculator's money, capital goods producers see at least a portion of their original investment recouped. With respect to the fourth possibility, the firm expends all its proceeds from the issuance of equity in making real capital on its own. Lastly, it can acquire other securities by, say, acquiring another company or taking a minority position in it. If the shares thus happen to be new securities, then the range of outcomes are covered by the four possibilities just described. If the stock has previously been trading, then the relevant consequences would be those applicable to old shares.

That brings us to the alternative group of scenarios that Machlup delineates for the more common occurrence of speculative activity in the secondary market. Now one possibility is that the speculator buys shares from someone that employs the monies to repay a loan. Here, the money is left at the disposal of whoever made the loan. Varying this scenario slightly, we can imagine the seller of the shares loaning out the proceeds themselves, in which case the money capital ends up serving the purposes of the borrower. Depositing the funds in the bank would effectively be the same thing, as this act is equivalent to lending it money. Similar to the third possibility with new shares, sellers of existing equity can apply their receipts to the purchase of already produced capital goods. As before in the primary market context, the money capital winds up with the capital goods maker, thus compensating them for their efforts. Of course, we can also mimic the fourth possibility from before and envision the seller of the old shares using the funds to construct real capital. Completing Machlup's rundown of all the potential outcomes, that seller can alternatively take the money they receive and spend it on consumption goods. In this instance, the money capital finds its way into the possession of the retailers who sold those goods, effectively displacing temporary savings from the stock market that an investor had originally put to work there.

In none of these cases – which also apply to the trading done by ordinary investors, not just professional speculators – can the stock market be seen as draining life out of the economy. In all the scenarios but three, the money capital merely changes hands. In two of these remaining three, the money capital is turned into real capital. And in the last, a stock trade brings about an act of consumption. Nowadays, given the influence of Keynes on the economic *zeitgeist*, this facilitation of consumption would not automatically be viewed askance. When Machlup was writing, though, the Keynesian glorification of demand had not yet taken hold of people's minds. So it was still considered a significant objection that profits generated on stock trades are more likely to be consumed, being viewed as a kind of free money, and thereby reduce the capital stock upon which productivity and economic growth ultimately depend. Machlup conceded this possibility, while further acknowledging that even non-realized profits could induce greater consumption by individuals out of their current income, what the Fed under Alan Greenspan would later call the wealth effect. But Machlup noted profits generated in other lines of business beyond the stock market can also be consumed, and no one seems to be concerned about that. Moreover, no definitive evidence exists to believe that the stock market is more liable to this outcome (pp. 32–33).

But what if investors suffer losses en masse? Does this not sap energy from the economy? Certainly, the media can always be expected, in the wake of an equity market collapse, to feature statements to the effect that a large swath of the national wealth has vaporized into nothing. Even trained economists have been known to fall into this error, including in Machlup's time (Reisch, 1929, 1930). To espy the fallacy here, Machlup goes through the various factors that can precipitate a decline in stock prices (pp. 57–60). As shares represent claims on a firm's capital, the value of those titles will naturally fluctuate with expectations concerning what that capital might return to stockholders. They will incur losses should the firm's capital assets be impaired or destroyed, if, for example, its plants and factories were to be hit by an earthquake. Traders could hardly be blamed for taking share prices down on this news, for they would be merely registering the implications of a material event. Likewise when the share price drops after a company has shown itself less capable of generating profits out of its capital goods. The same goes, too, where shares decline upon an increase in interest rates. Whether this change is owing to a reduced supply of money capital for lending, bad for society, or a heightened demand for it by companies looking to borrow, good for society, the resulting larger discount of future profits that gets embodied in lower stock prices merely reflects a larger economic reality. To be sure, Machlup recognizes these are not the sort of losses that are singled out by critics of the bourse. The losses that they have in mind are those arising after a speculative boom has allowed companies to direct capital into what turn out to be poor investments. As we will see shortly, Machlup has more to say about this charge, but suffice it to mention for now that it presumes that share price bubbles are endogenously generated. Whatever the origins of such run-ups, the subsequent collapse simply redistributes wealth, rather than destroying it. Machlup well reminds us that everyone that lost money after a bubble was popped originally bought their positions from other traders: "one does not have to be a very good detective in order to reason out … that the money which is being searched for must have gone to the person who sold at a high price, or to use the jargon of the stock exchange, to the person who got out in time" (p. 62). It is the latter who are the beneficiaries of the market's redistribution.

Keynesians might wonder whether this transfer of wealth affects the overall marginal propensity to consume. But that is not the Keynesian counter that Machlup chooses to address. The one he confronts involves the theory of liquidity preference, the notion that, in setting aside part of their current income for future consumption, people will demonstrate a rate at which they prefer to hold that reserve in cash as opposed to less liquid forms. Keynes (1991, pp. 194–209) argued that part of what motivates the desire for liquidity was the necessity of cash for impending purchases as well as a desire to hedge against future contingencies. It is a third motive, though, which Keynes laid down that is germane to the stock market: the speculative impulse by which people will move in and out of cash based on their predictions of how other assets will perform going forward. If individuals expect shares to decline, they will prefer to be in cash with the aim of buying those securities later; if they think these will rise, individuals will tend to stay out of cash. In *A Treatise on Money*, Keynes (1930) insisted that, as stocks ascend to lofty heights in a bull market, smart investors will sell their positions and shift to cash. This is significant, according to Keynes, because preferring liquidity is equivalent to hoarding money. By taking money out of circulation in this way, bearish traders are alleged to undermine the economy.

Interestingly, Machlup (2007) agrees with Keynes that hoarding could theoretically occur. Like the famed British economist, Machlup dismisses the notion that putting money in a bank account still leaves those funds available for economic uses, inasmuch as the bank can lend it to others who, in turn, either consume or invest it. Unlike Keynes, however, Machlup does not rely on the argument that the matching of savings to investment referenced in the traditional story wrongly supposes that national income is unaffected by a drop in savings. Instead, what Machlup does is observe that we no longer live in a monetary system where a new deposit typically involves the submission to the bank of coins or notes previously in circulation. Now, deposits are usually made by cheque or, to phrase Machlup's point more generally, via book entries between banks. So when an individual places money into their account, all that is transpiring is a transfer of funds, and their associated bank reserves, within the financial system. While that person's own savings go up, this amount remains unchanged from the point of view of society. "Deposits," Machlup observes, "do not put any funds at the disposal of the banks, if all are taken together" (p. 134).

Critical to Machlup's argument here is the distinction between chequing and savings accounts. When the transfer is made from the first to the second, the money is more apt to become idle, on the assumption that chequing accounts are used like cash in settling daily transactions, whereas savings accounts represent funds which the banks might choose to leave untouched. In Machlup's (2007) thinking, then, Keynes' thesis about liquidity preference has force to the extent that bearish traders put the proceeds of their sales into savings accounts (pp. 134). Still, a further assumption is necessary for the argument to work, on which Machlup explicitly asserts as a possibility (pp. 26–27), namely, that wages are downwardly sticky. Were that not the case, the decline in circulating money caused by the idling of savings would simply drive all prices down so as to leave the now reduced money wages of the workers with same purchasing power over goods as before. Where wages are sticky, however, firms must respond to lower prices for their goods by laying off workers.

Having conceded these theoretical points to Keynes, Machlup questions the empirics of his hypothesis. The distinction between chequing accounts that get used in transactions, and savings accounts that might not, is too neat. Individuals and firms have been known to treat the money in their chequing accounts as a reserve fund (pp. 134–135). In the United States at least, regulations permit banks to hold fewer reserves against savings accounts. Even where regulations do not mandate this difference, the rules of prudent banking would dictate the same policy. Machlup additionally presents statistical evidence that, heading into the 1929 stock market, individuals and firms who preferred to be liquid rather than invested did so by lending to bullish traders on the call loan market which, at the time, was the main provider of margin loans to stock buyers (pp. 140–141).[3] Rather than hoarding funds, the bearish camp financed the bulls. Perhaps small investors did not do this, but Machlup rightly points out they are the group most likely to be caught up in the speculative excitement that marks the latter stages of bull markets (p. 135). Larger players on the bearish side will not be so unsophisticated as to maintain liquid positions through savings accounts. To bring Machlup's argument to the present time, institutional investors today who adopt a negative view on stocks will shift into cash through treasury bills, commercial paper, repurchase agreements, money market instruments, the funds for all of which ends up being put to use by governments and corporations. Further supporting Machlup, the historical record since he wrote amply demonstrates that margin loans increase markedly as bull markets mature, thus furthering the circulation of the money.

WHEN MONEY CAPITAL IS DAMMED UP

Reflecting on this last phenomenon, however, it might be deduced that the stock market is liable to draw loanable funds in the credit market away from industrial and commercial purposes, if only in boom periods. It was in the process of responding to this charge that Machlup made his one concession to the advocates of equity market absorption of capital. It was a concession that ultimately pointed the finger away from the bourse to the central bank.

Yet, one might ask, was this challenge not already precluded by Machlup's tracing of the various paths which can money take after the execution of stock trades? For as he convincingly demonstrated, money capital flows through the stock market to either form real capital or to be translated into consumption. But leaving the argument in this form ignores the time element. In Machlup's (2007) view, economic theorizing properly removes the variable of time when initially tackling a problem, "but frequently commits the error of failing to recognize that such an abstraction is not permissible in the final stages of the analysis" (p. 43). No doubt, time may pass between the purchase of shares with money and its eventual deployment in the real economy by a seller of equity. Machlup specifies two ways this can occur: (1) the circumstances of payment are such that the seller in a particular transaction only receives the money at some point after the buyer has advanced the funds; (2) sellers continually use their proceeds to speculate on additional trades so that, for example, B having sold to A then buys from C who then buys from D who again buys from E and so forth down a long chain of transactions (p. 43).

Neither of these scenarios would involve any special demands on the money supply if there is a quick and efficient system of clearing trades. Acknowledging Mises' warning that caution is warranted before invoking a clearance mechanism to make up for an increase in business activity in the demand function for money, Machlup nevertheless insists that if there is any area of the economy where an exception to this rule is merited, it is the stock market. Among market professionals, trades are often settled without any transfer of funds, instead being simply netted out between the counterparties. Not having any contemporaneous data on hand, Machlup cites a 1905 book that estimated 90% of transactions on English stock exchanges were cleared by offsetting (p. 74, n4). While the "paperwork crisis" that hit Wall Street in the late 1960s showed that the back office systems in place for the clearing of trades may not always be up to the task of moving money quickly from buyers to seller, the situation today conforms with Machlup's contention (Norman, 2011, p. 124). The Depository Trust and Clearing Corporation (2010), which settles virtually all equity transactions in the United States, reports that even on peak days from 2006 to 2008, the netting out procedure cleared 98–99% of the dollar volume of trades (p. 14). The fly in the ointment here, as Machlup sees it, is that the netting out process chiefly applies to market professionals (pp. 77–78). To the extent that the public gets involved in trading, as it must for the stock market to be ultimately viable, cheque payments will come into play or, to update Machlup's point, electronic bank transfers – all of which adds time to trade settlement. That said, the investing public does not usually rely on cheques or bank transfers to pay for each and every transaction. Nor do they request that money be sent to them from their brokerage accounts every time they sell shares. Most will initially fund an account and then trade on that amount, making only periodic deposits and withdrawals should they have some money out of their paycheque to invest or they need funds for a large purchase. Noting this, Machlup holds that brokerage deposits constitute a distinct form of currency dedicated to the equity market, capable of facilitating transactions there without the necessity of drawing money from the rest of the community. "There is thus," he says, "a separate money so to speak ... which serves to effect security transactions between the regular customers of the brokers" (p. 87).

Still, this is not monopoly money. Unlike the currency in that famous board game, this medium of payment on the stock exchange can be cashed in for goods and services in the real economy. Insofar as brokerage deposits are debited and credited to finance prolonged sequences of speculative trades, the speed of the clearance mechanism will do little to stop the damming of money capital in the stock market. If anything, by encouraging trading, it will extend the amount of time that capital remains there. For this second source of time delay, Machlup a potential escape valve: the issuance of new equity by corporations. In the stock markets, these organizations act no differently in seeking equity financing than they do in the loanable funds market in search of debt financing. The lower the price of financing is, the higher the demand will be for it. Higher stock prices imply a lower cost of equity for companies, so one can expect them to issue more stock whenever an upward trend presents itself. And once new equity offerings come onto the market, the money capital at play there is more apt to leave that arena and finds its way into the real economy, as firm employed the proceeds garnered to either pay back or make loans, purchase already existing capital goods, or construct new ones. Everything else remaining equal, this addition of new share supply ought to stop upturns in stock prices from persisting. Yet, it is glaringly evident from historical experience that the stock market can head higher for protracted periods.

For Machlup, this is telling. Equity prices, he observes, can increase for a number of reasons: expectations of higher profits to be eventually distributed as dividends to shareholders, or a reduction in interest rates at which future dividends are discounted to the present. In either of these events, share prices should adjust more or less immediately – Machlup here invoking the sort of argument that advocates of the efficient market hypothesis would put forward. Stock charts would then feature a sequence of zigzag patterns punctuated by quick moves in one direction or another – precisely what the charts do not convey. While there are zigzags, underlying these are steady and enduring trends, whether up or down. When this happens to be up, there has to be more money capital in the market than leaving it through the issuance of new equity. Somehow, the latter, effectively a demand for money capital, is not keeping up with the supply of it that traders are wielding.

Here, according to Machlup, is that much vaunted absorption of capital. But it has not been autonomously produced by the stock market. Money capital can enter there if people and companies have decided to save a greater proportion of their income. It can also become more available if firms amortize their capital assets at a faster rate. However, these fonts of additional money capital are not especially sensitive to price changes on the stock exchange. People do not modify their savings versus consumption tradeoffs with every tick of the Dow Jones Industrial Average. This is a relatively inelastic supply factor. A more elastic source of money capital has to be at work. The obvious candidate, Machlup figures, is the currency that can be created at will above and beyond the community's stockpile of savings by the central bank orchestrated system of credit. "If it were not for the elasticity of bank credit," he says, "which has often been regarded as a good thing, a boom in security prices could not last for any length of time" (p. 92). To the immediate protest that this too can be quickly factored into stock prices by traders, Machlup calls attention to the uncertainty of the course and extent of any loose money campaign being run by the central bank. "Professional speculators cannot anticipate the entire development at one stroke because they do not know to what limits the credit expansion will go" (pp. 92–93). As the evidence of continued money supply inflation trickles into the marketplace, stock prices experience a steady ascent, setting the psychological conditions for a speculative fever that absorbs capital in a long chain of transactions. Bull markets, therefore, are fundamentally the consequence of central bank unpredictability during phases of monetary easing.

Machlup stresses that the resulting lock-up of money capital is far from lasting. Some investors do take advantage of lofty share prices to withdraw their funds entirely from the market. More significantly, new issue offers are ramped up as stocks accelerate upwards, a claim well supported in studies detailing how IPOs tend to occur in waves after periods of unusually strong market performance (Pastor & Veronesi, 2005). Machlup never takes note of this factor that runs against his argument, but the well-documented tendency of IPOs to be underpriced, particularly in the manic stages of bull markets, serves to confine money capital to the stock exchange (Daily, Certo, Dalton, & Roengpitya, 2003; Ljungqvist, 2008). An IPO that is underpriced, after all, is a stock that leaps upward, or undergoes a "pop" to use the market's parlance, on the first day of trading. Not only does this mean that the company has not obtained as much capital for its productive purposes as it would otherwise have with a higher issue price, the quick profits realized by the IPO pop add fuels to the speculative frenzy engrossing capital in lengthy series of trades. That said, Machlup (2007) is still not off the mark in stating, "stock exchange credits begin to 'work' only too quickly on production" (p. 96).

Phrasing it in this manner, especially with the quotation marks around work, Machlup insinuates that it would actually be nice if the effects of inflationary credit creation could be quarantined to the bourse. Alas, it cannot be contained there and, precisely because it cannot, the excess money that eventually escapes will distort the production structure in the real economy. While some of it will seep into consumption, thus favoring consumer goods industries, the stock market's primary role as a distributor of capital to industry entails that the bulk of the newly freed up money will finance additional projects in capital goods industries. Revealing himself as the good student of Hayek and Mises that he was (at least at this stage of his academic career),[4] Machlup echoes the fundamental lines of Austrian business cycle theory in noting that any money put into the pockets of business for investment without a correlative act of savings by someone else must, once it is employed, draw on existing factors of production. "Newly created credit," he points out, "places money capital at the disposal of the market without any corresponding release of productive factors" (p. 183).

Such resources, after all, cannot be brought into existence by manufacturing additional money; someone had to have refrained from consuming those resources. Take a piece of wood, for example, needed to construct real capital in the form of a sling shot with which to catch birds to eat in the future. If someone instead has decided to use that wood in a fire to warm themselves for the evening, no amount of credit that can be produced out of human willfulness is going to magically cause it to reappear from the ashes. Since the augmentation of money capital will cause interest rates to fall in the debt market, and the cost of equity to do the same in the stock market, businesses will be encouraged to invest in real capital and so bid up the prices of available production factors. This would not be a problem if firms could be assured of higher prices for the goods that their efforts in constructing capital will subsequently bring to the marketplace. But this future demand will fall short of the expected level because it was not provisioned for in prior savings. So though the initial activity in capital goods production catapults the economy, buoying an already rising stock market, this monetarily constructed edifice inevitably comes crashing down once the investment mistakes become evident – although this point will be reached sooner if the central bank, in an attempt to prevent the boom from escalating dangerously, decides to tighten the monetary spigot.

This conclusion cannot be resisted by insisting that central banks can keep the tide of prosperity going indefinitely. Keynes (1991) advanced this very idea: "The right remedy for the trade cycle is not to be found in abolishing booms and thus keeping us permanently in a semi-slump; but in abolishing slumps and thus keeping us permanently in a quasi-boom" (p. 322). To be fair to Keynes, he actually thought that the money supply should be raised only until full employment was realized. After that, it could be kept stable until the economy went below full employment again. In taking up Keynes' proposal, Machlup reiterates his agreement with him that savings do not automatically give rise to an equivalent amount of investment. As such, Machlup is willing to allow for credit expansion to neutralize the deflating effects of hoarding. On this basis, Machlup supports public expenditures on real capital to make up for the deficit in private investment, a position that put him in tension with the Austrian tradition. For as Mises saw it, increased spending on public works has to be financed either by taxing the public or borrowing from them. Either way, they are left with less to spend and invest to an amount equal to what the government employs. It is a wash, even from the Keynesian emphasis upon aggregate demand (Mises, 1963, pp. 798–799).

To this crowding-out argument, someone could come to the defense of Machlup by noting that, in circumstances of hoarding at least, the resources being transferred to the government is dead money in the hands of the private sector. No crowding out takes place here because individuals and firms are not competing with the state over the use of money capital. Underlying this counter to Mises, though, is the claim that hoarding is not simply a derisive term to describe what is really nothing more than an individual preference to hold cash beyond what someone else arbitrarily deems to be acceptable. The latter is exactly how Mises (p. 402) viewed it, whereas Machlup came to share the Keynesian concern that the downward stickiness of wages meant that higher cash balances could not get adjusted without a significant rise in unemployment. At bottom, the difference revolves around how to deal with the rigidity of wages that have become a distinguishing feature of economies since the early 20th century. Should we focus on removing the institutional structures responsible for those rigidities (Mises) or should we accept those as an unalterable fact of economic life (Machlup) to which monetary policy must willy-nilly accommodate?

Let us not, however, exaggerate the concessions that Machlup made to Keynes at this stage of his intellectual career. In a section of *The Stock Market, Credit, and Capital Formation* that he appended in 1940 – the only addition to which he alerts us in the course of the book via a footnote – Machlup (2007) took on a key plank of the Keynesian revolution that had been set in motion in the time between the first and second editions of his book (pp. 193–198). Rather than confining the amount of public investment to that contained in private hoards, Keynes insisted that it ought to be maintained as long as workers are unemployed, a standard which the Federal Reserve Board (2012) recently adapted in deciding to continue with its quantitative easing (QE) campaign. In opposing this, Machlup did advance a crowding-out type of argument. Labor is not the sole factor of production for companies, which means that any increase in capital expenditure on the part of the state is bound to extract resources from the private sector. That will raise costs there and slow commercial activity. So too, private firms are liable to be misled by the initial economic stimulus caused by the government's actions into undertaking unwise investments. As if that were not enough, if we take Keynes' counsel to its logical extent, investments made by the state need not pass the bar of promising returns sufficient to compensate for the initial outlay of funds and the associated risks. As Machlup (2007) wryly comments: "To judge the direction and extent of investment and production according to whether it will pay, that is, whether the undertaking is justified by the relations between costs and prices is, however, something more than a mere liberal-conservative prejudice" (p. 197).

Given all this, we can surmise Machlup's likely response to the only analysis of his arguments that has recently appeared in the scholarly literature. Statistically examining bank data from 1919 to 1929, this study determined that trading volumes on the New York Stock Exchange impacted the transactions demand for money (Field, 1984). Inasmuch as the Fed in the late 1920s was attempting to dampen speculative excesses on Wall Street with higher interest rates, the implication of that finding is that the Fed erred in compounding an already tight monetary situation. Machlup would comment on the study that the Fed erred in sowing the seeds of the 1920s bubble in the first place. To which we may add what some might dismiss as a simplistic observation, namely that no central bank has yet succeeded, despite the continually expressed desire for soft landings, in perpetuating a bull market. Clearly, there are forces which the central bank unleashes through its policies that are beyond its subsequent power to control.

Also empirically illustrative of Machlup's overarching claim that monetary policy lies behind the swings of equities is the practice of those who earn their livelihood in the financial markets. Investment firms devote significant resources to the task of divining the central bank's next set of moves. A multitude of popular investment strategies are built around notions about what the central bank is thought to be up to, all of them embodying the mantra, "don't fight the Fed." Academic evidence confirms that the market professionals know what they are doing. From 1955 to 2006, changes in the Fed Funds rate had a significant impact on subsequent stock returns over 3-, 6-, 9-, and 12-month periods. Increases in that rate were associated with lower than average market performance, while decreases were associated with higher than average performance (Siegel, 2008, pp. 196–198). Recently, with the Fed funds rate virtually at zero since December 2008, the capacity of this tool to further ease monetary policy has been neutered. Since then, the Fed has relied on QE: the outright purchase of debt securities with a view specifically to increasing the money supply and lowering rates at the longer end of the yield curve where central banks ordinarily do not tread. As the chart shown in Fig. 1 indicates, both of the QE campaigns which the Fed has undertaken in the aftermath of the 2007–2009 financial crisis correlate strongly with upswings in the stock market, as measured by the S&P 500 index.

Notice that shares began to extend their recovery from the March 2009 bottom after the Fed announced a major ramp-up in its bond purchasing

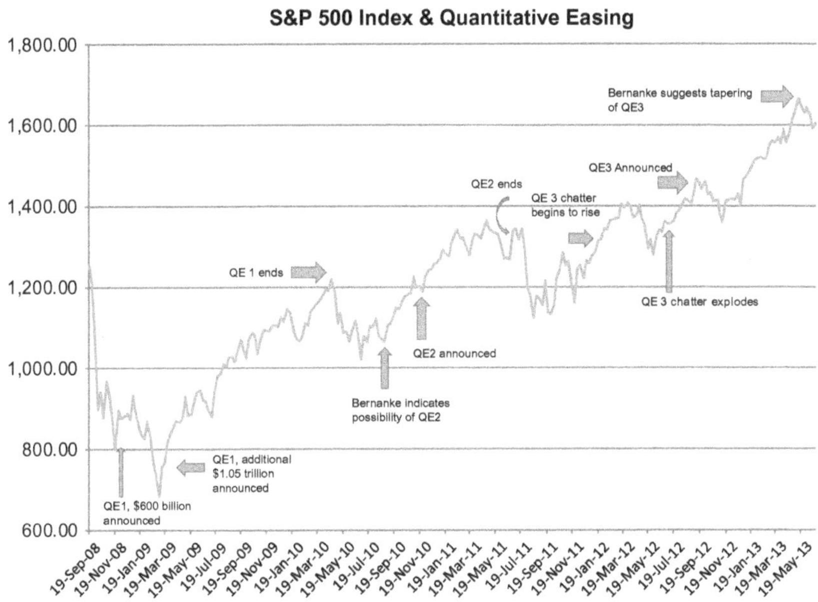

Fig. 1. S&P 500 Index and Quantitative Easing (2008–2013). *Sources*: Author's own creation (Adapted from Yahoo, Google).

program by $1.05 trillion to $1.605 trillion. Notice, too, that the market languished between the first and second rounds of QE. By the time the second dose had been delivered, the markets no longer considered the tactic as unprecedented as it did before and so no longer waited until a Fed declaration to react. With respect to the third round, traders began forming expectations of its onset a couple of months before the Fed divulged its intent in September 2012 to continue QE until employment conditions significantly improved (Federal Reserve Board, 2012). As the chatter (measured here by references to it in the Google News database) rose about QE3, the S&P 500 inched higher, eventually hitting its highest point since the financial crisis. Once Q3 came into effect, stocks rallied to all-time highs until prices slid back in May 2013 when Bernanke first suggested that the Fed might taper its monthly bond purchases.

Consistent with his arguments, Machlup advises policymakers to look at the stock market, instead of retail prices or gold, to gauge when the monetary situation has become overly stimulative. If only to assess the empirical merits of Machlup's case, this is an intriguing proposal, for if he is correct that money creation drives share prices upward, the stock market would be expected to do a better job of alerting us to unsustainable booms than other indicators. This was certainly the case in the 1920s, which Machlup himself observed, a period in which consumer prices were steady. The latter were also not flashing any cautionary signals in the 1990s when movements on the Nasdaq Composite Index were both mirroring and stoking a mania in the technology and Internet sectors. At this time, too, the gold market was moribund. Though the yellow metal went on to betoken the Fed's easy money policy of the 2000s leading up to the sub-prime mortgage debacle, the stock market once again did not fail in issuing a warning by rallying from its dotcom bust lows in 2002 back toward its dotcom boom highs, with the S&P 500 broaching the 1,500 level in 2007.

CONCLUSION

Repeating what happened during the 1920s and 1930s, early 21st century critics of the capital markets have expressed concerns about the financialization of society and economy. In response to the first wave of critics, Machlup gave a response that continues to be helpful in grappling with the second wave making its influence felt today. As a general matter, Machlup denied the proposition that the equity market absorbs capital that can otherwise be put to use by industry. For companies in need of external financing, the stock exchange offers an alternative to banks, one that allows them to tap a larger group of savers attracted by the exit option provided by the ability to liquidate their investments whenever they choose. By this liquidity, speculators advance this service that the bourse provides, and cannot justifiably be viewed as social parasites that prey on the vulnerability of other market participants. The funds which they, along with ordinary investors, deploy in the purchases of shares invariably ends up in the hands of sellers who, depending on their circumstances and preferences, use the proceeds to consume goods, buy existing capital assets, or to construct real capital. A crucial qualification to this that needs to be made concerns bull markets, particularly in their late manic phases. On such occasions, capital can be temporarily engrossed in prolonged concatenations of speculative transactions. But the fault here lies with excess money creation by unpredictable central banks. Hence, the phenomena of financialization that is so much complained about does not originate from the precincts of Wall Street or the City – its roots are political.

NOTES

1. The 1940 edition of the book elicited a number of reviews, including from Paish (1940), Neisser (1941), J.E.W. (1940), and Mitra (1943). There is no common thread of criticism in the reviews, though two of them do take issue with Machlup's advocacy of the Austrian business cycle theory, discussed later in this article.

2. The total dollar volume of shares traded on the world's equity marts was $49 trillion in 2012. During the same year, the total value of new equity capital raised was $621 billion.

3. This venue of stock market credit went into decline with the passage of legislation in the 1930s restricting financial institutions from acting as agents for corporations in the call loan market.

4. In his later years, reflecting his support of flexible exchange rates as a solution to the defects of Bretton Woods, Machlup would become quite critical of the enthusiasm that hard money supporters espoused for gold. It exacerbated a rift between him and Mises that had already developed after Machlup's move to the United States, where he drifted toward the prevailing anti-Austrian orthodoxy. (Hulsmann, 2007, p. 479)

REFERENCES

Barger, H. (1935). The banks and the stock market. *The Journal of Political Economy, 43*(6), 763–777.

Bohm-Bawerk, E. (1930). *The positive theory of capital.* New York, NY: G.E. Stechert & Co.

Brogard, J. A. (2010). *High frequency trading and its impact on market quality.* University Kellogg School of Management Working Paper. Retrieved from http://www.clasesdebolsa.com/archivos/HTF.pdf. Accessed on November 29, 2012.

Cassel, G. (1929). Does the stock exchange absorb capital? *Skandinaviska Kreditaktiebolagot,* (April), 21.

Clark, C. (2012, October). How to keep markets safe in the era of high speed trading. *Chicago Fed Letter.* Retrieved from http://www.chicagofed.org/digital_assets/publications/chicago_fed_letter/2012/cfloctober2012_303.pdf. Accessed on November 30, 2012.

Daily, C. M., Certo, S. T., Dalton, D. R., & Roengpitya, R. (2003). IPO underpricing: A meta-analysis and research synthesis. *Entrepreneurship Theory and Practice, 27*(3), 271–295.

Federal Reserve Board. (1930). *Seventeenth annual report of the Federal Reserve Board.* Washington: US Government Printing Office. Retrieved from http://fraser.stlouisfed.org/docs/publications/arfr/1930s/arfr_1930.pdf. Accessed on August 17, 2012.

Federal Reserve Board. (2012, September 13). *Press release: Federal Reserve Issues FOMC statement.* Retrieved from http://www.federalreserve.gov/newsevents/press/monetary/20120913a.htm. Accessed on November 30, 2012.

Field, A. J. (1984). Assets exchanges and the transactions demand for money, 1919–1929. *The American Economic Review, 74*(1), 43–59.

Haberler, G. (1983). Fritz Machlup: In memoriam. *Cato Journal, 3*(1), 11–14.

Hahn, L. A. (1927). Borsenkredite und Industries. *Frankfurter Zeitung,* (May), 341.

Hasbrouck, J., & Saar, G. (2013). Low-latency trading. Johnson School Research Paper Series No. 35-2010. *AFA 2012 Chicago Meetings Paper*. Retrieved from http://ssrn.com/abstract=1695460. Accessed on June 27, 2013.

Hendershott, T., Jones, C. M., & Menkveld, A. J. (2011). Does algorithmic trading improve liquidity. *The Journal of Finance*, *66*(1), 1–33.

Hulsmann, G. (2007). *Mises: The last knight of liberalism Auburn*. Alabama: Ludwig von Mises Institute.

J.E.W. (1940). Review of the book [The stock market, credit, and capital formation]. *Journal of the Royal Statistical Society*, *103*(3), 415–417.

Keynes, J. M. (1930). *A treatise on money*. New York, NY: Harcourt, Brace, and Company.

Keynes, J. M. (1991). *The general theory of employment, interest, and money*. San Diego, CA: Harcourt.

Lasswell, H. (1950). *Politics: Who gets what, when, how*. New York, NY: Peter Smith.

Ljungqvist, A. (2008). IPO underpricing. In B. Espen Eckbo (Ed.), *Handbook in corporate finance: Empirical corporate finance* (Vol. 1, pp. 375–422). Amsterdam: Elsevier.

Machlup, F. (2007). *The stock market, credit, and capital formation*. Auburn, AL: Ludwig von Mises Institute.

Mises, L. V. (1963). *Human action*. San Francisco, CA: Fox and Wilkes.

Mitchell, L. E. (2007). *The speculation economy: How finance triumphed over industry*. San Francisco, CA: Berrett-Koehler.

Mitra, R. N. (1943). Review of the book (The stock market, credit, and capital formation). *Sankhyā: The Indian Journal of Statistics*, *6*(3), 337–338.

Neisser, H. (1941). Review of the book (The stock market, credit, and capital formation). *Annals of the American Academy of Political and Social Science*, *231*(1).

Norman, P. (2011). *The risk controllers: Central counterparty clearing in globalized financial markets*. West Sussex, UK: Wiley.

Paish, F. W. (1940). Review of the book (The stock market, credit, and capital formation). *Economica*, *7*(28), 441–443.

Palyi, M. (1932). Significance of bank loans for stock market transactions. *Journal of Business*, *5*(1), 28–46.

Pastor, L., & Veronesi, P. (2005). Rational IPO waves. *The Journal of Finance*, *60*(4), 1713–1757.

Pecora Commission. (1934). *Report of the committee on banking and currency pursuant to senate resolution 84*. Washington, DC: United States Government Printing Office.

Reed, H. L. (1930). *Federal reserve policy 1921–1930*. New York, NY: McGraw-Hill.

Reisch, R. (1929). Ueber das Wesen und die Wirkungen der Borsenkredite. *Bankarchw*, *28*, 13.

Reisch, R. (1930). Ruickwirkungen der Borsenspekulation auf den Kreditmarkt. *Zeit-schrift fiur Nationalokonomie*, *1*(2), 205–221.

Securities and Exchange Commission. (2010, September 30). *Findings regarding the market events of May 6, 2010*. Retrieved from http://www.sec.gov/news/studies/2010/marketevents-report.pdf. Accessed on November 29, 2012.

Siegel, J. (2008). *Stocks for the long run* (4th ed.). New York, NY: McGraw-Hill.

The Depository Trust and Clearing Corporation. (2010). *Introduction to DTCC*. New York, NY. Retrieved from http://www.dtcc.com/downloads/about/Introduction_to_DTCC.pdf. Accessed on August 17, 2012.

World Federation of Exchanges. (2012). *Statistics*. Retrieved from http://www.world-exchanges.org/statistics. Accessed on June 27, 2013.

SYNTHESIZING STATE AND SPONTANEOUS ORDER THEORIES OF MONEY

Alexander W. Salter and William J. Luther

ABSTRACT

What role does government play in determining the medium of exchange? Economists weighing in on the issue have typically espoused one of two views. State theorists credit government with the emergence and continued acceptance of commonly accepted media of exchange. In contrast, spontaneous order theorists find little need for government, maintaining that money emerges and continues to circulate as a result of a decentralized market process. History suggests a more subtle theory is required. We provide a generalized theory of the emergence and perpetuation of money, informed by both approaches and consistent with recent theoretical and empirical advances in the literature.

Keywords: Chartalism; Menger; medium of exchange; search; spontaneous order; unit of account

JEL classifications: B53; E41; E42

Entangled Political Economy
Advances in Austrian Economics, Volume 18, 161–178

ISSN: 1529-2134/doi:10.1108/S1529-213420140000018008

What role does government play in determining the medium of exchange? Economists weighing in on the issue have typically espoused one of two views. Following in the tradition of Knapp (1924) and Lerner (1947), state theorists (also called chartalists) credit government with the emergence and continued acceptance of commonly accepted media of exchange. On the extreme end, state theorists claim money is always a creature of the state – deriving acceptability from legal tender status or public receivability – and, moreover, that the state can choose virtually anything to serve as money. More moderate state theorists recognize that granting legal tender status, requiring taxes to be paid in a particular medium, and making public expenditures in that medium might not be sufficient to generate or perpetuate widespread acceptance. Nonetheless, they maintain that *existing* monies are largely the product of sovereign support.

In contrast, spontaneous order theorists follow in the tradition of Menger (1892) by crediting a decentralized market process with the emergence and continued acceptance of monies. They maintain that historical commodity monies emerged in the absence of sovereign support, neither conceptualized nor intended by any single mind. Some even claim intrinsically worthless fiat monies can emerge without sovereign backing (e.g., Kiyotaki & Wright, 1989).

History suggests a more subtle theory is required. After reviewing efforts to launch fiat monies with varied success, Selgin (1994) concludes government-sponsored fiat currencies can only get off the ground if they are introduced at a fixed exchange with the historically accepted money.[1] In other words, there are limits to a government's ability to determine the commonly accepted medium of exchange. However, Selgin (2003) finds no evidence that intrinsically worthless monies have ever emerged in the absence of sovereign support. He suggests epistemic limitations preclude decentralized agents from coordinating on fiat money equilibria.

Whether a currency survives once launched also suggests a more subtle theory is in order. Informal dollarization in hyperinflation countries shows there is some limit to what governments might perpetuate as money. And although government might be necessary to launch a fiat money, King (2004) and Luther and White (2011) demonstrate that unbacked monies can continue to circulate after sovereign support disappears.[2]

Following Wagner (2009), we reject theories of government acting on market and market participants acting without regard to government in favor of a theory emphasizing interaction between various players of various types. Along these lines, we provide a generalized theory of the emergence and perpetuation of money informed by both state and spontaneous order theories and consistent with recent theoretical and empirical advances in the literature. The paper proceeds as follows: In the sections "Money as a Creature of the State" and "Money as a Spontaneous Order," we examine the hard line claims from each school. Then, in the section "Crossed Wires and Ships Passing in the Night," we demonstrate that small concessions by authors on both sides of the debate leave room for a unified theory that emphasizes the spontaneous order aspects of money without trivializing the role of government. We sketch our view in the section "Including the State as a Player in Spontaneous Order Theories" while surveying several recent works. We conclude by noting the potential for future research.

MONEY AS A CREATURE OF THE STATE

According to chartalists, money is a social phenomenon and, therefore, cannot be understood without relation to the institutions in which it is imbedded (Bell, 2001).[3] Specifically, they point to the historical record to show that money arose as a system of payments for the discharge of debt (Wray, 1998, 2004).[4] Hence, chartalists view money primarily as a balance sheet relation: to hold money is to hold an asset, a claim drawn on someone else. Although chartalists recognize money's function as a medium of exchange, they tend to focus on the unit of account and store of value properties (Bell, 2001, p. 154).

The state theory of money – a particular instantiation of chartalism – asserts that government is the prime mover in the determination of the medium of exchange through the obligations it imposes on its citizens. It also emphasizes the extra-market origins of money. According to Wray (2004, p. 7):

> ... [T]he state (or any other authority able to impose an obligation) imposes a liability in the form of a generalized, social unit of account – a money – used for measuring the obligation. This does not require the pre-existence of markets, and, indeed, almost certainly predates them. Once the authorities can levy such obligations, they can name what fulfills this obligation. They do this by denominating those things that can be delivered, in other words, by pricing them.

Hence, in Wray's view, money originates when the government imposes obligations (i.e., taxes).

The state theory was first fully presented by Knapp (1924), a student of the German Historical School. According to Knapp, state money begins when the government specifies the particular object and unit it will accept as a legitimate discharge for obligations it is owed. The cycle is complete when the government begins issuing the "money-object" it accepts. Intuitively, the principle means by which the state imposes these obligations is taxation. Hence, the state can create a demand amongst the citizens for any money-object it accepts as payment for that purpose. Goodhart (1998, p. 416) explains the symbiotic relationship between taxation and money in the state theory:

> First, without money, it would be hard to place taxes on anything other than the production, transport and trade of goods, since only goods (or labour time) could be delivered. Once money exists, poll, income, and expenditure taxes, as well as taxes on the production of services become easier to levy. When taxes are received in goods or labour, the balance of goods (and labour) obtained will not be that required for public sector expenditures; so, money reduces the transactions costs of governments, pari passu with that of the private sector. By the same token, taxes payable in monetary form raise the demand for base money. Since a government obtains seigniorage from money creation, this benefits the fiscal position twice over, not only from the taxes levied, but also from the seigniorage resulting from the induced monetary demand.

In other words, money is the product of taxation and, additionally, facilitates collection of taxes to an even greater extent.

Although there has long since been a consensus among chartalists on the historical validity and modern relevance of their theory, the extent to which legal tender status is required to generate widespread acceptance remains an open question. Knapp (1924, p. 21) thought it important for a state to name the money-object and accept it as payment; he was less sure of the necessity of specific legal tender laws. Lerner (1947, p. 313) held that legal tender laws were irrelevant: "general acceptability, which is its all-important attribute, stands or falls by its acceptability by the state." Recently, Starr (1974, 2003) and Goldberg (2012) revisit the question. Employing formal models wherein the state decides what it will receive as payment, they show that agents are induced to accept the chosen item in a wider range of transactions. In doing so, the authors show legal tender laws are unnecessary. Nonetheless, legal tender status might be a contributing factor to the acceptability of a currency.[5]

MONEY AS A SPONTANEOUS ORDER

Despite admonitions from chartalists, most modern monetary economists follow in the tradition of Menger (1892) by explaining the emergence of a commonly accepted medium of exchange as the unintended outcome of individual actions.[6] In the absence of a mutual coincidence of wants, Menger surmised, an economic actor finds it in her interest to trade for a more *saleable* object. In doing so, she improves her odds of finding a trading partner that has what she wants and wants what she has. However, she also increases the saleability of the object she initially accepts, thereby encouraging others to accept it as well. The result, according to Menger, is a narrow class of highly saleable objects that one might call money.[7]

For Menger, the origins of money can be traced to economic agents' attempts to deal with the problem of the mutual coincidence of wants. The importance of salability comes from the inherent uncertainty into the objective exchange ratios between goods in the barter economy. Salability ultimately is determined by the unmet wants of the consumer, the divisibility of the commodity in question, and the extent of the market, as well as spatial and temporal considerations (Menger, 1892, pp. 246–247). Menger realizes that consumers who deal in less saleable goods, such as cattle, will find themselves frustrated when they bring their products to market in an attempt to exchange them for goods which will satisfy more urgently felt wants. Eventually, clever sellers of relatively less saleable goods will, in anticipation of their difficulties, prefer to exchange their products not for the final goods they wish to consume, but goods which they believe are more likely to be accepted by fellow traders based on the circumstances listed above. Other agents, eager to find more economical ways to satisfy their wants, observe this practice and mimic it. Eventually what results is a handful of commodities being accepted in anticipation of their ease of acceptance; these commodities have now become *media of exchange*: "And so it has come to pass … those commodities, which relatively to both space and time are most saleable, have in every market become the wares, which it is not only in the interest of every one to accept in exchange for his own less saleable goods, but which also are those he actually does readily accept (Menger, 1892, p. 248)." Menger then explains that the precious metals, that is, gold and silver, have almost universally become media of exchange for human societies due to their high degree of salability – both metals are homogeneous, easily divisible, and cheap to store. Finally, Menger (1892, p. 255) briefly considers the role of the state in monetary acceptance: "Money has not been generated by law. In its origin it is a social, and not a state-institution. Sanction by the authority of the state is a notion alien to it." However, Menger makes it clear that this admonition only applies to the *emergence* of money; he explicitly acknowledges the role of the state in adapting the socially accepted money to the needs of commerce by providing for the minting of coins of reliable weight and convenient denomination.

Menger's insight was cited approvingly by Ludwig von Mises in his influential treatise on monetary economics. Mises (1953, p. 34) emphasizes even more strongly the supremacy of money's function as a medium of exchange:

> The simple statement, that money is a commodity whose economic function is to facilitate the interchange of goods and services, does not satisfy those writers who are interested rather in the accumulation of material than in the increase of knowledge. Many investigators imagine that insufficient attention is devoted to the remarkable part played by money in economic life if it is merely credited with the function of being a medium of exchange; they do not think that due regard has been paid to the significance of money until they have enumerated half a dozen further "functions" – as if, in an economic order founded on the exchange of goods, there could be a more important function than that of the common medium of exchange.

On the state's ability to create a new money, the chartalists' "money-object," Mises (1953, p. 72) is similarly dismissive: "One thing, however, must be made clear; even now the state has not the power of directly making anything into money, that is to say into a common medium of exchange. Even nowadays, it is only the practice of the individuals who take part in business that can make a commodity into a medium of exchange."[8] Mises (1953, p. 74) explicitly considers the state theory of money put forth by Knapp and rejects it: "By declaring an object to be fitted in the juristic sense for the liquidation of liabilities expressed in terms of money, the state cannot influence the choice of a medium of exchange, which belongs to those engaged in business." More explicitly,

> The establishment of a legal ratio for the discharge of obligations incurred under the regime of the superseded kind of money constitutes a merely secondary measure which is significant only in connection with the change of standard which is achieved by other means. The provision that taxes are in future to be paid in the new kind of money, and that other liabilities imposed in terms of money will be fulfilled only in the new money, is a *consequence* of the transition to the new standard. It proves effective only when the new kind of money has become a common medium of exchange in commerce generally. (Mises, 1953, p. 74)

Mises's most remembered critique, however, resulted from his investigation into the determinants of the purchasing power of money. Mises showed that individuals value money based on the ability of that money to command goods and services, that is, to satisfy wants. As such, a subjective valuation of money must be founded on the objective exchange ratios which exist in the market (Mises, 1953, p. 108). In particular, we base our subjective valuation of money on the exchange ratios which we observe in the *immediate past*:

> Once an exchange-ratio between money and commodities has been established in the market, it continues to exercise an influence beyond the period during which it is maintained; it provides the basis for the further valuation of money. Thus the past objective exchange-value of money has a certain significance for its present and future valuation. The money-prices of to-day are linked with those of yesterday and before, and with those of to-morrow and after. (Mises, 1953, p. 109)

Mises recognizes that this cannot be the end of the story, since we have merely moved the analysis back one stage in time. The process of deriving subjective value from the objective exchange ratios of the past continues until it terminates at a specific place in time: the point at which the money-object first became valued as money (i.e., acquired exchange value in addition to its use value). According to Mises (1953, pp. 109–110):

> To trace back the value that money has to-day to that which it had yesterday, the value that it had yesterday to that which it had the day before, and so on, is to raise the question of what determined the value of money in the first place. Consideration of the origin of the use of money and of the particular components of its value that depend on its monetary function suggest an obvious answer to this question. The first value of money was clearly the value which the goods used as money possessed (thanks to their suitability for satisfying human wants in other ways) at the moment when they were first used as common media of exchange. When individuals began to acquire objects, not for consumption, but to be used as media of exchange, they valued them according to the objective exchange-value with which the market already credited them by reason of their "industrial" usefulness, and only as an additional consideration on account of the possibility of using them as media of exchange. The earliest value of money links up with the commodity-value of the monetary material.

This result, dubbed the "regression theorem," has an important implication for the emergence of money: since the purchasing power of the money-object today is continuously linked to the value of the money-object the moment it became money, the money-object must have had its own independent use value as determined by the community's economic agents. This implies that no authority, state or otherwise, can arbitrarily chose any money-object as a method of payment and have it perform the role of money in the community. In other words, fiat money cannot exist indecently, without being tied to the money-object upon which the community had already arrived.[9] This result clearly stands in stark contrast to the implications of the chartalist theory.

CROSSED WIRES AND SHIPS PASSING IN THE NIGHT

The line in the sand between the two theories is clear. However, as is often the case when two strongly opposing points of view clash, there is a degree of misattribution and talking past each other on both sides. Consider, for example, the chartalists' views on what they call the metallist theory. The accusation that metallist monetary theorists defend the choice of metallic currencies due to their "intrinsic" values (Bell, 2001, p. 152; Goodhart, 1998, p. 408) is vague. It is unclear whether by "intrinsic" they imply the existence of some value apart from that which Mises (1953) had in mind (i.e., the value of money derives from its ability to command goods and services, and hence its objective market exchange values). Indeed, their attacks on the metallist paradigm are even more confusing in light of the distinction some authors make between a metallist and Mengerian paradigm (as Goodhart does) whereas others, such as Bell, lump all the nuances of opposing ideas into a single, more easily assailable category.

The hardline chartalist movement overstates its differences with the alternative paradigm in regards to the ability of state authority, through taxation, to augment the demand for a certain commodity. As Forstater (2006) notes, this insight was well-recognized by both classical and neoclassical economists such as J.S. Mill and Philip Wicksteed. Even Adam Smith acknowledged it: "A prince, who should enact that a certain proportion of his taxes should be paid in a paper money of a certain kind, might thereby give a certain value to this paper money; even though the term of its final discharge and redemption should depend altogether on the will of the prince (Smith, 1904, p. 312)."

On the other side, Mises (1953) appears to be attacking a straw man in part of his critique of Knapp (1924). As Selgin (1994, p. 818) notes, although Knapp insisted the state, in creating fiat money, did not need to make the new money redeemable in the pre-established commodity, it *did* need to tie it to that commodity (by establishing a fixed exchange value). Thus, even Knapp admitted that the operation of fiat money was somewhat constrained by historical path dependence, which is illustrative of, rather than an argument against, Mises's regression theorem.

The degree to which the two sides fail to appreciate each other's specific insight is rooted in the role of government, both in the creation of a new monetary order and the maintenance of one which already exists. The hardline chartalist and emergent views seem to deify and ignore the state's authority respectively, and even the more moderate positions have not well-integrated into their theories whether the central authority is more umpire or ordinary player. We take Mises's (1953, p. 73) view: the state is an important player, admittedly with more weight to throw around, but a player nonetheless in the sense that it is endogenous to the social process which results in a monetary order. In doing so we believe we can reconcile this more moderate chartalist approach with the spontaneous order conception to arrive at a theory of money with more explanatory power.

This is not a trivial distinction. Formally, we may say that the locus of the debate is the nature of the demand for money. The state theory maintains that obligation imposition and acceptance by powerful authorities is the key component of the demand to hold money, and thus the principle source of a commodity's value as money. The spontaneous order explanation goes one stage deeper: rather than treat the specifics of money demand as the starting point of the analysis, it seeks to explain the emergence of a demand to hold money in the first place. Thus theorists who point to the anthropologic record (e.g., Einzig, 1966; Quiggin, 1949; Ridgeway, 1892) for evidence that money arose to serve the interests of elites are begging the question.[10] Even acknowledging that "[b]arter was virtually nonexistent in primitive and ancient societies, and instead the first commercial transactions took place on the basis of elaborate credit systems whose denomination was typically in agricultural commodities, including cattle, grain by weight, and tools" (Benes & Kumhof, 2012, p. 13), we can progress no farther in our understanding without some explanation for why the precious metals almost universally became media of exchange, whereas "cattle, grain by weight, and tools" did not.

The interesting cases lie at the nexus of state and emergent theories. The state (or other elites) can contribute to the demand for holding a commodity for exchange purposes, but they cannot bypass the emergence process and declare a monetary order *ex nihilo*. How does augmenting the exchange value for a money-commodity affect the process of emergence when the latter has not completely played out? How do these forces interact? Can we arrive at a monocausal explanation? Or, are the lines of causality inseparable? By endogenizing the social elites – by including the state as a player in a spontaneous order theory of money – we are likely to produce a more useful framework for analyzing the historical record.

INCLUDING THE STATE AS A PLAYER IN SPONTANEOUS ORDER THEORIES

Our primary contention is that both views – that which presumes the government acts on the market as wells as that which presumes the market is unaffected by government action – are inadequate. In contrast to the traditional views, we emphasize interaction between various players of various types. One might crudely think of two player types: market players aiming to satisfy their own narrow interests and government players committed to some strategy that is a product of their unique behavioral characteristics, institutional processes, or combination thereof. Although we are certainly open to relaxing these assumptions – say, by allowing market players to act in a manner consistent with observations from laboratory experiments or by increasing the number of types to consider more narrow classes of individuals – the crude approach alluded to above suffices for our purposes here.

Allowing government players to act in a manner contrary to their own narrow interests will no doubt raise red flags for those working in the public choice tradition, where behavioral symmetry has been stressed. Though we are sympathetic to this tradition, and believe it served a useful function when the prevailing assumptions held naively that government decision-makers necessarily acted in the social interest, we see no reason to require behavioral symmetry at present. It seems quite reasonable to think filtering mechanisms might sort behavioral types such that government players are more, less, or equally concerned with the interests of others as compared to market players. Similarly, institutional decision-making processes might produce decisions that seem to be more, less, or equally concerned with the interests of others. Since these are ultimately empirical issues, we need not preclude them with our theoretical approach.

Rather than presenting a formal theory of the interaction between government and market players, we survey works from several distinct but related literatures that are consistent with (or can be interpreted in such a way that renders them consistent with) our view. Specifically, we consider search-theoretic matching models, agent-based computational models, and laboratory experiments. In doing so, we sketch a general theory of the emergence and perpetuation of money informed by both state and spontaneous order traditions, while demonstrating that our view is consistent with recent theoretical and empirical advances in the literature.

Aiyagari and Wallace (1997) and Li and Wright (1998) present views remarkably close to ours. Building on Kiyotaki and Wright (1989, 1993), these authors classify G agents in the population of size N as government agents. All N agents are randomly matched into pairs, where each agent decides whether to swap the item currently held in storage for the item held by its partner. Trades are accomplished when both agents in a pair agree to swap their items. Government agents are not endowed with special qualities in these models; they act *in* the market, rather than *on* the market. That is, they are randomly matched and employ trading strategies just like all other agents. The only significant difference between government and non-government agents in the model space concerns the selection of trading strategies. Non-government agents choose individual trading strategies to maximize their own private utility. In contrast, the trading strategies of government agents are exogenously determined. It is therefore possible to observe the pattern of interactions conditional on the trading strategy employed by government agents.

An important result emerging from Aiyagari and Wallace (1997) and Li and Wright (1998) is that only a "sufficiently big" government is capable of determining the commonly accepted medium of exchange. That is, government can determine the medium of exchange if and only if G/N is large enough given the "properties of the money, the presence of alternative means of payment, and other aspects of policy" (Li & Wright, 1998, p. 312).[11] In our opinion, these models provide a much-needed compromise from the two traditional positions outlined above. According to this new view, it is not the case that governments can always and everywhere determine the commonly accepted medium of exchange. At the same time, it is not the case that governments are altogether impotent in this capacity. Some governments – acting in some contexts – will find it relatively easy to determine the medium of exchange, while others – despite their best efforts – will be unsuccessful at doing so.

In demonstrating the existence of equilibria where governments can and cannot determine commonly accepted media of exchange, Aiyagari and Wallace (1997) and Li and Wright (1998) go a long way toward synthesizing state and spontaneous order theories of money. However, the authors offer little regarding the process of interaction whereby those equilibria might be obtained. Duffy (2001, p. 297) levies the same criticism against the older Kiyotaki-Wright models on which these works are built:

> They do not attempt to describe the process by which an equilibrium is achieved, or equivalently, give an account of how one or more commodities might emerge as conventional media of exchange. Since agents almost certainly do not begin a process of social interaction with equilibrium beliefs but must adjust their strategies to their evolving historical experiences within a given trading regime, the relevant question is whether the comparative static predictions of the theory are actually informative of how play evolves when agents are placed in the Kiyotaki-Wright environment.

Agreeing with Duffy, we contend that the models put forward by Aiyagari and Wallace (1997) and Li and Wright (1998) must be modified to consider disequilibrium dynamics with less heroic assumptions regarding the epistemic capabilities of agents.

Many authors have considered whether agents operating in the Kiyotaki-Wright environment can obtain beliefs necessary for the equilibrium pattern of behavior to emerge in a reasonable amount of time. Marimon, McGrattan, and Sargent (1990), Staudinger (1998), Basçi (1999), Giansante (2006), Kawagoe (2007), and Hasker and Tahmilci (2008) take an agent-based computational approach. The results are mixed. When the parameterization requires agents employ a medium of exchange with a lower storage cost than their production good, these authors typically find strong convergence to optimal behavior. Convergence to optimal behavior is much less likely under parameterizations where agents should trade their production good for an item that is more costly to store, even though doing so would enable them to trade for their consumption good so much more quickly as to warrant the additional cost. Similarly, Kawagoe (2007) shows that, contrary to theory, agents are reluctant to use perishable goods as money. Using the terminology common in the literature, agents are inclined to employ *fundamental strategies* – offering to trade for items with lower storage costs – even when they would do better to employ *speculative strategies* – accepting higher storage costs in order to consume sooner. Basçi (1999) finds that allowing agents to learn by imitating the successful strategies of other agents (in addition to one's own experience) increases the degree of equilibrium-consistent behavior under some parameterizations where speculative strategies are justified. Even still, the agent-based computational approach suggests parameterizations of the model exist where full convergence to equilibrium in a reasonable amount of time is unlikely.

Although the aforementioned computer simulations shed much needed light on the process of interaction in the model space considered herein, we are ultimately concerned with the behavior of human subjects. Along these lines, some have considered questions of belief acquisition and disequilibrium dynamics by observing human subjects in a laboratory version of the Kiyotaki-Wright environment (Brown, 1996; Duffy, 2001; Duffy & Ochs, 1999, 2002).[12] Controlled experiments generally yield results consistent with the agent-based computational models discussed above. Commodity monies emerge as predicted under parameterizations supporting fundamental strategies (Duffy & Ochs, 1999), but players are reluctant to employ speculative strategies (Brown, 1996; Duffy & Ochs, 1999). Similarly, in the context of fiat monies, players typically offer to trade for items that lower their storage costs, even under parameterizations where they would do better to accept an item with higher storage costs (Duffy & Ochs, 2002). As with the agent-based computational models, laboratory experiments with human subjects suggest full convergence to equilibrium in a reasonable amount of time is unlikely under some parameterizations of the model.

Whereas much work has been done in the Kiyotaki-Wright environment, no one to our knowledge has taken an agent-based computational or experimental approach to consider the role of government support in this environment. Duffy (2001) comes closest. In an effort to bridge the gap between agent-based computational and experimental approaches, the author constructs an agent-based computational model with an environment similar to that populated by human subjects in Duffy and Ochs (1999) and compares results across the two approaches. Then, Duffy (2001) proposes two new treatments and explores each using both techniques. Although the author aims to consider whether and to what extent changing the experimental design encourages subjects to adopt speculative strategies while gauging consistency across approaches, we maintain that he unintentionally contributes to the literature on state and spontaneous order theories of money in the process.

Of particular interest here is the second treatment proposed and considered by Duffy (2001), wherein a subset of the population is automated to employ an exogenously determined strategy. Specifically, he requires type 2 and 3 players employ fundamental strategies consistent with those predicted by theory in order to eliminate "noisy" trading and thereby make the optimal speculative strategy more salient for type 1 players. Although Duffy (2001) does not interpret it as such, the automation technique is similar to those employed by Aiyagari and Wallace (1997) and Li and Wright (1998) to model government.[13] His results – that automating a subset of the population can enable agents to obtain non-salient, but preferred equilibria – can therefore be interpreted to mean governments can, at least under some parameterizations, improve upon monies emerging naturally (i.e., in the absence of government). Moreover, it suggests an additional channel through which government action might significantly affect the commonly accepted medium of exchange: anchoring the beliefs of non-government players.

There are only two minor items we would like to add to this novel interpretation of Duffy (2001). First, it seems reasonable to think that a government capable of anchoring beliefs to improve upon the natural state of affairs could similarly use this power to favor an inferior money. In other words, government might anchor beliefs to introduce or sustain a money that makes the average individual worse off. Second, the belief-anchoring role of government would seem particularly relevant in a multiple equilibrium environment, especially in the absence of alternative focal points.

In contrast to the traditional Kiyotaki-Wright environment – where it is common to consider only three goods and a single intrinsically worthless item that might function as money – the real world is marked by an astounding number of goods and presumably an infinite number of intrinsically worthless items to potentially serve as money. If these extensions increase the number of equilibria, the need for a focal point would similarly increase. Hence, the identified channel might be more significant than the standard theoretical approach suggests.

Taken as a whole, the literature surveyed above creates an interesting starting point for those considering the role of government in determining media of exchange. In contrast to traditional state and spontaneous order approaches, the modern literature treats government as another player in the game. The theoretical literature concludes that a government of sufficient size is capable of determining the commonly accepted medium of exchange. Agent-based computational and experimental approaches reveal that the theoretical literature is lacking in an important respect: some parameterizations do not yield particularly salient strategies for agents not initially endowed with equilibrium beliefs. Duffy's (2001) work suggests government can help solve this problem, improving welfare by anchoring beliefs and thereby enabling the achievement of difficult equilibria. However, if Duffy's (2001) results are generalizable, the inclusion of government might also reduce welfare if government agents commit to employ strategies consistent with less desirable equilibria.

CONCLUSION

Although there is still much to learn concerning the role of government in the emergence and perpetuation of commonly accepted media of exchange, we believe traditional state and spontaneous order theories – at least in their extreme forms – offer little way forward. A more sophisticated theory allowing for the interaction of government and non-government players is required. We do not claim that government can circumvent the spontaneous order process and create a monetary order *ex nihilo*. Rather, we wish to emphasize that, among the set of relatively more saleable commodities, government action may be the decisive factor in creating or sustaining a monetary order. Drawing on works from multiple literatures, we have pieced together a generalized theory. We posit that in some – but certainly not all – cases, government is capable of determining the commonly accepted medium of exchange. Furthermore, we suggest that the welfare implications of government action in this capacity are ambiguous and should be considered on a case-by-case basis. Our view might thereby be viewed as a synthesis of traditional state and spontaneous order theories of money.

The value of any theory is its ability to shed light on history and thereby help one understand the world around us. At present, there is a dearth of empirical work regarding the role of government in determining (or failing to determine) media of exchange. Similarly, economists seem to know relatively little about scrip and other private monies prevailing throughout periods of history. The difficulty of approaching these topics in a way that most economists would accept as rigorous is perhaps partly to blame. Another potential reason is the lack of a general framework within which one might identify puzzles and pursue analytically satisfying solutions. We hope to have made some progress with regard to providing a general framework and intend to fill the empirical gap with future research.

NOTES

1. On the difficulties of launching a new currency resulting from network effects, see Dowd and Greenaway (1993) and Luther (2013a).
2. See also Luther (2013b).
3. The name "chartalism" derives from the Latin word "charta" meaning "ticket" or "token."
4. Wray (2004) approvingly cites Innes (1913, 1914, 1932) as a specific historical example illustrating how warring tribes used a system of credits and debits as a way of preventing inter-clan feuds.
5. Legal tender, in this context, refers to *exclusive* legal tender laws, meaning laws restricting the range of objects agents may use as a means of payment in private (non-state) transactions. However, as Goldberg (2008) explains, this definition is far more restrictive than the legal tender laws in most first-world countries. Part of the difficulty in pinning down the role of legal tender is likely due to the fact that the term is so often misused.
6. Although Menger (1892) is often credited with the spontaneous order theory of money, the view can be found in earlier works. See, for example, Galiani (1751).
7. Wallace (1980) questions whether there is a clear distinction between barter and indirect exchange with commodities.
8. Mises, like Menger, qualifies this statement by acknowledging the state can influence the choice of the money-object due to its size and hence importance as a buyer and seller. He also acknowledges its ability to use the mint to change the "character" of the money in circulation (p. 73).
9. Selgin (2012) and Luther (2013a) consider a possible exception in bitcoin.

10. It is sometimes claimed that the power of elites was so great that they were able to generate money from intrinsically useless objects. A famous example is the giant round stones that were currency on the island of Yap. These claims are refuted by Goldberg (2005).

11. It is worth comparing this view with that of Koppl (2002), who characterizes a "big player" as (1) big in the sense of influencing the relevant market, (2) more or less immune or insensitive to profit and loss, and (3) acts on discretion rather than rules. Although these views are similar with respect to (1) and (2), the exogenous trading strategy found in Aiyagari and Wallace (1997) and Li and Wright (1998) is, in effect, a binding rule.

12. Duffy (2010) provides a useful survey.

13. Aiyagari and Wallace (1997) and Li and Wright (1998) introduce a fourth player type labeled government, which, given the parameters, is analytically equivalent to automating an equal proportion of all three types. Duffy's (2001) automation technique differs – perhaps significantly – in that he automates 100 percent of type 2 and 3 players and 0 percent of type 1 players. Nonetheless, we maintain that the automation techniques are qualitatively similar.

ACKNOWLEDGMENT

The authors wish to thank the Mercatus Center at George Mason University for its generous support.

REFERENCES

Aiyagari, S. R., & Wallace, N. (1997). Government transaction policy, the medium of exchange, and welfare. *Journal of Economic Theory*, *74*(1), 1–18.

Basçi, E. (1999). Learning by imitation. *Journal of Economic Dynamics and Control*, *23*(9), 1569–1585.

Bell, S. (2001). The role of the state and the hierarchy of money. *Cambridge Journal of Economics*, *25*(2), 149–163.

Benes, J., & Kumhof, M. (2012). *The Chicago plan revisited.* IMF Working Paper No: WP/12/202.

Brown, P. M. (1996). Experimental evidence on money as a medium of exchange. *Journal of Economic Dynamics and Control*, *20*(4), 583–600.

Dowd, K., & Greenaway, D. (1993). Currency competition, network externalities and switching costs: Towards an alternative view of optimum currency areas. *The Economic Journal*, *103*(420), 1180–1189.

Duffy, J. (2001). Learning to speculate: Experiments with artificial and real agents. *Journal of Economic Dynamics and Control*, *25*(3–4), 295–319.

Duffy, J. (2010). Macroeconomics: A survey of laboratory research. In A. Roth & J. Kagel (Eds.), *The handbook of experimental economics* (Vol. 2). Princeton, NJ: Princeton University Press.

Duffy, J., & Ochs, J. (1999). Emergence of money as a medium of exchange: An experimental study. *American Economic Review*, *89*(4), 847–877.
Duffy, J., & Ochs, J. (2002). Intrinsically worthless objects as media of exchange: Experimental evidence. *International Economic Review*, *43*(3), 637–673.
Einzig, P. (1966). *Primitive money* (2nd Ed.). Oxford: Pergamon.
Forstater, M. (2006). Tax-driven money: Additional evidence from the history of economic thought, economic history, and economic policy. In M. Setterfield (Ed.), *Complexity, endogenous money, and macroeconomic theory* (pp. 202–220). Cheltenham: Edward Elgar.
Galiani, F. (1751). (1977). *On money: A translation of Della Moneta*. Ann Arbor, MI: Published for Department of Economics, University of Chicago by University Microfilms International.
Giansante, S. (2006). *Social networks and medium of exchange*. Working Paper. Retrieved from http://andromeda.rutgers.edu/˜jmbarr/NYComp/GiasanteEEA.pdf
Goldberg, D. (2005). Famous myths of fiat money. *Journal of Money, Credit, and Banking*, *37*(5), 957–967.
Goldberg, D. (2008). *Legal tender*. Working Paper. Retrieved from http://www.drorgoldberg.com/tender.pdf?attredirects = 0
Goldberg, D. (2012). The tax-foundation theory of fiat money. *Economic Theory*, *50*(2), 489–497.
Goodhart, C. A. E. (1998). The two concepts of money: Implications for the analysis of optimal currency areas. *European Journal of Political Economy*, *14*(3), 407–432.
Hasker, K., & Tahmilci, A. (2008). *The rise of money: An evolutionary analysis of the origins of money*. Working Paper. Retrieved from http://hasker.bilkent.edu.tr/Research/Hasker-Tahmilci-evolution-of-money-08-05-15.pdf
Innes, A. M. (1913). What is money? *Banking Law Journal*, *30*(5), 377–408.
Innes, A. M. (1914). The credit theory of money, *Banking Law Journal*, *31*(2), 151–168.
Innes, A. M. (1932). *Martyrdom in our times: Two essays on prison and punishment*. London: Williams and Norgate, Ltd.
Kawagoe, T. (2007). Learning to use a perishable good as money. *Multi-Agent-Based Simulation VII*, *4442*, 96–111.
King, M. (2004). The institutions of monetary policy. *American Economic Review*, *94*(2), 1–13.
Kiyotaki, N., & Wright, R. (1989). On money as a medium of exchange. *Journal of Political Economy*, *97*(4), 927–954.
Kiyotaki, N., & Wright, R. (1993). A search-theoretic approach to monetary economics. *American Economic Review*, *83*(1), 63–77.
Knapp, G. F. (1924). *The state theory of money*. London: Macmillan.
Koppl, R. (2002). *Big players and the economic theory of expectations*. New York, NY: Palgrave Macmillan.
Lerner, A. P. (1947). Money as a creature of the state. *American Economic Review*, *37*(2), 312–317.
Li, Y., & Wright, R. (1998). Government transaction policy, media of exchange, and prices. *Journal of Economic Theory*, *81*(2), 290–313.
Luther, W. J. (2013a). *Crypto-currencies, network effects, and switching costs*. Mercatus Center Working Paper No. 13-17.
Luther, W. J. (2013b). Friedman versus Hayek on private outside monies: New evidence for the debate. *Economic Affairs*, *33*(1), 127–135.

Luther, W. J., & White, L. H. (2011). *Positively valued fiat money after the sovereign disappears.* Working Paper No. 11–14. George Mason University, Department of Economics.

Marimon, R., McGrattan, E. R., & Sargent, T. J. (1990). Money as a medium of exchange in an economy with artificially intelligent agents. *Journal of Economic Dynamics and Control, 14*(2), 329–373.

Menger, C. (1892). On the origin of money. *Economic Journal, 2*(6), 239–255.

Mises, L. von. (1953). In H. E. Batson (Trans.) *The theory of money and credit.* New Haven, CT: Yale University Press.

Quiggin, A. H. (1949). *A survey of primitive money: The beginnings of currency.* London: Metheun.

Ridgeway, W. (1892). *The origin of metallic currency and weight standards.* Cambridge: Cambridge University Press.

Selgin, G. (1994). On ensuring the acceptability of a new fiat money. *Journal of Money, Credit, and Banking, 26*(4), 808–826.

Selgin, G. (2003). Adaptive learning and the transition to fiat money. *Economic Journal, 113*(484), 147–165.

Selgin, G. (2012). *Synthetic-commodity money.* Working Paper. Retrieved from http://papers.ssrn.com/sol3/papers.cfm?abstract_id=2000118

Smith, A. (1904). In E. Cannan (Ed.), *An inquiry into the nature and causes of the wealth of nations.* London: Muethen and Co. Book II, chapter II.

Starr, R. M. (1974). The price of money in a pure exchange economy. *Econometrica, 42*(1), 45–54.

Starr, R. M. (2003). Why is there money? Endogenous derivation of "money" as the most liquid asset: A class of examples. *Economic Theory, 21*, 455–474.

Staudinger, S. (1998). *Money as a medium of exchange: An analysis with genetic algorithms.* Working Paper. Technical University of Vienna.

Wagner, R. E. (2009). Property, state, and entangled political economy. In W. Schäfer, A. Schneider, & T. Thomas (Eds.), *Markets and politics: Insights from a political economy perspective* (pp. 37–49). Marburg: Metropolis.

Wallace, N. (1980). The overlapping generations model of fiat money. In J. H. Kareken & N. Wallace (Eds.), *Models of monetary economies* (pp. 49–82). Minneapolis, MN: Federal Reserve Bank of Minneapolis.

Wray, L. R. (1998). *Understanding modern money: The key to full employment and price stability.* Cheltenham, UK: Edward Elgar.

Wray, L. R. (2004). Conclusion: The credit money and state money approaches. In L. R. Wray (Ed.), *Credit and state theories of money: The contributions of A. Mitchell Innes.* Cheltenham, UK: Edward Elgar.

GAME MINING: HOW TO MAKE MONEY FROM THOSE ABOUT TO PLAY A GAME

James W. Bono and David H. Wolpert

ABSTRACT

It is well known that a player in a non-cooperative game can benefit by publicly restricting his possible moves before play begins. We show that, more generally, a player may benefit by publicly committing to pay an external party an amount that is contingent on the game's outcome. We explore what happens when external parties – who we call "game miners" – discover this fact and seek to profit from it by entering an outcome-contingent contract with the players. We analyze various structured bargaining games among such miner(s) and players that determine such an outcome-contingent contract before the start of the original game. These bargaining games include playing the players against one another as in the original game, as well as allowing the players to pay the miner(s) for exclusivity and first-mover advantage. We establish restrictions on the strategic settings in which a game miner can profit and bounds on the game miner's profit.

Entangled Political Economy
Advances in Austrian Economics, Volume 18, 179–211

ISSN: 1529-2134/doi:10.1108/S1529-213420140000018009

We also find that game miners can lead to both efficient and inefficient equilibria.

Keywords: Game mining; contracts; side-payments; bargaining

JEL classification: C72; D86

INTRODUCTION

How to Mine a Game

Suppose corn producers compete with sugar producers in the market for sweeteners, and this market is characterized by Cournot quantity competition. Corn producers seeking a market advantage could lobby for a sugar tariff. However, there are other laws they could lobby for that would also benefit them. For example, they could lobby for a law in which they themselves are punished unless they produce the Stackelberg leader quantity of high fructose corn syrup. Because the sugar producers know such a law means that the corn producers are forced to produce the Stackelberg leader quantity, the sugar producers have no choice but to choose their best response, which is the Stackelberg follower quantity. Since the Stackelberg equilibrium yields the leader greater profits than the Cournot equilibrium, corn producers would be willing to pay for the passage of such a law. This could even be seen as a basis for lobbyists feeling induced to make campaign contributions, as enterprising lawmakers may initiate such an arrangement.

This way that a player in a game could benefit by having a third agree to punish them in certain circumstances is fairly obvious. But can the same kind of phenomenon occur even when the third party does not have regulatory power over the first two parties but is just a private firm or citizen? Suppose the external party is a private firm called Game Mining Inc. This firm has a crack legal team that can draft a bullet-proof contract with the corn producers specifying sums of money that corn producers must pay to Game Mining Inc. if certain market outcomes are obtained. Can Game Mining Inc. design such an outcome-contingent contract that the corn producers will sign?

That players can benefit in games by entering contracts that distort payoff functions is well documented in the economic literature (see e.g. Jackson & Wilkie, 2005; Renou, 2009; Schelling, 1956; Sobel, 1981; Vickers, 1985).

This literature focuses on the outcomes that can occur when binding commitments are possible separately by the players in the game or among those players. In this paper, we focus on games where binding commitments by the players separately are not possible in the original game, but an external party – the "game miner" – can provide the ability to make such commitments to the players, in exchange for a payment to that third party.

As a graphic example, there are situations where the game miner can extract money from player i by promising to pay the opponent of player i, player j, an outcome-contingent amount. The game miner's proposition to player i in such a scenario would be: "if you pay me x dollars now, then I will pay player j a total of y dollars after the game if outcome z occurs." Player i will accept this contract because the payment to player j changes j's payoffs in a way that benefits player i in the equilibrium of the resultant game. Note that this overall outcome involving the game miner and two players is a renegotiation-proof equilibrium; player j cannot credibly commit to not accepting y dollars from the game miner after the game has ended. Moreover, the game miner's commitment to make that payment can be made before start of play, publicly, using any conventional binding contract mechanism.

Perhaps even more strikingly, in a variant of this scenario the game miner can profit by "threatening" player j: "pay me x dollars now, or after the game has completed I will pay you an outcome-contingent amount." An illustration is given in the following example.

Example 1. Consider a game between two players, (A)ngry and (C)onfused, with utilities given, respectively, by the row and column entries of the following bimatrix

		C: L	C: R
A	T	−12, 0	−1, −1
	B	−11, −10	0, 0

The unique Nash equilibrium is (B,R), leading to a payoff to A of 0.

Now say that the game miner asks A for a payment of 9.5 before A plays the game with C. The game miner says that if A does not make this payment, and if A plays T in the game with C, then the game miner will pay 2 to A. This contract and all other transactions are visible to all players.

If A does not accept the offer by the game miner, then due to the output-contingent payment they would receive from the game miner, the game between A and C effectively changes to the following new bimatrix:

		C: *L*	C: *R*
A	*T*	−10, 0	−1, −1
A	*B*	−11, −10	0, 0

This new game has the unique Nash equilibrium (T,L), leading to a payoff for A of −10.

So if A does not pay 9.5 to the game miner, A plays the new game with C, and A's total payoff is −10. In contrast, if A pays 9.5 to the game miner, then A and C play the original game, and A's payoff (including the payment to the game miner) is −9.5. Accordingly, A will agree to pay the game miner 9.5, thereby saving 0.5.

In effect, in this scenario A agrees to pay 9.5 to the game miner under the threat that if he does not, the game miner will pay him an (output-contingent) amount after the end of the game with C.[1,2] So we have an example of "Pay me now, or else I will give you some money later."

This is an odd kind of extortion indeed, in which the worst that the extorter can do to their victim is to give them some money.

Clearly the full set of possible structured bargaining games involving an arbitrary set of players offering contacts to one another and to those playing the original game is quite elaborate. To limit the scope of our analysis, in this paper we only consider scenarios where a player i may benefit by publicly committing to pay an external party an amount that is contingent on the game's outcome, and explore what happens when external parties discover this fact and seek to profit from it. The following simple example clarifies the types of outcome-contingent contracts that are the foundation of our analysis.

Example 2. There are two cell-phone manufacturers, Anonymous (A) and Brandname (B). They must simultaneously decide how many cell phones to produce. Each firm has two options, high output (H) or low output (L). Anonymous, like its name suggests, is not well known. Therefore, no matter what level of output Brandname produces, Anonymous prefers to produce high output to gain brand recognition. On the other hand, Brandname's choice of output does depend on Anonymous's choice. If Anonymous produces low output, then Brandname prefers to keep prices high by also producing low output. However, if Anonymous produces high output, then Brandname prefers to safeguard its recognized name by also producing high output. The moves and payoffs (in millions of dollars) are summarized by the following matrix.

		B: *H*	B: *L*
A	*H*	1, 0.5	2, 0
	L	0, 0	1, 1

The NE is (*H*,*H*), and payoffs are (1.5).

A firm called Game Mining Inc. (G) watches this, and just before Anonymous and Brandname declare their output decisions, G offers Anonymous the following contract, making sure Brandname sees them do this: "Pay us \$1.5 million right now. Then we will pay you back a certain amount after you and Brandname make your decisions. The following matrix shows how much we will pay you, in millions of dollars, for the four possible joint decisions by you and Brandname:"

$$\begin{bmatrix} 0 & 1.01 \\ 1.5 & 2.0 \end{bmatrix}$$

Note that this matrix does not include the \$1.5 million upfront payment. So if Anonymous accepts the contract, then the final payoff matrix for the game (including the upfront payment) becomes

		B: *H*	B: *L*
A	*H*	−0.5, 0.5	1.51, 0
	L	0, 0	1.5, 1

In this modified game, the unique NE is very close to (2/3, *L*), where 2/3 is the probability that A chooses *H*. For Anonymous, this results in an average payoff of approximately \$1.5 million. This is a \$500,000 improvement over its payoff without the contract. On average, G makes approximately \$160,000 for their trouble. Brandname, on an average, makes approximately \$333,333. This is a \$166,666 decrease in Brandname's payoff compared to the situation where Anonymous and G do not have a contract.

Note that the Coaseian outcome of the game without G would be for Anonymous to pay at least \$500,001 to Brandname for the outcome (*H*, *L*) (see Coase, 1960). So G is not merely facilitating the Coaseian outcome.

Note also that the outcome in Example 2 cannot be achieved by a commitment by either player to play or not play either one of their actions. In general, the presence of G creates an entirely new strategic setting. However, in this simplest of game mining scenarios, a commitment by A to play the mixed strategy (2/3, 1/3) would achieve the same equilibrium as the game miner's outcome-contingent contract. This is not the case for the other game mining scenarios discussed in this paper.

In Example 2, G makes considerable profit from recognizing that Anonymous benefits from an output-contingent contract. However, Anonymous also benefits from this contract. So game mining can be seen as a natural result of profit-seeking behavior, rather than as the result of economic planning and regulation. It requires no mechanism other than enforceable contracts between players and game miners.

Since profit-seeking behavior creates the game mining setting in Example 2, it is natural to think about what other types of game mining settings can arise this way. By studying various structured bargaining games between game miners and players, we find a range of new phenomena. For example, in some cases, it may be that the miner can create a prisoner's dilemma scenario between the players by offering contracts that each player has an incentive to accept regardless of whether their opponent accepts. If both players accept, the outcome is that they are both worse off than if neither accepts, and the game miner profits considerably. There are also important timing issues in game mining. When players sequentially sign contracts with game miners, there can be a significant first-mover advantage to the first-signing player. This provides the game miner with yet another opportunity for profit; they can charge the players to move first. In addition, game mining has complicated effects on efficiency. The effects depend on the underlying game as well as the bargaining structure between players and the game miner. In this paper, we explore situations where the presence of a game miner can both increase and decrease equilibrium efficiency.

Related Literature

The ideas underlying the game mining concept are implicit in a large body of economic literature. As an illustration, in the model presented in Jackson and Wilkie (2005) (JW), every player specifies outcome-contingent side-payments that they will make after a non-cooperative strategic form game is played and the payoffs are resolved. These side-payments are binding contracts, so the players are ex ante determining their preferences over the game's outcomes. In this regard the game that the players actually play is endogenously determined. JW examine whether a mechanism that allows players to make such outcome-contingent side-payments generally results in efficient outcomes and conclude that it does not.

The simplest game mining scenario, for example, Example 2, can be viewed as a variant of JW. In this variant, the only outcome-contingent side-payments are between the players and the game miners, and the game miners would be indifferent over outcomes of the game if not for the fact that they will be receiving side-payments dependent on those outcomes. Furthermore, the game miners play no part in the game between the players other than to accept contracts for outcome-contingent side-payments and make the contracts public.

In contrast to JW, we do not assume that a social planner installs a mechanism for players to make side-payments. Instead, we look at a game without formal mechanisms and ask whether external parties will create contracts for outcome-contingent side-payments in pursuit of profit. In addition, we relax the assumption in JW that all side-payments are non-negative. That is, we allow game miners to pay players for certain outcomes. This will be important when examining optimal contracts as well as the extent to which a monopolist game miner can extract profits from players. Hence, game mining can be seen as the version of JW's setting that arises as the natural result of profit-seeking in the absence of JW-type regulation. We also consider how outcomes change when the game miner can enter contracts with both players, when mining contracts are offered to players in sequence, and when we change the underlying bargaining structure between the players and the game miner. These considerations do not arise in JW's setting.

In another related paper, Renou (2009) analyzes what happens when players are able to embed the original game in a new two-stage game. In the second stage of that new game the players play the original game. However before they do so, in the first stage, the players each simultaneously commit not to play some subset of their possible moves in that game in the second stage. These *commitment games* can be seen as the result of placing three restrictions of the JW setting: (1) player *i*'s side-payments are only contingent on *i*'s action (rather than on the full profile of actions), (2) the side-payments are made to external players, and (3) the side-payments are effectively infinite. Renou's restricted setting means that there are fewer commitments available but that there are also fewer deviations available. This means the set of equilibria sustainable in Renou's restricted setting can differ significantly from the set sustainable in the less restricted JW setting.

Renou's setting and analysis are too restricted to cover the full game mining scenario. This is because there are many circumstances in which both the player and the game miner prefer to make contracts that are fully outcome-contingent and that have non-infinite side-payments. One example can be found in Example 2, where the player and game miner find it optimal to agree on a contract that results in a unique equilibrium in which the player uses a mixed strategy with full support (and therefore does not make any commitment in the first stage of Renou's two-stage game).

In Garcia-Jurado and Gonzalez-Diaz (2006), the types of commitments are similar to those studied in Renou (2009). The main difference is that the former studies a repeated game in which commitments to play mixed strategies are possible. They show that when such commitments are available, standard folk theorem results can be obtained with milder assumptions on the stage game. A key difference between our work and that of Garcia-Jurado and Gonzalez-Diaz (2006) is that our settings are all single-shot. Still, it should be possible to make commitments to play mixed strategies in a single-shot game. In the simplest game mining scenario, the set of equilibria is the same as what can be sustained by commitments to play mixed strategies. However, when mixed strategies do arise in our framework, they do so as the result of contracts that produce games with unique mixed NE rather than being required by the commitments themselves. And beyond the simplest game mining scenario, the set of equilibria under commitments to play mixed strategy differ from game mining equilibria. Like Garcia-Jurado and Gonzalez-Diaz (2006), the work of Kalai, Kalai, Lehrer, and Samet (2010) also obtains a folk theorem for commitments. They study a setting in which players can make commitments that are conditional on the commitments of their opponents. For two-player strategic games, they show that all feasible and individually rational payoffs can be obtained in the equilibrium set of a game with conditional commitments. Such conditional commitments are not explored in the game mining framework but remain of interest for future work.

Another well-studied aspect of commitment in games is the role of timing. Papers such as Hamilton and Slutsky (1990), van Damme and Hurkens (1996), and Romano and Yildirim (2005) concern endogenous timing and Stackelberg-like commitments. Emanuele and Levent (2012) examine the effect of renegotiation on such commitments with third parties and find that there is a large class of games in which third party contracts have strategic implications even when they are renegotiable. Wolpert and Jamison (2011, 2012) introduce the idea that players might also commit to using certain personas before the start of a game. These papers analyze the possibility that experimentally observed non-rationality is in fact rational, because by committing to play the game with a non-rational "persona," a player may increase her ultimate payoff. This persona has the same effect as a side-payment or commitment, as it is reflected in a temporary change to the player's utility function. The *persona games* model has been successful in explaining non-rational behavior in non-repeated traveler's dilemma and even in versions of the non-repeated prisoner's dilemma. Timing is also studied in the current paper. Here, the focus is on how the sequence of contracts between the game miner and players determines the outcome. As is the case in persona games, there is often a first-mover advantage in game mining even when players have dominant strategies.

Finally, there is a subset of the principal-agent literature concerning delegation games that is closely related to game mining. In these models, the principal is able to contract with an agent that will engage in a game with the principal's opponent (or agent of the principal's opponent). One concern of this literature is detailing the optimal contract for a principal (see Fershtman, 1985; Fershtman & Judd, 1987; Sklivas, 1987; Vickers, 1985). Another concern is whether a mechanism that allows specific types of contracts can lead to Pareto efficiency (see Fershtman, Judd, & Kalai, 1991; Katz, 1991). Game mining is closely related to a previously unexplored aspect of principal-agent scenarios: the degree to which the agents can profit from delegation contracts. Similar ideas are also present in the "budget-breaking" manager of Holmstrom (1982).

The important difference between the work here and the related literature is that we concentrate on the potential role of a third party, seeking to make profits by interacting with the players, rather than focus on situations where all relevant decisions are by the original players alone.

Overview

We start by introducing the game mining model and notation in the section "Notation". Then, in the section "Maximal Mining," we assume that one player interacts with the game miner and conduct a foundational analysis of the types of contracts and outcomes they can achieve. The properties derived in the section "Maximal Mining" serve as the foundation for more in-depth analysis that appears later in the paper. For example, here we derive bounds on the aggregate payoffs that the game miner and player can earn together. We show that they can select a contract to divide these payoffs in any way between them. We also show that outcome-contingent contracts cannot be profitable for both the game miner and contracting player if the other player has a strictly dominant strategy.

In the section "Game Mining Bargaining Structures" we consider various market structures, that is, various structured bargaining games involving the players of the underlying non-cooperative game and an external party that tries to mine that underlying game. We begin the section "G Accepts One Contract" with a game based on the assumption that players offer contracts to the game miner, and the game miner must choose either one of the offered contracts or neither contract. We show that the game miner can profit by more than the maximal payoff to either player in the game without contracts. This is because players can suffer a loss if their opponent outbids them for the right to contract with the game miner. We derive an upper bound on the game miner's equilibrium profit. We also characterize the set of equilibria for a simple example and show that the opportunity to make contracts with the game miner can make both players worse off. That is, a Pareto efficient equilibrium of the underlying game is not an equilibrium when game mining is possible. Note, that JW find a similar result using their contingent transfers mechanism.

In the section "G Accepts Both Contracts," we allow the game miner to accept both offers if she chooses so. This reduces the game miner's bargaining power, and we find that the game miner can always do at least as well by restricting herself to accept only one contract.

In the section "Sequestial Contracts," we discuss the role of timing and first-mover advantage, establishing that the players may be willing to pay for the right to contract first with the game miner. Therefore, in contrast to the simultaneous contract case in the section "Sequestial Contracts," G can engage players in a bidding war even when she can accept both contracts. Furthermore, this can happen when one or both of the players have a strictly dominant strategy. Two examples illustrate this and further analyze the difference between game mining and Renou-type commitments.

In the section "G Makes Offers," we analyze the case where the miner has the bargaining power, that is, G is the one making the offers. We show that this allows the game miner to "play the players against one another" and thereby increase her profit. We also derive an upper bound on this profit. An interesting feature of this scenario is that the game miner moves the players from an inefficient equilibrium to an efficient one. However, as a profit seeker, the game miner is able to capture *more* profit than the efficiency gain.

In the section "Discussion," we briefly discuss several new research areas opened by game mining. These areas include games of more than two players, and risk aversion on the part of the game miner. We briefly consider unstructured bargaining among the players and the miner to determine the contract. We also touch on an "inverted" version of this topic, where the underlying game is itself unstructured, while the miner(s) negotiate with the player(s) via structured bargaining to determine a contract for that underlying game. We end by discussing the idea that one player might sign a contract that obligates him to pay the other player outcome-contingent amounts. This obligation may actually help the payer and hurt the payee.

NOTATION

We study a two-player, one-stage simultaneous-move game of complete information. However, we relax the usual assumption that the two players cannot make outcome-contingent contracts (or simply contracts) with players external to the game.

Specify the two-player *pre-contract* game as

$$\Gamma \equiv \{\mathrm{A},\mathrm{B}\},\{X_{\mathrm{A}},X_{\mathrm{B}}\},\{U_{\mathrm{A}},U_{\mathrm{B}}\}$$

where $X_i \in \{\mathrm{A,B}\}$ is finite and U_i is an $|X_{\mathrm{A}}|$-by-$|X_{\mathrm{B}}|$ matrix for which the (m, n) entry gives the payoff to i when A chooses his mth pure strategy and B chooses his nth pure strategy. Player i's set of mixed strategies is Δ_i, $i=\mathrm{A}$, B, and the set of mixed strategy profiles is $\Delta \equiv \Delta_{\mathrm{A}} \times \Delta_{\mathrm{B}}$. We write all of i's pure and mixed strategies as $|X_i|$-by-one vectors σ_i for which the mth entry gives the probability that σ_i assigns to playing i's mth pure strategy. Therefore, player i's expected payoff from $\sigma=(\sigma_{\mathrm{A}}, \sigma_{\mathrm{B}})$ as

$$\mathbb{E}_{\sigma}(U_i)=\sigma_{\mathrm{A}}^{\mathrm{T}} U_i \sigma_{\mathrm{B}}$$

where superscript T indicates matrix transpose.

Player i's best response correspondence is given by $R_i^{\Gamma}(\cdot) : \Delta_j \to 2^{\Delta_i}$, so that

$$R_i^{\Gamma}(\sigma_j) \equiv \left\{\sigma_i \in \Delta_i : \ \sigma_{\mathrm{A}}^{\mathrm{T}} U_i \sigma_{\mathrm{B}} \geq \sigma_{\mathrm{A}}^{\prime\mathrm{T}} U_i \sigma_{\mathrm{B}} \quad \forall \sigma_i' \in \Delta_i\right\} \tag{1}$$

Therefore, the set of Nash equilibria of game Γ is given by

$$\mathrm{NE}(\Gamma) = \left\{(\sigma_{\mathrm{A}}, \sigma_{\mathrm{B}}) : \sigma_{\mathrm{A}} \in R_{\mathrm{A}}^{\Gamma}(\sigma_{\mathrm{B}}) \quad \text{and} \quad \sigma_{\mathrm{B}} \in R_{\mathrm{B}}^{\Gamma}(\sigma_{\mathrm{A}})\right\}$$

An outcome-contingent contract between player i and the game miner G is a matrix D_i that specifies a (possibly negative) transfer from i to G for every outcome of Γ. We assume D_i is finite. If players use strategies (σ_A, σ_B), then under contract D_i player i expects to pay $\sigma_A^T D_i \sigma_B$ to G. Defining $U_i^{D_i} \equiv U_i - D_i$, player i's expected payoff is $\sigma_A^T U_i^{D_i} \sigma_B$. Therefore, we can view D_i as a transformation of Γ. We write the *post-contract* game as $\Gamma(D,i) \equiv \{\{A,B\},\{X_A,X_B\},\{U_i^{D_i},U_j\}\}$ for $i \neq j$, where the second argument of the post-contract game identifies the player with whom G has contracted. Note, that we simplify this notation by dropping this second argument whenever the context makes clear the identity of the player with whom G has contracted. We write the set of possible contracts as $\mathscr{D} \equiv \mathbb{R}^{|X_A|} \times \mathbb{R}^{|X_B|}$. The notation D_0 denotes the null contract, where all entries are zero.

MAXIMAL MINING

Before introducing a formal strategic setting for game mining in the next section, we first explore the way that a player A and the game miner can work together to extract gains from Γ. This is the simplest game mining scenario.

The first step is to define the *aggregate payoffs* from a contract. These are the amounts that the contracting parties can earn in equilibrium and divide among themselves. Suppose A and G are the contracting parties and D_A is their contract. Then the aggregate payoff that is apportioned between A and G is given by the payoff that A gets at a NE in $\Gamma(D_A)$ *before* A pays to G the amount specified in D_A.

Definition 1. The aggregate payoff set for A and G from DA is:

$$M_A(D_A) \equiv \{\sigma_A^T U_A \sigma_B : (\sigma_A, \sigma_B) \in \text{NE}(\Gamma(D_A))\}$$

A's payoffs are the only difference between Γ and the post-contract game $\Gamma(D_A)$. Here D_A distorts U_A, thereby distorting A's best response function. By varying D_A, we can give A any best response function in $\Gamma(D_A)$. This includes best response functions that designate dominant strategies as well as indifferences. Therefore, when A exclusively contracts with the game miner, any profile such that B chooses a best response can arise as an equilibrium of $\Gamma(D_A)$ for some D_A. The same thing can be said for the situation where A has the exclusive opportunity to make commitments on mixed strategies.

We denote by $M_A^*(D_A)$ the maximum of the aggregate payoff set from D_A. The maximum over all aggregate payoff sets is $\mathcal{M}_A \equiv \max_{D_A \in \mathcal{D}} \{M_A^*(D_A)\}$. It is the maximum that A and G can possibly have to divide among themselves in any NE of any game in which they sign a contract. We refer to this quantity as the *maxagg* (maximum aggregate payoff). The maxagg is the subject of our first result.

Proposition 1.

$$\mathcal{M}_A = \max_{\sigma_A, \sigma_B} \{\sigma_A^T U_A \sigma_B : \sigma_B \in R_B^\Gamma(\sigma_A)\} \tag{2}$$

Proof. From the definition of maxagg we have:

$$\mathcal{M}_A = \max_{D_A} \{\max\{\sigma_A^T U_A \sigma_B : (\sigma_A, \sigma_B) \in NE(\Gamma(D_A))\}\} \tag{3}$$

Recall that the contract D_A does not affect B's payoffs U_B. This means that $\text{NE}(\Gamma(D_A)) = \left\{\sigma \in \Delta : \sigma_A \in R_A^{\Gamma(D_A)}(\sigma_B) \text{ and } \sigma_B \in R_B^\Gamma(\sigma_A)\right\}$. The trouble is to choose D_A so that A's best response correspondence meets B's best response function at the maximizers that correspond to $\mathcal{M}_A$,(σ_A, σ_B). This problem is solved trivially by choosing D_A such that A is indifferent among all strategy pairs. Then every action of A is a best response to every action of B, including σ_B, which, by assumption is in $R_B^\Gamma(\sigma_A)$.

So Eq. (3) becomes

$$\mathcal{M}_A = \max_{D_A} \{\max\{\sigma_A^T U_A \sigma_B : \sigma_B \in R_B^\Gamma(\sigma_A)\}\}$$

which is the same as Eq. (2) because the set $\{\sigma_A^T U_A \sigma_B : \sigma_B \in R_B^\Gamma(\sigma_A)\}$ is independent of D_A. □

Proposition 1 means that to find the maximum aggregate payoffs for A and G, we simply search B's best response correspondences to all of A's moves for the one giving maximum payoff to A. This allows us to restrict our analysis to the values of U_A along B's best response correspondence. Note that certain outcomes in the aggregate payoff set correspond to profiles in which A does not choose a best response to B's strategy. Only B is being forced to make a best-response. So, maxagg is nothing more than an upper bound on what is possible for A and G to obtain by making a contract.

In some cases, a game miner might be concerned with maximizing the minimum of the aggregate payoff set as a way of guaranteeing a sufficient minimum payoff. We write the minimum of the aggregate payoff set $M_A(D_A)$ as $\underline{M}_A(D_A)$. Maximizing $\underline{M}_A(D_A)$ over all contracts D_A, we get the maximum minimum aggregate payoff $\underline{\mathcal{M}}_A$, called the *maxminagg*:

$$\underline{\mathcal{M}}_A \equiv \max_{D_A} \min_{\sigma} \left\{ \sigma_A^T U_A \sigma_B : \sigma \in \mathrm{NE}(\Gamma(D_A)) \right\}$$

Trivially, $\underline{\mathcal{M}}_A \geq \underline{M}_A(D_0)$. Comparing maxminagg with maxagg, we also know that $\underline{\mathcal{M}}_A \leq \mathcal{M}_A$. And when there exists a contract D_A such that $M_A(D_A) = \{\mathcal{M}_A\}$, we have $\underline{\mathcal{M}}_A = \mathcal{M}_A$. That is, if there exists a contract D_A such that the only NE of $\Gamma(D_A)$ yields the maxagg to A and G, then the maxagg and maxminagg are the same.

The next example continues from Example 2 in the introduction, using maxagg and maxminagg to illustrate a distinction between the equilibrium outcomes in game mining and commitments to play pure strategies. In this example, maxagg is associated with a NE strategy for A, σ_A, that is a mixed strategy with full support. However in this example, a commitment by A to play (or not play) certain pure strategies will never allow A and G to achieve the maxagg.

On the other hand, contracts that achieve the maxagg may also give rise to a NE with an aggregate payoff lower than the maxagg or the NE aggregate payoff for the original game. So we may expect that a conservative miner would avoid such contracts that achieve the maxagg but also have bad equilibria. To address this, we show that there are contracts that yield a unique mixed NE σ_A for which the aggregate payoff is arbitrarily close to the maxagg. Because this NE is unique, the aggregate payoff is also the maxminagg that concerns the conservative game miner. Therefore, a conservative game miner would choose such a contract over one that involves a commitment to play (or not play) a specific strategy.

Example 3. Consider again the game Γ presented in Example 2:

	H	L
H	1, 0.5	2, 0
L	0, 0	1, 1

where A is the row player. Write $p \equiv \sigma_A(H)$. Then B's best response correspondence is

$$R_B^\Gamma(p) = \begin{cases} H & \text{if } p > \frac{2}{3} \\ L & \text{if } p < \frac{2}{3} \\ q \in [0,1] & \text{if } p = \frac{2}{3} \end{cases}$$

If A chooses $p < 2/3$, then B will choose L, and the payoff to A will be $2_p + 1(1-p) = 1 + p$. Likewise, if A chooses $p > 2/3$, then B will choose H, and the payoff will be p. If A chooses $p = 2/3$, then B chooses any combination of H and L yielding payoffs to A between 2/3 and 5/3. Therefore, the maximum payoff for A along R_B^Γ is when $\sigma_A = (p, 1-p) = \left(\frac{2}{3}, \frac{1}{3}\right)$ and $\sigma_B = (0,1)$:

$$\mathcal{M}_A = \sigma_A^T U_A \sigma_B = \begin{bmatrix} \frac{2}{3} \\ \frac{1}{3} \end{bmatrix}^T \begin{bmatrix} 1 & 2 \\ 0 & 1 \end{bmatrix} \begin{bmatrix} 0 \\ 1 \end{bmatrix} = \frac{5}{3}$$

In other words, the maxagg payoff for A and G is achieved by a mixed strategy. The problem is that there is no contract D_A such that $\Gamma(D_A)$ has a unique NE that achieves the maxagg payoff to A and that results in a non-negative payoff for G. Moreover, for those D_A's such as there is a NE of $\Gamma(D_A)$ with A's payoff equaling the maxagg payoff, there are other NE with A's payoff less than 1, which is already A's payoff in every NE of the original game Γ. So it would appear that A has no incentive to form a contract with Game Mining, Inc. However, there are contracts that produce a unique NE under which the aggregate payoff is arbitrarily close to the max-agg of 5/3. An example of such a contract that gets arbitrarily close to the maxagg is

$$D_A = \begin{bmatrix} 1.5 & 0.5 - \varepsilon \\ 0 & -0.5 \end{bmatrix}$$

With this contract A's payoffs are now given by

$$U_A^{D_A} = \begin{bmatrix} 1 & 2 \\ 0 & 1 \end{bmatrix} - \begin{bmatrix} 1.5 & 0.5-\varepsilon \\ 0 & -0.5 \end{bmatrix} = \begin{bmatrix} -0.5 & 1.5+\varepsilon \\ 0 & 1.5 \end{bmatrix}$$

There is a unique NE for all $\varepsilon > 0$. As ε approaches zero, that NE approaches (2/3, L), so the maxminagg approaches 5/3. As mentioned previously, this outcome is also possible if A can commit to playing his NE mixed strategy.

The preceding results consider the aggregate payoffs that A and G can achieve by contracting. We next address the way in which A and G are able to divide those aggregate payoffs. The following result says that they are able to incorporate any division of the aggregate payoffs directly into the contract without affecting the best response correspondence of A or B. (Whether A and G would accept such a division is a different issue.)

Proposition 2. For any $a \in \mathbb{R}$ and $\sigma^* = (\sigma_A^*, \sigma_B^*)$ such that $\sigma_B^* \in R_B^{\Gamma}(\sigma_A^*)$, there exists a contract D_A^* such that:

1. $(\sigma_A^*, \sigma_B^*) \in NE(\Gamma(D_A^*))$ and
2. $\sigma_A^{*T} U_A^{D_A^*} \sigma_B^* = a$

Proof. By Proposition 1 there exists a contract D_A such that $(\sigma_A^*, \sigma_B^*) \in NE(\Gamma(D_A))$. Let $\underline{1}$ stands for a matrix all of whose entries are 1. So $(\sigma_A^*)^T \underline{1} \sigma_B^* = 1$. Therefore there is a scalar $x \in \mathbb{R}$ such that

$$(\sigma_A^{*T} (U_A - D_A - x\underline{1}) \sigma_B^*) \underline{1} = a\underline{1}$$

This gives us $D_A^* \equiv D_A + x\underline{1}$. Since $U_A^{D_A^*} = U_A^{D_A} - x\underline{1}$, $(\sigma_A^*, \sigma_B^*) \in NE(\Gamma(D_A^*))$. □

Proposition 2 says that the aggregate payoffs that A and G get by mining are not affected by a restriction on the way in which A and G divide those payoffs. So the way $\mathcal{M}_A$ is divided between A and G in equilibrium will be determined by strategic rather than technical considerations. This will be convenient when we introduce a formal strategic environment in the next section.

In some settings, there is no contract such that A and G can both benefit in any NE of $\Gamma(D_A)$. This is always the case when B has a strictly dominant strategy.[3] The intuition is that A's contract with G will never change B's payoffs. Therefore, B will always play his dominant strategy, no matter what the contract says. Therefore there is nothing that a contract can do to help A. This intuition is formalized in the following result.

Proposition 3. If B has a strictly dominant strategy, then there is no contract D_A such that A and G both strictly benefit in any NE of $\Gamma(D_A)$.

Proof. Suppose $\tilde{x}_B$ is a strictly dominant strategy for player B. Then $\tilde{x}_B = R_B^{\Gamma(D_A)}(\sigma_A) = R_B^{\Gamma}(\sigma_A)$ for all $\sigma_A \in \Delta_A$. Hence the set of NE in Γ is

$$\left\{\sigma^* \in \Delta : \sigma_A^* = \arg\max_{\sigma_A} \ \sigma_A^T U_A \tilde{x}_B \ \text{ and } \ \sigma_B^* = \tilde{x}_B\right\}$$

and the set of NE in $\Gamma(D_A)$ is

$$\left\{\tilde{\sigma} \in \Delta : \tilde{\sigma}_A = \arg\max_{\sigma_A} \ \sigma_A^T U_A^{D_A} \tilde{x}_B \ \text{ and } \ \tilde{\sigma}_B = \tilde{x}_B\right\}$$

If G benefits by entering contract D_A, then $\tilde{\sigma}_A^T D_A \tilde{x}_B > 0$.

But this means that $\tilde{\sigma}_A^T U_A \tilde{x}_B > \tilde{\sigma}_A^T U_A^{D_A} \tilde{x}_B$. Since $\sigma_A^{*T} U_A \tilde{x}_B \geq \tilde{\sigma}_A^T U_A \tilde{x}_B$, by combining we have $\sigma_A^{*T} U_A \tilde{x}_B > \tilde{\sigma}_A^T U_A^{D_A} \tilde{x}_B$ for all $\sigma^*, \tilde{\sigma}$. Accordingly, A will not benefit by signing D_A. □

Proposition 3 puts a restriction on the set of games Γ in which A will benefit from the services of a game miner. However, as shown in later sections, there are ample opportunities for A and G to benefit from contracts when player B has a strictly dominant strategy. In general, such a situation requires that B also has an opportunity to make a payoff-contingent contract with the miner.

The next result establishes limits on game mining when one player has a weakly dominant strategy.

Proposition 4. If B has a weakly dominant strategy, then there is no contract D_A such that both A and G strictly benefit in every NE of $\Gamma(D_A)$ compared to not signing any contract.

Proof. By contradiction. Suppose x_B^* is weakly dominant and D_A is a contract such that both A and G benefit in every NE of $\Gamma(D_A)$. There is a NE (x_A^*, x_B^*) of Γ. For every $x_A \in X_A$ we have that

$$x_A^T U_A x_B^* \leq x_A^* U_A x_B^*$$

If A is better off in every NE of $\Gamma(D_A)$, then for $x_A \in R_A^{\Gamma(D_A)}(x_B^*)$

$$x_A U_A^{D_A} x_B^* > x_A^* U_A x_B^*$$

which implies

$$x_A D_A x_B^* < 0$$

which in turn contradicts the fact that G is better off. □

Proposition 4 tells us that A and G cannot eliminate the risk of loss in a NE of $\Gamma(D_A)$ if B has a weakly dominant strategy in Γ. If A and G are both conservative and require that they gain in every NE of $\Gamma(D_A)$, then no contract will be made between them.

GAME MINING BARGAINING STRUCTURES

G Accepts One Contract

Consider a situation in which players A and B encounter each other in a simultaneous move game, $\Gamma=\langle\{A,B\}\{X_A,X_B\}\{U_A,U_B\}\rangle$. There is only one external party, G, that is willing to accept publicly observable outcome-contingent contracts. Before A and B play Γ, they simultaneously offer contracts to G. These contracts are called D_A and D_B, respectively.

After observing D_A and D_B, G chooses either D_A, D_B or D_0 (the null contract). Players A and B observe this contract and recognize its legally binding nature. A and B then engage in the simultaneous move game $\Gamma(D,i)$. $\Gamma(D, i)$ is the *post-contract subgame*, where again we simplify the notation by dropping the second argument when the identity of the player with whom G has contracted is clear.

Formally, this is an extensive form game with three stages:

Stage 1: Players A and B simultaneously offer contracts D_A and D_B to G.
Stage 2: G chooses D_A, D_B or the null contract D_0.
Stage 3: Players A and B play $\Gamma(D, i)$.

A strategy S_i for $I=A,B$ in the extensive form game is a pair $S_i \equiv (D_i, S_i)$. The first component, $D_i \in \mathcal{D}$, is the offer that i makes to G in the first stage. The second component is a function from the space of all possible contracts and contractees, $\mathcal{D}\times\{A,B,0\}$, to the space of probability distributions over *i*'s action set X_i, that is, $s_i : \mathscr{D} \times \{A, B, 0 \mapsto \Delta_i$. In other words, $s_i(D, j)$ gives *i*'s strategy (pure or mixed) in the post-contract subgame induced by G choosing contract *D* from player *j*. Here, we also simplify the notation by dropping the second argument when the identity of the player with whom G has contracted is clear, for example, $s_A(D_B) = s_A(D_B, B)$. The profile of strategies of player A and player B are written as S_{-G}, where $S_{-G} = (s_A, s_B)$.

In stage two, G selects an element of the choice set $\mathcal{I}_G \equiv 0, A, B\}$. S_G is the function that takes as input the history $\mathcal{D}_G = (D_A, D_B)$ and returns an element of $\mathcal{I}_G$ indicating which player's contract has been chosen. We let $D_{S_G(\mathscr{D}_G)} = 0$ indicate the game miner chooses not to contract with either player.

Given a full strategy profile (S_A, S_B, S_G), G's payoffs are

$$U_G(S_A, S_B, S_G) = s_A\left(D_{S_G(\mathscr{D}_G)}\right)^{\mathrm{T}} D_{S_G(\mathscr{D}_G)} s_B\left(D_{S_G(\mathscr{D}_G)}\right)$$

$D_{S_G(\mathscr{D}_G)}$ is G's stage two choice given the stage one actions (D_A, D_B), and $s_A\left(D_{S_G(\mathscr{D}_G)}\right)$ is A's stage three reaction to that choice. For $i = A, B$, the payoffs are

$$U_i(S_A, S_B, S_G) = s_A\left(D_{S_G(\mathscr{D}_G)}\right)^{\mathrm{T}} U_i^{D_{S_G(\mathscr{D}_G)}} s_B\left(D_{S_G(\mathscr{D}_G)}\right)$$

if G chooses *i*'s contract and

$$U_i(S_A, S_B, S_G) = s_A\left(D_{S_G(\mathscr{D}_G)}\right)^T U_i s_B\left(D_{S_{G(\mathscr{D}_G)}}\right)$$

otherwise. As shorthand, we represent this extensive form game as

$$\Gamma_G \equiv \langle \{A, B, G\}, \Gamma, \{\mathscr{S}_i\}_{i=A}^{B}, \mathscr{S}_G, U_G \rangle$$

Definition 2. A subgame perfect equilibrium (SPE) of Γ_G is a strategy profile $S = (S_A, S_B, S_G)$ such that:

1. $\left(s_A\left(D_{S_G(\mathscr{D}_G)}\right), s_B\left(D_{S_G(\mathscr{D}_G)}\right)\right) \in \mathrm{NE}\left(\Gamma\left(D_{S_G(\mathscr{D}_G)}\right)\right)$ for all contracts $D \in \mathbb{R}^2 \times \mathbb{R}^2$.
2. S_G is optimal given S_{-G} for all pairs (D_A, D_B), that is

$$U_G(S_A, S_B, S_G) \geq U_G\left(S_A, S_B, S_G'\right)$$

for all S_G'.

1. D_A is optimal given S_G, s_A, and S_B, that is

$$U_i((D_A, s_A), S_B, S_G) \geq U_i\left(\left(D'_A, s_A\right), S_B, S_G\right)$$

for all D'_A (mutatis mutandi for B).

We turn our attention to finding the maximum amount that can be mined from Γ. To do so, we introduce a concept that is related to the aggregate payoff set from Definition 1:

Definition 3. The aggregate payoff function for A and G from D_A is:

$$m_A(D_A|s_{-G}) \equiv s_A(D_A)U_A^{D_A}s_B(D_A)$$

The aggregate payoff function differs from the aggregate payoff set. Whereas the aggregate payoff set includes payoffs for all NE of $\Gamma(D_A)$, the aggregate payoff function simply returns the sum of A and G's payoffs when s_{-G} is played in $\Gamma(D_A)$. For example, if s_{-G} selects a NE of the post-contract subgame $\Gamma(D_A)$, then the aggregate payoff function $m_A(D_A|s_{-G})$ selects one element from the aggregate payoff set $M_A(D_A)$. We denote by $\hat{D}_A$ a contract that maximizes A's aggregate payoff function.

In an SPE, G will choose whichever contract yields her the highest payoff as determined by (s_A, s_B). Given that, i's should offer more to G than j's offers whenever j's contract offers less than $m_i(\hat{D}_i|s_{-G}) - s_A(D_j)^T U_i s_B(D_j)$. The most that i will ever be willing to offer G is therefore determined by finding the contract of j that results in the smallest payoff for i, called $\underline{D}_j$. Following this logic reveals that, loosely, G will contract with the player that has the greatest willingness to pay. In other words, there will not be an SPE in which G accepts a contract from one player while the other has a greater willingness to pay. From the players' willingness to pay, we get the maximum SPE payment to G in the following proposition.

Proposition 5. The upper bound SPE payment to G is

$$\overline{U}_G = \max_i \left\{ \mathcal{M}_i - \min_{\sigma_A, \sigma_B} \left\{ \sigma_A^T U_i \sigma_B : \sigma_i \in R_i^\Gamma(\sigma_{-i}) \right\} \right\}$$

Proof. First, let $\underline{D}_j(s_{-G}) \equiv \arg\min_{D_j} s_A(D_j)^T U_i s_B(D_j)$. That is, $\underline{D}_j$ is the contract that minimizes i's payoff given s_{-G}. Also let

$$\delta_i(D_i|s_{-G}) \equiv m_i(D_i|s_{-G}) - m_i(D_0|s_{-G})$$

be the change in i's payoff by going from Γ to $\Gamma(D_i)$. Similarly define

$$\delta_i(D_i, D_j|s_{-\mathrm{G}}) \equiv m_i(D_i|s_{-\mathrm{G}}) - m_i(D_j|s_{-\mathrm{G}})$$

as the change in i's payoff by going from $\Gamma(D_j)$ to $\Gamma(D_i)$.

The proof follows from the strategic considerations of the players. Either (1) neither player pays G, or (2) player i pays G. In the case of (2), i will offer G no more than necessary, which is the minimum increment above what G would get by accepting j's offer, D_j. Player i will only be willing to pay this amount if it is less than the amount that she gains by changing the game from $\Gamma(D_j)$ to $\Gamma(D_j)$, that is, $\delta_i(D_i,D_j|s_{-\mathrm{G}})$ This difference is maximized by choosing D_j to minimize i's payoff in $\Gamma(D_j)$ and choosing D_i to maximize i's payoff in $\Gamma(D_i)$. Given $s_{-\mathrm{G}}$, these arguments are $\underline{D}_j$ and $\hat{D}_i$, respectively. So we have that the maximum i will pay in an SPE of Γ_{G} given $s_{-\mathrm{G}}$ is $\delta_i\left(\hat{D}_i, \underline{D}_j|s_{-\mathrm{G}}\right)$.

Maximizing i's payoff over all functions $s_{-\mathrm{G}}$ and contracts D_i we get the maxagg $\mathcal{M}_i$. Minimizing i's payoff over all functions $s_{-\mathrm{G}}$ we get $\min_{s_{-\mathrm{G}}} \underline{D}_j(s_{-\mathrm{G}})$ where the minimizer,

$$s^i_{-\mathrm{G}} = \arg \min_{s_{-\mathrm{G}}} s_{\mathrm{A}}\left(\underline{D}_j(s_{-\mathrm{G}})\right)^{\mathrm{T}} U_i s_{\mathrm{B}}\left(\underline{D}_j(s_{-\mathrm{G}})\right)$$

yields $\underline{D}_j(s^i_{-\mathrm{G}})$. However, we know that since $s^i_{-\mathrm{G}}$ is part of an SPE, that $s^i_{-G}\left(\underline{D}_j\right)$ is a NE of $\Gamma\left(\underline{D}_j\right)$. Therefore, $s^i_i\left(\underline{D}_j\right) \in R^{\Gamma}_i\left(s^i_j\left(\underline{D}_j\right)\right)$. In other words, the only requirement in constructing $s^i_{-\mathrm{G}}$ is that i is always playing a best response. This is because D_j can be such that $s^i_j\left(\underline{D}_j\right)$ is a best response to i. Therefore,

$$s^i_{\mathrm{A}}\left(\underline{D}_j\right)^{\mathrm{T}} U_i s^i_{\mathrm{B}}\left(\underline{D}_j\right) = \min_{\sigma_i,\sigma_j} \left\{\sigma_{\mathrm{A}}^{\mathrm{T}} U_i \sigma_{\mathrm{B}} : \sigma_i \in R^{\Gamma}_i(\sigma_j)\right\}$$

Putting this together with i's maxagg and choosing i we get the result. □

Proposition 5 gives an upper bound on the amount that the monopolist game miner can extract from a game between A and B. This is achieved when player i chooses the contract that minimizes j's payoff given the strategies for the resulting post-contract game, $\underline{D}_i$. At the same time, the amount offered to the game miner by the contract $\underline{D}_i$ is equal to the maximum amount that j is willing to pay to change the game from $\Gamma(\underline{D}_i)$ to $\Gamma(\hat{D}_j)$. The amount paid to the game miner in this situation is bounded by the players' payoff functions. So a monopolist game miner cannot, in this situation, extract arbitrary profits.

The SPE concept here allows for some behavior that is unreasonable from a trembling hand perspective. For example, in order for G to achieve her maximum payment, i must choose contract $\underline{D}_i$. However, i might actually *prefer* the outcome under $\hat{D}_j$ to the outcome under $\underline{D}_i$. That is, to support the equilibrium in which j offers her maximum willingness to pay, i offers quite a bit of money to G for a deal she wants not to take effect. i's offer is only a best response to j's slightly greater offer because G will choose j's contract, so that this unreasonable offer by i, $\underline{D}_i$, will never be accepted by G. But, if G trembled and chose $\underline{D}_i$, the outcome could be disastrous for i. In short, for some Γ_G, there exist SPE in which G achieves her maximum payoff only if one of the players acts in a manner that seems unreasonable.

Instead of considering all possible equilibria, perhaps a more reasonable set of outcomes is one in which players only offer contracts $\hat{D}_i$ (i = A,B) that maximize the aggregate payoff function, $m_i(D_i|s_{-G})$. It is reasonable to restrict the analysis to this set of contracts because at least one aggregate payoff maximizer, $\hat{D}_i$, is a best response to every D_j and s_{-G}. Note that in some games, this restriction on players' choice of contracts can reduce G's maximum SPE payoff.

Fig. 1 is a flow diagram that illustrates how the aggregate payoff maximizing contracts translate into the monopolist miner's payoffs. Positive quantities represent movements in the direction of the associated arrow.

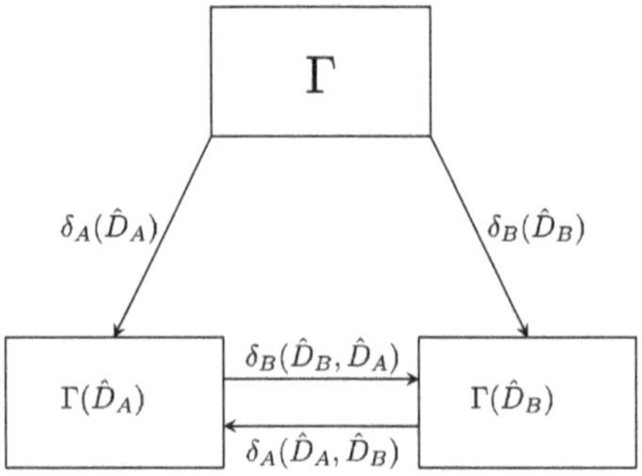

Fig. 1. This Diagram Depicts a Flow between Γ, $\Gamma(\hat{D}_A)$, and $\Gamma(\hat{D}_B)$ based on the Willingness to Pay of Players A and B.

So if $\delta_B(\hat{D}_B) > 0$, we know that B is willing to pay to change the game from Γ to $\Gamma(\hat{D}_B)$. Hence, Γ will not be the post-contract subgame in an SPE. Next, if $\delta_B(\hat{D}_B, \hat{D}_A) > \delta_A(\hat{D}_A, \hat{D}_B) > 0$, then B is willing to pay more to change the game from $\Gamma(\hat{D}_A)$ to $\Gamma(\hat{D}_B)$ than A is willing to pay to change it from $\Gamma(\hat{D}_B)$ to $\Gamma(\hat{D}_A)$. B will offer G a contract such that G's payment is just greater than A is willing to pay to change the game from $\Gamma(\hat{D}_B)$ to $\Gamma(\hat{D}_A)$.

Another implication of Proposition 5 is that G's payoff can be greater than $\max\{\mathcal{M}_A, \mathcal{M}_B\}$. In other words, the winning contract may pay G more than the maxagg for either player. The following example illustrates how a monopolist miner can make both players worse off than they were without the opportunity to mine. We demonstrate that this is the case even when players are restricted to choosing contracts that maximize aggregate payoff functions.

Example 4. Consider the game Γ:

	x	y	z
x	−1, 2	−1, 3	0, 0
y	−1, −1	0, 0	3, −1
z	−2, −2	−1, −1	2, −1

where A is the row player. The unique NE of Γ is (y,y). Calculating A's aggregate payoff function for $\hat{D}_A$, $\hat{D}_B$, and $\hat{D}_0$ as well as A's willingness to pay, we get:

$$m_A(\hat{D}_A|s_{-G}) = 2, \quad m_A(\hat{D}_B|s_{-G}) = -1, \quad \text{and} \quad m_A(D_0|s_{-G}) = 0$$

$$\Rightarrow \quad \delta_A(\hat{D}_A, \hat{D}_B) = 3 \quad \text{and} \quad \delta_A(\hat{D}_A) = 2$$

By symmetry the quantities for B are the same as the corresponding quantities of A.

The fact that $\delta_i(\hat{D}_i) = 2 > 0$ for i = A,B means that both players are willing to pay to change the game from Γ to $\Gamma(\hat{D}_i)$, so D_0 will not be the outcome. Next, because $\delta_i(\hat{D}_i, \hat{D}_j) = 3 > 0$ for i = A,B, we know that G will get a payoff of $\delta_i(\hat{D}_i, \hat{D}_j) = 3$ in equilibrium. This payoff is greater than $\mathcal{M}_i - m_A(D_0|s_{-G}) = 2$. In other words, if i's contract is accepted, then the contract between i and G pays G more than the increase in aggregate payoffs $\mathcal{M}_i - m_A(D_0|s_{-G}) = 2$. The reason is that i is paying to avoid having $\Gamma(\hat{D}_j)$ become the equilibrium game.

We also observe that $s_A(\hat{D}_i)^T U_i^{D_i} s_B(\hat{D}_i) = -1 < 0 = m_A(D_0|s_{-G})$. This says that i gets less by having the equilibrium contract with G than i would get if neither player had the opportunity to offer contracts. For j, the player that does not win the equilibrium contract, the SPE payoff is also −1. Therefore, the both players are worse off with the opportunity to mine.

G Accepts Both Contracts

We now relax the assumption that G must choose between D_A and D_B. After all, if G is a true monopolist game miner and there are gains to be made by simultaneously contracting with both parties, then G will certainly want to do this.

The strategies in Γ_G must be modified to accommodate this new possibility. First, a strategy S_G for G selects an element of G's choice set $\mathcal{D}_G$ after the history $(D_A,D_B) \in \mathcal{D}^2$. Since G can now choose to accept both contracts if she wishes, the choice set $\mathcal{D}_G$ is now given by:

$$\mathscr{D}_G = \{(D_A, D_B), (D_A, D_0), (D_0, D_B), (D_0, D_0)\}$$

This induces the game $\Gamma(D_i,D_j)$ where D_i ($i=$A,0) is the contract between A and G and D_j ($j=$B,0) is the contract between B and G. Therefore, the game $\Gamma(D_i,D_j)$ is one in which A's preferences are $U_B^{D_i}$ and B's preferences are $U_B^{D_j}$. This means that the stage three strategy profile $s_{-G}=(s_A,s_B)$ is defined on $\mathcal{D}^2$ so that $s_i : (\mathscr{D})^2 \mapsto \Delta_i$ ($i=$A,B). In other words, players select a strategy for every possible post-contract subgame of the form $\Gamma(D_i,D_j)$.

We refer to the stage three game that is played in equilibrium of Γ_G as the *equilibrium game*. If G accepts only D_A, then the equilibrium game is $\Gamma(D_A)$. If G accepts D_A and D_B, then the equilibrium game is $\Gamma(D_A,D_B)$ and so on. The game $\Gamma(D_A,D_B)$ was not possible when G could only accept a single contract. However, when G can accept both contracts it is possible.

This raises the issue of determining how A chooses D_A given that B is choosing D_B. Given a function $s_{-G}=(s_A,s_B)$, B's contract D_B and G's decision S_G, A chooses a contract in order to maximize his payoff.

$$\max_{D_A} \; s_A\left(D_{S_G(\mathscr{D}_G)}\right)^T U_A^{D_A} s_B\left(D_{S_G(\mathscr{D}_G)}\right) \tag{4}$$

This gives rise to a best response correspondence for A.

Definition 4. Player A's best contract response correspondence given s_{-G} is a set valued function $\Phi_A(\cdot|s_{-G}) : \mathscr{D} \mapsto 2^{\mathscr{D}}$ that gives all of the contracts D_A that maximize Eq. (4) when B makes contract D_B given s_{-G}.

By requiring that s_{-G} selects a NE of every post-contract subgame, we guarantee that $s_A\left(D_{S_G(\mathscr{D}_G)}\right)$ is a best response to $s_A\left(D_{S_G(\mathscr{D}_G)}\right)$ and vice versa. When s_{-G} meets this requirement, the best contract response correspondence amounts to a best response correspondence for the extensive form game. The following result uses the concept of a best contract response correspondence to categorize a monopolist game miner's payoffs when able to accept both contracts.

Proposition 6. The monopolist game miner's equilibrium payoffs under the restriction that G can only accept one contract are always as good and sometimes better than her payoffs without that restriction.

Proof. Suppose $\delta_A\left(\hat{D}_A\right) \geq 0$ and/or $\delta_B\left(\hat{D}_B\right) \geq 0$ and $\delta_A\left(\hat{D}_A, \hat{D}_B\right) \geq \delta_B\left(\hat{D}_B, \hat{D}_A\right) \geq 0$, then with the restriction, G gets $\delta_B\left(\hat{D}_B, \hat{D}_A\right)$. However, without the restriction, there is the possibility that for some D_A and D_B, A and B both prefer $\Gamma(D_A, D_B)$ to $\Gamma\left(\hat{D}_A\right)$ and $\Gamma\left(\hat{D}_B\right)$. If $D_A \in \Phi_A(D_B)$ and $D_B \in \Phi_B(D_A)$ given s_{-G}, then this will be an equilibrium. When the equilibrium game is $\Gamma(D_A, D_B)$, neither player is paying for exclusivity, so G's payoff is zero instead of $\delta_B(D_B, D_A)$.

Further, the threat of an outcome $\Gamma(D_A, D_B)$ can never induce i to pay more than $\delta_j\left(\hat{D}_j, \hat{D}_i\right)$ for exclusivity. This is because $\delta_j\left(\hat{D}_j, \hat{D}_i\right)$ is the value for j of going from $\Gamma\left(\hat{D}_A\right)$ to $\Gamma\left(\hat{D}_B\right)$. Given that i pays for exclusivity, there is no payment that j can make to change the game from $\Gamma\left(\hat{D}_A\right)$ to $\Gamma(D_A, D_B)$ because i's contract is contingent on exclusivity. □

Proposition 6 says that a monopolist game miner cannot be made worse off by restricting herself to accept a single contract. The reason is that when G does not restrict herself, then she does not give up D_A in order to accept D_B. Therefore, if G accepts D_B, then her best response is to accept any contract D_A for which her payoff under $\Gamma(D_A, D_B)$ is at least her payoff under $\Gamma(D_B)$. Knowing this, A will choose D_A such that G's payoff under $\Gamma(D_A, D_B)$ is exactly what it is under $\Gamma(D_B)$. The same holds for B. Therefore, G is made worse-off by the ability to make contracts with both players. Put differently, the threat of an equilibrium game $\Gamma(D_A, D_B)$ never induces the players to pay more, and it is sometimes better for the players.

The above suggests that the one-contract restriction might be the result of payoff maximizing behavior. That is, G's payoff in equilibrium of the one-contract game might be equivalent to a payment not to contract with the other player. Hence, the restricted game is equivalent to a game in which A and B submit two-element stage-one offers, (D_i,z_i), where D_i is the matrix of strategy-contingent transfers and z_i is a payment not to make a contract with j. If $z_i=0$, then i places no exclusivity restriction on G's acceptance of D_i. Therefore, G's payoff from accepting A's contract is $z_A + s_A(D_A,D_0)^T D_A s_B(D_A,D_0)$. If $z_A=z_B=0$ then G's payoff from accepting both contracts is $s_A(D_A,D_B)^T(D_A+D_B)s_B(D_A+D_B)$.

Sequential Contracts

We now examine the role of timing on game mining outcomes. The game is exactly as previously described, except that A first selects a contract to be observed by B before B selects a contract. In this setting we find that A may have a first-mover advantage and also that contracts are not equivalent to the pre-commitments of Renou (2009). Both points are demonstrated in Example 5.

Example 5. Consider the game Γ where A is the row player. The unique NE of this

	x	y	z
x	2,5	0,0	5,4
y	1,3	1,2	2,0
z	0,3	0,1	2,0

game is(x,x). Note that x is a strictly dominant strategy for B. By Proposition 3, there is no contract D_A such that A gets a better payoff in a NE of $\Gamma(D_A)$ than in a NE of Γ. Despite this fact, there is a contract D_A such that

$$s_A\left(D_A, D_B^*\right)^T U_A^{D_A} s_B\left(D_A, D_B^*\right) > s_A(D_0)^T U_A s_B(D_0)$$

where $D_B^* \in \Phi_B(D_A|s_{-G})$ is a best contract response to D_A given s_{-G}. In other words, there is a contract D_A such that when B chooses his best contract response to D_A, A gets a higher payoff in $\Gamma\left(D_A, D_B^*\right)$ than in any NE of Γ. To illustrate, suppose A signs a contract with G to pay G2 whenever the outcome is (x,x), then the unique NE of $\Gamma(D_A)$ is (y,x). The post-contract game, $\Gamma(D_A)$, is given by:

	x	y	z
x	0,5	0,0	5,4
y	1,3	1,2	2,0
z	0,3	0,1	2,0

Then B's best contract response is a contract D_B^* that promises to pay G4 if the outcome is (y,x) and 3 if the outcome is (y,y). This will make (x,z) the unique NE of $\Gamma\left(D_A, D_B^*\right)$.

	x	y	z
x	0,5	0,0	5,4
y	1,−1	1, −1	2,0
z	0,3	0,1	2,0

The final outcome gives A his highest payoff from U_A, and it gives B his maxagg. G gets zero in the equilibrium of Γ, $\Gamma(D_A$, and $\Gamma\left(D_A, D_B^*\right)$. Therefore, this outcome is the unique SPE of Γ_G.

Note that if B was the first to select a contract, then B would choose D_0 to which 's best contract response is D_0. Both players would be willing to pay for the right to move first. *A* would pay the difference between his payoff in $\Gamma\left(D_A, D_B^*(D_A|s_{-G}\right)$ and Γ, which is 5. However B would only be willing to pay the difference between his payoff in Γ and $\Gamma\left(D_A, D_B^*\right)$, which is just 1.

This example draws a sharp distinction between game mining and pre-commitments to play or not play certain strategies. Suppose A instead selected a contract that made x a never-best-response. Then B's best response is D_0, and the outcome is (y,x), which is worse for A. A does not want to commit to not playing x because (x,y) is the ultimate goal. He rather wants to commit to (x,x) not being the outcome, so that B will commit to (y,x) and (y,y) not being the outcome.

Exploiting contract timing is yet another way that game miners can extract profits from players even when players are making the offers. Since A has a first-mover advantage, and B has a second-mover disadvantage, both are willing to pay to move first. Suppose A recognizes this advantage before B and approaches G with his desired contract D_A. G could potentially put A on hold and notify B to start a bidding war over the first-mover advantage. The first-mover advantage is worth more to A than it is to B, five versus one, so A would end up paying B's maximum willingness to pay for the first-mover advantage. In contrast to the discussion above where players make simultaneous offers and G accepts one contract, this type of bidding war can happen even though G is free to accept both the contracts.

G Makes Offers

Until this point we have assumed a particular bargaining structure in which A and B make take-it-or-leave-it offers to G. This implies that G's only bargaining power is in rejecting contracts that result in negative payoffs. Suppose now that we change the game so that G makes publicly observable offers to A and B. Then A and B simultaneously accept or reject the offers G has made. So A and B will now accept any contract that does not make them worse off, given the other's choice. This clearly places more power in the hands of G.

To accommodate the new structure of the game, we alter the definition of strategies. Now G's stage one strategy is $s_G \in \mathcal{D}^2$. A and B have binary stage two strategies $s_i^2 : \mathscr{D}^2 \mapsto \{\text{accept}, \text{reject}\}$ and stage-three strategies $s_i^3 : \mathscr{D}^2 \mapsto \Delta_i$ $(i = \text{A,B})$, which we sometimes shorten to be s^2_{-G} and s^3_{-G}. So G selects a contract for each player, s_G. Then each player chooses to accept or reject the contract they are offered, s^2_{-G}. Finally, the players play the post-contract game according to s^3_{-G}.

We want to characterize G's payoffs in an SPE. To do so, consider the following devious plan where G can sometimes create a high-order prisoner's dilemma between A and B. This is illustrated in the example below.

Example 6. Consider the game Γ where A is the row player and both players have a strictly dominant strategy to choose z.

	x	y	z
x	5, 5	1, 5	1, 6
y	5, 1	1, 1	2, 2
z	6, 1	2, 2	3, 3

The unique NE is (z, z), and both players get a payoff of 3. Then if G offers the following contract to A

$$D_A = \begin{bmatrix} 2.99 & -2 & 0 \\ 3 & -1 & -3 \\ 4 & 0.5 & 0 \end{bmatrix}$$

the unique NE of $\Gamma(D_A)$ is (y,z). A's payoff in $\Gamma(D_A)$ is $2-(-3)=5$, so A would accept D_A, getting 5 rather than 3. B's payoff in $\Gamma(D_A)$ is 2. If G offers $D_B = D_A^T$ to B, then the equilibrium of $\Gamma(D_A,D_B)$ is (x,x). The payoff to B is $5 - 2.99 = 2.01$. Therefore, B would accept D_B given that A accepts D_A because he will get 2.01 rather than 2. By the symmetry of Γ, D_A, and D_B, we know that each player i prefers to accept D_i regardless of whether $j \neq i$ accepts or rejects his offered contract.

This is very similar to a prisoner's dilemma game because each player $i = A,B$ has an incentive to accept D_i regardless of whether $j \neq i$ accepts D_j. This moves the players from Γ, where the unique NE gives them (3,3), to $\Gamma(D_A,D_B)$, where the only NE gives them (2.01,2.01). By playing A against B the game miner gets $2(5-2.01)=5.98$.[4] The situation can be visualized alternatively as the following PD game where A is the row player and B is the column player, and the payoffs are given by the unique NE of the resulting post-contract games:

	accept D_B	reject D_B
accept D_A	2.01, 2.01	5, 2
reject D_A	2, 5	3, 3

Note that G once again moves the game from an inefficient equilibrium to an efficient one. However, as a profit maximizer, the game miner captures the efficiency gains.

The example above shows that G can potentially do better for herself by selecting contracts that both A and B will accept than by contracting with one player exclusively. The intuition for why this is possible is that G relies on the fact that $\Gamma(D_A)$ and $\Gamma(D_B)$ will never obtain in equilibrium. Therefore, G is free to offer contracts D_A and D_B such that she loses money in the unique NE of $\Gamma(D_A)$ and $\Gamma(D_B)$. This allows her the flexibility to make sure the NE of $\Gamma(D_A,D_B)$ is in her favor. Note that this result does not rely on the fact that both players have strictly dominant strategies. It is simple to construct examples for games in which only one player has a dominant strategy or neither player has a dominant strategy.

The following proposition provides an upper bound on the game miner's payoff when she extracts profits according to this scheme.

Proposition 7. The maximum that a monopolist game miner can profit by offering contracts (D_A,D_B) such that A and B have weakly dominant strategies to accept is

$$\max_{x_A, x_B} x_A^T(U_A + U_B)x_B - \min_{x'_A, x'_B} \{x'^T_A U_B x'_B : x'_B \in R^\Gamma_B(x'_A)\}$$
$$- \min_{x''_A, x''_B} \{x''^T_A U_B x''_B : x''_A \in R^\Gamma_A(x''_B)\}$$

Proof. The first term is the maximum amount that A and B can earn in any outcome of Γ. The second term is the minimum amount that G can force B to get by designing D_A such that x'_A is a best response to x'_B. This is because G is constrained so that x'_B must lie on B's best response correspondence for Γ. The third term is the equivalent of the second term for A rather than B.

Suppose G earns more than this maximum, then

$$s_A(D_A, D_B)^T(D_A + D_B)s_B(D_A, D_B) > \max_{x_A, x_B} x_A^T(U_A + U_B)x_B \ldots \tag{5}$$

$$- \min_{x'_A, x'_B} \{x'^T_A U_B x'_B : x'_B \in R^\Gamma_B(x'_A)\} - \min_{x''_A, x''_B} \{x''^T_A U_B x''_B : x''_A \in R^\Gamma_A(x''_B)\}$$

but because A and B each have a weakly dominant strategy to accept, we know that

$$s_A(D_A, D_B)^T(U_A - D_A)s_B(D_A, D_B) \geq s_A(D_0, D_B)^T U_A s_B(D_0, D_B)$$

and

$$s_A(D_A, D_B)^T(U_B - D_B)s_B(D_A, D_B) \geq s_A(D_A, D_0)^T U_B s_B(D_A, D_0)$$

Together, these inequalities imply

$$s_A(D_A, D_B)^T(D_A + D_B)s_B(D_A, D_B) \leq s_A(D_A, D_B)^T(U_A + U_B)s_B(D_A, D_B)\ldots$$

$$- s_A(D_0, D_B)^T U_A s_B(D_0, D_B) - s_A(D_A, D_0)^T U_B s_B(D_A, D_0)$$

The left-hand side is G's profit, and the maximum of the right-hand side is given by the right-hand side of inequality 5. Therefore, we have a contradiction. □

This result is important because it says that the game miner cannot make an arbitrary profit from the players by giving each a dominant strategy to accept her offer. Therefore, the game miner's profit and any efficiency loss for the players are always limited.

DISCUSSION

As mentioned in the introduction, the game mining analysis opens up several new research areas. One natural extension is to consider game mining situations in which there are more than two players or even with multiple game miners. With multiple players simultaneously choosing contracts, the blocking and exclusivity concerns we address above are likely to become much more complicated. An open question is how the market structure affects the game miner's opportunity to profit.[5]

Yet another research question is whether replacing the structured bargaining between players and game miners with unstructured bargaining will change the profitability of game mining. One might also consider the reverse situation in which the stage game Γ is a game of unstructured bargaining between A and B, but the negotiations between players and game miners follow structured bargaining. Here, we would have that players sign contracts through structured bargaining in an attempt to gain an advantage in the unstructured bargaining that follows. The question is how would players design contracts to distort their utility possibilities set in such a way that benefits them in the ensuing unstructured bargaining. An interesting technical issue arises in deciding whether to allow players to sign contracts that lead to utility possibility sets that are non-convex. If so, then a solution concept other than the Nash Bargaining Solution is needed (see e.g. Kalai & Smorodinsky, 1975; Nash, 1950).

All of this raises a crucial question: Why are not real game mining firms wreaking havoc on real markets? Game mining appears to be very possible according to basic game theory, so if it is not generally possible in the real world, what assumptions are being violated?

There are many potential answers to this question. One tempting explanation is that the payoff structure of most real world games makes them unable to be mined. This seems a strange assertion because, as shown, even games in which both players have strictly dominant strategies can be mined for profit depending on the market structure. Other potential answers are that the calculations are too difficult in practice, that the time frame in real world games is too short, that game mining could be considered illegal, that imperfect information limits game mining opportunity, or that some kind of strategic uncertainty makes game mining impractical. These explanations should be explored in future work because they might shed light on the way game theory applies to real world strategic settings.

There are other questions to explore. For instance, does game mining imply that certain games should never exist because the minute they appear they will be mined into an alternate game? In some sense this gives rise to a meta-game whereby a player that finds himself involved in an easily mineable game might assume that the game will be mined and therefore conclude that he is actually playing a different game. Or, in a game with multiple equilibria, one equilibrium might make the game susceptible to mining by an outside party that ultimately makes both parties worse off (like what happens when a game miner makes offers that give players strictly dominant strategies to accept). Therefore, that susceptible equilibrium might become less likely than an equilibrium that is more robust. In this way game mining introduces an equilibrium refinement: choose the equilibrium that makes game mining least profitable.

These questions and others are not only interesting for their ability to shed light on game mining concepts, but also generally for their ability to shed light on the non-cooperative theory.

NOTES

1. It might be objected that the threat of the game miner to pay A an amount after the game has ended is not credible, since after the game has ended, a payment by the game miner to A will not change the game's outcome. It is simple to circumvent this, for example, by introducing a fourth external player, and have the game miner enter a binding contract with that fourth player under which the fourth player gets 3 now, and agrees to pay 2 to A if A does not pay the game miner before the game with C and also makes moves *T* in that game. (In essence, the game miner subcontracts out their threat-enforcement to the fourth player.)

2. Note that A cannot simply say to C before they play with C that A would refuse to take any funds at the end of the game from the game miner. This claim by A is not renegotiation-proof, and therefore not credible.

3. Later we introduce the possibility that A and B both make contracts with G in a sequential structure. Here, there are contracts such that A and G both benefit in $\Gamma(D_A, D_B)$ even though B has a strictly dominant strategy.

4. Of course, the game miner could reduce the contract payoffs for $D_i(w,w)$ $(i = A,B)$ from 2.01 to $2+\varepsilon$, where $\varepsilon > 0$ is an arbitrarily small number, and the game miner's payoff would strictly increase without changing any of the equilibria. The number 2.01 is used here for simplicity.

5. An earlier version of this paper analyzes perfect competition and duopoly competition among game miners.

REFERENCES

Coase, R. (1960). The problem of social cost. *Journal of Law and Economics*, *3*(1), 144.

Fershtman, C. (1985). Managerial incentives as a strategic variable in a duopolistic environment. *International Journal of Industrial Organization*, *3*, 245–253.

Fershtman, C., & Judd, K. L. (1987). Equilibrium incentives in oligopoly. *American Economic Review*, *77*(5), 927–940.

Fershtman, C., Judd, K. L., & Kalai, E. (1991). Observable contracts: Strategic delegation and cooperation. *International Economic Review*, *32*(3), 551–559.

Garcia-Jurado, I., & Gonzalez-Diaz, J. (2006). The role of commitment in repeated games. *Optimization*, *55*, 1–13.

Gerratana, E.. & Koçkesen, L. (2012). Strategic effects of renegotiation-proof contracts. *The B.E. Journal of Theoretical Economics*, 12(1), 1–49.

Hamilton, J. H., & Slutsky, S. M. (1990). Endogeneous timing in duopoly games: Stackelberg or Cournot equilibria. *Games and Economic Behavior*, *2*, 29–46.

Holmstrom, B. (1982). Moral hazard in teams. *The Bell Journal of Economics*, *13*(2), 324–340.

Jackson, M. O., & Wilkie, S. (2005). Endogenous games and mechanisms: Side payments among players. *The Review of Economic Studies*, *72*(2), 543–566.

Kalai, A., Kalai, E., Lehrer, E., & Samet, D. (2010). A commitment folk theorem. *Games and Economic Behavior*, *69*, 127–137.

Kalai, E., & Smorodinsky, M. (1975). Other solutions to Nash's bargaining problem. *Econometrica*, *43*(3), 513–518.

Katz, M. L. (1991). Game-playing agents: Unobservable contracts as precommitments. *The RAND Journal of Economics*, *22*(3), 307–328.

Nash, J. (1950). The bargaining problem. *Econometrica*, *18*(2), 155–162.

Renou, L. (2009). Commitment games. *Games and Economic Behavior*, *66*(1), 488–505.

Romano, R., & Yildirim, H. (2005). On the endogeneity of Cournot–Nash and Stackelberg equilibria: Games of accumulation. *Journal of Economic Theory*, *120*, 73–107.

Schelling, T. C. (1956). An essay on bargaining. *American Economic Review*, *46*, 281–306.

Sklivas, S. (1987). The strategic choice of management incentives. *The Rand Journal of Economics*, *18*, 452–458.

Sobel, J. (1981). Distortion of utilities and the bargaining problem. *Econometrica*, *49*, 597–617.

van Damme, V., & Hurkens, S. (1996). Endogenous Stackelberg leadership. *Games and Economic Behavior*, *28*(1), 105–129.

Vickers, J. (1985). Delegation and the theory of the firm. *Economic Journal*, *95*(suppl.), 138–147.

Wolpert, D., & Jamison, J. (2011). The strategic choice of preferences: The persona model. *Berkeley Electronic Journal of Theoretical Economics*, *11*(1), 1–37.

Wolpert, D. H., & Jamison, J. (2012). Schelling formalized: Strategic choices of non-rational behavior. In *Evolution and rationality: Decisions, cooperation, and strategic behavior*. Cambridge: Cambridge University Press.

A NEW ALGORITHMIC APPROACH TO ENTANGLED POLITICAL ECONOMY: INSIGHTS FROM THE SIMPLEST MODELS OF COMPLEXITY

Philip Z. Maymin

ABSTRACT

Economic models based on simple rules can result in complex and unpredictable deterministic dynamics with emergent features similar to those of actual economies. I present several such models ranging from cellular automaton and register machines to quantum computation. The additional benefit of such models is displayed by extending them to model political entanglement to determine the impact of allowing majority redistributive voting. In general, the insights obtained from simulating the computations of simple rules can serve as an additional way to study economics, complementing equilibrium, literary, experimental, and empirical approaches. I culminate by presenting a minimal model of economic complexity that generates complex economic growth and diminishing poverty without any parameter fitting, and which, when modified to

Entangled Political Economy
Advances in Austrian Economics, Volume 18, 213–236

ISSN: 1529-2134/doi:10.1108/S1529-213420140000018010

incorporate political entanglement, generates volatile stagnation and greater poverty.

Keywords: Algorithms; economy; complexity

JEL classifications: C62; C63; D58; E17; G00

INTRODUCTION

Even the simplest economies display universal concepts such as trade, specialization, currencies, consumption, production, and resource allocation. These concepts seem natural and are often taken as given, with firms assumed to take on the role of production and consumers the role of consumption, or particular types of market-making mechanisms to set equilibrium prices, or a specific algorithm for individual decision-making. But to explore the emergence of such concepts requires modeling at a more fundamental level to see which ones arise and under what conditions, and which ultimately need to be assumed.

A similar problem arises in finance. Financial complexity comes in many forms, from conventional noise and random events like bankruptcies to bubbles, crashes, and systemic risks. As in economics, most financial models take this rich randomness and complexity as given, and explore conditional questions such as valuation or hedging in the presence of the assumed risk.

As two exceptions, agent-based models and deterministic chaotic models are able to generate complexity from within. However, agent-based models tend to also imbue significant structure onto the agents and their method of interaction while deterministic chaotic models tend to have many free parameters and no natural relation to the behavior of investors.

Fortunately, in the case of financial complexity, a simple minimal model does exist (Maymin, 2011a). It requires neither multiple agents nor multiple assets, and is intimately related to the behavior of investors. With only a single representative investor trading a single-market asset, and making his decisions by looking over a few days of recent price changes, only one unique trading rule is able to generate financial complexity, and the character of the complexity is similar for various lookback windows. This is the unique minimal model of financial complexity.

Even more surprising, this minimal model seems to generate not merely random noise, but all of the various troubling features we find in real markets: fat tails, severe crashes, and rich autocorrelations. Extending it to allow for multiple agents, and therefore trading volume, seems to result in similarly realistic results for liquidity and volume and their relationships with the price movements (Maymin, 2013).

The minimal model of financial complexity is a simple algorithmic model from which real-world phenomenon emerge. Furthermore, the minimal model has no free parameters that can be tweaked, making the real-world match all the more serendipitous.

A similar approach can be used to model the broader economy. This paper presents a roadmap of several novel possibilities along this vein, ranging from the use of cellular automata and register machines to interpretations based on quantum computation. The algorithmic models are then extended to allow the simple agents to vote to change either the rules driving their evolution or to enact redistributions. The paper culminates with a minimal model of economic complexity that exhibits a complex growth path, rising income inequality, and diminishing poverty even for as few as five agents in the economy.

The algorithmic simulation approach has four advantages relative to equilibrium modeling.

First, the results are in general computationally impossible to know ahead of time and can only be revealed through simulation; cf. the Principle of Computational Irreducibility of Wolfram, 2002 or the theme of Chaitin, Doria, and da Costa (2011).

Second, the proper approach to algorithmic simulation modeling involves combining a process of constantly simplifying to find the smallest possible template of rules, and a comprehensive search among all possible rules within that type, followed by an exploration of the simulated results, rather than choosing rules and dynamics ahead of time based on desired results.

Third, policy and other interventions or regimes can be specifically tested and evolved, and their various dynamics and results compared directly, beyond merely the marginal changes at a purported optimum of equilibrium-based approaches. Specifically, we can explore the entangled political economy sketched by Wagner (2006) and Wagner (2007) and detailed in Smith, Wagner, and Yandle (2011). The insights of entangled political economy are that the outputs of the economy of course depend on the political environment, but also that the political environment depends on the economy, and thus analyzing both together, critically including their interactions, could yield more and deeper insight than analyzing either one on its own. The approach taken here aims to show

how they can be productively analyzed together in cohesive algorithmic frameworks.

Fourth, this approach offers the elusive intermediate step of modeling promoted by Mirowski (2004) that does not require a "general architecture of the mind."

COMPLEXITY IN ECONOMICS

There are various definitions of complexity and emergence. In this paper, we will treat these terms loosely and intuitively rather than strictly and formally. We will recognize complexity visually, and we will take emergence to mean outcomes that cannot be efficiently solved analytically ahead of time.

Koppl (2009) and Rosser (2012) discuss the long relationship that Austrian economics has had with notions of complexity. Individual behavior is neither purely rational nor purely psychological but reflects computational tradeoffs. Simon (1997) calls this "boundedly rational" behavior. Gigerenzer, Todd, and ABC Research Group (2012) dubs such behavior "ecological rationality" to reflect the fact that particular heuristics are helpful in particular circumstances, and are neither universally good nor universally bad. Maymin (2011b) shows that computational complexity is essentially identical to financial complexity by proving that markets are efficient if and only if $P = NP$.

Rosser (2010) notes that complexity and emergence are not precisely defined terms. Rosser then provides a useful taxonomy of complexity definitions ranging from "small tent" complexity involving local interactions of heterogeneous agents, to "broad tent" or dynamic complexity generalizing complexity to non-linear dynamics, to metacomplexity acknowledging the myriad possible definitions of complexity.

Holt, Rosser, and Colander (2011) point out that the new complexity era in economics embraces such complexity as part of economic reality, and they predict that models based on a priori assumptions and solvable equations will be replaced by simple models that build up from basic experimental and empirical data.

For our purposes, we can rely on the intuition of Wolfram (2002) that our mind's pattern-matching ability has evolved to be able to recognize complexity when we see it, combined with his Principle of Computational Equivalence which states that any system that is complex enough beyond some low hurdle has maximal complexity. In other words, any complexity tends to be both easy to spot and representative of some kind of universal complexity.

Similarly, we use the term emergence to mean that the features observed in the results are not predictable from the simple rules used to evolve the system without effectively simulating it, conforming to Wolfram's Principle of Computational Irreducibility.

VOTING CELLULAR AUTOMATA

A cellular automaton is a localized, decentralized model of parallel computation where each cell evolves following a static rule applied to its and its neighbors' current values.

The simplest useful example is a 1-dimensional, 2-color, 3-neighbor cellular automaton that evolves a possibly infinite tape of black and white cells by evaluating each cell separately according to a rule that depends on the current value of the given cell and its two immediate neighbors.

Wolfram (2002) provides a convenient numbering scheme for these 256 possibilities by ordering them in the following way. Any rule is defined by what the new value of the middle cell will be, based on what that cell, and its neighbors on either side, were previously. Those three cells, the middle cell and its two neighbors, could have had one of eight possible starting configurations: they could have all been white, all black, or any combination in between. There are eight total possible starting configurations. Expressing them in 1s for black and 0s for white, they can be written as these eight possibilities: 111, 110, 101, 100, 011, 010, 001, and 000.

How many different rules can there be? Each of the eight initial conditions could be mapped either to white (0) or to black (1); thus there are $2^8 = 256$ possible elementary rules, representing the number of ways of mapping each of the eight possible current conditions into one of two possible colors. For example, the rule that keeps the middle cell the same as it was looks like this: $111 \to 1$, $110 \to 1$, $101 \to 0$, $100 \to 0$, $011 \to 1$, $010 \to 1$, $001 \to 0$, and $000 \to 0$. We can assign a decimal number to each rule by interpreting the sequence of white and black cells they map to as a number written in binary. In the example of the rule that keeps the middle cell the same, we interpret the binary number 11001100 in base 10; thus, this is rule 204.

Of the 256 possible elementary cellular automaton rules, 88 are inequivalent; the remainder are mirror images or color-switched (or both) versions of those 88 distinct rules.

Precious few of these elementary cellular automaton rules generate complexity. Fig. 1 shows 100 time steps starting from one black square surrounded by 25 white neighbors on each side for the 88 inequivalent elementary automata with the size of the graph approximately proportional to the resulting complexity as proxied by the length of the compressed string representing the evolution. Wolfram (2002) has shown that rule 110 is capable of universal computation. Rule 110 is: 111→0, 110→1, 101→1, 100→0, 011→1, 010→1, 001→1, and 000→0. We know this because we can convert the decimal number 110 into binary: 01101110.

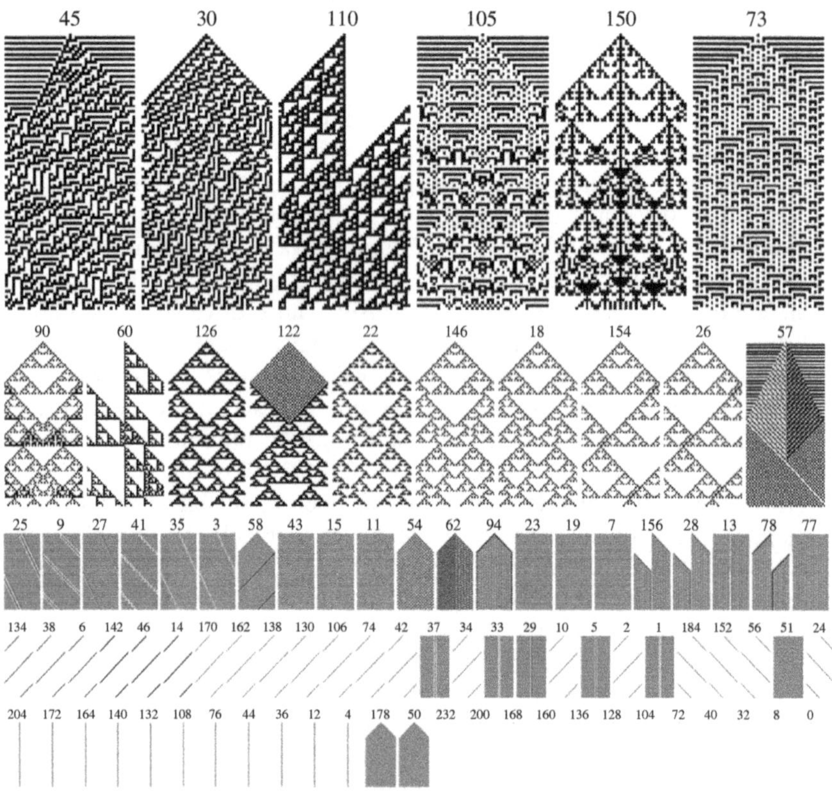

Fig. 1. The 88 Fundamentally Inequivalent Elementary Cellular Automata Evolved for 100 Steps from an Initial Single Central Black Cell Surrounded by 25 White Neighbors on Each Side.

If we interpret the cells as individual production and consumption decisions, with individuals deciding whether or not to produce or consume following some rule based on what they and their neighbors did in the previous period, and starting with only a single black cell, then in only a handful of the possible economies is complexity generated. For maximally complex rules such as rule 110, it is in general impossible to predict any single individual's future behavior without effectively simulating the underlying computation. This is what we experience as emergence.

What happens if the individuals are allowed to vote for what rule they would prefer to drive their evolution? If we evaluate at each step in an evolution which of the 88 distinct elementary rules results in a black square for the most number of cells, starting again from a single central black cell, we would end up with a single winner for the first round: rule 23.

Rule 23 is quite simple. It replaces any triplet with zero or one white cells with a white cell, and any triplet with two or all white cells with a black cell. So in our case it turns all the cells black, and then, if allowed to run further, would alternate between white and black each time step.

However, the voters are no fools. After voting themselves all black cells in the first time step, they now re-evaluate their options, and choose some other rule, one that will continue to make black cells for everybody rather than alternating. There are many such rules to choose from, such as rule 232; any rule that evolves a triplet of black cells into a black cell will do.

Thus, when allowed to vote for the underlying rules, cellular automaton find a way to vote themselves into utopia, with zero complexity.

A more reasonable extension of voting would be to allow redistribution, but maintain the underlying evolutionary rule. When the majority of cells are black, the vote changes nothing, but when the majority are white, they can vote to switch the colors of all cells, thereby bringing themselves into the majority as black cells.

Consider an evolution of an elementary cellular automaton that allows a vote to switch colors every k steps, for example, $k=1$ or $k=25$.

Some rules remain absolutely unchanged, regardless of voting, for examples rules 60, 90, and 126. Of the rules that change, three different effects occur: the birth of complexity, the death of complexity, and a different complexity.

The birth of complexity occurs, for example, in rule 106, which without voting produced a simple repeating pattern. With voting, complexity emerges, and indeed the complexity increases for more frequent voting. Note, however, that for some rules such as rule 134, complexity emerges only for some voting frequencies but not for others. Fig. 2 shows this effect.

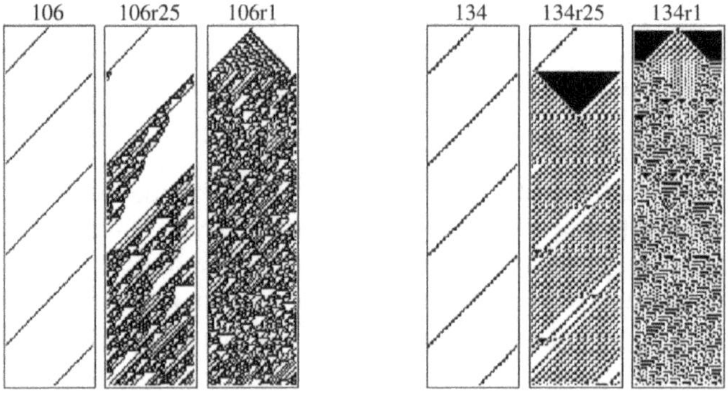

Fig. 2. The Elementary Rules 106 and 134 Cellular Automata Evolved for 200 Steps from an Initial Single Central Black Cell Surrounded by 25 White Neighbors on Each Side, with No Redistributive Voting (Left), or Redistributive Voting Every 25 Time Steps (Middle), or Redistributive Voting Every Time Step (Right).

The death of complexity occurs, for example, in rules 30 and 45, but only for high-frequency voting. Fig. 3 shows these examples.

Different complexity occurs in some rules such as the universal rule 110, which used to be complex without voting, and now continues to be complex even with voting, although the actual evolution differs. Fig. 4 shows these dynamics.

It may seem that no practical conclusion can be drawn from these simulations. Indeed, all of the possible effects of voting do happen in the cellular automaton models of entangled political economy: the complexity either increases, decreases, or stays the same. Nevertheless, there are actually two important conclusions to be drawn.

Note first of all that natural economies without redistributive voting will tend to select toward complexity. Kauffman (1999) discusses how all living systems are typically non-equilibrium systems, Arthur (1994) describes how systems that emerge from the inductive reasoning actually employed by humans tend to both result in and be caused by complexity, and Arthur (1999) writes explicitly that complex systems arise naturally in the economy. Indeed, real-world economies are complex almost by definition. And complexity past a low threshold is essentially maximal complexity due to the Principle of Computational Equivalence. Therefore, real-world economies untainted by redistributive voting are likely to have maximal complexity, and the best that introducing redistribution can do is to not harm it; it can never improve it.

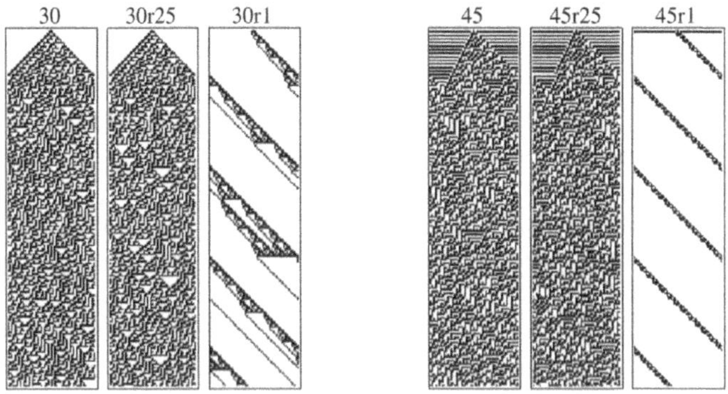

Fig. 3. The Elementary Rules 30 and 45 Cellular Automata Evolved for 200 Steps from an Initial Single Central Black Cell Surrounded by 25 White Neighbors on Each Side, with No Redistributive Voting (Left), or Redistributive Voting Every 25 Time Steps (Middle), or Redistributive Voting Every Time Step (Right).

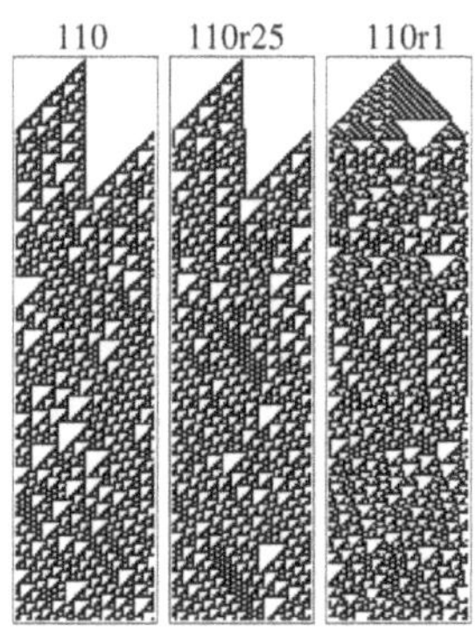

Fig. 4. The Elementary Rule 110 Cellular Automaton Evolved for 200 Steps from an Initial Single Central Black Cell Surrounded by 25 White Neighbors on Each Side, with No Redistributive Voting (Left), or Redistributive Voting Every 25 Time Steps (Middle), or Redistributive Voting Every Time Step (Right).

Secondly, the question of whether redistribution will harm is a fragile one and highly sensitive to the particulars of the redistribution, specifically the frequency of voting. For some frequencies, complexity is relatively undamaged, but for others, the economy collapses totally. And the effect is essentially unpredictable ahead of time due to the Principle of Computational Irreducibility.

In other words, even in these models with simple rules, we can see that complexity is a major feature of the economy, that redistribution can only harm and cannot improve the economy, and that the effects of redistribution are inherently intractable a priori, and therefore represent a purely negative gamble that one can only hope does not inflict its harm immediately.

Of course, the algorithmic approach to examining entangled political economy does not require one to use cellular automata. Because just about any computational paradigm can model any other, the amount of complexity generated is the same regardless of which paradigm is chosen. Thus, we can choose algorithmic representations that are most useful to us in easing interpretation. From cellular automaton we have learned that complexity is prevalent and that redistribution harms in an unpredictable way. In the next sections, we explore the implications of alternative algorithmic formulations.

VOTING REGISTER MACHINES

A register machine is the model of computation most similar to actual computer hardware. A fixed number of registers each store non-negative integers: $0, 1, 2, \ldots$, without bound. The machine is programmed with instructions to, for example, increment or decrement a particular register, move to another line of the instructions, or add the values of two registers and store the result in a given destination register. This language is similar to low-level assembly language on modern computers. In theory, the kinds of possible instructions are determined ahead of time, and one can search the space of all possible languages generated by those instructions to explore the evolution of the system and possibly find complexity.

Wolfram (2002) explores two-register, two-instruction machines, where the two instructions are to increment a given register, or to decrement a given register unless it is already zero in which case jump to a different line in the program. He reports that none of the more than a quarter million possible programs of less than eight instructions exhibit complexity, and that only 126 out of the more than 11 billion possible programs of length eight do.

Here we examine 51-register, one-instruction machines, where the single instruction is a NOR of the current register with either the previous, current, or subsequent register depending on the relative rankings of the three registers, with the result stored in the current register, and the current register also incremented by one each time the current register does a NOR with itself.

A NOR, or not-or, of bits returns true if and only if they are all false, and false if at least one is true. Generalizing to integers, the NOR of two integers is the pairwise NOR of the bits of the two integers in base-two representation with the smaller number padded with zeros to the left.

If each register represents the property allocation of the individual, with each bit in its base-two representation indicating possession, a NOR operation with a neighbor can be interpreted as a kind of combination of trade and innovation, where the current individual takes possession of any goods neither party had before in exchange for giving up any other property he used to own.

Fig. 5 shows both the definition and the evolution of rule 7179 (out of $3^9 = 19{,}683$ possible). Clear complexity emerges.

The nature of rule 7179, and in general of the integer-NOR approach, is such that the registers quickly reduce only to holding either zero, one, or two. Nevertheless, a complex web of trade emerges in the evolution.

To introduce redistribution, we can follow the same approach as before. If redistribution is to occur every k-th round (each round comprises 51 steps to ensure each register has been updated), then when it does occur, we can take the total of all the registers except the current one and distribute them as equally as possible to the left and right. Fig. 6 plots the non-complex results. Once again, we see the impact of redistribution: complexity tends to

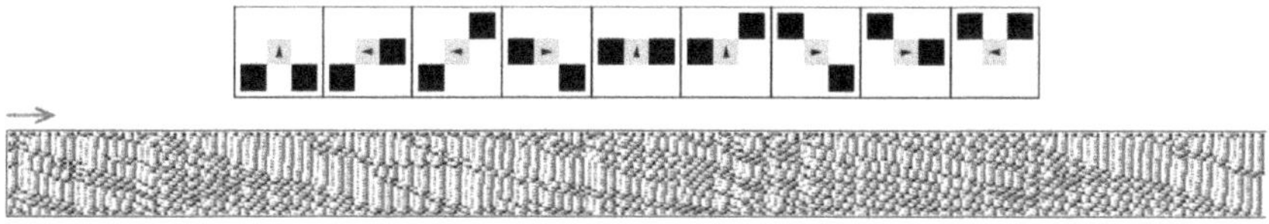

Fig. 5. A register machine comprising 51 registers all initialized to zero, except the middle one initialized to one, and instructions given by rule 7179 of the integer-NOR mapping, is simulated for 20,000 steps. Above are the rule description and the evolution, condensed by omitting all but every 25th step and oriented left-to-right. The rule conditions are depicted by the relative positions of the black squares and the comparison register is depicted by the arrow in the gray box: for example, when all three registers are equal (box 5), the comparison register is the current register, so its value becomes its integer-NOR with itself, incremented by one. When the current register is lower than both of its neighbors (box 9), then the comparison register is the previous register and there is no incrementing.

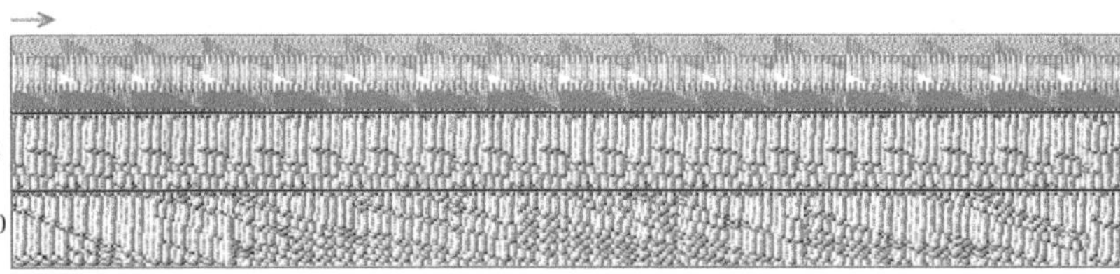

Fig. 6. The Same Register Machine Now Evolves with Redistribution after Every 1, 10, or 100 Evaluation Rounds.

decrease, and it tends to decrease more when redistribution occurs more frequently.

QUANTUM ELECTIONS

Typically models based on simple rules that generate complexity do so deterministically, without any outside source of randomness. There are exceptions, particularly when quantum computation is part of the model, where entangled randomness is critical. An alternative way to think about these models as still being deterministic is to imagine that the subject of the model is not the outcome but the distribution of possible outcomes.

As an example, consider random walks and quantum walks. A random walk of n steps is a probability distribution representing how far from his starting spot a person will be if he essentially tosses a fair coin each step to decide whether to stumble left or right. A quantum walk is the same thing except the outcome of the coin flip is not measured at each step and instead remains entangled with the position. Quantum probabilities or *amplitudes* differ from standard probabilities in that, in addition to their magnitude which can be interpreted as the standard probability, they also have an associated angle or direction. Intuitively, unlike standard probabilities, combinations of quantum probabilities can cancel out or magnify up depending on how the angles line up. Two quantum observations are entangled if measuring one, and collapsing its possibilities, immediately yields perfect information about the other, even though the other one is not itself directly observed and could be an arbitrary distance away. Note that a quantum walk can still ultimately be viewed as a regular probability distribution even though it involves amplitudes and entanglement in its intermediate computation. For a review and formal definitions of quantum walks, see Kempe (2003).

For our purposes, we will use the standard unbiased quantum coin. We are interested in the effect of repeated *measurement*. Measurement or observation in quantum mechanics is usually defined as a collapse of the wave function, meaning the quantum superposition collapses into a single observed variable. However, we are interested in the continuing evolution of the system from all possible values of the observed variable, weighed by their probability. Rather than collapsing each time we measure to a single number, we will instead rely on the following lemma.

Lemma. Intermediate measurement is equivalent to normalizing amplitudes.

Proof. A quantum superposition is a vector of possibilities associated with amplitudes. An amplitude is a vector, the combination of a probability and a direction. It is the associated direction that allows amplitudes, unlike probabilities, to combine like waves and either magnify or cancel out. A collapse occurs on measurement when each possibility is chosen with probability equal to the associated amplitude's squared modulus. On a final measurement, exactly one outcome is observed. The standard approach is that an intermediate measurement is the same as a final measurement, collapsing to a single one of the possibilities. However, this is unnecessary. Imagine the same experiment is run an infinite number of times, so that each outcome occurs exactly with its associated probability during an intermediate measurement, and then a further combination of quantum effects and final measurement occurs along each path. The final histogram will be a weighted average of the distributions resulting from each of the extended paths following the initial intermediate measurements. Thus, we do not actually need to do an infinite number of simulations or rely on any law of large numbers in the hope of achieving a good estimate; instead of a collapse to a single observation, intermediate measurement can be modeled as simply normalizing the amplitudes, meaning the amplitude as a complex number is simply replaced by its absolute value. The same proof extends to any number of intermediate measurements. ■

Fig. 7 shows the difference in probability distributions for different observation frequencies. If the quantum state is observed every step, quantum entanglement has no effect, and the quantum walk is identical to the random walk. Slightly less frequent observation, for example, every fifth or tenth step, results in a tighter terminal distribution, an effect which gradually dissipates until vanishing at every fifteenth step, at which point the distribution is again nearly identical to the random walk. From then on, less

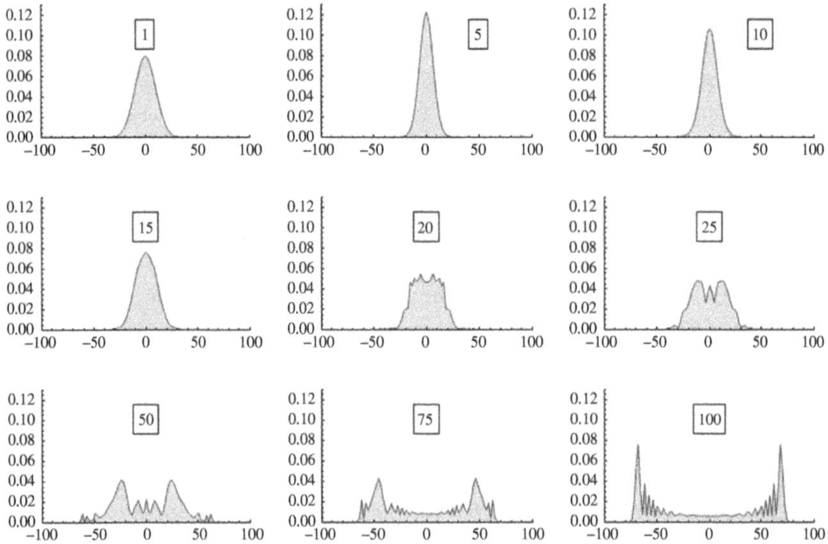

Fig. 7. A Quantum Walk of 100 Steps with the Position Observed Every 1, 5, 10, 15, 20, 25, 50, 75, or 100 Steps.

frequent measuring leads to longer-lived quantum entanglement and more drastic results until ultimately the likeliest locations are at the extremes.

To be clear, modeling with quantum walks does not assume actual quantum entanglement among humans, just as the use of random walks does not assume actual coin tossing by the economy.

If one views politics and elections as random left-right deviations, then frequent measurement will result in essentially normally distributed policies. While still a second-best to a society operating solely under a strict rule of law, a normal distribution is far more manageable by entrepreneurs and other economic actors than the highly erratic one that can result from a quantum entangled political economy. The same insight applies to evaluations of the impact of transparency on politics: the greater the transparency, and therefore the more frequent the measurement of political actions, the closer the terminal policies will be to a normal distribution.

Elections between two major parties by an opaque government would therefore produce the most extreme distribution. Compared to a normal distribution where the outcome is almost surely between −20 and +20, with greater likelihood nearer zero, the extreme distribution has about an equal chance to be any outcome from −50 to +50, with no greater likelihood near zero, and has an even greater chance to be further away, with the modes occurring at the two extremes.

RELATIONSHIP NETWORKS

Unlike agent-based models for which a decision-making algorithm needs to be embedded into each agent, the approach of using simulations of simple rules to search for complexity allows modeling at the most useful level of abstraction. In particular, to find a minimal model of economic complexity, namely one that is as simple as possible, perhaps the key modeling elements are not the individual agent, but the relationships among agents.

Specifically, consider contracts. Suppose there are five individuals: A, B, C, D, and E. Then there are $2^5 - 1 - 5 = 26$ possible contracts, corresponding to all of the possible subsets except for the empty set, because contracts require at least two parties but can accommodate more. For example, a dinner at a restaurant may be considered a four-party contract between the customer, cook, waiter, and owner.

The state of the world is a list of which contracts have actually consummated. There are therefore $2^{26} = 67,108,864$ possible states of the world.

How does one state of the world evolve into the next? A suitable device is an iterated finite automaton (IFA), defined by Wolfram (2003). An IFA is a state machine that reads a line of input and simultaneously writes a line of output. Fig. 8 shows an example transition diagram.

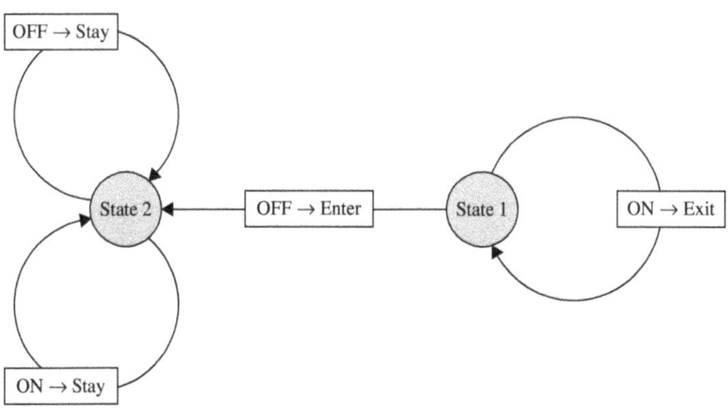

Fig. 8. Transition Diagram of Rule 62 of a 2-State, 2-Symbol Iterated Finite Automaton.

Suppose we are in a state given by {1,1,1,0,0,0,0,0,0,0,0,0,0,0,0,0,0,0,0,0,0,0,0,0,0,0,0,0,0,0,0}, meaning that only the first three out of the 31 possible contracts are in force. Then when rule 62 is applied, it always starts in state 1, and then begins reading item-by-item. It reads the first 1, meaning the contract is already ON, so it follows the arrow out of state 1 labeled ON → Exit. The portion after the arrow indicates what symbol the IFA will write: in this case, Exit, meaning 0; in other words, this contract is now void. Because the arrow led back to state 1, the IFA is still in state 1. Thus it does the same thing two more times. Having written out three zeros in a row, it now is still in state 1 but encounters a 0, so it follows the OFF → Enter arrow, and outputs a 1. The remaining off contracts stay off because the IFA follows the OFF → Stay arrow, meaning void contracts remain void, and the machine continues to be in state 2.

Once it is complete, the new state is {0,0,0,1,0,0,0,0,0,0,0,0,0,0,0,0,0,0,0,0,0,0,0,0,0,0,0,0,0,0,0}, and the IFA begins anew, again starting from state 1.

Following the canonical IFA numbering scheme of Wolfram (2003), we can run all 256 possible 2-state, 2-symbol machines to see which ones result in complexity. Fig. 9 displays the results.

The evolution of rule 62 appears second from the right on the second row, and is a nested but not complex pattern where, as Wolfram (2003) notes, the evolution is simply the binary form of successive digits. Indeed, none of these elementary IFAs directly exhibit complex behavior.

But for our purposes, we are not interested in the complexity or simplicity of the sequence of contracts, but of the individuals on whom those contracts act. Given an evolution of contracts, we can compute at each step the number of contracts that each individual is a party to. For example, if contracts {A, B}, {A, C}, and {A, B, D} are the only ones in force, then A is involved in three contracts, B in two, C and D in one each, and E in

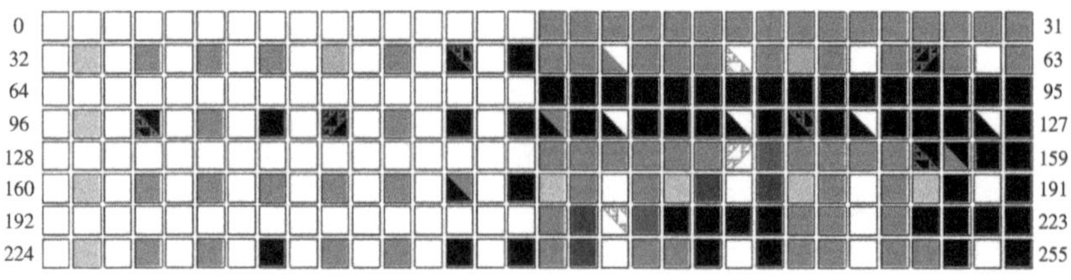

Fig. 9. Evolution of 100 Steps of Each of the 256 Possible IFAs Starting from 100 Blank Cells.

none. Fig. 10 shows the evolution of these contractual counts for each of the elementary IFA rules.

Note that rule 62 (and its essentially identical color-reversed twin 158) appears to be the only one that generates any complexity. Coincidentally, the minimal model of financial complexity in Maymin (2011a) was also an IFA; there, it was rule 54 that turned out to evolve complexity.

We can examine the evolution of rule 62 in greater detail, as shown in Fig. 11. Because the evolution is so thin – only five cells across for the five individuals – the graph of the evolution is partitioned into 50 columns of

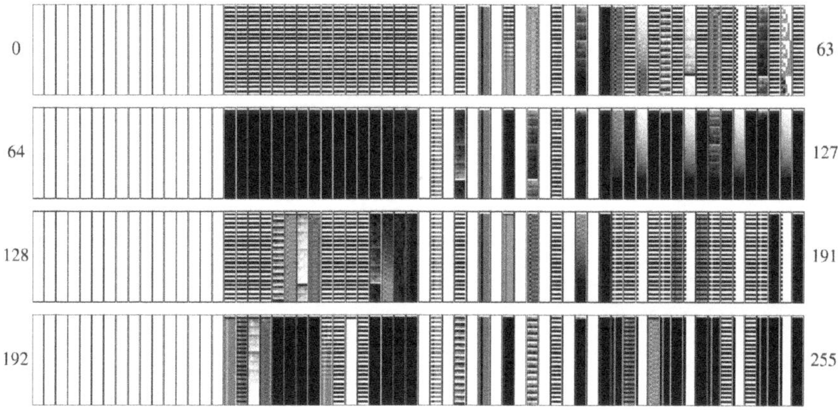

Fig. 10. Forty Steps of the Contractual Counts for the 256 Possible Rules for Five Individuals Starting with No Contracts.

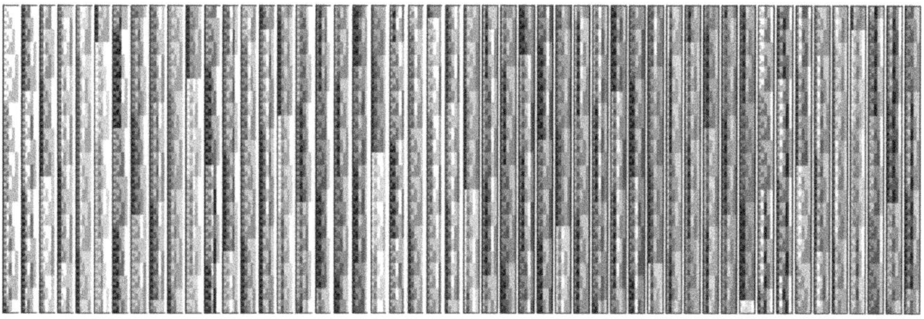

Fig. 11. Five Thousand Steps of the Contractual Counts under Rule 62 for Five Individuals Starting with No Contracts.

100 time steps each: the 50th time step at the bottom of the first column is followed by the 51st time step at the top of the second column, and so on.

This is a highly complex evolution of wealth and trade. Standard economic indicators can be computed for this economy if we use as a proxy for an individual's income the total number of active contracts he is involved in. Fig. 12 shows the resulting indicators.

The GDP, computed as the number of active contracts, trends steadily up with some noise but also experiences rare sharp downward reversals. The maximum GDP that can be achieved in our model occurs when all possible contracts are active and each of the five individuals participates in $2^4 - 1 = 15$ contracts. Thus the maximum GDP is $15 * 5 = 75$. After the 1 million time steps shown in Fig. 12, the GDP has increased less than halfway to its maximum.

The income gap, computed in each period as the difference in the number of contracts between the highest and lowest individual, is for all

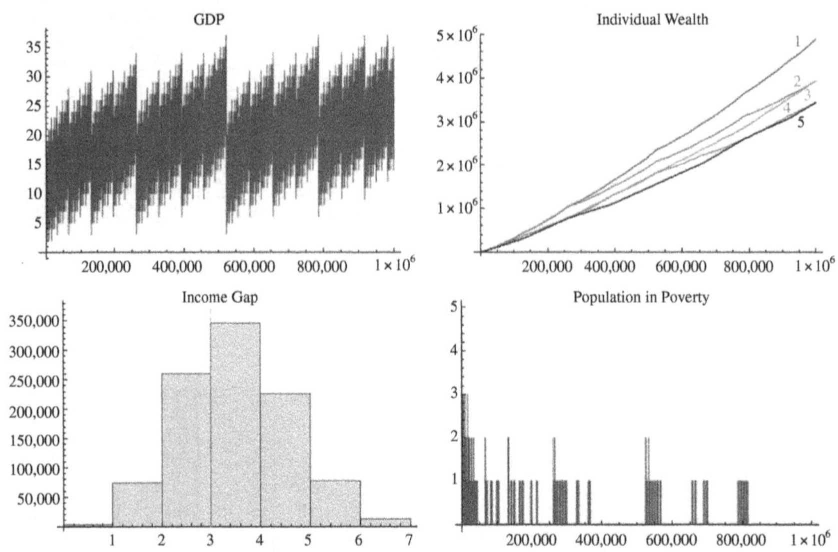

Fig. 12. Standard economic indicators of the simulated economy of rule 62 are shown for 1 million steps. The GDP is the total number of active contracts, the income gap histogram is the difference between the highest number of contracts and the lowest, the population in poverty is the number of individuals involved in zero contracts, and the individual wealth is the cumulative total number of all contracts each individual has ever been part of.

practical purposes flat: though it trends up microscopically, it barely increases after a million time steps. The histogram shows the symmetric nature of the income gap, centered on an average (displayed as a dashed vertical line) of three contracts. Similarly, the population in poverty, the number of individuals involved in zero contracts, trends toward zero, with occasional short-lived occurrences of poverty.

The wealth of each individual, that is, the cumulative number of contracts that individual has ever been involved with to that point, grows steadily for each individual. After 1 million time steps, the earlier individuals still have a slight lead over the later individuals. This is due to their being involved in more of the possible contracts early. By the time the GDP reaches its maximum, however, this lead should vanish because all possible subsets of contracts will have occurred.

In all of these effects, the minimal model of economic complexity broadly matches stylized facts about real-world economies, and it does so without any explicit assumptions about individual decision-making, without any fitting to data, and indeed without any parameter tweaking or calibration at all.

To integrate political entanglement, we can harness the insights of Friedman (2003) and Friedman (2004), in which the notion of a "radically minimalist model" is put forth in the context of Austrian economics in rejecting all of the traditional assumptions of perfect knowledge, perfect competition, and even self-interest. The results of rule 62 show that such a minimalist model is indeed possible, and does in fact match the complexities and intricacies of advanced economies.

Friedman argues that the essence of political entanglement with the economy can be regarded as restrictions on exit. It is with an eye toward this insight that the transition diagram in Fig. 8 was labeled with actions of "Enter" or "Exit." Friedman notes that freedom is essentially defined by the ability to voluntarily enter into or exit contracts with others. He shows that it is this ability to exit that is important for free-market economics, not any tautological notion of self-interest or error-free choices by individuals.

We can integrate the Friedman concept of "no exit" as the basis for political involvement in our model. The effect is to make contracts with one of the individuals permanent.

Implicit in Friedman's "no exit" approach is a "mandatory entrance." An entrance to a contract can only be practically mandatory if exit is impossible; Friedman gives the example of national defense. It would be possible to further extend the minimal model to enforce certain contracts with particular individuals; however, the more realistic model is the simpler one. New goods and services are first introduced to the market through private initiative, and only later do they become governmentally provided and therefore mandatory.

To emulate the "no exit" political entanglement in our model, we run a second pass after each complete run through of the IFA to ensure that any contract involving the designated mandatory party (Individual 1) that was active in the previous period remains active in the next period.

Fig. 13 plots the resulting contractual counts under this modification. The complexity vanishes, replaced by a darkening pattern.

Fig. 14 plots the corresponding economic indicators, making the lack of complexity all the more striking. In the corresponding calculations, the no-exit contracts involving the government are not tabulated in order to get measures of the private economy.

The GDP now simply vacillates between 0 and 32. There is no long-term growth at all, let alone complex growth. Even worse, recessions are both more severe and more frequent.

The population that is either in poverty or involved with contracts with the government now starts off higher, and does not diminish over time, instead suffering regular peaks of widespread poverty or government assistance.

The private income gap has higher peaks which also occur more frequently, though the average of two contracts is lower than before.

The lower private income gap is even better reflected in the accumulated wealth, which is virtually identical across private individuals, and approximately equal to the poorest individual in the free-market scenario.

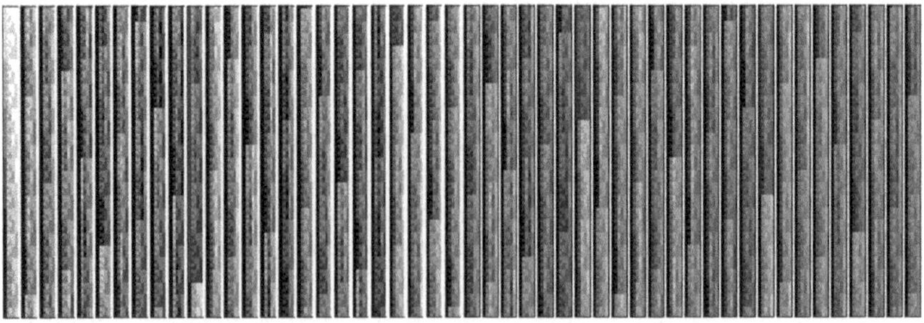

Fig. 13. Five Thousand Steps of the Contractual Counts under Rule 62 for Four Individuals and One Designated No-Exit Individual (Individual 1), All Starting with No Contracts.

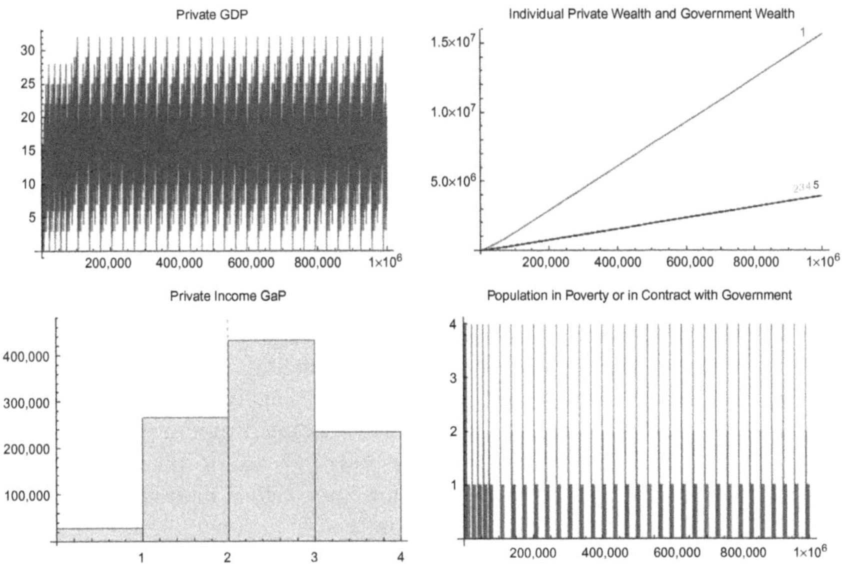

Fig. 14. Standard economic indicators of the simulated economy of rule 62 adjusted to disallow exiting contracts with the government (individual 1) are shown for 1 million steps. All numbers except the government wealth in the final plot reflect the private economy, so the mandatory contracts with the government are not counted. The private GDP is the total number of active non-government contracts, the income gap histogram is the difference between the highest number of non-government contracts and the lowest, the population in poverty or in contract with the government is the number of individuals involved in zero non-government contracts, and the individual wealth is the cumulative total number of all non-government contracts each individual has ever been part of.

Government wealth, however, grows substantially, due to the inability of people to exit from those contracts.

CONCLUSION

Computer simulations of simple rules governing interactions are valuable because they can generate complexity and they cannot in general be efficiently predicted ahead of time. As such, simulations of simple rules can usefully augment the equilibrium, literary, empirical, and experimental approaches in an economist's toolbox.

One unique benefit that this algorithmic approach has over the others is the ability to directly explore what would happen under different scenarios. In an equilibrium approach, one can either solve for two different equilibriums and compare their differences or look at the marginal change in the optimal equilibrium for a small change in some of the parameters, but neither way acknowledges let alone attempts to model the complex dynamics of the economy. In a literary approach, one can logically argue about the truth of an assertion, but many effects may not be computationally knowable without actually performing the simulations. In an empirical approach, one can tease out causality through statistical inference and creative experimental design, but it is impossible to know what would happen under a regime never before seen. In an experimental approach, laboratory subjects can be observed under different conditions and tests of different regimes can be conducted, but no simple theoretical model emerges from those results, and instead must be assumed ahead of time for testing purposes. Thus, the algorithmic simulation approach is unique in its ability to quickly explore the complex implications of a variety of simple possible models.

This paper presented several examples of such approaches ranging from cellular automata to register machines to quantum computation. Further, those examples were extended to explore the implications of allowing agents to vote for redistribution. The typical result has been that redistributive voting augmented onto a complex evolution will never increase the complexity but is likely to, first, reduce complexity if it has an effect at all; second, be inherently unpredictable ahead of time in its effect; and third, be fragile and highly sensitive to the specifics of the redistribution including the frequency with which it is performed.

Finally, a minimal model of economic complexity was developed and presented. This unique minimal model generates complex growth in the economy through voluntary trade. In addition, augmenting it with restrictions on existing contracts with a given individual as a way to model entangled political economy results in less complexity, greater poverty, and a worse economy.

ACKNOWLEDGMENTS

The author is grateful for the comments and suggestions of Francisco Doria, Roger Koppl, J. Barkley Rosser, Jr., Richard Wagner, David Wolpert, an anonymous reviewer, and the participants at the 2012 Wirth Institute Workshop on Austrian Economics.

REFERENCES

Arthur, W. B. (1994). Inductive reasoning and bounded rationality (The El Farol problem). *American Economic Review (Papers and Proceedings)*, *84*, 406–411.

Arthur, W. B. (1999). Complexity and the economy. *Science*, *284*, 107–109.

Chaitin, G., Doria, F. A., & da Costa, N. C. A. (2011). *Gödel's way: Exploits into an undecidable world.* Boca Raton, FL: CRC Press.

Friedman, J. (2003). *Theory gets a reality check: Philosophy, economics, and politics as if verisimilitude mattered.* The Dissident 1. Retrieved from http://the-dissident.com/theory.shtml

Friedman, J. (2004). *Death to homo economicus: A minimalist model of markets* (Seminar notes). Retrieved from http://econfaculty.gmu.edu/pboettke/workshop/fall04/friedman.doc

Gigerenzer, G., Todd, P. M., & ABC Research Group. (2012). *Ecological rationality: Intelligence in the world.* New York, NY: Oxford University Press.

Holt, R. P. F., Rosser, J. B., Jr., & Colander, D. (2011). The complexity era in economics. *Review of Political Economy*, *23*, 357–369.

Kauffman, S. A. (1999). Whispers from Carnot: The origins of order and principles of adaptation in complex nonequilibrium systems. In G. A. Cowan, D. Pines, & D. Meltzer (Eds.), *Complexity* (pp. 83–160). Cambridge: Perseus Books.

Kempe, J. (2003). Quantum random walks: An introductory overview. *Contemporary Physics*, *44*, 307–327.

Koppl, R. (2009). Complexity and Austrian economics. In J. B. Rosser, Jr. (Ed.), *Handbook of complexity research* (pp. 393–408). Cheltenham, UK: Edward Elgar.

Maymin, P. Z. (2011a). The minimal model of financial complexity. *Quantitative Finance*, *11*, 1371–1378.

Maymin, P. Z. (2011b). Markets are efficient if and only if P = NP. *Algorithmic Finance*, *1*, 1–11.

Maymin, P. Z. (2013). Schizophrenic representative investors. *Complex Systems*, *22*(1), 61–73.

Mirowski, P. (2004). Computable economics: The Arne Ryde memorial lecture series: Kumaraswamy Velupillai (Ed.), Oxford University Press, Oxford, 2000 (A book review). Journal of Economic Behavior & Organization, *55*, 125–127.

Rosser, J. B., Jr. (2010). Is a transdisciplinary perspective on economic complexity possible? *Journal of Economic Behavior & Organization*, *75*, 3–11.

Rosser, J. B., Jr. (2012). Emergence and complexity in Austrian economics. *Journal of Economic Behavior & Organization*, *81*, 122–128.

Simon, H. (1997). *Models of bounded rationality*. Cambridge, MA: MIT Press.

Smith, A., Wagner, R. E., & Yandle, B. (2011). A theory of entangled political economy, with application to TARP and NRA. *Public Choice*, *148*, 45–66.

Wagner, R. E. (2006). Choice, catallaxy, and just taxation: Contrasting architectonics for fiscal theorizing. *Social Philosophy and Policy*, *23*, 235–254.

Wagner, R. E. (2007). *Fiscal sociology and the theory of public finance*. Cheltenham, UK: Edward Elgar.

Wolfram, S. (2002). *A new kind of science*. Champaign, IL: Wolfram Media.

Wolfram, S. (2003). *Iterated finite automata*. Informal essay. Retrieved from http://www.stephenwolfram.com/publications/recent/iteratedfinite/

ON AN EXTENSION OF RICE'S THEOREM AND ITS APPLICATIONS IN MATHEMATICAL ECONOMICS☆

N. C. A. da Costa and Francisco A. Doria

ABSTRACT

Rice's Theorem is a notorious stumbling block in Computer Science. We review some previous work of us that shows that we can extend Rice's result to large segments of everyday mathematics, so that similar stumbling blocks appear in many areas of mathematics, as well as applied areas such as mathematical economics; one of its applications (Koppl's conjecture) is discussed in some detail. Note: this paper has been written in an informal style.

Keywords: Mathematical foundations of economics; Goedel's theorem; regulatory models

JEL classification: C650

☆ Dedicated to the memory of Professor Saul Fuks (1929–2012).

Entangled Political Economy
Advances in Austrian Economics, Volume 18, 237–257

ISSN: 1529-2134/doi:10.1108/S1529-213420140000018011

INTRODUCTION

> A huge range of questions – mostly algebraic or combinatorial – has since been proven undecidable. [The authors] show that undecidability extends to many basic questions in dynamical systems theory. These include whether the dynamics is chaotic, whether a trajectory starting from a given initial point eventually passes through some spacific region of phase space, and whether the equations are integrable. [...] Indeed virtually any "interesting" question about dynamical systems is – in general – undecidable.

This quote comes from a comment by I. Stewart (1991) on the results that we are going to sketch here. However, the last sentence in Stewart's text is intriguing (and is to be taken *cum grano salis*). But can we extend it and say that:

> In mathematics, if something is interesting, is it then undecidable?

We are going to discuss that issue here.

We have a blueprint to follow, Rice's Theorem in recursive function theory. Rice's Theorem (1953) is a major stumbling block in the joint field of logic and computer science. Roughly, it asserts that you cannot test for properties of programs, in the general case. Quite informally, it says that given a property P so that there is a program x with $P(x)$ (i.e., P holds for x), and another, different program y so that $\neg P(y)$ (P doesn't hold of y), then for arbitrary programs there is no general algorithmic procedure that separates the programs so that P holds from those where P doesn't hold any such P.

In 1990 (da Costa & Doria, 1991, Prop. 3.28) the authors managed to extend a version of Rice's Theorem to most areas of mathematics. We present here a summary of our results in that direction.

Rice's Theorem, Original Version

For the original version of Rice's Theorem, we deal with a set of languages, where a language is a collection of strings of symbols – and as programs are written as strings of symbols, they fit into the result. Let us be given an arbitrary set of languages so that for language x we can algorithmically decide that $P(x)$, and for language $y \neq x$, $\neg P(y)$, where both x,y are in the prescribed set of languages. Then we cannot algorithmically decide for arbitrary z in the set, whether $P(z)$ or $\neg P(z)$.

($P(x)$, which formally translates what we have called a "property," is a 1-variable formula.)

Rice's Theorem is a very restrictive result. Suppose that you have developed a complex software which you wish to test for desirable (or undesirable) behavior. There is no general procedure to do so. One must go by trial and error. And, yes, it implies that there are no universal virus-controlling programs, no universal "vaccines." Any general procedure for testing the output behavior of software is impossible, according to Rice's Theorem.

A Generalization of Rice's Theorem

Yet, such a damaging fact extends to much of "useful" mathematics: there are no general algorithmic procedures to test for anything that can be formulated as a predicate in (adequate extensions of) set theory.[1] That is the result which we want to discuss now; we already know, essentially from the work of Gödel and Turing (and again informally) that:

> There are no general algorithmic decision procedures in ordinary mathematics.

Or, simply:

> Mathematics as we do it cannot be reduced to a mechanical procedure.

Mathematicians will be needed as long as we conform to the current views about the nature of mathematics: axiomatic systems, computable procedures and the like. However we might hope to be able to develop algorithmic "testing procedures" for each P, separately, in a rather general framework.

Yet it won't do. Here is why.

Let P be a predicate in the language of our formal theory S (which is seen as an adequate fragment of ZFC, Zermelo–Fraenkel set theory, or one of its extensions) and let $x \neq y$ be such that S proves $P(x)$ and S proves $\neg P(y)$. Then:

> There is no general algorithmic procedure to test, for an arbitrary z, whether $P(z)$ or $\neg P(z)$.

(Crucial concepts are contained in the keywords "general" and "arbitrary.")

The present paper sketches the proof of this result and presents some applications to mathematical economics.

More on Informal Arguments

One of the most beautiful proofs of the incompleteness of arithmetics has been given by Kleene in 1936: it deals with Π_2 sentences and can be presented almost in a casual way. We try to do the same here with Rice's Theorem: our argument can be rigorously formalized, but the extra rigor will only cast a cloud over its main lines, we think. So we opted for intuition and clarity in the place of rigor.

Main Ideas

The main idea of the argument is quite simple: suppose that we have $x \neq y$ (and of course the + operation) so that our theory S proves $P(x)$ and $\neg P(y)$. Then:

$$z = \beta x + (1 - \beta) y$$

is undecidable given our conditions for β, which is a term in our theory S: either $\beta = 0$ or $\beta = 1$, but there is no decision procedure to test which will be the case.

Does an object such as β exist? The answer is, it does. We have:

- *The function $\theta(n)$*: We can build a function $\theta(n)$ in our theory S, where n ranges over the natural numbers, which is undecidable – there is no general algorithm to check – whether $\theta(n)$ is 0 or 1, arbitrary n.
- *The term β*: We exhibit a term β about which we prove in theory S that it is either 0 or 1, but such that theory S neither proves $\beta = 0$ nor $\beta = 1$.
- *Different formulations for θ and β*: There is an infinite variety of formulations for these objects, which include a rather simple one inspired by the construction of Chaitin's Ω number (Chaitin, da Costa, & Doria, 2011).

There is an even simpler construction:

η is the object that satisfies $[(x = \xi \wedge a) \vee (x = \zeta \wedge \neg a)]$, where a is an undecidable sentence in S and ξ, ζ are two constant terms.

It leads to analogous results.

We can extend in several ways the preceding ideas. For instance, given theory S supposed consistent, we can generate a recursively enumerable sequence of undecidable sentences $\xi_1, \xi_2, \ldots$, so that out of them we induce a sequence of constants $\beta_1, \beta_2, \ldots$, and make a simultaneous construction that involves a recursively enumerable sequence of predicates in the language of S (or in an adequate extension), $P_1,P_2,\ldots$.

The idea here is that, if Ps is the Diophantine polynomial that codes the proof machinery for S, the formal sentence $Ps(\xi_i,\ldots) > 0$, $i = 1,2,\ldots$, is undecidable – it is true in the standard model for arithmetic and false in some nonstandard ones – and out of it we obtain our β_i.

Applications to Economics

There are manifold situations where this result can be used in mathematical economics. We emphasize here three results:

1. *Undecidability and incompleteness of Nash games*: This is presented in some detail at the end of the technical section. It is the best known result obtained out of those tools we've developed.
2. *Undecidability and incompleteness of market equilibria*: For competitive markets it follows from the previous result.
3. *Koppl's conjecture*: Koppl communicated to us a conjecture on the impossibility of general regulatory schemes. Given an adequate formalization, it can be derived from our extended formulation for Rice's Theorem.

REMARKS ON KOPPL'S CONJECTURE

Koppl's Conjecture can be formulated as the question: *Can we develop a regulatory system for financial markets so that every issue in those markets is adequately addressed?* Common wisdom would most certainly say that it can't be done, but can we find a more rigorous argument for it?

Actually Velupillai proved that result for economic systems seen as complex systems (Velupillai, 2007), but can we give an alternative proof based on the techniques we describe in this paper?

Here are two possible ways to formally deal with it; they will depend on different, nonequivalent, ways to depict the actual economic system. The first one is quite general while the second one is based on the representation of economic systems as networks.

First formalization of the conjecture: Suppose that we are given a formal model of an economic system in an adequate mathematical language that includes arithmetic and is based on classical logic. In that language

p represents the state of the economy (say, price level, gnp, interest rates, whatever) and let P be a (possibly but not necessarily algorithmic) set of policies. Let $P(p') \neq P(p'')$ be the action of P on states p', p'', $p' \neq p''$. Suppose also that we can construct both θ and β in the language of our theory. Then:

Proposition 1. Given the preceding conditions, there is a state of the economy p''' which is undecidable with respect to policies P.

Proof. $p''' = \theta p' + (1-\theta)p''$ is an undecidable state of the economy, and therefore we cannot algorithmically predict the effect of P on p''', that is, we cannot compute $P(p''')$. □

So this result arises out of our version of Rice's Theorem. It can be paraphrased as:

> For any set of policies P there will be a state p of the economy for which the action of those policies will be algorithmically unpredictable.

We notice that the above result is valid for many different and possibly contradictory formal depictions of an economic system – that is to say, it is quite free from major theoretical constraints (but for the assumption of a formal treatment in a reasonable mathematical language). In particular we do not require the assumption that an economy be a complex system; a linear system will be as undecidable in that respect as a complex nonlinear one. The undecidable state p''' isn't an outlandish construction either, as it equal p' or p''. Only we don't know which one.

We can even formulate a Gödel-like incompleteness theorem out of the preceding result. Suppose that the axiomatic set theory of Zermelo–Fraenkel (ZF) is consistent and has a model with standard arithmetic. Axiomatize our economic theory within it with the help of Suppes predicates (da Costa & Doria, 1991, 2007). Then for our axiomatization E:

Proposition 2. If $p''' = \beta p' + (1-\beta)p''$ then the sentence $p''' = p'$ is formally undecidable in theory E.

Proof. Follows from the fact that we cannot decide whether β is 0 or 1 in theory E. □

(Suppes predicates are essentially a tool to reconstruct an intuitive mathematics-based theory within axiomatic set theory.)

Alternative formalization of the conjecture: This is just a sketch; here we formalize our economic system as a network, that is, as a lattice.

- Code the natural numbers ω on networks (we will be using lattices here).
- Induce arithmetical operations on networks via that coding.
- If the lattices are rich enough we can represent partial recursive functions as operations on networks.
- Now represent operations on networks (adding a branch, pruning, joining, etc.) by recursive operations.
- Define "state of financial networks" as some specific configuration of networks.
- Use the standard version of Rice's Theorem in computer science to show that we cannot decide whether recursive operations ("economic policies") can decide specific configurations of networks (outcomes of policies).

The corresponding theorem is self-explanatory:

Proposition 3. If an economic market is represented by networks described by lattices and if these lattices are rich enough to code:

1. The set ω of natural numbers;
2. The arithmetic operations;
3. An universal Diophantine equation;

then all nontrivial economic policies which are represented by algorithmic procedures on the network are undecidable.

Comment: The result directly follows from the standard Rice's Theorem; the only part we have left undescribed in detail is the way we code arithmetical operations on networks.

Notice that there is an analogous theorem for economic processes coded as cellular automata. There are also corresponding incompleteness theorems for the axiomatized versions of these theories. □

Notice that the above two results are not equivalent, as the first one is well more general; it requires a formal framework where one can build the θ or β objects, and such a framework goes beyond arithmetic,[2] while the second one is more specific and valid for rich enough networks. In fact there is a lot to be explored here; Koppl's Conjecture is a conceptually very promising domain.

We also wonder whether there is a proof of Koppl's Conjecture along the lines of the main argument in Arrow's Impossibility Theorem.

The interesting point here is that each of these alternative arguments is nested in a different formal and conceptual framework, which may indicate totally diverse viewpoints for the question.

PERSPECTIVES

Let us start this section with a brief historical note on the development of this extension of Rice's Theorem and on its application to mathematical economics.

To our knowledge, Scarpellini (2003a, 2003b) was the first to describe undecidable problems in the language of classical analysis. He also noticed that an ideal analog computer would be able to settle undecidable problems (what happens with real analog computers in such situations is so far unexplored (Doria & Costa, 2006). Then follows Richardson's (1968) map of exponential Diophantine equations onto real-valued smooth functions; such maps translate all undecidable problems about exponential Diophantine equations into corresponding problems in analysis. After the solution of Hilbert's 10th Problem by Matyasevich in 1970 (based on the work of Davis and Robinson) (Davis, 1982), we learned that Diophantine theory is, in some sense, a version of computability theory, and we can extend Richardson's results to the more restricted area of Diophantine theory. Finally Kreisel's major 1975 paper on the concept of mechanical proof tops all these results. See also Koppl (2008); Velupillai (2005a, 2005b, 2006).

We were unaware of Kreisel's paper when we exhibited in 1990 (da Costa & Doria, 1991) an explicit expression for the halting function in the language of analysis; we had been directed to Richardson's paper by Suppes, who also noticed that we were dealing with an extension of Rice's Theorem to the whole of analysis. Our original constructions heavily depend on Richardson's map, but we later learned how to circumvent it with a version of our θ function which is close to Chaitin's Ω number.

In 1991 we got in touch with Alain Lewis, who sent us his (then unpublished) results (Lewis, 1992) on the undecidability of recursively presented games (for the complete set of references, see Bartholo, Cosenza, Doria, & de Lessa, 2009). Tsuji, who was then a doctoral student in our group, noticed that we could extend Lewis' results with the help of our techniques. We announced Tsuji's result in 1994; the full paper only appeared in 1998 in a logic journal, (Tsuji, da Costa, & Doria, 1998) as we had lots of difficulties with referees in mathematical economics journals.

Velupillai published his lectures (Velupillai, 2000) on undecidability and economics in 2000. We learned about his work and contacted him in 2002. At his invitation one of us (Doria) presented these ideas at a workshop in April 2005 at Galway. There are still many venues to be explored in these directions, and about the theme of undecidability and economics in a general way.

Undecidability and Incompleteness in Economics

Of course undecidability and incompleteness in economics aren't restricted to the techniques described here. Lewis used forcing to show the independence of a formalized version of Edgeworth's Conjecture from axiomatic set theory (Lewis, 1991) and Prasad has several remarkable results on game theory with the help of different tools (Prasad, 1991, 2004).

S. Zambelli asked one of us[3] whether by using finite automata instead of Turing machines as economic agents one would avoid undecidability and incompleteness because of the finiteness of the objects involved. The answer is however, no.

As a blueprint, consider the slightly more general case of space-bounded and time-bounded Turing machines (our notebooks when running a program may be seen as concrete realizations of those). We can represent such machines by a triple $\langle M_n, p_{1,F}, p_{2,F'} \rangle$. Here M_n is a Turing machine of Gödel number n and the p_i are (algorithmic) time bounding and space bounding devices. (The time bounding device can be seen as a clock that shuts down the Turing machine when it reaches a given computable bound; the space bounding device acts in a similar way). We have parametrized the bounding devices by functions F, F' which are taken as intuitively total recursive functions (functions which are total in the standard model for arithmetic) that however cannot be proved total within our axiomatic framework. Let that formal theory be S, supposed consistent. This is enough to prove:

Proposition 4. There is an infinite set of intuitively bounded Turing machines

$$B = \{\langle M_n, p_{1,F}, p_{2,F'} \rangle\}_k$$

$k = 0,1,2,\ldots$ such that the sentence "B is a set of bounded Turing machines" cannot be proved or disproved in S. □

A similar result holds for finite automata. Intuitive here means: which holds true of the standard model for arithmetic.

So, there is much to be explored here. The advantage of using Rice-like constructions to study undecidability and incompleteness is that one verifies that such phenomena appear everywhere and in essentially all domains.

RICE'S THEOREM EXTENDED

Now some technical details. Below one finds a summary (or road map) of our main technical constructions; we base it on the works by Bartholo et al. (2009), da Costa and Doria (1991, 2005), and da Costa, Doria, and Bir (2007). The presentation splits into several topics:

- Formalized arithmetic and Turing machines.
- Richardson's maps.
- The halting function in formal languages that extend arithmetic.
- Applications to economics: axiomatic treatment of game theory and the main undecidability and incompleteness result.

We will here use results which appear in our papers (Bartholo et al., 2009; da Costa & Doria, 2005).

Preliminary

For concepts from logic see Mendelson (1997). We use: $\neg$, "not," $\vee$, "or," $\wedge$, "and," $\rightarrow$, "if... then...," $\leftrightarrow$, "if and only if," $\exists x$, "there is a x," $\forall x$, "for every x." $P(x)$ is a formula with x free; it roughly means "x has property P." Finally $T \vdash \xi$ means T proves ξ, or ξ is a theorem of T. ω is the set of natural numbers, $\omega = \{0,1,2,\ldots\}$.

We deal with algorithmic functions. These are given by their programs coded in Gödel numbers e (Rogers, 1967). We will sometimes use Turing machines (noted by sans-serif letters with the Gödel number as index M_e) or partial recursive functions, noted $\{e\}$.

We start from a very simple theory of arithmetic, noted $A1$. Its language includes variables $x,y,\ldots$, two constants, $\mathbf{0}$ and $\mathbf{1}$, the equality sign $=$, and two operation signs, $+,\times$. Basically $A1$ has axioms for the operations $+$ and $\times$, the behavior of constants $\mathbf{0}$ and $\mathbf{1}$, and the trichotomy axiom, that is, given two natural numbers x and y, either $x<y$ or $x=y$ or $x>y$. $A1$ contains no induction axiom.

We will also require Russell's ι symbol (Kneebone, 1963). $\iota_x P(x)$ is, roughly, the x such that P.

The *standard interpretation* for $A1$ is: the variables $x,y,\ldots$ range over the natural numbers, and **0** and **1** are seen as, respectively, 0 and 1. The only requirements we impose on $A1$ is: that theory should be strong enough to formally include all of Turing machine theory. Recall that a Turing machine is given by its Gödel number, which recursively codes the machine's program. Rigorously, for $A1$, we must have:

Definition 1. A Turing machine of Gödel number e operating on x with output y, $\{e\}(x)=y$ is representable in theory $A1$ if there is a formula $F_e(x,y)$ in the language of $A1$ so that:

1. $A1 \vdash \{F_e(x,y) \wedge F_e(x,z) \rightarrow [y=z]\}$, and
2. For natural numbers a,b, if $\{e\}(a)=b$, then $A1 \vdash F_e(a,b)$. □

Then we have the representation theorem for partial recursive functions in $A1$:

Proposition 5. Every Turing machine is representable in $A1$. Moreover there is an effective procedure that allows us to obtain F_e from the Gödel number e. □

Remark 1. We mainly consider here theories that are *arithmetically sound*, that is, which have a model with standard arithmetic for its arithmetical segment. □

A First Example of Generalized Incompleteness; Rice's Theorem

The example we now give shows that incompleteness is a pervasive phenomenon, from an arithmetic theory like $A1$ upwards, that is, it affects all theories that contain $A1$, are based on a first-order classical language, have a model where arithmetic is standard and have a recursively enumerable set of theorems.

Suppose that the theory S we deal with has also the ι symbol. Let P be a predicate symbol so that for terms $\xi \neq \zeta$, $S \vdash P(\xi)$ and $S \vdash \neg P(\zeta)$ (we call such P, nontrivial predicates). Then, for the term:

$$\eta = \iota_x[(x=\xi \wedge \alpha) \vee (x=\zeta \wedge \neg\alpha)],$$

where α is an undecidable sentence in S:

Proposition 6. $S \nvdash P(\eta)$ and $S \nvdash \neg P(\eta)$. □

This shows that incompleteness is found everywhere within theories like S.

Remark 2. Notice that this implies Rice's Theorem (Machtey & Young, 1979; Rogers, 1967) in computer science. Briefly: suppose that there is an algorithm that settles $P(n)$, for each $n \in \omega$. Then by the representation theorem we may internalize that algorithm into S, and obtain a proof of $P(n)$ for arbitrary $n \in \omega$, a contradiction given Proposition 6. □

Richardson's Map

Our main tool here will be an explicit expression for the halting function, that is, the function that settles the halting problem (Rogers, 1967). We will show that it can be constructed within the language of classical analysis. We use the Richardson transforms (da Costa & Doria, 2005). We start from a strengthening of Proposition 5:

Proposition 7. If $\{e\}(a)=b$, for natural numbers a,b, then we can algorithmically construct a polynomial p_e over the natural numbers so that $[\{e\}(a)=b] \leftrightarrow [\exists x_1, x_2, \ldots, x_k \in \omega p_e(a,b,x_1,x_2,\ldots,x_k)=0]$. □

Follows:

Proposition 8. $\alpha \in R_e$, where R_e is a recursively enumerable set, if and only if there are e and p so that $\exists x_1, x_2, \ldots, x_k \in \omega[p_e(a, x_1, x_2, \ldots, x_k)=0]$. □

Richardson's map (da Costa & Doria, 2005) allows us to obtain in an algorithmic way, given any $p_e(a, \ldots)$, a polynomial over the natural numbers, a real-defined and real-valued function $f_e(a, \ldots)$ that has roots if and only if $p_e(a, \ldots)$ has roots as a Diophantine equation.

We can be more specific: let A be the algebra of subelementary functions (polynomials over the reals, sines, cosines; everything closed under $+,-$, products by real numbers and by the functions that generate the algebra, to which we add function composition). Let R denote the real line.

Richardson's Map: Multidimensional Version

We now state the first of Richardson's main results: given that $A1_{\mathrm{ZFC}}$, and if P is the set of all finite-length polynomials over ω:

Proposition 9. (Richardson's Map, I) There is an injection $\kappa_p: P \to A$, where P denotes the algebra of ω-valued polynomials in a finite number of variables, and A is the algebra of subelementary functions described above, such that:

1. κ_p is constructive, that is, given the expression for p in $A1$, there is an effective procedure so that we can obtain the corresponding expression for $F = \kappa_p(p)$ in ZFC.
2. κ_p is $1-1$.
3. For $\vec{x} = (x_1, \ldots, x_n)$, $\exists \vec{x} \in \omega^n(m, \vec{x}) = 0$ if and only if $\exists \vec{x} \in R^n F(m, \vec{x}) = 0$ if and only if $\exists \vec{x} \in R^n F(m, \vec{x}) \leq 1$, for $p \in P$ and $F \in A$.
4. The injection κ_p is proper. □

The crucial property is given in step 3: it allows us to translate the existence of roots for Diophantine equations into roots of the corresponding transformed real-defined and real-valued function, with some extras.

Next step gives us a one-dimensional version of Richardson's map.

Richardson's Map: One-Dimensional Version

Corollary 1. (Richardson's Map, II) Let A_1 be the algebra of subelementary functions over a single real variable x. Then there is a map $\kappa' : P \to A_1$ such that:

1. κ' is constructive.
2. κ' is $1-1$.
3. The inclusion $\kappa'(P)_{A_1}$ is proper.
4. $\exists \vec{x} \in \omega^n(m, \vec{x}) = 0$ if and only if $\exists x \in RL(m,x)=0$ if and only if $\exists x \in RG(m,x) \leq 1$. □

Undecidability of the Computation of Fixed Points

Remark 3. This is enough to imply the algorithmic unsolvability of the following problem: *given the interior D of a square, there is no general algorithm to decide whether a given curve described by elementary functions meets some straight line in D.* It suffices to compactify the previous function over the interval $[-1,+1]$ and consider its restriction to $(-1,+1)$. □

Remark 4. Also notice that, for an adequate D_{R^n}, if $f: D \rightarrow D$, the computation of fixed points is in general undecidable. For the fixed-point condition:

$$f(x) = x$$

is simply $f(x) - x = 0$, and there is no general algorithm to solve that equation.

There is no need to stress the importance of that result to theories in mathematical economics. □

The Halting Function

One of the main results in Alan Turing's great 1937 paper, "On computable numbers, with an application to the Entscheidungsproblem," (Turing, 1937) is a proof of the algorithmic unsolvability of a version of the halting problem: given an arbitrary Turing machine of Gödel number e, for input x, there is no algorithm that decides whether $\{e\}(x)$ stops and outputs something, or enters an infinite loop.

Remark 5. Let $M_m(a)\downarrow$ mean: "Turing machine of Gödel number m stops over input a and gives some output." Similarly $M_m(a)\uparrow$ means, "Turing machine of Gödel number m enters an infinite loop over input a." Then we can define the halting function θ:

- $\theta(m,a)=1$ if and only if $M_m(a)\downarrow$.
- $\theta(m,a)=0$ if and only if $M_m(a)\uparrow$.

$\theta(m,a)$ is the halting function for M_m over input a. □

θ isn't algorithmic, of course (Rogers, 1967; Turing, 1937), that is, there is no Turing machine that computes it.

Remark 6. As we now show, we can explicitly write an expression for a function in the language of classical analysis that settles the halting problem. We proceed as follows:

- Given Turing machine $M_m(a)=b$, for natural numbers a,b, we can algorithmically obtain (Davis, 1982) a polynomial $p_{\mathrm{m}}(\langle a,b\rangle, x_1,\ldots, x_k)$ so that:

$$M_m(a) = b \leftrightarrow \exists x_1, \ldots, x_2 \in \omega[p_m(\langle a, b\rangle, x_1, \ldots, x_k) = 0]$$

- Given F_m, real-defined and real-valued, we have that:

$$\exists x_1, \ldots, x_2 \in \omega [p_m(\langle a, b \rangle, x_1, \ldots, x_k) = 0] \leftrightarrow$$

$$\leftrightarrow \exists x_1, \ldots, x_k \in \mathrm{R} F_m(\langle a, b \rangle, x_1, \ldots, x_k) \leq 1$$

and

$$\forall x_1, \ldots, x_2 \in \omega [p_m(\langle a, b \rangle, x_1, \ldots, x_k) \neq 0] \leftrightarrow$$

$$\leftrightarrow \forall x_1, \ldots, x_k \in \mathrm{R} F_m(\langle a, b \rangle, x_1, \ldots, x_k) > 1$$

- That is to say: $M_m(a)\downarrow$ if and only if $F_m(a,\ldots)$ goes below 1, and $M_m(a)\uparrow$ if and only if $F_m(a,\ldots)$ stays above 1.

This is the property we use in order to construct the halting function θ_m. □

We now need the concept of an *universal Diophantine polynomial.* Davis (Davis, 1982) describes an algorithmic procedure out of which, given a Turing machine with input *a* $M_m(a)$, we obtain a polynomial $p_m(a,x_1,\ldots)$ so that it has roots if and only if $M_m(a)$ converges. Now, if $U(m,a)$ is an universal Turing machine (Rogers, 1967; Turing, 1937), we can similarly obtain a polynomial $p(\langle m,a \rangle,\ldots)$ which stands for $p_m(a,\ldots)$.

Precisely, if $[\exists x_1,\ldots, x_k p_m(\langle a,b \rangle,x_1,\ldots, x_k)=0] \leftrightarrow [M_m(a)=b]$, then, for the universal polynomial $p(\langle m,a,b \rangle,\ldots)$:

$$[\exists x_1, \ldots, x_r p(\langle m, a, b \rangle, x_1, \ldots, x_r) = 0] \leftrightarrow$$

$$\leftrightarrow [\exists x_1, \ldots, x_k p_m(\langle a, b \rangle, x_1, \ldots, x_k) = 0]$$

From the preceding considerations, if σ is the sign function, $\sigma(\pm x)=\pm 1$ and $\sigma(0)=0$:

Proposition 10. (The Halting Function). The halting function $\theta(n,q)$ is explicitly given by:

$$\theta(n, q) = \sigma(G_{n,q})$$

$$G_{n,q} = \int_{-\infty}^{+\infty} C_{n,q}(x) \mathrm{e}^{-x^2} \, \mathrm{d}x$$

$$C_{m,q}(x) = |F_{m,q}(x) - 1| - (F_{m,q}(x) - 1)$$

$$F_{n,q}(x) = \kappa_P p_{n,q} \quad \square$$

Here $p_{n,q}$ is the two-parameter universal Diophantine polynomial

$$p(\langle n, q \rangle, x_1, x_2, \dots, x_r)$$

and κ_p is as in Proposition 9.

Remark 7. Notice that there are infinitely many alternative explicit expressions for the halting function θ (da Costa & Doria, 2005). □

General Undecidability and Incompleteness Results

Everything proceeds within ZFC (or within any similarly powerful axiomatic system $S \supset A_1$), so that we can obtain all the maps given by Richardson's functor into A and extensions. Let also $B \supseteq A$ be any similar extension; let P be a predicate (a formula with a free variable $P(x)$) defined for B such that P is nontrivial.

If ξ is any word in that language, we write $||\xi||$ for its complexity, as measured by the number of letters from ZFC's alphabet in ξ. Also we define the *complexity of a proof* $C_{\mathrm{ZFC}}(\xi)$ of ξ in the language of ZFC to be the minimum length that a deduction of ξ from the ZFC axioms can have, as measured by the total number of letters in the expressions that belong to the proof.

Then:

Proposition 11. If ZFC is arithmetically sound, then:

1. There is an $h \in B$ so that neither ZFC $\nvdash \neg P(h)$ nor ZFC $\nvdash P(h)$, but $\mathbf{M} \vDash P(h)$, where $\mathbf{M}$ makes ZFC arithmetically sound.
2. There is a denumerable set of functions $h_m(x) \in B$, $m \in \omega$, such that there is no general decision procedure to ascertain, for an arbitrary m, whether $P(h_m)$ or $\neg P(h_m)$ is provable in ZFC.
3. Given the set $K = \{m : \mathrm{ZFC} \vdash \phi(\hat{m})\}$, and given an arbitrary total recursive function $g: \omega \to \omega$, there is an infinite number of values for m so that $C_{\mathrm{ZFC}}(P(\hat{m})) > g(||P(\hat{m})||)$.

Proof. Let θ be as above. Let f_0, g_0 satisfy our conditions on P, that is, ZFC $\vdash P(f_0)$ and ZFC $\vdash \neg P(g_0)$. Then define:

$$h(m,x) = \theta(m,x)f_0 + (1-\theta(m,x))g_0$$

This settles (2). Now let us specify θ so that the corresponding Diophantine equation $p=0$ is never solvable in the standard model for arithmetic, while that fact cannot be proved in ZFC. We then form, for such an indicator function,

$$h = \theta f_0 + (1-\theta)g_0$$

This settles (1). Finally, for (3), we notice that as K is recursively enumerable but not recursive, it satisfies the conditions in the Gödel–Ehrenfeucht–Mycielski Theorem about the length of proofs. □

Higher-Level Intractability

The next results are somewhat off the main road but they give an idea of how intractable those problems can be (we stress the first one):

Proposition 12.

1. There is a term ξ so that $P(\xi)$ isn't arithmetically expressible.
2. Given theory S as in this paper, then there is a partial recursive function F so that S neither proves nor disproves it to be total, and for some arbitrarily chosen constructive ordinal α in the Turing–Feferman hierarchy over S, $S_\alpha \vdash [F$ is total$]$, but for no $\beta < \alpha$ does S proves that F is total.
3. Given axiomatic set theory ZFC plus some large cardinal hypothesis, there is a partial recursive function F so that ZFC thus enlarged neither proves nor disproves F to be total. □

For the second statement is given a detailed, constructive proof in Carnielli & Doria (2008). For the third statement see the construction of F in da Costa et al. (2007) and references therein.

Now: can we give an interpretation for those phenomena, when we meet them in the realm of mathematical economics?

NONCOOPERATIVE NASH GAMES; THEIR AXIOMATIZATION

We now apply the preceding ideas to mathematical economics. From the usual mathematical definitions in game theory (Nash, 2002):

Definition 1. A noncooperative game is given by the von Neumann triplet

$$\langle N, S_i, u_i \rangle$$

with $i = 1,2,\ldots N$, where N is the number of players, S_i is the (finite) strategy set of player i, with elements $s_i \in S_i$, and u_i is the real-valued utility (or payoff) function u_i:$S_1 \times S_2 \times \ldots S_N \rightarrow R$, for every $i = 1,2,\ldots N$. □

Then,

Definition 2. A strategy vector $s^* = \langle s_1^*, \ldots \rangle$, $s_k^* \in S_k$ is a Nash equilibrium vector for a finite noncooperative game Γ if for all strategies and all i,

$$0u_i(s^*) = u_i\left(\langle s_1^*, \ldots, s_k^*, \ldots \rangle\right) \geq u_i(\langle s_1, \ldots, s_k, \ldots \rangle) \qquad \square$$

We call those games *Nash games* for short. If we work within some strong theory S (like ZFC), it is easy to transform the above two informal definitions into formal ones by means of set-theoretical concepts. The result is therefore a Suppes predicate, that is, a set-theoretic predicate that allows us to axiomatize this portion of game theory within ZFC; for details see da Costa & Doria (2005) and references therein; for details on the axiomatization via Suppes predicates, see da Costa et al. (2007). Then:

Proposition 13. If S is arithmetically sound, then there is a noncooperative game Γ where each strategy set is finite, but such that for some s^* the (formal version of the) sentence "s^* is a Nash equilibrium for Γ" is undecidable.

Proof. We can easily obtain from the preceding constructions a β so that $S \nvdash \beta = 0$ and $S \nvdash \beta = 1$, but for a model $\mathbf{N} \models S$ with standard arithmetic, $\mathbf{N} \models \beta = 0$. Then for such a β and for two games Γ' and Γ'' with the same number of players but with different utility functions u_i', $u'\prime_i$, form the game $\hat{\Gamma}$ with the same players as Γ' and Γ'', and with utilities:

$$\hat{u}_i = \beta u_i' + (1 - \beta) u_i'' \qquad \square$$

The idea is the following: of course if we are given a game with explicitly given actual values for the u_i, we can calculate the corresponding Nash equilibria. Trouble only arises when we give the u_i by some complicated expressions, which may be the case when we are dealing with a "model" (in the current sense of depiction of portions of reality) of some market.

The main result here is:

Proposition 14. If S is arithmetically sound then:

- Given any nontrivial predicate $P(\Gamma)$, where Γ is a Nash game, there is an infinitely denumerable family of Nash games Γ_m such that for those m, given $S \vdash P(\Gamma_m)$, for an arbitrary total recursive function $g{:}\omega \rightarrow \omega$, there is an infinite number of values for m such that the complexity of proof $C_s(P(\Gamma_m)) > g(||P\Gamma_m||)$.
- For any nontrivial predicate $P(\Gamma)$ as above, there is one Γ_0 such that $T \vdash P(\Gamma_0)$ if and only if $S \vdash$ Riemann's Hypothesis.
- There is a Γ for which each strategy set sigma_i is finite but such that we cannot compute its Nash equilibria.
- There is a Γ for which each strategy set sigma_i is finite and such that the computation of its equilibria is S-arithmetically expressible as a Π_{n+1} problem, but not to any $\sum_k$ problem, $k \leq n$.
- There is a Γ for which each strategy set σ_i is finite and such that the computation of its equilibria is not arithmetically expressible. □

NOTES

1. Intuitively a 1-variable predicate $P(x)$ translates as "x has property P." More technically we recall that one can introduce by definition out of $\in$ and $=$ the notion of predicate in axiomatic set theory.
2. Actually Peano Arithmetic plus the possibility of writing down an infinite sum will do.
3. FAD; in private conversation.

ACKNOWLEDGMENTS

The authors are members of the Brazilian Academy of Philosophy. F. A. Doria wishes to thank R. Koppl who kindly invited him to present these ideas at the Wirth meeting; the authors also thank Koppl for many comments on his conjecture. The authors also thank an anonymous referee for many detailed criticisms that greatly improved the present paper. This paper was supported in part by CNPq, Philosophy Section. It is part of the research efforts of the Advanced Studies Group, Production Engineering Program, at Coppe-UFRJ and of the Logic Group, hcte-ufrj. Finally, the authors thank Profs. R. Bartholo, C. A. Cosenza, S. Fuks (in memoriam), S. Jurkiewicz, R. Kubrusly, and F. Zamberlan for support.

REFERENCES

Bartholo, R., Cosenza, C. A. N., Doria, F. A., & de Lessa, C. T. R. (2009). Can economic systems be seen as computing devices? *Jebo*, *70*, 72–80.

Carnielli, W. A., & Doria, F. A. (2008). Are the foundations of computer science logic-dependent? In C. Degrémont, L. Keiff, & H. Rückert (Eds.), *Dialogues, logics and other strange things*. London: College Publications.

Chaitin, G. J., da Costa, N. C. A., & Doria, F. A. (2011). *Gödel's way*. Boca Raton, FL: CRC Press/Taylor & Francis.

da Costa, N. C. A., & Doria, F. A. (1991). Undecidability and incompleteness in classical mechanics. *International Journal Theoretical Physics*, *30*, 1041–1073.

da Costa, N. C. A., & Doria, F. A. (2005). Computing the future. In K. V. Velupillai (Ed.), *Computability, complexity and constructivity in economic analysis*. Oxford: Blackwell.

da Costa, N. C. A., & Doria, F. A. (2007). Janus-faced physics: On Hilbert's 6th problem. In C. Calude (Ed.), *Complexity and randomness: From Leibniz to Chaitin (Festschrift in Honor of G. Chaitin on his 60th Birthday)*. World Scientific.

da Costa, N. C. A., Doria, F. A., & Bir, E. (2007). On the metamathematics of the P vs NP question. *Applied Mathematics and Computation*, *189*, 1223–1240.

Davis, M. (1982). Hilbert's tenth problem is unsolvable. In *Computability and unsolvability*. Mineola, NY: Dover Publications.

Doria, F. A., & Costa, J. F. (Eds.). (2006). Special issue on hypercomputation. *Applied Mathematics and Computation*, 178.

Kleene, S. C. (1936). General recursive functions of natural numbers. *Mathematische Annalen*, *112*, 727–742.

Kneebone, G. T. (1963). *Mathematical logic*. Van Nostrand.

Koppl, R. (2008). Thinking impossible things: A review essay. *Journal of Economic Behavior and Organization*, *66*, 837–847.

Kreisel, G. (1975). A notion of mechanistic theory. In P. Suppes (Ed.), *Logic and probability in quantum mechanics*. D. Reidel.

Lewis, A. A. (1991). *On the effective content of asymptotic verifications of Edgeworth's conjecture*. preprint. Irvine, CA: University of California.

Lewis, A. A. (1992). On Turing degrees of Walrasian models and a general impossibility result in the theory of decision making. *Mathematical Social Sciences*, *24*, 141–171.

Machtey, M., & Young, P. (1979). *An introduction to the general theory of algorithms*. North-Holland.

Mendelson, E. (1997). *Introduction to mathematical logic* (4th ed.). Chapman & Hall.

Nash, J. F., Jr. (2002). Non-cooperative games. In H. W. Kuhn & S. Nasar (Eds.), *The essential John Nash*. Princeton.

Prasad, K. (1991). Computability and randomness of Nash equilibria in infinite games. *Journal of Mathematical Economics*, *20*, 429–449.

Prasad, K. (2004). Constructive and classical models for results in economics and game theory. *Metroeconomica*, *55*, 141–154.

Rice, H. G. (1953). Classes of recursively enumerable sets and their decision problems. *Transactions of the American Mathematical Society*, *74*, 358–366.

Richardson, D. (1968). Some unsolvable problems involving elementary functions of a real variable. *Journal Symbolic Logic*, *33*, 514–520.

Rogers, H., Jr. (1967). *Theory of recursive functions and effective computability*. McGraw-Hill.

Scarpellini, B. (2003a). Two undecidable problems of analysis (translation from the 1963 original text). *Minds and Machines*, *13*, 49–77.

Scarpellini, B. (2003b). Comments on "two undecidable problems of analysis". *Minds and Machines*, *13*, 79–85.

Stewart, I. (1991). Deciding the undecidable. *Nature*, *352*, 664–665.

Tsuji, M., da Costa, N. C. A., & Doria, F. A. (1998). The incompleteness of theories of games. *Journal of Philosophical Logic*, *27*, 553–564.

Turing, A. M. (1937). On computable numbers, with an application to the entscheidungsproblem. *Proceedings of the London Mathematical Society*, *50*, 230.

Velupillai, K. V. (2000). *Computable economics*. Oxford.

Velupillai, K. V. (Ed.). (2005a). *Computability, complexity and constructivity in economic analysis*. Blackwell.

Velupillai, K. V. (2005b). The unreasonable ineffectiveness of mathematics in economics. *Cambridge Journal of Economics*, *29*, 848–872.

Velupillai, K. V. (2006). Algorithmic foundations of computable general equilibrium theory. *Applied Mathematics and Computation*, *179*, 360–369.

Velupillai, K. V. (2007). The impossibility of an effective theory of policy in a complex economy. In D. Colander & M. Salzano (Eds.), *Complexity hints for policy*. Springer-Verlag.

ON ETHICAL AND INTELLECTUAL FAILURES IN CONTEMPORARY ECONOMICS

Stuart Kauffman

ABSTRACT

Contemporary Anglo-American economics, which I admire, faces two major obstacles. First, in its drive at least since Milton Freedman to be a positive science free of normative issues, it ignores its own current intellectual foundations buried at the heart of its analysis of the "advantages of trade": Fairness. Second, the major driver of economic growth in the past 50,000 years has been the explosion of goods and production capacities from perhaps 1,000 to 10,000 long ago, to perhaps 10 billion goods and production capacities today. Economics, lacking a theory for this explosion, deals with this explosion by ignoring it and treating it as "exogenous" to its theory.

The "Edgeworth Box" carries the heart of advantages of trade, demonstrating for properly curved isoutility curves a region where you and I are better-off trading some of my apples for some of your pears. The ratio of these in trade constitutes price. But spanning the region of advantages of trade is the famous CONTRACT CURVE, where we have

Entangled Political Economy
Advances in Austrian Economics, Volume 18, 259–282

ISSN: 1529-2134/doi:10.1108/S1529-213420140000018012

exhausted all the advantages of trade. Different points on the curve correspond to different prices. But the Contract Curve is Pareto Optimal, motion on the curve can only make one of us better-off at the expense of the other. Critically, economics has NO THEORY for where we end up on the Contract Curve. Nor, since different points on the curve correspond to different prices, can PRICE settle the issue.

Using the Ultimatum Game I will show that FAIRNESS typically drives where we settle on the Contract Curve, as long as we do not have to trade with one another. Thus ethics enters economics at its foundation, yet cannot be mathematized, so is ignored in Freedman's name of a positive science.

Perhaps more important, unlike physics, no laws entail the evolution of either the biosphere or the "econosphere." There are no laws of motion whose integration would entail that evolution. Lacking an entailing theory of the growth of the economy in diversity, often of new goods and production capacities, economists ignore the most important feature of economic growth, wrongly treating it as "exogenous."

The failures above are likely to play major roles in the lapse to mere greed in our major financial institutions, and in our inadequate capacities to help drive growth in much of the poverty-struck world.

Keywords: Contract curve; Pareto efficient; fairness; Ultimatum Game; economic webs; economic growth beyond entailing laws

JEL classifications: A13; D63; O40

INTRODUCTION

Anglo-American economics is dominated by an unrelenting drive for mathematical formulation. The triumphs of this passion are clear. One needs to understand the Arrow Debreu Theory of Competitive General Equilibrium with its elegant fixed point theorem, to appreciate its intellectual power. Indeed, this theory remains the only overarching mathematical framework in economics, along with game theory and Rational Expectations as additions. All this is truly beautiful work.

In contrast, the Austrian school, long ignored, eschewed overreliance on mathematical formulation. In part, I will be supporting the centrality of issues in the evolution of the economy, or "econosphere," that appears to be beyond mathematical formulation, yet drives our lives. I will discuss new results, to be found in "No entailing laws, but enablement in the evolution of the biosphere," with French mathematicians Giuseppe Longo and Mael Montevil of the Ecole Polytechnique, Paris, and biologist Stuart Kauffman, on line at Physics ArXhiv (Longo, Montevil, & Kauffman, 2012a, 2012b). They argue that no laws whatsoever entail the evolution of the biosphere, and a fortiori, the evolution of the economy, law, or culture. If true, we cannot mathematize this evolution, for we can neither write equations of motion for the evolving biosphere or economy, nor lacking foreknowledge of the "niche" boundary conditions, whether biological or economic, could we integrate those equations of motion even were we to have them. These results are new, seem true, and if so, must change our integrated view of what economics should be, theory or praxis.

Another feature of the drive to mathematize is a deep commitment to avoiding that which cannot be mathematized, including ethical considerations. Here a kind of "physics envy" reigns in a desire for an intellectual rigor, fine for physics, but, I hope to show, entirely wrong for economic theory. Indeed the first subject I shall discuss is that ethics lies at the very center of standard economic theory, at the heart of the Pareto Efficient Contract Curve of the famous Edgeworth Box. No theorem establishes where on the Contract Curve the trading parties will settle in a final agreement. Ethics here plays a central role that is both unavoidable, and not mathematizable.

An effort to hope to mathematize ethics was given birth by Bentham and Mill in Utilitarianism. Though neither figure attempted a mathematization, they inspired later figures such as F. Y. Edgeworth (2008) to do so. But in addition to its familiar issues, which I will describe briefly, the sort of Utilitarianism Edgeworth attempted fails in the deepest way: I will argue, indeed, I hope so, based on the Longo et al.'s paper, that we cannot know ahead of time the economic variables that may become relevant, therefore cannot know the "sample space" of economic evolution, therefore cannot CALCULATE Utility Theory's "Greatest Good for the Greatest Number." All this is radical: Often not only do we not know what WILL happen, we do not even know what CAN happen, nor can we even formulate a probability for those unknown possibilities, for we lack foreknowledge of the sample space. Life is not what we have thought and living it is beyond the ken of reason alone, for we cannot reason about that which we cannot know.

ETHICS IN THE EDGEWORTH BOX

The Edgeworth Box lies at the center of understanding a simple bilateral exchange economy. Behind the Edgeworth Box lies the hope by Walras to mimic the potential energy function, one part of the heart, with kinetic energy, of the Hamiltonians of physics. The fundamental idea is that agent A has a desire for each of two products, apples and oranges. So does agent B. But their relative desires for different ratios of apples and oranges differ. Given that, there can be an advantage of trade between A and B, given an "initial endowment" to each of the set of apples and oranges, such that each is happier. Walras reasoned that this advantage of trade was analogous to the driving force in physics of a potential energy that was minimized, as when a ball rolls down a gravitational potential.

The Edgeworth Box is typically depicted as a square. Agent A is located at the lower left corner. Agent B is located at the upper right corner. The *X* axis shows the total amount of apples in the endowments of A and B. A point on the *X* axis depicts the amount of the apples owned initially by A, read as the distance from A at the lower left corner of the Box, to that point on the *X* axis. The distance from that point to the lower right corner represents the remaining apples owned by B.

Similarly, on the *Y* axis, the total number of oranges in the endowments of A and B is depicted by the entire *Y* axis. A point on the *Y* axis shows the fraction of the oranges in B's endowment, read as the distance from the upper left corner down to that point on the *Y* axis. The remaining distance from that point to the lower left corner depicts the fraction of the oranges in the endowment of A.

To continue, it is necessary to know the importance to A of owning for himself any given numbers of apples and oranges. Different points within the Edgeworth Box correspond to different numbers of apples and oranges, with no apples or oranges owned by A himself, at the lower left corner. The upper right corner would correspond to A owning all the apples and oranges. Similarly, B is represented in the upper right corner, which point represents B owning NO apples or oranges. The lower left corner represents B owning for himself all the apples and oranges.

For each agent, a set of roughly parallel "utility curves" each represent the "trade-off" of apples to oranges that make either agent A or agent B "equally happy," hence each such curve is called an "isoutility curve." The set of curves for agent A starts near the lower left corner with few apples and oranges owned by A for himself, and he is not very happy, so has "low" utility. As one "ascends" up the set of roughly parallel isoutility curves for A, agent A becomes ever happier as the upper right corner is approached.

In parallel for agent B, a set of nearly parallel isoutility curves show his trade-off of apples for oranges. Near the upper right corner, B owns for himself almost no apples or oranges, so is not very happy and his isoutility curves near that corner are of low utility for him. As HIS set of nearly parallel isoutility curves are crossed, going from the upper right to lower left corner, he owns for himself ever more of the apples and oranges and his utility goes up, reaching a maximum at the lower left corner.

At this point in the development of the Edgeworth Box theory, the way each of A's isoutility curves are "bent" in the *X Y* space of the Edgeworth Box, and the way the isoutility curves of agent B are "bent" become critical. By convention as given, for example, by different algebraic expressions for this bending of isoutility curves, the curves are bent in such a way that for EACH isoutility curve of A, there are a SET of neighboring isoutility curves for B, EACH of which is bent such that there is a convex space between the two isoutility curves between two points where the A and B isoutility curves CROSS.

We need one more initial idea: At the start of time, agent A has some fraction of the apples and some fraction of the oranges in his "endowment." B has rest of the apples and oranges in HIS endowment. These endowments pick a single point inside the Edgeworth Box which is the initial state of the economy.

The initial state corresponds to some point where two isoutility curves, one of A's and one of B's, cross.

Now the magic happens, thanks to the magical curvature of the isoutility curves leaving the convex space between A's and B's isoutility curves between the two points where they cross, one of which is the initial state of the economy. Why? Because any point INSIDE that convex region is a point where the isoutility curves of BOTH A AND B are greater, higher, than the initial state of the economy.

This is the crucial step that Walras saw and Edgeworth mathematized. By exchanging apples for oranges from the initial state of the economy, A and B can jointly move to a state INSIDE the convex region noted. In doing so each is "happier," so the two have "AN ADVANTAGE OF TRADE." It is to the benefit of BOTH A AND B to exchange their initial endowments of apples and oranges, such that they move from the initial state of the economy, corresponding to both their initial endowments of apples and oranges, to a point inside the convex curve.

It is this increase in happiness for both A and B that Walras saw as the analogue for a ball rolling down a gravitational potential and his hopes to align economics in a trade economy with physics.

THE CONTRACT CURVE

But the wonderful Edgeworth Box hides another bit of magic where ethics in some form often enters. The Box is filled with A's isoutility curves, densely packed, filling the space in the Box. So too is the Box filled with B's isoutility curves densely packed, filling the space in the Box. Thus, for EACH isoutility curve of A, there is exactly ONE isoutility curve of B which is exactly TANGENT to A's isoutility point at a single spot. In short, the two crossings of many pairs of A and B isoutility curves, for these special pairs of curves, come together at this single point of "tangency." But at that special point, there is NO LONGER a convex space within the Box between these two curves which are tangent at a single point. IF the economy is at such a point of tangency, there IS NO FURTHER trades that agents A and B can do that makes both A and B happier! All the advantages of trade have been "used up" once a point of tangency is achieved by, say, a series of early trades of apples for oranges by A and B.

Now consider the initial state of the economy and the pair of A and B isoutility curves that cross at the initial state of the economy. The entire convex regions between these curves are the entire region of advantages of trades between A and B. But because the A and B isoutility curves each densely fill the Box, the entire convex region of advantages of trade is "bisected" by a line of points connecting all the adjacent pairs of A and B isoutility curves where they are exactly tangent. This line, or more generally "curve" through all these points of tangency, is the "Contract Curve."

Now the very special properties of the Contract Curve itself are that: (1) no trades that move A and B OFF the contract curve can make both happier and (2) the most critical property is that NO MOTION ON the Contract Curve can make BOTH A AND B happier at the same time. Either A becomes happier and B less happier, or A less happy and B happier. The curve is said to be "PARETO EFFICIENT." Note that motion ON the contract curve constitutes a change in the ratio of trade of apples to oranges, hence is a change in the PRICE of apples in terms of oranges. Thus, no change in price can determine where on the contract curve A and B eventually "settle." Price does not determine the outcome!

Why should we care? Because the Edgeworth Box mathematizes the advantages of trade as well as can be done in mathematical economics. BUT NOTHING in that mathematics, including any change in price, tells us where on the Contract Curve the two trading parties may end up!

The two could end up at one or the other end of the Contract Curve, then either A or B gets ALL the advantages of trade. Here "market power" may come into play and often does.

But what else may determine where on the Contract Curve the two parties end up? Ethics!

THE ULTIMATUM GAME AND ETHICS

I now describe a famous "game" tried around the world. I am the game organizer. You and another person, say Mary. Here are the rules of my game, known equally to you and Mary. I tell YOU, "I will give you $10,000, but you must make a single offer to Mary to share some fraction of the $10,000 with her. IF and only IF she accepts, I give you the $10,000 and you give her the agreed upon share. BUT IF she does NOT accept your offer, I give you nothing and neither of you get a cent."

That is the "Ultimatum Game." OK. How much do you offer Mary? Think about it. How much DO you really offer Mary? Around the world, the fraction is between 30% and 50% in almost all cultures. WHY? Because if you offer Mary $1.00, you fear that she may be angry at you for your greed and would rather forego the $1.00 that let you be so UNFAIR.

UNFAIR? WHY THAT IS AN ETHICAL NOTION

Monkeys behave the same way. Here is the experiment. A group of monkeys are in cages and can see each other. Each day the experimenter enters and gives each monkey 10 grapes. One day he enters, gives all but one monkey 10 grapes and gives the remaining monkey 10 bananas. What happens? In what I hope is rage, the other monkeys hurl their grapes from their cages! UNFAIR.

We evolved as social primates. Sharing good fortune was part of sharing, for example, food in a fluctuating environment. I see you on the trail. You caught a rabbit, I nothing. "Can I borrow half your rabbit, I'll pay you back as soon as possible. And here is a marked stick I give you to help us remember my promise to you," I say. You share your half rabbit with me, and I pay you back with a half squirrel two days later. In doing this we have mastered by sharing a fluctuating environment, who knows who will find food each day? And we invented "credit," my stick is money marking my promise and your lending me the half rabbit is credit. We have bound time by our intertemporal trade.

It is FAIR, we need the sharing to survive. It is a roughly FAIR trade. Ethics just entered.

So, I claim, your giving Mary $4,200.00 is a fair trade, an ethical one.

But I claim the same ethical demand helps determine where we end up on the contract curve.

Caveats. If many can trade apples and oranges, and few have apples, those few have market power and can get more of the advantages of trade. But take the housing market. How many of us have gone through the above calculation about how to offer or demand, taking account of the anger we may generate with our greedy behavior. FAIRNESS.

Ethics is central, not peripheral to the Edgeworth Box, so central to the cornerstone of the economic theory of advantages of trade that drive trade and economic activity.

An even stronger case is the Dictator game. Here I have been given $1000.00 and I can determine how much I give you, you must agree. I keep the rest whether you agree or not. Typically we give a reasonable fraction of the $1000.00. Why? This is NOT the behavior of "Economic Man." In the Dictator game, there is no argument that I share with you, as in the Ultimatum Game, calculating what your response will be and act for my own advantage. We give in the Dictator game because we sense it is "fair," a moral issue, perhaps evolved as social primates.

THE INADEQUACY OF ECONOMIC GROWTH THEORY

I believe our current familiar theories of economic growth are fundamentally inadequate, if not even fundamentally flawed, strong statements from a noneconomist.

I begin with this rough truth. How many goods and services were in the global economy 50,000 years ago? Perhaps a few hundred to a few thousand. How many are in the global economy today? By good estimates,

New York City boasts about 10,000,000,000 goods and services. The global economy with its diversity is obviously greater.

How did this explosion of goods and services arise? The truth is, we have no theory for it, certainly no theory whatsoever the specific goods and services that have come to exist.

Note that the growth of the economy is the growth of an economic WEB of goods and production capacities, where new goods and production capacities arise as new economic opportunities, or "adjacent possible" economic niches, arise as new substitutes or complements of existing goods. The standard theories of economic growth are single-sector models that entirely miss the role of the economic web in economic growth, as discussed below (Hanel, Kauffman, & Thurner, 2005; Kauffman, 1995; Wagner & Ashkenasy, 2009), where the very diversity of the web is a positive factor in its own growth. Indeed, we will find subcritical and supracritical economic growth as a function of the diversity of renewable goods and production capacities in the economy (Hanel et al., 2005; Kauffman, 1995; Wagner & Ashkenasy, 2009).

But it will be my deeper claim, a radical one, that we CAN HAVE NO ENTAILING THEORY for the specific goods and services and production capacities that have come to exist. More I shall claim, as an extension of a set of ideas based on an analysis of the evolution of a similar explosion of diversity among species in the last 3.5 billion years, that we can have NO entailing theory for the evolution of the biosphere or, a fortiori, for the evolution of the econosphere (Longo et al., 2012a, 2012b). More I shall claim that the evolving biosphere, without natural selection "acting" to achieve it, creates its own future possibilities of becoming. In a rather parallel way, the evolving econosphere creates, often with no intent or foresight, its own possibilities of becoming.

This claim is truly radical. Newton taught us how to think. Given his three laws of motion and universal gravitation, formulated in differential equations, he gave us the mathematization of Aristotle's Efficient Cause. Were we to ask Newton how to analyze six billiard balls rolling on a billiard table he would tell us to measure the initial positions and momenta of all the balls, the initial conditions. Then he would tell us to measure the shape of the billiard table, the boundary conditions. Then he would tell us to INTEGRATE his equations in differential equation form giving the forces between the balls to derive the future trajectories of the balls. But integration IS deduction and deduction IS entailment, so Newton taught us an entailed deterministic worldview.

With Laplace and his Demon in the sky knowing the initial positions and momenta of all the particles, then using Newton's laws, we could deduce the entire future and past of the universe. (Newton's equations are time reversible.) This is the birth of modern reductionism, the faith that there is a theory "down there," that entails the entire unfolding of the universe. Laplace thought determinism implied predictability. With Poincare' and the three gravitating body problems, we encountered deterministic chaos where nearby states lie on trajectories that diversify exponentially at least initially. Since we cannot measure positions and momenta to infinite accuracy, Poincare' taught us that determinism did not imply predictability, contra Laplace, but left us in an entailed universe.

Even quantum mechanics does not change this in a fundamental way. From the Schrodinger equation and Born rule, we derive the deterministic entailed trajectory of a probability distribution – still we live in an entailed world.

Longo, Montevil, and Kauffman, in "No entailing laws, but enablement in the evolution of the biosphere," (2012a, 2012b), think this view is wrong for the becoming of the evolving biosphere. I urge you to read this difficult paper, beyond the scope of this paper. But I give part of its core now.

We begin by noting that in physics one can always PRESTATE the phase space, Newton, Einstein, Schrodinger. From this we get equations of motion and trajectories in that space. But we argue, and to say that we cannot prestate the ever changing phase space itself of the evolving biosphere (or econosphere), so can write no laws of motion. Nor, lacking foreknowledge of the boundary conditions afforded by biological or economic niches, could we integrate the equations of motion in differential form, even if we had them. Hence no laws entail the becoming of the biosphere, nor the economy, where in the former we need not consider human intent but do in the latter.

I begin with the biological notion of a Kantian whole. Kant told us that in an organized being, the parts exist for and by means of the whole, and the whole exists for and by means of the parts.

An example is in the hands of Gonen Ashkenasy at Ben Gurion University. Ashkenasy has constructed nine small proteins, called peptides (Kauffman, 1995; Wagner & Ashkenasy, 2009). Each peptide catalyzes, that is, speeds up, the gluing together, or ligation, of two smaller peptide fragments which, when ligated, form the NEXT of the nine peptides. This catalysis proceeds around a rough cycle among the nine peptides, such that the set as a WHOLE is "collectively autocatalytic." Critically, no peptide catalyzes its OWN formation, the set as a WHOLE catalyzes its own formation, hence is collectively autocatalytic. If we call "catalyzing a reaction" a "catalytic task," then the nine peptide set achieves "Task Closure." All the reactions requiring catalysis are catalyzed by at least one of the nine peptides.

Such an autocatalytic set is a simple example of a Kantian whole; the parts exist for and by means of the whole and the whole exist for and by means of the parts.

Now consider a dividing bacterium in an environment. It too achieves some vast task closure far beyond mere catalysis, for it replicates DNA, makes membranes, chemosmotic pumps, transmembrane proteins, and divides.

I now take an odd step: Can you name ALL the uses of a screw driver? Try it: Screw in a screw, open a can of paint, stab an assailant, tie to the end of a stick as a fish spear, rent to the locals and take 5% of the fish catch as rent, an objet d'art, wedge open a door, scrape putty off a window ... . I think, and this is critical, that we agree to the following: (1) The number of uses of a screw driver, alone or with other things, is INDEFINITE. (2) Unlike the integers which are ORDERABLE, THERE IS NO NATURAL ORDERING AMONG THE USES OF THE SCREW DRIVER.

But (1) and (2) mean something profound: there is no effective procedure to LIST ALL THE USES OF A SCREW DRIVER. That is, there is no algorithm to list the uses of a screw driver.

Now let us try one use of a screw driver: open a can of paint. Can you list all the other things or processes that alone or together can be used to open a can of paint? Again, the number of things that can be used to do this is indefinite and unorderable. So there is no effective procedure, or algorithm, to list all those objects.

ADAPTATIONS IN EVOLUTION ARE NON-PRESTATABLE AND NO LAWS ENTAIL EVOLUTION

Now let us consider an evolving bacterium in some niche. ALL that has to happen is that some one or more cellular or molecular screw drivers FIND SOME USE that enhances the fitness of the bacterium in its niche, then if those screw drivers have heritable variations, natural selection will tend to pull out the fitter variants. This IS adaptation. It is also "The arrival of the Fitter" in evolution.

But can we prestate the USE that the cellular or molecular screw driver finds? No! The evolution of novel functionalities is nonalgorithmic. Here is why, first, as above, we cannot algorithmically list those uses, nor the entities that can fulfill some use. Second, the bacterium achieves its task closure via effects that pass through the environment. But selection acts at the level of the Kantian whole bacterium, not its molecular or cellular screw drivers. More we cannot prestate the aspects of the actual niche by which the organism finds some new task closure until selection reveals AFTER THE FACT what worked. That is, the task closure via the niche and the rest of the organism that achieves that task closure are CIRCULARLY DEFINED. We cannot define the actual niche of the evolving organism beforehand. We can only recognize it after the fact of success under selection at the level of the Kantian whole bacterium evolving.

But these facts mean that there is no algorithm or effective list of features of cellular or molecular screw drivers that find some use, nor any way of prestating the actual niche in which task closure by the Kantian whole is achieved. We cannot SAY IT beforehand.

In turn this means that when the adaptation occurs, the phase space of the biosphere has changed in a way we cannot prestate. Thus, we can write no laws of motion for the evolving biosphere. Nor, if the niche is the boundary condition, can we prestate it either, thus we could not know beforehand the boundary conditions, so could not integrate the equations of motion of the biosphere in differential equation form, even if we had those equations, which we do not. In short, no laws entail the evolution of the biosphere.

We are beyond the reductionism of Newton and Laplace and contemporary physics at the watershed of life.

DARWINIAN PREADAPTATIONS ARE NOT PRESTATABLE

I discuss next the reality of the lack of entailment in light of what are called Darwinian preadaptations, which are not prestatable.

Darwin discussed not only functions, as the function of the heart is to pump blood, for which he gave a selective account, we discovered what are now called Darwinian preadaptations or "exaptations." His point was that a causal feature of an organism of no selective use in the current environment might come to have a new use in a different environment. Here is an example: Some fish have swim bladders, sacs partially filled with air and partially with water whose ratio adjusts neutral buoyancy in the water column.

Now paleontologists claim the swim bladder evolved from the lungs of lung fish as water entered some lungs. Assume this is true.

First, did a new function arise in the biosphere? Yes, neutral buoyancy. Second, did the preadaptation affect evolution? Yes, new fish with swim bladders, new proteins and critically, ONCE the swim bladder exists, it affords what I will call a "new Adjacent Possible" empty niche, for a worm or bacterium or both might evolve to live in the swim bladder alone. I return to this in a moment.

Finally, now that you know what preadaptations are, can you prestate all human preadaptations in the next 3 million years? We all say NO. Why? How would we prestate and list all selective conditions? This parallels prestating and listing ALL USES of screw drivers for which there is NO effective procedure. How would we prestate all features of organisms that might fulfill such a use? This parallels the lack of an effective procedure to list all the objects that can be used, like a screw driver, to open a can of paint.

In short, we cannot prestate the evolution of the biosphere into its adjacent possible. Not only do we not know what WILL happen, we do not even, typically, know what CAN happen. This means that we do not know all the possibilities of the evolution of the biosphere. Thus we do not know its "sample space." Thus we cannot even make probability statements about that evolution.

Further, if we do not know what CAN happen, we cannot reason about it. Reason is an insufficient guide for living our lives, for the evolution of the econosphere, like the biosphere cannot be prestated, nor, I believe, is it entailed or mathematizable in its detailed unfolding, more on this below. For if this thesis is true, that often we do not even know what CAN happen, then top down management, as if life were a solvable optimization problem whose relevant variables were knowable beforehand, is typically a profound illusion. We must reshape how we govern ourselves to enable, not to command.

THE EVOLVING BIOSPHERE CREATES, WITH NO "ACTION" OF SELECTION, ITS OWN FUTURE POSSIBILITIES

The next issue is, for me stunning, and has changed forever my view of reality. Without selection "acting" to achieve it, the biosphere creates its own future possibilities of becoming. We will see the parallel in the evolution of the econosphere below, where, typically with no intent or foresight, the evolving econosphere also creates its own possibilities of becoming. These possibilities are at the heart of the unprestatable course of economic growth that has led from 10,000 to 10 billion or more goods and services in the past 50,000 years.

I invite you to consider this with me: Above I asked, Did the evolution of the swim bladder, ONCE IT CAME TO EXIST, change the future possible evolution of the biosphere? Of course the answer is YES. It is true, true, that once the swim bladder exists it constitutes an Adjacent Possible Empty Niche in which a bacterium or worm or both might evolve to live. Thus, once it exists, the swim bladder changes the future possibilities of evolution.

But now ask: DID Natural Selection, to anthropomorphize it harmlessly, "struggle" to create the swim bladder as a new Adjacent Possible Empty Niche? Well, ask first, did natural selection "act" on a population of evolving fish with lungs to evolve functioning swim bladders? Of course. In this falsely anthropomorphized view of selection, selection "acted" to achieve functioning swim bladders.

But did Natural Selection "struggle" to achieve the swim bladder AS A NEW ADJACENT POSSIBLE EMPTY NICHE? NO! Selection was indifferent to the fact that, once achieved, the swim bladder would constitute a new Adjacent Possible Empty Niche.

Yet this means something stunning: Without selection in any way acting to "achieve it," evolution is creating its own future possibilities! The evolving biosphere creates its own possibilities of becoming.

How far we are from the entailed reductionistic worldview spawned by Newton? In this worldview, at least for life in its becoming, that becoming is not entailed by any law, and without any natural selection "acting" to achieve it, evolution creates the very possibilities it shall become. Moreover, we cannot prestate this becoming.

THE NEW ADJACENT POSSIBLE EMPTY NICHE ENABLES BUT DOES NOT CAUSE THE NEW POSSIBLE EVOLUTION

Evolution requires mutations in contemporary DNA-based life. Typically, these mutations are quantum events, hence indeterminate and acausal. Thus, the new niche afforded by the swim bladder does not "cause" the evolution of the bacterium or worm that comes to live in it. Rather the new adjacent possible niche ENABLES the new possibilities afforded to evolution by the coming into existence of the swim bladder. Thus not only do we live in the familiar web of cause and effect, we also live in a web of new niche opportunities that enable, make possible, new future directions in evolution.

The vastness of this change in worldview is captured by a statement by Max Weber, early sociologist, "With Newton we became disenchanted and entered Modernity." Yes, for with Newton, we entered an entailed becoming of the universe to be captured by some final theory, with no room for, if you will, magic. But is not the creation by the biosphere of its own possibilities of becoming a "natural magic" that is re-enchanting?

Our living world is not the world of Newton, Einstein, Schrodinger, or even amazing Darwin who did not yet see that the biosphere, beyond selection, creates its own future possibilities. We live in a different reality than we have thought. Ultimately we will come to BE in this reality in a new way. From this must follow a slow transition beyond Modernity, born of Newton, the Enlightenment and its Age of Reason, the resulting Industrial Revolution and entry into a Modernity in which we are, I think, inarticulately partially lost.

THE EVOLVING ECONOSPHERE IS NOT MATHEMATIZABLE, AND CREATES ITS FUTURE POSSIBILITIES

The arguments above require no consideration of human conscious intent, for they apply to the biosphere's evolution with no consideration of intent at all. The evolution of the economy surely involves human intent. But simultaneously, the evolving econosphere creates its own empty economic niches which afford, not causes, but opportunities, for its future possible evolution.

Consider these familiar facts: In the 1930s Turing invented the Turing machine. This did not cause, but enabled von Neuman to invent the present computer architecture. This did not cause, but enabled the invention of the mainframe computer. The wide sale of the computer created a new economic niche opportunity for the invention of the personal computer. The wide sale of the personal computer did not cause, but enabled the invention of word processing. The invention of word processing enabled sharing files.

The wide spread sharing of files did not cause, but enabled the opportunity to invent the World Wide Web. The invention of the Web did not cause, but enabled the invention of sales on the Web. Wide spread sales and other content on the web did not cause, but enabled the new economic niche opportunity for Web browsers. And the Web did not cause but enabled social networks, and Facebook arose and enabled the Arabic Spring.

We have lived this history. Did Turing either intend or foresee Facebook? NO. The growth of the multifaceted economic web is here before us. Can we prestate it? No. Do we know the ever new Adjacent Possible Opportunities that this growth enables and into which we become? No. Is reason a sufficient guide for a road map command and control top down decision process, as if we, at Turing's time, knew the variables, the WEB and Facebook, that would become relevant? No. Is the phase space of the evolving econosphere persistently changing in unprestatable ways? Yes. Can we therefore write an entailing set of laws of motion for economic growth in the ever new goods and services sprawling into ever new adjacent possible but unprestatable economic niche opportunities? NO. Could we prestate the new economic niches which are the boundary conditions on that economic evolution, allowing us to integrate the equations of motion of the evolving econosphere, even if we had them? No. Hence no laws entail the evolution of the econosphere.

Then, beyond Anglo-American economic growth theory, we cannot mathematize the detailed becoming of the econosphere.

More, does this evolution, typically with no intent or foresight, create its own new Adjacent Possibilities of its future becoming? Yes. In turn these new Adjacent Possibilities constitute new enabling constraints that define the new Adjacent Possible, and into which we become. In turn that becoming engenders new Adjacent Possibilities with yet new enabling constraints. We can rarely prestate any of this. The living world is not that of Newton, Einstein, Schrodinger, Darwin, or Arrow Debru, for with regard to Arrow Debru, we cannot prestate the future possibilities, so can have NO probability distribution over them, so cannot carry out the splendid fixed point theorem of Competitive General Equilibrium for an evolving econosphere.

Finally, most theories of economic growth are SINGLE-SECTOR ECONOMIC MODELS. But this entirely misses the history above in which the vast WEB of sprawling diversity of ever new goods and services create, in typically unprestatable ways, ever new empty economic niche opportunities into which entrepreneurs, the heroes of Schumpeter who eschewed premature mathematization, create their gales of creative destruction.

It is not that single-sector models are useless; it is that they miss the main drive that has led from 10,000 goods and services 50,000 years ago to billions today. Almost certainly, the very diversity of the current "economic web" enables, but does not cause, the growth of the ever new Adjacent Possibilities into which the economy becomes.

SUBCRITICAL AND SUPRACRITICAL ECONOMIC GROWTH

Alberta, Canada, has an export economy, exporting wheat, timber, oil, and beef. It is the richest Provence in Canada, thanks largely to oil revenues. It has a stable government, stable banks, well-educated people, stable money, and fine infrastructure. Yet the diversity of goods and services produced by Alberta has not increased much at all over decades.

Call an economy whose diversity of produced goods and services and production capacities does not increase, "Subcritical." Alberta is subcritical.

The global economy has produced a diversity of goods which has exploded from some 1,000 to 10,000, say 50,000 years ago, to billions today. The US and First World economies are producing ever new goods and services. Call such economies "Supracritical economies." This distinction is a fact of the economic world. Yet standard economic growth theory, largely single-sector growth models, has no account for this phenomenon.

It is intuitively plausible that the rate of growth of the Adjacent Possible economic niche opportunities is itself an increasing function of the existing diversity of goods and production capacities. If so, diversity itself helps drive economic growth.

Our incapacity to write equations of motion for the detailed, nonalgorithmic, unprestatable growth of new goods and services and production capacities seems real, and precludes detailed prediction via laws of motion in differential equation form and their integration by prestatable boundary conditions. As above, the evolution of the econosphere is not "entailed."

However, it IS possible to construct more limited algorithmic models (Hanel et al., 2005; Hanel, Kauffman, & Thurner, 2007; Kauffman, 1995), several of which are now published. In general, one gives up detailed prediction for statistical laws. These laws, in their simplest form, plot the extant diversity of renewable resources on the X axis and diversity of production capacities on the Y axis. A critical line separates a subcritical region below that line and a supracritical region above that line. Theorems establish these results (Hanel et al., 2005, 2007). Thus, while we cannot predict the specific unfolding of the real economy, we can make policy guiding science that strongly suggests that the diversity of production capacities and renewable resources in a trading region play major roles in economic growth. All this is beyond the reach of single-sector economic growth models which formed the basis of the Washington Consensus, and may play a role in the failure of the IMF and World Bank to drive real growth for a half century.

We misunderstand economic growth. It is strongly dependent upon the diversity of the economy and the way that diversity itself enables, but does not cause, the emergence of few or many new Adjacent Possibilities for new economic activities into which the econosphere "becomes," enabling yet new Adjacent Possibilities we typically cannot prestate. And we misconstrue the roles of command and control in companies, and governance and policy, as IF we knew and could optimize that which we cannot know, but still cocreate. We must learn to enable wisely, both new Actuals and new Adjacent Possibles, a new intellectual task, in economic growth and in governance around the globe.

THE FAILURES OF UTILITARIAN AND SIMPLE DEONTOLOGICAL ETHICS

Utilitarian ethics was, famously, founded by Bentham and Mill in the 19th century. The maxim of Utilitarian ethics says, in Bentham's words, "An action then may be said to be conformable to the principle of utility ... when the tendency it has to augment the happiness of the community is greater than any it has to diminish it" (Bentham, 1921). Because Bentham identified the "interest of the community" with "the sum of the interests of the several members who compose it," it may not be unfair to say that Bentham seeks to maximize average or mean utility.

F. Y. Edgeworth interpreted the "Greatest Happiness" principle of Utilitarian ethics to seek "the greatest sum-total of pleasure summed through all time and over all sentience" (p. vii). Thus, Edgeworth is clearly maximizing mean utility given population, and we may call this sort of utilitarianism "mean-utilitarianism."

Peart and Levy (2005, pp. 180–203) discuss what we might call "median-utilitarianism," which they associate with Adam Smith and J. S. Mill (pp. 184–185). Adam Smith and J. S. Mill upheld an ethical principal of reciprocity, whereby we should have sympathy for one another and each counts for one. With reciprocity in that sense, it becomes harder to justify dispossessing the powerless. On the contrary, reciprocity demands that we ensure all persons capable of free exchange are empowered to join the network of trade. If "utilitarianism" is understood to include a principle of reciprocity, then the welfare of the median individual is a fairly good barometer of policy, whereas the welfare of the mean individual is not. In the ambiguous formula "greatest good for the greatest number," the phrase "greatest number" may be more important than the phrase "greatest good."

Perhaps we should not consider median-utilitarianism to be a form of utilitarianism at all because it does not consider all pains and pleasures to be equal. Instead it considers all persons to be equal. However, it is not clear whether the general notion of enhancing "utility" implies the one principle of equality rather than the other. Moreover, we should certainly view J. S. Mill as a utilitarian. If Peart and Levy are right to view him as a median-utilitarian, then perhaps such views should be considered a legitimate variant of the species "utilitarian ethics." In any event, median-utilitarianism and mean-utilitarianism lead to different conclusions.

Edgeworth seems to have been sensitive to the difference between median-utilitarianism and mean-utilitarianism. He criticizes Bentham's phrase "Greatest happiness of the greatest number," and hints that it may have led "Bentham's followers" into "exaggerating the democratic or isocratic tendencies implicit in *Utilitarianism*" (p. 117, n. 1). Edgeworth rejected "the assumption that *Equality* is necessarily implied in Utilitarianism." He thought "some classes of sentients" have a greater "*Capacity for happiness*," which implied that "there is no presumption that equality of circumstances is the most felicific arrangement" (2008, p. vii). Edgeworth did not hesitate to draw illiberal conclusions from his mean-utilitarianism. The final paper of *Mathematical Psychics*, "On the Present Crisis in Ireland," was intended as an illustration to answer the question "of what possible use can Psychical Mathematics be in real life" (p. 126). The first part of this paper was devoted to showing that his more refined mathematical version of utilitarianism defeated "the authority of Mill, conveying an impression of what other Bethamites have taught openly, that all men, if not equal, are at least *equipotential*, in virtue of equal educability" (p. 132). Those who speak of "some metaphysical 'rights of man' " are "demogues" (p. 129). Edgeworth does not explicitly say that the Irish are somehow inferior to the English. It seems evident, however, that he thinks his mean-utilitarian knocks away one of the main supports of Irish liberation, median-utilitarianism.

Unfortunately, it was Edgeworth's mean-utilitarianism that came to inform standard economics. This type of utilitarian ethics gave rise to the economic concept of "utility" and "utility functions" as in the Edgeworth Box discussed in the "Introduction" section.

There are famous and familiar problems with Utilitarian ethics of this sort. One of the most obvious is: how do we partition the "Good" among the "numbers." Thus, if the good is monetary, say $10,000, and the number is 100 people, does one get all $10,000? Is the $10,000 equally split? Indeed, given a finite sum, here $10,000, the distribution of these among the 100 people is, like the famous Contract Curve in the Edgeworth Box, PARETO EFFICIENT. There is no way to give more of the money to any one person without making the others less happy.

Thus, just as the Contract Curve does not solve the ETHICAL problem of what is a fair partition of the advantages of trade, neither does Utilitarian ethics solve the problem of the ETHICAL and FAIR distribution of the "good," whatever it may be, among the "number" of people.

A second well-known problem, familiar to all students of Ethics 101, is this: One hundred of us are randomly seized by thugs who promise to shoot to death one of us, and then let the rest free. How do we choose "the one"? For most of us, although we realize that under Utilitarian ethics, it is surely better for just one of us to be shot to death, most normal humans would not participate in this act. We would consider it to be UNFAIR and immoral. But then on what ethical grounds do we so consider this action to be immoral and unfair if Utilitarianism is our only recourse?

Interestingly, if true, I have read of a small lesion in the brain of normal humans which renders those with the lesion perfect Utilitarians. If true, this suggests that normal humans have evolved brain structures which override Utilitarianism.

But there is a still deeper problem with Utilitarian ethics that I wish to stress: Utilitarian ethics presumes that we can, ahead of time, calculate the consequences of our action, then act for the greatest good of the greatest number. Some philosophers have tried to get around this problem by switching from "act utilitarianism" to "rule utilitarianism" or even "indirect utilitarianism" (see Williams, 1973). But if the econosphere is as creative as I have been arguing, then it may be necessary to rethink the epistemic guidance they can offer us. In any event, the mean-utilitarianism that undergirds standard economics is clearly ill suited to guide us into the future of a creative world.

The entire argument above about our inability to prestate the evolution of the biosphere, the economy, and culture, the unprestatable emergence of ever new Adjacent Possibles which are enabling constraints that enable us to enter into new activities, business opportunities, cultural activities, human activities, implies that we do not even know what CAN happen. But then we not only cannot reason about such consequences of our acts, we surely cannot calculate those consequences. Thus, in many or most real-life situations, Utilitarianism is simply moot. It can make no ethical statements at all, let alone solve the Pareto optimality issue raised above.

As a concrete example, consider a venture capitalist confronted with a young enthusiastic entrepreneur, eager to start his or her new business. The risks and rewards can be roughly stated, but too much depends upon what we cannot know for any firm calculation of the risks. Assume the venture capitalist is taken with the young entrepreneur and wishes to be of help. Still, how does the venture capitalist decide to risk capital? How does the venture capitalist decide to keep investing in the fledgling company to keep it afloat until it finds a pathway to success – if it does?

KANT AND DEONTOLOGICAL ETHICS

Immanuel Kant (1951) famously proposed a logical test for moral maxims: "Act such that the maxim of your action can be universalized." Thus, it is wrong to lie. Why? If we all tell the truth, the maxim can be universalized. If we all lie, there is no POINT in lying, so the maxim cannot be universalized.

But the problem Kant faces is that real moral problems often place moral maxims in conflict. Again, the Ethics 101 question. You are in your home. Your spouse is asleep in the bedroom. A former, angry lover of your spouse enters and demands to know if your spouse is asleep in the bedroom. Lying is wrong. Letting your spouse be killed is wrong. Two moral aims are in conflict, the typical situation in real moral discussion.

But the number of moral maxims is indefinite. More, there IS no natural ordering among our moral aims, the sumum bonum sought by the Greeks, the sumum bonum −1, −2, −3. Lacking an ordering, or even partial ordering. Thus we have no effective procedure, or algorithms even to list all moral maxims. Hence we have NO ALGORITHMIC WAY to decide moral issues. I think this is of fundamental importance. Given a morally laden situation, we engage in nonalgorithmic moral argument and may or may not ultimately agree.

Yet, on the Contract Curve, with the monkeys faced with grapes while one gets bananas, and in Utilitarian ethics, we nevertheless find a way to what we come to consider FAIR. We cannot, it seems, do so algorithmically.

THE HUMAN MIND IS NOT ALGORITHMIC AND THE FRAME PROBLEM

Thus I close this broad discussion of ethics, economic growth, and the inadequacy of Utility theory by briefly trying to show that human reasoning is not algorithmic. This shows up in the famous FRAME problem of computer science with algorithmic computers. A robot is in room, computer on board. Many features of the room and robot are given a FINITE LIST of "affordances," such as "X is a," X does a," X uses a," X needs a." Given that finite list of affordances, the computer can compute any logical consequence of the finite list of affordances.

But it cannot compute consequences that are not logically derivable from the finite list of affordances.

Is the human mind so bound? No, I claim and give several examples. A number of engineers are trying to invent the tractor. They know they need a huge engine block, find one, mount it on a chassis, which promptly breaks. They try ever bigger chassis. All break. At last, one of the engineers says, "You know, the engine block is so big and RIGID, we can hang everything off the engine block itself and USE IT as the chassis." That was a patentable invention and it is how tractors are made.

Now if the finite list of affordances about engine blocks had not included the rigidity of the engine block, no algorithmic computer could have solved the problem as the engineer did. His doing so exemplifies the FRAME problem. There IS no predefinable statement of the broad context, and there is no algorithm, as discussed above, for the USES of a screw driver or rigid engine block – here as a chassis – which uses are indefinite in number and unorderable, so not listable algorithmically. But this IS the FRAME problem, hence no algorithm can solve the frame problem. Indeed computer science using Turing machines has never solved the frame problem. Yet we find those uses all the time. So does evolution by Darwinian preadaptations and without conscious mind.

A second funny personal example: My wife and I, years ago, were driving from the University of Pennsylvania parking lot to take me to the airport. Elizabeth drove into the intersection. A car rushing through a red light at right angles to her almost hit us. The driver smashed his horn, then advanced adjacent to our car and proceeded to bang into our right side several times. We both stopped at a red light. He rolled down his driver window and brandished a pistol at us. A car pulled up and stopped behind this pistol brandishing threat. No one was stopped behind us. Elizabeth brilliantly jammed our car into reverse and backed up 60 feet. The light changed, the angry man could not back up to us and drove off. We were saved from a ridiculous way to die, reported the incident in 1 minute, with description of driver, car and license number to a passing policeman who did nothing whatsoever about this felony. And we drove to the airport.

Now Elizabeth solved the frame problem. How would we program a computer to solve the affordances created by this extremely complex and context-laden situation? There is no definite prestatable list of the features of situations which allow such a finite list of affordances to suffice, just as there is no algorithm to list all the uses of a screw driver.

The human mind and evolution of life are not algorithmic. With this, our ethical reasoning is also not algorithmic.

Yet as the Edgeworth Box shows, our nonalgorithmic sense of fairness and moral arguments central to the operation of the economy, from the Contract Curve to the Occupy movement rightly decrying the 1% versus the 99%, where the 1%, driven by unending greed for wealth and power, operates largely in today's first world for its own benefit, corrupting our political and social lives. Human morality, honor, integrity, and generosity are broader than Gordon Gekko. The economy must evolve serve our humanity, not we the economy.

ACKNOWLEDGMENT

This work was partially funded by the TEKES FOUNDATION which supported the author's Finnish Distinguished Professorship at Tampere University of Technology.

REFERENCES

Bentham, J. (1821). *On the Liberty of the press, and public discussion*. London.

Edgeworth, F. W. (2008). In Schotter, A. (Ed.), *Microeconomics: A modern approach* (p. 524). Cengage Learning. ISBN: 978-0-324-31584-4

Hanel, R., Kauffman, S., & Thurner, S. (2005). Phase transition in random catalytic networks. *Physical Review E*, *72*, 036117.

Hanel, R., Kauffman, S., & Thurner, S. (2007). Towards a physics of evolution: Critical diversity dynamics at the edges of collapses and bursts of diversification. *Physical Review E, 76*, 036110.

Immanuel, K. (1951). In, J. H. Bernard (Ed.), *Critique of judgment*. New York, NY: Hafner Publishing. (Original publication date 1892.)

Kauffman, S. (1995). *At home in the universe*. New York, NY: Oxford University Press.

Longo, G., Montevil, M., & Kauffman, S. (2012a). No entailing laws, but enablement in the evolution of life. Physics ArXhiv posted.

Longo, G. Montevil, M., & Kauffman, S. (2012b). No entailing laws, but enablement in the evolution of the biosphere. In *Proceedings of the fourteenth international conference on genetic and evolutionary computation conference companion* (pp. 1379–1392). doi:10.1145/2330784/2330946. Retrieved from http://dl.acm.org/citation.cfm?id=2330163

Wagner, N., & Ashkenasy, G. (2009). Symmetry and order in systems chemistry. *The Journal of Chemical Physics, 130*, 164907.

Williams, B. A. O. (1973). A critique of utilitarianism. In J. J. C. Smart & B. A. O. Williams (Ed.), *Utilitarianism for and against* (pp. 77–150). Cambridge: Cambridge University Press.